Praise for

# COLOSSUS

*Washington Post* Best Books of 2010
*Los Angeles Times* Bestseller
*New York Times* Political Bestseller
*Good Morning America* "Great Summer Reading"

"Masterly. In the grand tradition of David McCullough. [Hiltzik] fixes the endeavor in its time and captures the personalities of the people involved. May inspire in readers a longing for something . . . that will summon up once again America's famous self-confidence and daring."

—John Steele Gordon, *The Wall Street Journal*

"Hiltzik tells the dam's tale well, with majestic sweep . . . every iota of material fits snugly into the narrative, which, unlike the river, flows freely."

—*San Francisco Chronicle*

"[A] superb new history of the dam's conception, construction and legacy . . . And in Hiltzik's hands, it makes very good history, indeed."

—*Cleveland Plain Dealer*

"The parade of grim particulars might make *Colossus* a depressing read were it not for the vigor of Hiltzik's prose and the lively gallery of individual portraits and anecdotes that convey a wonderfully textured sense of what it was like to work on Hoover Dam."

—*Los Angeles Times*

"Fascinating. . . . A construction epic reflecting Depression-era America. . . . Astutely conveying the characters of its creators, Hiltzik marvelously captures the times."

—*Booklist*

## Also by Michael Hiltzik

*A Death in Kenya: The Murder of Julie Ward*

*Dealers of Lightning: Xerox PARC and the Dawn of the Computer Age*

*The Plot Against Social Security: How the Bush Plan
Is Endangering Our Financial Future*

# COLOSSUS

## The Turbulent, Thrilling Saga of the Building of Hoover Dam

## Michael Hiltzik

Free Press
New York  London  Toronto  Sydney

Free Press
A Division of Simon & Schuster, Inc.
1230 Avenue of the Americas
New York, NY 10020

First Free Press trade paperback edition May 2011

*Sources for Photo Insert*
1: From J.C. Ives, *Report upon the Colorado River of the West* (1861); 2, 3: From H.T. Cory, *The Imperial Valley and the Salton Sink* (1915); 4, 5, 7, 11-15, 17-31, 34: United States Bureau of Reclamation; 6: San Bernardino Public Library; 8, 9: Library of Congress; 10: UNLV Libraries, Special Collections; 16: Nevada State Museum, Las Vegas; 32, 33: *Los Angeles Times*

FREE PRESS and colophon are trademarks of Simon & Schuster, Inc.

For information about special discounts for bulk purchases,
please contact Simon & Schuster Special Sales at 1-866-506-1949
or *business@simonandschuster.com*

The Simon & Schuster Speakers Bureau can bring authors to your live event.
For more information or to book an event contact the Simon & Schuster Speakers Bureau
at 1-866-248-3049 or visit our website at *www.simonspeakers.com*.

Designed by Carla Jayne Jones

Manufactured in the United States of America

3   5   7   9   10   8   6   4   2

Library of Congress Cataloging-in-Publication Data

Hiltzik, Michael A.
Colossus : the turbulent, thrilling saga of the building of Hoover Dam / Michael
Hiltzik. —1st trade pbk ed.
p. cm.
Includes bibliographical references and index.
1. Hoover Dam (Ariz. and Nev.)—History. 2. Dams—Colorado River
(Colo.-Mexico)—Design and construction—History. I. Title.
TC557.5.H6H55 2010b
627'.820979313—dc22
2010051592

ISBN 978-1-4165-3216-3
ISBN 978-1-4165-3217-0 (pbk)
ISBN 978-1-4391-8158-4 (ebook)

*To Deborah, Andrew, and David*

# CONTENTS

# CONTENTS

# INTRODUCTION

*September 30, 1935: Roosevelt Comes to the River*

The president's train lumbered across the desert in the dead of night. The darkness was opportune, for it spared the passengers—those still awake as Sunday night edged into Monday morning—the sight of the wasteland they were traversing on this, the fourth day of an exhausting coast-to-coast journey. One of the most desolate landscapes in the United States, it was a vast flat desert without a hint of green, its few human settlements separated from one another by hundreds of waterless miles. For generations, hardy (or foolhardy) Americans had crossed this territory in search of fortune or fulfillment, looking for gold, water, a patch of land to homestead, or the answer to a dream. Thousands had perished in the quest.

In making the same crossing, Franklin Delano Roosevelt was on a quest of his own. He aimed to appropriate as a tangible symbol of the New Deal, his Democratic administration's economic recovery program, a great dam on the Colorado River conceived and launched by Republicans.

To that end he had resolved to dedicate this landmark of human achievement in person, at a ceremony scheduled for the coming day. He would speak directly to a crowd of ten thousand from a shaded podium beside the monumental work while his words were carried across the land on a nationwide radio hookup.

# INTRODUCTION

FDR worked long past midnight, laying down his words on yellow lined tablets in his angular longhand. This was his second full draft, the first having been unanimously panned earlier that evening by a review chorus composed of Interior Secretary Harold Ickes, Federal Reserve Chairman Marriner Eccles (whose own Utah Construction Company had helped build the dam), and his press secretary, Stephen T. Early. "All thought it was below par and did not do the President justice," Ickes reported in his diary. "The result was that he had to do it all over again." The new version would carry a full helping of the Roosevelt magic.

As he began to speak just before noon on that sizzling Monday, the president, strapped uncomfortably upright into a steel frame attached to a shaded lectern, first evoked the arid landscape on which thousands of Americans had scratched out a living for years in thrall to the menacing moods of the Colorado River. "For a generation the people of Imperial Valley had lived in the shadow of disaster from this river," he said. "Every spring they awaited with dread the coming of a flood, and at the end of nearly every summer they feared a shortage of water would destroy their crops." The dam had already vindicated the foresight of its builders, he observed, for only a few months earlier a great flood had cascaded down from the mountains and would surely have ruined the settlers of the valley had it not been "caught and safely held" behind the huge concrete rampart.

Next he turned his attention to the future, describing the rich bounty of electricity, water, and recreation to be provided by the man-made lake, 115 miles long, that already had begun to fill behind the dam. Transmission lines of unprecedented length already spanned the desert, ready to bring electricity to factories, streetlights, and household appliances in towns and cities hundreds of miles away. The cities of Southern California had broken ground for yet another engineering marvel, an immense aqueduct to transport the Colorado's waters over the mountains to quench the thirst of millions of residents on the coastline. More gifts were in the offing. Agriculture, mining, and manufacturing, not to speak of industries yet unforeseen, all would be nourished by the dam. "They await the development of cheap power," Roosevelt said. "The national benefits which will be derived from the completion of this project will make themselves felt in every one of the forty-eight States."

FDR envisioned the project in a way that his predecessor, Herbert Hoover, the once and future namesake of what was then known as Boulder Dam, would have found entirely alien: as a symbol. The dam signified not only man's mastery over nature, Roosevelt observed, but also a people's ability to find greatness by coalescing into a social and economic community. The dam's $108 million cost (including interest) might seem daunting at first blush, he added, but as the price of nationwide inspiration and the creation of a template for further public works it would be reckoned modest indeed.

As the largest federal project of its kind, Hoover Dam—to use the name Congress made permanent in 1947—inaugurated an age of grand national undertakings. Emboldened by the successful effort to harness the Colorado, the United States embarked on a campaign to place more of its rivers and streams under human domination. Within a year of Roosevelt's address, three more dams—Bonneville, Grand Coulee, and Shasta—would be under construction, all ranking with Hoover Dam as among the biggest in history. The Tennessee Valley Authority, born in the Hundred Days, the frenzy of legislative action at the very inception of Roosevelt's term, would eventually encompass twenty-nine hydroelectric dams. FDR called constantly for even more projects, like a man under a spell. "How about it?" he would scribble to Ickes during cabinet meetings. "Can we survey? Can we take money from here and put it there? Can we do it?" Seven more dams would rise on the Colorado itself, choking it so completely that its once mighty flow into the Gulf of California has been reduced today to a brackish stream of runoff from Mexican farms.

Hoover Dam inspired much more than irrigation works. Even before its last concrete was poured, construction of the Golden Gate Bridge was underway, involving some of the same contractors. More bridges and tunnels followed, along with the first freeways. The power of America's concerted will and intellectual resources, demonstrated so decisively by Hoover Dam's construction, would continue to reveal itself over the succeeding years—in times of acute crisis, as after Pearl Harbor, at D-Day, and in the Manhattan Project; and in times of more placid if not entirely tranquil aspiration, as during the 1950s and 1960s, which bequeathed us the interstate highway system and man's landing on the moon.

Franklin Roosevelt instinctively grasped the totemic power of what he called "the greatest dam in the world," its elegant machine beauty and opalescent majesty. He foretold in his opening words the spell it would cast on every visitor: "This morning I came, I saw and I was conquered, as everyone would be who sees for the first time this great feat of mankind." Hundreds of thousands of visitors had preceded him, peering over the canyon rim during the construction phase at the antlike workers seven hundred feet below; afterward, a million tourists a year would heed his call "to come to Boulder Dam and see it with your own eyes."

Movie companies set their melodramas against the backdrop of the dynamiting of cliffsides and the pouring of concrete, novelists nudged their plots into motion with mysterious events unfolding in the dam's shadow, advertisers posed their cars and trucks against its elegant outlines, poets sang of its flawless beauty. To the leftist English novelist and playwright J. B. Priestley, the structure heralded the advent of the new socialist man: "This is what he can do when given a real job. This is a first glimpse of what chemistry and mathematics and engineering and large-scale organization can accomplish when collective planning unites and inspires them," he wrote. "You might be tempted to call it a work of art; as if something that began with civil engineering ended somewhat in the neighborhood of Beethoven's Ninth Symphony."

As a federal project, Hoover Dam was the first manifestation of the clamorous, ascendant West's expanding influence in Washington, and became the instrument of the region's further empowerment. Its water and hydroelectricity helped turn California into the most politically weighty state of the union; fueled the development of the isolated cities of the Southwest into bustling Sunbelt metropolises, which continue today to drain Eastern cities of money, population, and talent; and transformed the entire region into a seedbed of new industries.

Had the dam never been built, the West would look very different today. The growth of the urban areas most dependent on the river for water and power—Los Angeles, Phoenix, Denver, Salt Lake City, and San Diego— would have been stunted, leaving them at a fraction of their current size. The largest city on the West Coast today might well be San Francisco or Seattle, which get their water and power from other sources.

But it was built. The transformation of America that took place during the post–World War II period really began a decade earlier, with the completion of Hoover Dam. The story of America in the last half of the twentieth century is the story not of the postwar era, but the post-dam era.

The United States became in that post-dam era a country very different from the United States that built it. It was transformed from a society that glorified individualism into one that cherished shared enterprise and communal social support. To be sure, that change was not all the making of the dam itself; Social Security, the Works Progress Administration, and other New Deal programs forged in the crucible of the Depression played their essential role, as did the years of war. But the dam was the physical embodiment of the initial transformation, a remote regional construction project reconfigured into a symbol of national pride.

The dam's durability in that role warrants a new examination of its creation and its legacy. Gazing upon it today, we are reminded of a more innocent era when American might and engineering seemed invincible, even under the crushing weight of economic crisis. The dam's imposing mass seems to ask whether we as a nation are still capable of such an undertaking today—whether we would still have the drive and resourcefulness to conceive it, build it, and even finish it an astonishing two years ahead of schedule.

A modern perspective requires us also to ask other, darker questions. Among them is whether it was right to build the dam even then. For all that Los Angeles and the other great regional capitals owe their evolution into modern metropolises to the dam, they have also become its prisoners, and the would-be masters of the Colorado have become, in a real sense, its dependents. Thirty million Americans—10 percent of the country's population—were enticed westward by the Colorado's abundance; but the region's population now faces the sobering truth that the river's gift was never as extravagant as generations of reclamation promoters had promised. The Colorado could give only so much, and in recent decades it has reached its limits. The question of how to conserve the river's bounty in an era of drought is also part of the story of Hoover Dam.

Hoover Dam made a new West, but also confined it in a straitjacket. The millions lured across the frontier to settle and build soon discovered that they were still subject to the river's ancient vicissitudes. To be sustained by the river their descendants still must understand its rhythms and moods, even placate its spirits. For when the river's flow dwindles, as it will do from time to time, much more is at stake than ever before: The beneficiaries of the river are no longer tribespeople growing staples on its banks between floods and droughts, but great cities and great industries. The ancients knew that attempting to control the Colorado was folly, but the moderns have had to learn the lesson anew. This book tells the story of that discovery and its consequences.

Hoover Dam was not solely the product of the thousands of men who applied tools to rock and poured concrete from 1931 to 1935 and whose work was honored by Franklin Roosevelt in the closing words of his dedication: "Well done." The impulse to build it was born long before it began rising in concrete columns from the bedrock. Before the dam came there were ten thousand square miles of desert peopled by a few scattered tribes and penetrated by a few lonely pioneers hoping to claim that land for vigorous cultivation by taming the river. But the river would not be easily subdued.

# PART ONE

# The Sinful River

# 1

## The Journey of Death

B y any customary measure, the Colorado River is an unremarkable
stream. It does not rank as the longest river in North America, nor the
widest, nor the most abundant. Its drainage basin of a quarter-million
square miles barely falls within the ten largest in the United States, and
much of it covers inaccessible range or desolate wasteland. Unlike the Mississippi, Hudson, and St. Lawrence, to name three great riparian thoroughfares of the continent, the Colorado has never been a significant bearer of
commercial traffic.

Throughout history, what has set the Colorado River apart from all
other waterways of the Western Hemisphere is its violent personality. The
Colorado has always been best known for the scars it left on the landscape,
among them the greatest of all natural works, the Grand Canyon, a testament to the river's primordial origin and its compulsive energy. No river
equaled its maniacal zeal for carving away the terrain in its path and carrying it downstream, sometimes as far as a thousand miles. No river matched
its schizophrenic moods, which could swing in the course of a few hours
from that of a meandering country stream to an insane torrent.

It is hardly surprising that from ancient times, the humans who coexisted with the Colorado depicted it not as a beneficent life-giving force but
as a fiery red monster, a dragon or serpent beyond man's ability to tame.

The basin's first recorded inhabitants, the native tribespeople of the southern plains, had no option but to accommodate themselves to the river's implacable temperament. They pastured their livestock on the grass that sprang up in the wake of its floods, planted crops on its rich alluvial deposits, imagined their gods and spirits housed within its labyrinthine canyons, assembled their myths and legends from the raw material of its natural mystery.

The American settlers of a later era, driven by the demands of commerce and dreams of wealth, were not so inclined to defer to nature's unpredictable willfulness. From their earliest encounters with the river, they pondered how to corral it, divert it, drain it, and consume it. The California engineer Joseph Barlow Lippincott, dispatched to the river by the city of Los Angeles in 1912, pronounced it "an American Nile awaiting regulation"—to be best treated "in as intelligent and vigorous a manner as the British government has treated its great Egyptian prototype."

Lippincott's judgment reflected a new conservation policy then taking root in the United States. It was based on defining conservation not as protection or preservation but as exploitation. Woodrow Wilson's interior secretary, Franklin K. Lane, laid out the new approach with striking directness. "Every tree is a challenge to us, and every pool of water and every foot of soil," he proclaimed. "The mountains are our enemies. We must pierce them and make them serve. The sinful rivers we must curb."

Lane's successors answered his call to arms. Over the following decades, the U.S. government carried out an ambitious program to harness the sinful Colorado, working the river until the volume remaining to trickle into the sea scarcely merited an asterisk on a hydrological graph. The architects of this program couched their intentions in moral terms, as though they were not altering the natural order but restoring the watershed to a state of grace. "The Colorado River flows uselessly past the international desert which Nature intended for its bride," wrote William Ellsworth Smythe, the most prominent water evangelist of his era, in 1900. "Some time the wedding of the waters to the soil will be celebrated, and the child of that union will be a new civilization."

\* \* \*

What first lured Europeans to the banks of the Colorado, however, was not its potential to nurture crops. It was gold. Or, more precisely, the mirage of gold.

The Spanish conquistadors, led by Hernán Cortés and Francisco Pizarro, had completed their plunder of the Inca and Aztec empires of the New World before the sixteenth century was three decades old. They had looted the Indians' storehouses, exhausted their mines, and worked legions of slaves to death. Yet their appetite for gold, silver, and gemstones remained unquenched.

Fortuitously, hints of new treasures soon emerged from the uncharted north, reenergizing the Spanish quest. In the mid-1530s, adventurers returned from Indian imprisonment in the Sonoran Desert—present-day New Mexico and Arizona—laden with news of a land called Cibola, where stood seven magnificent cities in which (according to the yarn one traveler spun for his relatives) "the women wore strands of gold and the men golden waistbands" and the palace walls were encrusted with emeralds.

Lured by this vision of wealth, the conquistadors probed along the Sea of Cortez (the Gulf of California) until they encountered, inevitably, the Colorado delta. The first advance parties were driven back by the ferocious tides at the confluence of the river and gulf. Finally, in 1539, a ship under the tenacious command of Captain Hernando de Alarcón managed to sail upriver about 150 miles, penetrating well into Sonora. He was shortly followed by an immense force under the command of General Francisco Vásquez de Coronado, dispatched to explore the beckoning golden empire by land.

Coronado's scouts were soon filling in the blank maps of the Southwest. They renamed the Colorado the Río del Tison, or Firebrand River—not because of its willfulness, but for the torches the local Indians bore on their travels—and they came upon the Grand Canyon, reporting the immense natural formation with appropriate wonderment.

But their quest for gold failed. A pueblo city that scouts had described as ringed with gilded ramparts proved to be built of mere mud and clay, which happened to glimmer deceptively in the setting sun. The other majestic cities of Cibola remained as elusive as phantasms. For two more years

Coronado searched for gold, finally returning home empty-handed and deeply in debt.

Yet there was gold in the north, just not where he had been looking for it. Another three centuries would pass before its discovery would attract white Americans in great numbers back to what had long since been written off as a hopelessly unprepossessing territory. The Gold Rush of 1849 would draw ninety thousand fortune seekers, known as Forty-niners or Argonauts, to ford the Colorado River—part of a migration of men, women, and families that has been called "the largest single western movement in the nation's history."

The frenzy began with an unassuming item on an inside page of the *San Francisco Californian* of March 15, 1848, headlined, "GOLD MINE FOUND." It did not fully take root in the national consciousness until nine months later, when President James K. Polk gave the federal government's imprimatur to the discovery at Sutter's Mill. As an expansionist, Polk made no effort to downplay a discovery likely to encourage new settlement in an underpopulated region. Instead, he reported in his annual message to Congress on December 5 that "the explorations already made warrant the belief that the supply is very large."

Some 300,000 Argonauts struck out for the West, a third of them taking what became known as the southern routes—overland byways converging at Yuma, Arizona, where the Gila River joined the Colorado, and continuing along one or another waterless trail, or jornada, toward the Pacific coast. These trails acquired a vicious reputation. One in particular, a desert crossing paralleling the Rio Grande in New Mexico, bore a label that presently was applied to the entire unspeakably harsh road west. It was known in Spanish as *la jornada de la muerte*; in English as "the journey of death."

Perils of every variety confronted travelers on the jornada: disease, brigands, hostile tribes, and the daunting terrain itself. Not even the best-outfitted expeditions were immune. This was shown by the dire experience of John Woodhouse Audubon, the renowned naturalist's younger son, who left New York for the Texas coast and points west with a party of eighty, backed by what was regarded as lavish capital of $27,000.

On the day of his departure, Audubon was a youthful thirty-six, "tall, strong and alert," in the words of his daughter Maria. When he returned home a year later he was broken, "worn out in body and spirit" by his travails on the jornada and the loss at sea of all his sketches and most of his notebooks.

The first blow to strike Audubon's company had been cholera, which killed five members within days of their landing in Texas and reduced a dozen others to dehydrated wraiths. The survivors pressed on, Audubon collecting botanical specimens and sketching wildlife in his father's style. In mid-October he and his remaining companions reached the junction of the Gila and the Colorado, which he dismissed as merely a "muddy stream." Crossing to the opposite bank and clambering up a sand dune, he perceived a further omen of the dismal prospects facing the expedition. He was perched upon a desert ridge that belonged to the "walking hills" of California, a natural barrier that would obstruct men's activities in the region for the next half-century. "There was not a tree to be seen, nor the least sign of vegetation, and the sun pouring down on us made our journey seem twice the length it really was."

The next day Audubon's group came upon a chain of fetid lagoons, where they deduced the fate of their numberless predecessors from the detritus scattered on the ground. "Truly here was a scene of desolation," he wrote.

> Broken wagons, dead shriveled up cattle, horses and mules as well, lay baking in the sun, around the dried-up wells that had been opened, in the hopes of getting water. Not a blade of grass or green thing of any kind relieved the monotony of the parched, ash-colored earth, and the most melancholy scene presented itself that I have seen since I left the Rio Grande.

They could hardly have suspected, slogging through the vacant wastes and slaking their thirst from pools of water described by a fellow traveler as "a tincture of bluelick, iodides of sulphur, Epsom salts, and a strong decoction of decomposed mule flesh," that they were crossing the grounds of a future paradise. The introduction of fresh water to the Imperial Valley and the dam that would impound it lay decades in the future. But the Argonauts' journeys marked a vital step in the process. The Gold Rush awoke official Washington to the military and economic significance of America's western territories and to the necessity of acquiring firsthand testimony about what lay between the frontier and the Pacific coast.

One of the prime movers of what became known as the Great Reconnaissance was President Franklin Pierce's secretary of war, Jefferson Davis.

The desert held a peculiar fascination for Jeff Davis. As a U.S. senator, he had risked public ridicule by proposing to deploy camels in the Southwest as a military experiment. Upon joining the cabinet in 1853, he put his plan into action by importing fifty of the animals for his department, but the program collapsed four years later, following his and President Pierce's departure from power.

A more enduring mark was left by the survey Davis commissioned to identify a Southwestern route for an intercontinental railroad. The reports from his five survey parties later published in twelve majestic volumes—America's most important exploratory record since Lewis and Clark—contained a wealth of information about the vast region's topography, geology, wildlife, and natural history.

Attached to the survey was William Phipps Blake, a young geologist from a prominent Eastern family. Blake's party failed to discern a suitable railroad route, but he did stumble upon a remarkable geologic feature in the trackless desert. His first clue that he had found something extraordinary came on November 17, 1853, when from the edge of a windswept ridge in the San Bernardino Mountains (not far from the site of modern Palm Springs) he noticed "a discoloration of the rocks extending for a long distance in a horizontal line on the side of the mountains."

With great excitement, Blake worked his way down the gradient. From the valley floor the line "could be traced along the mountain sides, following all the angles and sinuosities of the ridges for many miles—always preserving its horizontality—sometimes being high up above the plain, and again intersecting long and high slopes of gravel and sand; on such places a beach-line could be read."

The conclusion was inescapable: he was standing in the dry bed of an immense ancient sea, and the white line was its high water mark.

Blake named the sea Lake Cohuilla, after the local Indian tribe. The white deposit, he determined, was composed of the fossilized shells of freshwater animals. His barometer told him that his location measured at least one hundred feet below sea level. From the Indians he learned that the valley served as the traditional locus of their own flood legend, "a tradition they have of a great water (agua grande) which covered the whole valley and was filled with fine fish. . . . Their fathers lived in the mountains and used to come down to the lake to fish and hunt. The water gradually subsided 'poco,' 'poco,' (little by little,) and their villages were moved down from the mountains, into the valley it had left. They also said that the waters once returned very suddenly and overwhelmed many of their people and drove the rest back to the mountains."

The desert was shaped like an oblong bowl rising from a central depression, or "sink," about one hundred miles west of the Colorado River and deeper at its lowest point than Death Valley. The region's rainfall of less than three inches a year, the continent's most meager, had created over the eons a terrain as empty as the Arabian wastes. Where there was any vegetation at all, it was of the lowliest variety, resinous greasewood and creosote whose roots clung like talons to the sun-hardened earth.

Yet Blake was not fooled by the apparent lifelessness of the cracked and sere clay veneer. "The alluvial soil of the Desert is capable of sustaining a vigorous vegetation," he reported. "If a supply of water could be obtained for irrigation, it is probable that the greater part of the Desert could be made to yield crops of almost any kind."

The desert was in fact a deposit of rich soil eroded by the Colorado River from the basin upstream and transported south at the rate of 160 million tons a year. Working on millennial time, the silt filled in the shallow headwaters of the Gulf of California, shifting its shore 150 miles southward. This process turned the gulf's northernmost arm into the landlocked lake later known as the Salton Sea. As the lake slowly evaporated, it left behind a crust of mineral salt and calcified shells, the remnants of which Blake had spotted.

Meanwhile, the river built up its bed with its own silt deposits year after year, like a train laying its own tracks. Eventually the river would be flowing within parallel levees elevated high above the desert floor. In time the levees would become unstable, their walls would collapse, and the stream, freed of its constraints, would inundate the desert basin, recharging the inland sea. Centuries would pass, a new accumulation of silt would stopper the errant flow, and the river would return to its old delta, resuming its journey to the gulf. Again the sea would evaporate, again the river would build up and tear down its levees, and again the sea would fill up, in a never-ending cycle.

How many such oscillations took place over the ages no one can say. A filled sea was encountered by travelers in the 1500s. Another inundation was recorded in the first half of the eighteenth century. Between 1824 and 1905, the lake filled and evaporated eight times; in 1891 it was known as a modest impoundment covering 100,000 acres, about half the surface area of the modern Salton Sea.

Blake knew none of this geological history. But his intuition told him that the Colorado could irrigate the valley year-round through the judicious cutting of canals and channels to take advantage of its periodic overflows. He even pictured the valley as a sort of reclaimed aquatic wonderland: "It is, indeed, a serious question whether a canal would not cause the overflow of a vast surface, and refill, to a certain extent, the dry valley of the Ancient Lake," he wrote.

He was the first American to perceive that this was a grand natural system of inexhaustible economic value—a desiccated Eden requiring only a water supply to make it bloom. Because of the region's remoteness and inaccessibility, however, this vision would have to be discovered and rediscovered several times before it would permanently take hold in the national imagination.

Blake would live long enough to see his predictions come to pass in the new century. At the time of his survey's publication, however, his perceptions went largely unheeded. Unheeded, that is, by all except another man, afflicted by a restless, visionary cast of mind, who had come west like so many others, searching for gold.

A thirty-four-year-old Ohio-born physician, Oliver Meredith Wozencraft had contracted an acute case of wanderlust from the Argonauts passing through his hometown of New Orleans. Early in 1849 he left behind his wife and children and set forth to scratch his itch. Reaching the eastern bank of the Colorado in May to find the river at floodtide, he and his traveling companions accomplished a precarious crossing in a makeshift kayak of ox hide.

Taking the long way around the Saharan dunes, they traveled by night and by day slept huddled under blankets that were buried in sand by the time they awoke. This stratagem failed to shield them from the ravages of the climate.

> The heat was so intense [Wozencraft confided to his diary] that on the third day two of my men failed. It occurred to me, as there was nothing I could do there, to mount my patient and gentle mule and at a distance of some eight miles I reached the border of the desert and water with which I filled a bag and brought it back to them.

"It was then and there," he wrote later, "that I first conceived the idea of the reclamation of the desert."

This was, at best, a romanticized version of his epiphany, tailored for public consumption. In fact, Wozencraft's conception of an irrigated desert gradually took form over the following decade, inspired in part by Blake's report. He unveiled his plan for public consumption in 1859 by laying a cunning proposal before the California legislature: if the state would grant him title to the desert, he would crosshatch it with canals and turn it into an agricultural wonderland.

The tract he sought encompassed the land between the Colorado River and San Bernardino Peak all the way south to the Mexican border, roughly sixteen thousand square miles or ten million acres, of which about half was flat terrain suited for agriculture. It would rank as one of the largest outright gifts of territory to an individual ever proposed in the youthful United States. On April 16, 1859, the California legislature approved it with barely a murmur of debate and with the sole condition that Wozencraft persuade Congress to agree to the transfer. This mission would consume him for the next twenty-eight years.

While Wozencraft was formalizing the first plan to exploit the Colorado for the reclamation of the desert, the federal government pondered the river's greater virtues. Davis's railroad survey had whetted the War Department's thirst for geographic knowledge. The task of achieving the next great leap in understanding was assigned to a young officer of the Army Corps of Topographical Engineers bearing the evocative name of Joseph Christmas Ives.

Ives was a slender New Yorker with deep-set eyes and a dandified bearing who had been born to a family of socialites on December 25, 1828—hence his middle name. Upon his graduation from West Point in 1852, he was dispatched by the engineering corps to distant Arizona, where he was still cooling his heels in 1857 when Secretary of War John B. Floyd, Davis's successor, ordered him to probe the Colorado River as far upstream as he could go. The goal was to determine exactly how much of it was navigable, and therefore whether it could be used to supply the proliferating army garrisons strung across New Mexico and Utah like a giant necklace. These were served over land routes stretching as long as 1,500 miles, and the army hoped that river transport might shorten the supply lines enough for a round-trip to be measured in days, not weeks.

But the river was a closed book to the army quartermasters—indeed, to the entire federal bureaucracy—beyond Yuma, which stood a mere 150 miles upstream of the head of the Gulf of California. Among the questions for which the government sought answers was the exact location of what was called the "Big Cañon"—a "rather mythical" feature, as Ives wrote in his expedition journal, which became one of the seminal documents of the Great Reconnaissance. Little was known of the canyon, he wrote, other than the descriptions bequeathed by "the accounts of one or two trappers, who . . . propagated among their prairie companions incredible accounts of the stupendous character of the formation."

Ives would be the white man who finally located the Grand Canyon. He found its downstream entrance roughly 450 miles from the gulf, or about a hundred miles beyond the point he marked as the river's "practical head of navigation," where he had been forced to abandon his waterborne vessels and continue his expedition on dry land.

From the rim of the canyon he would unburden himself of a misjudgment that still echoes along the corridors of history: "Ours has been the first, and will doubtless be the last, party of whites to visit this profitless locality," he wrote in his journal. "It seems intended by nature that the Colorado river, along the greater portion of its lonely and majestic way, shall be forever unvisited and undisturbed."

Ives had been ordered to depart from the mouth of the Colorado by December 1, which gave him less than six months to assemble and equip his crew. From a Philadelphia forge he commissioned a fifty-foot flat-bottomed steamer, christened the *Explorer*, which was transported in disassembled form via rail to San Francisco. There it was loaded aboard the schooner *Monterey* for onward shipment to the expedition's starting place at the head of the Gulf of California.

On November 1, the *Monterey* lumbered out of San Francisco Bay, carrying the *Explorer* and Ives's traveling party of twenty-four, including a captain and engineer, a boat crew of eight, and his official topographer, a gifted Bavarian draftsman named Baron Frederick W. von Egloffstein. Blessed with a favorable wind she reached Cabo San Lucas, at the southern tip of Baja California, in seven days, only to spend three weeks beating laboriously back against the same northerly gusts along the eastern shore of the Baja peninsula, toward the Colorado delta.

At the head of the gulf, Ives memorably encountered the phenomenon known as the "bore," a tidal surge capable of reducing a vessel to splinters. Caused by the thirty-six-foot difference between high and low tide in the narrow head of the gulf, the bore announced itself with a fall in the water level so abrupt that the *Monterey,* anchored peaceably over a shoal, suddenly found herself beached atop a hummock of sand. Then conditions turned sinister.

> About nine o'clock, while the tide was still running out rapidly, we heard, from the direction of the Gulf, a deep, booming sound, like the noise of a distant waterfall [Ives recollected]. Every moment it became louder and nearer, and in half an hour a great wave, several feet in height, could be distinctly seen flashing and sparkling in the moonlight, extending from one bank to the other, and advancing swiftly upon us. . . . [T]he broad sheet around us boiled up and foamed like the surface of a caldron, and then, with scarcely a moment of slack water, the whole went whirling by in the opposite direction. . . . For a long time, in the stillness of the night, the roaring of the huge mass could be heard reverberating, until at last it became faint and lost in the distance.

The next day the *Monterey* sidled up to land and the crew transferred the *Explorer*'s parts from the schooner for assembly on the riverbank, a job hampered by the tendency of the waterlogged clay to swallow the men up to their knees.

Four weeks later, on December 30, Ives inspected his "pigmy, but prettily modeled, boat," fully assembled. In truth the *Explorer* was an odd-looking contraption, a glorified skiff so unbalanced by the huge boiler placed amidships that lengths of timber had to be riveted to the hull to keep it from buckling. A small pilothouse stood aft, and a paddlewheel at the stern with a cowl on which crewmen were inclined to drape themselves in calm weather. At the bow a four-pound howitzer was mounted—proof, it was hoped, against an Indian ambush.

With an earsplitting blast from her whistle minutes before midnight on New Year's Eve, the *Explorer* slid out of her muddy berth and headed up the Colorado. Word of her progress passed rapidly along the river from tribe to tribe, so she was often greeted by throngs of Indians massed on the banks. Sensitive to his role as chronicler of the meeting of two cultures with a mutual, if not necessarily reconcilable, interest in the Colorado, Ives filled his journal with tolerant judgments of the onlookers. ("The women generally have modest manners, and many are good looking.")

For seven weeks he made his way upriver. The flat featureless terrain of the delta gave way to stone palisades and rocky canyons, framed by the vivid reds and browns of distant mountains. By day Egloffstein perched on the wheelhouse, notebook in his lap, producing an incomparable artistic record of the unspoiled West: bighorn sheep drinking serenely from the riverbanks, storks skimming inches from the surface, towering rocks of every shape and description—lighthouses, pyramids, obelisks, stone cathedrals of awe-inspiring grace and immeasurable grandeur.

During the last week of February the *Explorer* reached the Black Mountain range in Arizona's Mojave country. Ives, eyeing the steep walls of a distant gorge, thrilled himself with the conviction that he was about to enter the Big Cañon of legend. "Every point of the view is scanned with eager interest," he jotted.

What he had actually found was the mouth of Black Canyon—some one hundred miles short of his myth-shrouded objective but spectacular enough in its own right. The five days needed to reach it after it first appeared on the horizon had been fraught with danger: a dozen rapids, violent eddies that whirled the *Explorer* around "like a teetotum," interspersed with innumerable reaches through which the boat had to be towed by a dozen men hauling upon fraying ropes or by a battered skiff with splintered oars.

At the very last moment, just before entering the canyon itself, the *Explorer* nearly came to grief. She had gunned her engines to conquer one final rapid and then, suddenly reaching calm water, shot heedlessly up the river and slammed at full speed into a submerged rock at the center of the channel. "For a second the impression was that the canyon had fallen in," Ives reported. Several men pitched overboard. The boiler jolted loose from its moorings, the wheelhouse tore away, and the boat seemed on the verge of coming apart in mid-river.

The damage, while serious, was not as bad as it could have been. Limping to shore, the *Explorer* proved to need only a few days of repair. Ives left his crew to the task, assigned himself a spare skiff, and headed into the ravine. As his two oarsmen pulled against the stiff current, he marveled at the perpendicular walls towering more than a thousand feet above him from the very edge of the water.

> The river was narrow and devious, and each turn disclosed new combinations of colossal and fantastic forms, dimly seen in the dizzy heights overhead, or through the sunless depths of the vista beyond . . . amphitheaters, rotundas, castellated walls, and rows of time-stained ruins, surmounted by every form of tower, minaret, dome, and spire.

Darkness closed over this passage in the mountains with the abrupt finality of a lid shutting a coffin. In the last gleams of twilight Ives sketched his impressions of the brooding gorge. These he presently delivered to Egloffstein, who sifted them through his own gothic imagination to produce a classic, if exaggerated, portrayal of nature at her most portentous. In his etching, the walls of Black Canyon tower out of the frame, behind a line of serrated crags and a whitewater rapid, like a dark valley in Norse myth. The entire scene is bathed in a premonitory gloom hinting at shadowy wonders ahead, beyond a blind turn.

This was the Black Canyon Ives's readers got to know, among them officials in the War Department who were surely discouraged by his report of the poor navigability of the Colorado beyond Black Canyon. None of them could have imagined that many years later, just a few hundred yards upstream from where the *Explorer* almost broke to pieces, the natural spectacle of Black Canyon would be eradicated by a huge arch of white concrete, a man-made thing to take the place of nature's handiwork as a wonder of the world.

When Ives's report was published, Wozencraft was in his second year of harrying Congress for a land grant. Monitoring the debate over his proposal from the visitors' gallery, he could not have been uplifted by his bird's-eye view of Congress at work.

The legislation was introduced by a Unionist congressman, John W.

Crisfield of Maryland, with a nonchalant condemnation of the Colorado Desert as utterly worthless territory "not in a condition that a rattlesnake could live on it."

The House of Representatives nevertheless was wary of giving it away. Members demanded to know if the territory was truly worthless or if it did not, in fact, harbor vast mineral wealth and comprise thousands of arable acres. They bickered over the idea of bestowing a lavish gift on a private citizen, and considered the alternative of granting half the request, in alternating tracts like a checkerboard, and waiting to see what California could make of that. Finally, having worried the matter to exhaustion like dogs fighting over scraps, they tabled the bill.

War and Reconstruction intervened, and the measure did not reappear on the House floor for another fourteen years. By then, the Forty-niners and the prewar Great Reconnaissance had shriveled into quaint memories, and Wozencraft's project came to be viewed as the delusion of an aging crackpot.

In a sense, Wozencraft arrived both too early and too late. His scheme had been conceived before official Washington was ready to grasp the concept of a reclaimed desert. When it resurfaced in 1876, Congress was more inclined to take seriously the development of what it now labeled "the Arid Lands," a formal designation that invested the region with the status of a national patrimony. By then the lawmakers had come under the spell of John Wesley Powell, a one-armed Civil War hero and explorer who had rediscovered the Grand Canyon in 1869, entering it from upstream. Powell's contention that desert land could be conserved and reclaimed through judicious irrigation would be pursued by bureaucrats and commercial promoters for the next half-century. But his parallel warning that there was not enough water in the river to supply even a fraction of their increasingly ambitious proposals—that their visions promised "a heritage of conflict and litigation," as he thundered in 1893—would be just as assiduously ignored. In any case, the idea that a vast tract of potentially arable government land should be turned over to a single developer, as Wozencraft proposed, was deemed eccentric at best.

Wozencraft was the first American to surrender his fortune and health to the dream of a resplendent desert fed by the Colorado's waters. He last visited Washington in pursuit of his land patent in 1887. He was seventy-three, a shriveled shadow of the burly entrepreneur of a quarter century earlier. His financial resources were as exhausted as his frame.

On a chilly day that November he watched again from the gallery as the House buried his bill under a shower of ridicule for the last time. He trudged back to his Washington rooming house, where for some reason—whether poverty, dementia, or a spirit of impotent protest is unknown—he refused all food for ten days. Finally, on November 22, his landlord summoned one of his Washington friends to witness his last hours and inform his family in San Bernardino of his lonely end.

For his family, Wozencraft's dream left a bitter aftertaste. As his daughter wrote after his death:

> My dear father lost a fortune on it . . . he spent large sums for travel to Washington and home again, and for heavy burdens of expense while at the capital. His last sacrifice was a beautiful home in San Francisco. Everything went to the desert. Dear father was confident of success; he gave his very life to achieve its reclamation.

With his passing the dream slumbered, but only briefly. The lure of a desert in profitable bloom was too potent not to stir again. Five years after his death, in 1892, it gripped another Western pioneer, one who would finally turn Wozencraft's dream into reality, with disastrous, yet historic, consequences.

## 2

# Born of the Desert

**C**harles Robinson Rockwood stares out from the frontispiece of his memoirs with the look of an afflicted man. His brow is furrowed, his eyes glazed, the corners of his mouth set hard as though bracing for yet another blow from a hostile fate. In 1909, the year of the book's publication, he was a prematurely aged forty-nine-year-old man looking back at a dream that had beckoned to him from just beyond reach for most of his life.

He called his book *Born of the Desert*—the title hinting at the great things he had hoped to bring forth from the arid California valley stretching west from the Colorado River nearly to the Pacific shore. But his chapter headings hinted at something darker, a downward spiral of unrelenting disappointment leading to personal ruin: "Financial Troubles Begin" . . . "Hopes Rise and Fall" . . . "The Irony of Fate" . . . "Every Cent Gone."

Rockwood harbored no doubts about where to place the blame for his misfortunes: on venal investors, dishonest partners, fickle financial markets, and, most vexing of all, the unruly river—on everyone and everything, indeed, except his own unsteady judgment. Contemporary opinion of his character was split. Some lionized him as the father of the Imperial Valley ("To no other man belongs as much credit, nor a tenth part as much," asserted a local newspaper editor). Some cursed him as a criminally negligent blunderer (a description favored by President Theodore Roosevelt) and denounced him for imperiling the lives and livelihoods of thousands of innocent persons. Some regarded him as a selfless visionary, others as one of the most unprincipled businessmen of his day. In *The Winning of Barbara Worth,* a dialect-ridden 1911 Western by the popular novelist Harold Bell Wright, he is depicted as "the Seer," a master engineer whose vision of a verdant desert sets the melodramatic plot in motion. ("They call him the Seer because av his talk av the great things that will be doin' in this country av no rain at all.")

Rockwood failed to get rich from his scheme to irrigate the desert. But he did succeed in one respect that had eluded his predecessor Oliver Wozencraft: his project brought river water to the valley for the very first time. Even if he was responsible for the catastrophe that almost ruined the valley for cultivation forever, that catastrophe led directly to the recognition that the only agency that could be relied on to place the Colorado permanently under control was the government of the United States, and that the only dependable instrument of that control would be a massive dam of poured concrete.

Charles Rockwood's origins could hardly have been further removed from the desert. His mother traced her lineage back to John Robinson, the English pastor whose Puritan congregation sailed for the New World on the *Mayflower* in 1620. (Robinson chose to stay behind in exile in Holland with most of his flock when the ship sailed. Like his descendant, he died without achieving his dream—in his case, resettlement in a tolerant America.)

Before Charles Rockwood's birth in 1860, the family moved west to take up farming in Michigan. By the time he reached the age of twenty-one, he possessed an incomplete engineering education from the University of Michigan, which he had been forced to abandon shy of a degree because of failing eyesight. Hoping that work in the outdoors would relieve his chronic eyestrain, he accepted a railroad surveying job in Denver.

His infirmity aside, Rockwood was a burly man with the farm-bred constitution to survive long sojourns in the wilderness. The popular historian David O. Woodbury depicted him as a man with "great hands that amazed everybody with their delicacy of touch. . . . Though he could crush an apple in one palm, he could set the fine adjustment on a transit instrument with unerring accuracy." Woodbury cites no authority for this Bunyanesque description, but its kernel of truth is that Rockwood's reputation as an irrigation engineer spread rapidly. Before he was thirty he had won appointment as chief engineer of the Northern Pacific Railroad, which was building a pioneering reclamation project in the water-rich Columbia River basin.

Two years later, Rockwood's career was diverted by a letter he received from a Denver speculator with a plan to develop a very different patch of territory. John C. Beatty claimed to hold title to a million and a half acres of the Mexican desert. His proposal involved irrigating it from the Colorado River, then sitting back as money rolled in from homesteaders clamoring for a piece of the glorious future.

After a month of surveying, Rockwood flatly declared the project unfeasible. Beatty's land lay higher than the river, and water does not flow uphill. But during a side trip through the California portion of the Colorado Desert Rockwood recognized, as though by revelation, that this territory could be watered from the river by gravity. Returning to Denver, he informed Beatty that his backers would lose every cent they put into Mexico, but that California could make them rich. There was only one catch: a ridge of sand dunes as impassable as the Sahara blocked the direct route between the river and the valley. Rockwood's survey showed that the river could be diverted by cutting into the western bank a few miles north of the Mexican border, but the canal carrying irrigation water then would have to curve south across the border, passing through Mexico for up to sixty miles before veering north again. Obtaining permission from the Mexican government and the owner of the right of way, a Mexican hidalgo named General Guillermo Andrade, would require a great deal of capital.

Unfortunately, what Beatty brought to the partnership was guile, not money. He was a sharp dresser and smooth talker imbued with the mysterious charm of the confidence man, an expert cadger of handouts from relatives, friends, and total strangers. A project to make the desert bloom with water diverted from a storied river was the ideal lure for a certain kind of starry-eyed investor, and Beatty aimed to squeeze the breed for every penny he could. He cast his net to snare everyone from "cabinet ministers to hotel bell boys" (as a critic observed), but had no intention of putting any of the invested money into the ground.

His most important mark was Rockwood, who had come out of the Colorado Desert possessed by the dream of a rejuvenated wilderness. Rockwood's was a dangerous obsession, especially when yoked to his poor judgment of human nature. "He took all men at their own valuation and liked them all," Woodbury wrote, accurately identifying Rockwood's critical flaw as an inability to "distinguish between real friends and those who would exploit him."

Beatty played on this weakness mercilessly, taking pains to maintain an impressive front. At one point Rockwood discovered him ensconced in a lavish top-floor suite in the finest building in Providence, Rhode Island, among "show cases and tables filled with oranges, lemons, bananas, figs, apricots, all products of the Colorado Desert, which at that time was producing nothing but a few horn toads and once in a while a coyote." Beatty was energetically exploiting this fakery to flog irrigation company shares to investors all across New England.

Yet Rockwood's innocent faith in his partner persisted. At the outset of one picaresque journey to Mexico, where Beatty said he was going to secure the canal right-of-way from the government, he extracted $10 from Rockwood before parting from him at the Yuma train depot. "After getting his supper at the station, he put his foot on the car step, then turned to me and said, 'Rockwood, I believe I am a little short of cash.'" The startled Rockwood could not help observing that "he had on a new suit and looked as if he had come from a tailor's shop," but dipped into his pocket nonetheless.

Rockwood and Beatty spent more than a year together trying to scare up investors. One sweltering evening at the Southern Pacific Railroad hotel in Yuma, their dinner conversation about the project was overheard by a fellow guest, who expressed interest in the undertaking. Dr. William T. Heffernan was one of those intriguingly broad-minded individuals who often surface in remote places around the globe. He spent the 1890s and early 1900s serving as a camp medic for a succession of army brigades in unforgiving postings across the Southwest. Yet he must have had private means, for between 1892 and 1900 he advanced Rockwood at least $20,000, and possibly as much as $40,000—the equivalent of nearly $1 million today.

At the time of their first encounter, he was the army surgeon at Fort Yuma and a habitué of the railroad hotel, which he described as a "sort of a central meeting place at meal time for the community." An avuncular man with twinkling eyes, he was a sharp judge of character, taking Beatty's measure instantly and disapprovingly as "a glad hand artist, the type of promoter known in a mining town as 'a booster.'" He was more favorably impressed by Rockwood's glittering idealism. "Of all the men, myself included, who were interested in the irrigation of the Imperial Valley lands, Rockwood was the one least influenced by the hope of financial reward," he wrote later.

For fifteen years, Heffernan would serve as Rockwood's closest confidant and most steadfast financial backer. Under his influence Rockwood eventually cut his ties to Beatty, preserving from the scam only his surveys and equipment—and the vision of an irrigated Colorado Desert bringing forth an agricultural bounty.

Reorganizing as the California Development Company, Rockwood continued to beat the bushes for capital and to recruit settlers for the farmland he expected to open to cultivation. An encouraging response came from the Boston millionaire William Hathaway Forbes. The Forbes fortune originated in the Far East opium trade, but it had been scrubbed and sanitized through the family's acquisition of the U.S. rights to Alexander Graham Bell's telephone. The aging W. H. Forbes, who was searching for ventures to occupy his two college-educated sons, agreed to send his own engineer to substantiate Rockwood's representations, on condition that if any of the claims proved questionable Rockwood would pay for the trip.

Despite a glowing report from the engineer, however, Forbes cooled on the venture. Rockwood scorned the proffered explanation, which was that Forbes's health was failing. The investment, after all, was to have been for his sons' benefit, not his own. At length Rockwood discovered that Forbes had quietly made separate inquiries with a source in San Diego, who warned him that the desert was too hot to support white settlers, that it was hopelessly barren, and that a financial disaster awaited any man foolish enough to sink even a dollar in it. Rockwood nursed a grudge against Forbes's un-identified correspondent to the end of his days. "I have been trying all these years to find out the name of that man, but so far have failed to do so," he wrote late in life. "I still have hopes of meeting him."

Forbes's caution reflected a stark reality: To investors in the humid Northeast, where the word "farmland" evoked expanses of dark, moist, loamy soil under temperate skies, the very idea that the desert could be made to bloom reeked of fantasy. Then there was the issue of scale. Rock-wood's grandiose scheme demanded investors of fortitude and foresight, thin on the ground in any era but especially so just prior to the turn of the century, while the Panic of 1893 was still painfully fresh in people's memo-ries. Rockwood's project did not lend itself to unambitious design; the water had to come from the Colorado in a torrent or it would not come at all. The same doubts would recur among investors and public officials decades later when the idea of corralling the Colorado behind a towering dam was first broached, and they would take a decade more to overcome.

Despite this, a promising overture came in 1898 from Silas B. Dutcher, president of the Hamilton Trust Company of Brooklyn. Dutcher was an enterprising backer of the sort Rockwood had been seeking from the start. He had spent weeks scrutinizing engineers' reports and vetting Rockwood's background, and on Monday, February 14, 1898, he informed Rockwood that his attorneys had approved a substantial investment in the California Development Company. The last formality, a vote by the bank's board of directors, would be disposed of the following Friday morning.

Rockwood was overcome by optimism. The next evening, he and An-thony H. Heber, a prim Chicago land agent who had joined the California Development Company as a partner, treated themselves to a festive din-ner in Manhattan, "believing without doubt that our financial troubles were over for the present." If in their celebratory mood they overlooked the cautionary dispatches filling the New York newspapers about a brew-ing civil war in the Spanish Caribbean—particularly those of the Hearst *Journal* and Pulitzer *World,* which had been inflating rebel activity in Cuba into the semblance of a menace to the United States—that was un-derstandable.

The following morning there was no overlooking the war. They awoke to a changed world. The front page of the Hearst *Journal* told the story with a headline that screamed "CRISIS IS AT HAND" and "SPANISH TREACHERY" over an engraving of the USS *Maine* half-sunk and ablaze in Havana harbor. President William McKinley had dispatched the battleship, emblematic of growing American naval might, to Cuba as a "friendly" guardian of American interests on the island; the explosion, ostensibly the product of an attack by Cuban insurgents or Spanish provocateurs, was one of those once-in-a-lifetime events that become a shared memory for an entire generation. Rockwood's heart sank as he made his way to Dutcher's office along avenues thronged with shocked and infuriated New Yorkers. As he suspected, the deal was off. In *Born of the Desert,* his title for the section encompassing this crisis is "Darkness Once More."

More disappointment lay in store. Heffernan regretfully ended his contributions to the company, pleading that his personal investments had crashed. In actuality, he had come to realize that his piecemeal infusions of capital would never be enough to get a single spade turned in the ground, much less attract other investors to Rockwood's side. "I advised him to give up all further attempts to carry out the promotion," he recalled, "as I felt the enterprise was entirely too great for our feeble effort." Rockwood tried to smile through the disappointment, but the depth of his despair was evident. "He pressed my hand and, placing a hand on my shoulder, said smilingly, 'Buck up, the worst is yet to come,'" Heffernan recalled of the painful interview. "He left me with a feeling that was anything but pleasant."

Heffernan's withdrawal left the California Development Company in possession of an option to acquire the Mexican right-of-way, but no way of raising the money to exercise it. For the first time since he had come under the desert's spell, Rockwood contemplated the end of the dream. "I believe I shall be obliged to . . . seek some other means of earning a livelihood," he confided to Heber.

For so many years Rockwood and his partners had "struggled through adversity, laughed at by big capitalists, and by others dubbed pipe dreamers and rainbow chasers," Heber recollected later to a congressional committee. The looming collapse was a bitter pill. But then, as sometimes happens to gamblers down to their very last coin, Rockwood's luck turned and salvation, of a sort, finally appeared. Its bearer was George Chaffey.

Chaffey in 1899 was a stout, bullet-headed man of fifty-one who reigned as the leading irrigationist in America, a man with an almost mystical ability to find water under the most parched terrain and to put it to profitable use. The news that he had affiliated with the California Development Company transformed the firm's image instantaneously from pipe dream to potential gold mine. Squadrons of formerly dismissive bankers lined up to advance the venture $150,000 without murmur. What Chaffey demanded as his price to deliver this bounty to the CDC was control of the company.

Chaffey's roots, like Rockwood's, lay far from the Colorado Desert—in his case in Ontario, Canada, where his family had farmed for three generations. In 1880, at the age of thirty-two, he followed his father and two younger brothers to an irrigated citrus farm they had acquired in Riverside, California. A self-taught engineer and a born entrepreneur, within two years he had founded the model irrigation colonies of Ontario and Etiwanda below the foothills of the San Gabriel Mountains, where canyons collected the rainfall in winter and spring and funneled it downgrade to his land.

The colonies' names hint at one of Chaffey's skills: marketing. They referred to his native Canadian province and to an Indian chief who had been a family friend. But their seductively exotic ring to nineteenth-century American ears proved useful in attracting settlers. Another lure was the colonies' high level of technical innovation. The 2,500-acre Etiwanda was the first irrigation colony in the Western United States to conserve water by lining its irrigation ditches with concrete, the first to use pressurized water pipelines on a large scale, and the first to exploit its water flows for hydroelectric generation (all features that would become associated with Hoover Dam and its works). The inventive hydroelectric arrangement turned power into "the best cash crop of an irrigation project," observed Elwood W. Mead, an irrigation engineer whose name later became attached to one of the grandest sources of hydroelectric power in the world, Hoover Dam's vast reservoir. Perhaps the communities' most important innovation was a mutual water company system, which Chaffey devised to guarantee an irrigation supply to settlers free of the legal entanglements that often complicated water rights in the West.

Etiwanda and Ontario were unalloyed successes. The firm of Chaffey Brothers sold 1,400 acres of arid, coyote-ridden land in eight months to settlers who transformed it over the following years into a marvel of citrus groves, orchards, and vineyards. Soon Chaffey would replicate the models of Etiwanda and Ontario in a valley he called Imperial.

In the years before he joined with Charles Rockwood, Chaffey had experienced successes and reversals that his new partner would have found familiar. Etiwanda and Ontario were world-famous, but a failed eleven-year effort to repeat their success in the Australian outback had left Chaffey financially ruined and tainted by scandal. He was saved from poverty by a summons back to Ontario, which was staggering under an unyielding drought. His dowsing skills as sharp as ever, he sank a new line of artesian wells and brought forth a torrent of underground water. This was more than enough to restore Ontario's viability, his own wealth, and, at least in the United States, his reputation. He was once again basking in the lifestyle of a water baron when an acquaintance induced him to take a look at Rockwood's irrigation plan in 1899.

Intrigued, Chaffey disappeared into the desert that December for a three-week survey with an Indian guide for company. With a few minor differences, Chaffey concurred with Rockwood: the canal cut could be made on American territory, but the water would have to flow through Mexico in a dry channel known locally as the Rio Alamo. He arranged to have the route mapped and the costs estimated. The only objection raised to his participation came from his son Andrew, who was armed with professional banking experience and a level business head. Andrew's private investigation of the California Development Company unearthed its past association with the scoundrel Beatty, and showed it to be destitute besides. He begged his father to give the venture a pass.

But George Chaffey had fallen under the same implacable spell that had gripped Wozencraft and Rockwood before him. The dream of the resplendent desert had entered his soul. It would cost him dearly, as it did those other pioneers. But he rejected his son's entreaties.

"Let me do one more big thing before I die," he said, and signed up.


It could not have taken long for Chaffey to regret his rashness. His son's misgivings proved accurate, even conservative, for he soon discovered that the California Development Company had allowed two crucial land options to expire. These were "vital misrepresentations," in Chaffey's view, for the options covered both the parcel where the canal was to be cut into the Colorado's western bank and the 100,000 acres the canal would cross south of the border. What Chaffey identified as "the sine qua non of the whole scheme" was therefore in doubt.

Every new particle of information Chaffey discovered about the company's finances darkened the picture. The CDC was not simply penniless, but deeply in the red, having transferred $1 million in stock and $350,000 in water scrip to Rockwood, Heffernan, and a few other insiders at 10 cents on the dollar. Beyond these financial maneuvers, Chaffey discovered to his displeasure, Rockwood "had taken not one single practical step" to consummate his grand scheme.

Strictly speaking, Chaffey's contract required him merely to cut into the Colorado River at a spot known as Pilot Knob, just north of the Mexican border, and to build a four-mile canal crossing the border to the Rio Alamo. The canal was to cost no more than $150,000, which Chaffey was to raise. As compensation he was to receive one-quarter of CDC's shares and $60,000 in cash or water rights "payable when the company was able to pay it," as he later recounted. In practical terms, this meant that he would earn nothing until the company began to deliver water to settlers and collect water fees, which could not happen until he completed the headworks for the canal and water began to flow. On the plus side of the ledger, the contract did give him near-dictatorial power over the company for five years, or until April 1905. This was reason enough for him to press on, notwithstanding the CDC's parlous financial condition.

Chaffey wasted little time before taking charge. Pledging his personal credit, he persuaded bankers in Los Angeles to lend him the money to reinstate the crucial land options. From merchants whose trust he had earned while building Ontario and Etiwanda, he obtained supplies of lumber, construction equipment, and groceries for his work crews "without so much as the scratch of a pen."

Perhaps his most important step was to erase from the map any hint of the region's desolation. Reasoning that few humans would willingly commit their life savings to a place known as the "Colorado Desert" or, worse, the "Salton Sink," the man who had founded dreamscapes with the exotic names of Etiwanda and Ontario decreed that henceforth the territory stretching a hundred miles from the Colorado River toward the sea would carry the name "Imperial Valley." After all, he reasoned, "the project, by creating a new province in its own territory for the United States, was Imperial in the truest and best sense of the word."

The change was inspired; with its new name adorning advertising circulars, the valley quickly attracted settlers from all over the country. The very first arrived just after New Year's Day 1901, a party comprising three families: Mr. and Mrs. W. A. Van Horn with their six children; Mr. and Mrs. W. F. Gilett with seven children; and the widower L. M. Van Horn, with his four motherless offspring. They had been eking out a poor existence in Arizona's Salt River valley when Chaffey's promotional campaign lured them to a man-made paradise where "the land is free to all comers for a small government fee." (The fee was $1.25 an acre.) Laden with crates of chickens, five cows and a bull, and two Fresno scrapers—a horizontal plow hauled behind a horse to excavate and grade terrain—they made their way laboriously down the Gila River to Yuma, where they transported their goods and animals across the Colorado on a crude raft. The crossing took them seven days.

Upon reaching the promised land, they discovered that the California

Development Company had yet to deliver a drop of water to the Imperial Valley. Left without the necessary resources for farming, the crestfallen families subsisted for the next year on the only steady employment available in the region: working for the irrigation company. Hitching up their Fresnos, the men etched the first canal ditches into the valley floor. The two ladies established a commissary to feed a workforce that soon grew to more than thirty men (mostly would-be farmers awaiting the coming of water), while also caring for the seventeen children. Fresh food was impossible to come by, so the tiny community survived on tinned provisions imported by horse cart from the nearest Southern Pacific railhead, thirty miles to the north.

In the spring of 1901, Chaffey completed his cut into the river at Pilot Knob and gouged out a channel to the Rio Alamo with mule-drawn scrapers. On May 14, he opened the wooden headgate he had installed at the diversion point, and for the very first time Colorado River water flowed through a man-made channel into the Imperial Valley. Sixty miles from the river, the Alamo curved north and reentered the United States at a location known as Sharps Heading—or as some preferred, Buzzards Roost, after the thousands of foreboding birds that used its mesquite trees as launching points for their forays over the desert. Chaffey marked the occasion by dispatching a terse telegram from the border hamlet of Ogilby to his son Andrew in Los Angeles.

"Water turned through gate at 11 A.M.," he wrote. "Everything all right."

This judgment would prove to be wildly optimistic. Chaffey's gate design incorporated a flaw that would initiate a chain of disastrous events. Of more immediate import, the flow of water from Chaffey's canal, like the infusion of capital from his bankers, did nothing to alleviate the California Development Company's fundamental defect: it was still insolvent. In other words, by no means was "everything all right."

News that the water was finally flowing redoubled the influx of settlers, but failed to lessen the shock of their initial encounters with the valley.

They would arrive by rail or wagon with all their worldly goods, perhaps trailing a few head of household livestock, expecting at any moment to come upon the expanses of lush field and orchard conjured up by Chaffey's advertising campaign. Instead they discovered rutted roads and desolate fields, often obscured behind a haze of windblown sand. The most prominent vegetation was greasewood—tenacious bushes, poisonous to animals, as fire-resistant as asbestos and, thanks to their prehensile roots, clearable only by teams of horses dragging heavy chains. There was not a tree to be seen, no source of timber for home building or firewood, and "only a trickle of muddy red water which had to be strained before it could be drunk," one pioneer recalled.

For many, the first glimpse of their new home came at a depot named, inaptly, Flowing Well, which had been established by the Southern Pacific Railroad as a bivouac for its work crews. Flowing Well comprised the foreman's ramshackle frame house, several huts built out of discarded rail ties, and a population of mangy dogs "of questionable pedigree and suspicious behavior" (recalled Dr. Heffernan). Desert extended as far as the horizon on every side.

Scarcely any territory in the Western Hemisphere seemed more hostile to the accumulation and husbanding of water. One could drill a thousand feet into the ground without finding moisture. Months could pass without a drop of rain falling from the cloudless sky. When the rain did arrive, it fell in torrents too brief to nourish crops, but intense enough to create a sea of mud that immobilized settlers' wagons like tar. Upon reemerging, the sun baked the mud into a cracked and gullied carapace as resistant to the plow as a layer of granite.

Yet concealed behind this unprepossessing scrim were plentiful hints of the valley's potential richness. The stench of the black mud that churned up in the wake of a flood or downpour arose from its surfeit of biological nutrients. The territory may not have been overlaid with topsoil like the loamy earth cherished by farmers back east, but that was because the entire valley was topsoil. The river, an earthmover nonpareil, had transported this treasure hundreds of miles and deposited it as an immense alluvial fan, creating "a 500,000-acre bowl filled with a conglomeration of soils transported here by the Colorado River . . . not the usual six to ten inches deep, but a full mile or more."

Still, the toil required to extract sustenance from this harsh landscape drove countless disillusioned homesteaders back where they had come from. They felt hopelessly isolated and bullied by the pitiless elements. The mail service was erratic, wire communication nonexistent. They battled poisonous sidewinders and rattlesnakes for possession of their claims, the creatures slithering under the settlers' beds while they slept, leaving serpentine tracks on the dirt floors to be discovered in the morning by the unnerved householders.

Disease and infirmity were constant menaces. Typhoid, possibly carried by the brackish ditch water used for household purposes, was a particular threat.

My brother, Harold, was stricken at 14 [the youngster of a settler family recalled]. He lay for days in a delirious fever. Robert got "walking typhoid," I was still sick from the train, my mother took a dreadful cold from the sudden change of hot days and cold nights. The climax was reached when my father came in one morning with a swollen jaw from an ulcerated tooth, and surveying the utterly miserable group said, "God bless our happy home."

Strangely enough, another threat in this fantastically remote place was litigation. At any moment a homesteader might be confronted by the dreaded "contesters," who were schemers exploiting the haphazard drawing of property lines throughout the valley by challenging claims in court, hoping to extort quick monetary settlements.

The confusion arose from a bungled government survey of the desert in 1854. The survey party had filed maps of their work, but these were largely a sham, as the survey contract had been a patronage payoff to some long-forgotten politician's cronies. No one had actually gone into the field; popular legend held that the maps had been drafted "in the back room of a saloon in Yuma." But the consequences for the hapless settlers could be dire, as clouded property could not be posted as collateral on a loan. One settler recalled spending $20,000—in 1902!—to clear a contested claim on a single square mile of farmland.

Such an expenditure hinted at the wealth that awaited any farmer hardy enough to prevail against the challenges thrown up by nature and man. Indeed, those willing to stay were well positioned to benefit from the failings of their fellows. "Quitters helped a lot, they sell cheap and on credit," recalled T. D. McCall, who devoted thirty years of his life in an "unfaltering, laborious grind" to turn his square mile of valley into a thriving grapefruit grove.

What was quite properly described at the start of 1901 as "an accursed region of shimmering heat, mocking mirage and racking thirst" without a single white or European resident was supporting some two thousand settlers by the end of 1902, after the water began to flow. One year later, the census was seven thousand; it doubled again over the following twelve months. The Southern Pacific soon had a branch line bisecting the valley to provide regular passenger and freight service. At the turn of the year 1905, the Imperial Valley boasted seven towns, each with its complement of banks and shops; nearly eight hundred miles of distribution canals; and 120,000 acres under cultivation. The value of its alfalfa, cotton, and barley crop approached $2 million a year. Irrigation had turned the onetime desert into the envy of the nation.

The California Development Company should have been among the greatest beneficiaries of this astounding growth. Chaffey had contrived an elaborate financial structure to profit from the valley's development, even though it did not own the land it was helping to populate with farmers and ranchers—the real estate belonged to the United States government, which offered it to citizens in blocks of up to 320 acres for that fee of $1.25 per acre. All that the CDC owned was the canal and the water in it.

Chaffey's corporate structure, however, allowed the CDC to involve itself in almost every detail of the Imperial Valley's economy. The CDC brought the water from the Colorado River, sold it to one of its own subsidiaries in

Mexico, and transferred the rights to another subsidiary upon its recrossing the border—maneuvers designed largely to foil efforts by the state of California to regulate local water rates. It dictated the terms of water sales to landholders, lent them the money to buy it, and took a mortgage on their lands to guarantee repayment. If they defaulted, it took possession of their farms. Unsurprisingly, the CDC soon became the valley's largest landlord.

Yet with every sale by the California Development Company of a share of water stock (representing a commitment to supply a newly developed acre with irrigation), it sank deeper in debt—"swamped by prosperity," in the words of Godfrey Sykes, a local geographer.

The problem stemmed partially from Rockwood's original undercapitalization of the company, partially from its sale of water rights on credit, and partially from its overspending on advertising, which left almost nothing for the crucial work of digging canals and erecting headgates.

The company had hoped to finance the construction of canals and waterworks by borrowing against the credit notes it held from the settlers, but Los Angeles banks refused to accept the notes as collateral. Consequently, as Imperial filled up with settlers, the company became committed to supplying more water at greater expense and, as Rockwood acknowledged later, "with no money in sight to do the work."

Matters were not improved by the personal animosity between Chaffey and Rockwood. Chaffey blamed the company's fragile financial position on fraud by Rockwood. The latter, for his part, resented how Chaffey had taken credit for the irrigation plan he had nurtured in his own breast for the better part of a decade. As the company fell deeper into the red, the mutual hostility grew until it rendered impossible even routine decision making by the two principals.

This was the situation only months after water filled the Alamo channel and began reaching settlers in the Imperial Valley. The California Development Company should have been riding a tide of engineering triumph and financial success. Instead, as Chaffey's biographer would describe matters years later, the company was "a craft loaded below the plimsoll with liabilities, and carrying a mutinous crew waiting for a chance to scuttle it." Nature and man were about to collude on a capsizing blow.

# 3

## Rockwood's Gamble

The California Development Company was back under Rockwood's management in 1902, thanks to a series of backroom maneuvers through which he had quietly accumulated proxies for a majority of CDC shares. Chaffey, realizing that Rockwood's shareholdings punched holes in what he thought was his ironclad contract, decided to avert a long and costly court showdown with the company's founder. He sold his interest in the CDC to Rockwood for a $100,000 note and $25,000 in cash. Rockwood obtained the funds from Dr. Heffernan, who had resurfaced as a reliable backer.

In recognition of Heffernan's loyalty Rockwood named him treasurer. This was something of a poisoned chalice, Heffernan later acknowledged, as it led him to the shocked discovery of the company's true financial condition. "I fell heir to an empty cash box," he recalled.

Chaffey's access to capital had saved the company from extinction only two years earlier. Yet now, at the very moment when it desperately needed money to redouble its ditch digging to bring water to its customers, Chaffey had been driven off. In the words of Otis Tout, one of the valley's pioneering businessmen and its earliest historian, as soon as Chaffey quit, the "birds of evil omen began again to hover" over the CDC.

The main source of its problems was the implacable river. The awe-inspiring Grand Canyon only hinted at the Colorado's capacity to scour soil and stone from its path and redeposit the material downstream. For all that the Nile and Mississippi are renowned for their alluvial deltas, the Colorado outstripped their ratio of silt to water by a factor of seven. On average, the river carried enough material to build a levee twenty feet high, twenty feet wide, and a mile long every single day. Put another way, in any given year it could bury the entire Imperial Valley under six inches of sediment.

The turbid red stream inspired a host of folk epigrams. The Colorado was damned as "too thick to drink and too thin to plow" and wags swore that on windy days dust could be seen blowing off the water's surface. As exaggerated as these jests sound, they were uncomfortably close to the truth. Silt clogged the canal faster than the CDC could dredge it out. The influx of settlers only aggravated the situation, for the greater the volume of water flowing through the Alamo, the more sediment was deposited there and the more rapidly the channel was choked off. In the winter of 1902, the barricade of mud produced a water shortage in the valley for the first time since George Chaffey had turned on the flow at Pilot Knob.

Some of the blame surely belonged to Chaffey himself, for he had installed the Pilot Knob headgate improperly: it sat so high above the channel floor that in the winter, the water level fell too low to pass over its sill. The gate, as it happened, failed to conform to Rockwood's specifications, a point he never failed to mention when complaints of water shortages began to reach the CDC's offices.

Whoever deserved the blame, the situation was untenable. Any extended dry spell would jeopardize a king's ransom in crops. The company's remedy every autumn was to excavate a bypass around Chaffey's gate to ensure that water reached into the canal, and to dam up the bypass every spring to prevent the canal from being overwhelmed by summer floods. The bypass, meanwhile, caused another problem, which was that the erratic flow allowed greater quantities of sediment to collect in the main channel, choking it off even faster than before.

The right way to keep the channel clear was constant dredging, but that task, requiring thirty dredges operating twenty-four hours a day, was well beyond the CDC's meager financial capacity. So every year the company fell further behind in its pitched battle with the muddy river. The canal blockages produced a major drought, affecting fourteen thousand settlers then tilling farmland in the valley, in 1904. Damage claims of more than $500,000 piled up in the CDC's offices, adding to Rockwood's financial torment.

Four miles of the main canal had become solidly clogged. Rockwood decided to try blasting out the silt with the full force of the summer current. This, he supposed, would scour the canal clear much as one might clean out a clogged gutter with a high-pressure hose. Put into action, this stratagem worked exactly as expected—at first. The torrent sluiced two feet of silt out of the canal, ensuring a suitable supply of irrigation water for the spring. But Rockwood had not reckoned with one of the peculiarities of a silt-bearing stream like the Colorado, which is that under certain conditions the river can deposit more sediment than it removes. This is exactly what happened when the current began to slacken in late summer. By the end of the season, despite all of Rockwood's careful planning, the silt level measured one foot higher than it had been at the beginning.

Another winter of parched crops would ruin the California Development Company. Plainly, the situation required a more decisive approach. Whether the CDC was capable of delivering it seemed doubtful.

The 1904 drought dealt a fatal blow to the company's standing in the Imperial Valley, which had already been hopelessly undermined by several seasons of erratic water deliveries. Rockwood, proud of his stature as the valley's pioneering developer and in his usual state of denial about his own responsibility for the company's ebbing reputation, was certain he could detect the government's hand in the surge of damage claims and the settlers' growing agitation for a federal takeover of the irrigation program. Specifically, he blamed the anti-CDC sentiment on the U.S. Reclamation Service, which the government had established in 1902 to put John Wesley Powell's ideas into practice.

But there was another agitator behind the settlers' growing militancy: a transplanted New England journalist operating out of San Diego named William Ellsworth Smythe. Distinguished by his close-trimmed Van Dyke beard and cultivated bearing, Smythe was the most eminent of a breed of characters who had begun to appear on the American political scene in the 1890s and might best be described as water evangelists. They resembled Wozencraft and Rockwood in their devout belief in the potential of irrigation to reclaim arid lands. But where Wozencraft and Rockwood saw irrigation chiefly in commercial terms, Smythe and his fellows saw it as an instrument of social reform and moral revival.

Irrigation, Smythe contended, was by its nature a communal enterprise, requiring the weaving of a fabric of community institutions that would perforce supplant the dismal individualism of the small-farm and urban economies. Irrigation was "not merely a matter of ditches and acres, but a philosophy, a religion, and a programme of practical statesmanship rolled into one." A spellbinding orator, Smythe nominated himself as the standard-bearer of this "new crusade."

Disenchanted with the CDC and its commercial orientation, Smythe made common cause with the Reclamation Service to eradicate the private commercial administration of irrigation. In the Imperial Valley he orchestrated public meetings to agitate for a government takeover of the CDC, and in Washington pressed Congress to impose "Government ownership of the Imperial system . . . as the nucleus of a magnificent system of public works on the lower Colorado."

Thirty years later, this vision would become reality. In the meantime, however, the valley was still at the CDC's mercy. The company had sold irrigation rights over 217,000 acres—three times as many as it could reliably supply with water. In the winter, persistent canal blockages made deliveries so unreliable that some farmers simply gave up planting winter crops. Fees were too high, the wait for water too long, the CDC's promises too threadbare.

Rockwood's ultimate solution to the clogging of the river was to cut an entirely new diversion point downstream from Pilot Knob, four miles south of the Mexican border. He claimed to have designed the project in accordance with the most rigorous professional considerations. In fact it was another cheap, quick, and dirty CDC solution to a pressing problem, a glorified ditch 3,300 feet long and fifty feet wide, detouring around the silted-up portion of the Alamo but lacking even the most rudimentary control gates. The entire excavation took three weeks. The cut was located just opposite a long ovoid sandbar that forked the river into two parallel streams. This feature presently would acquire the bleakly appropriate name of Disaster Island.

Rockwood's decision to cut into the riverbank at this location was an act of heedless folly, as would soon become plain—"a blunder so serious as to be practically criminal," in the considered judgment of one expert. Geologists working on the lower river had already noticed decreasing stability on the Colorado's banks, with breaches and localized floods becoming more common and severe. The volume of driftwood cascading downstream on floodtides had increased, too, possibly because grazing and farming along the tributary Gila River had stripped the watershed of grasses that protected the land from erosion and prevented the uprooting of its willows and poplars. Experts familiar with the great geological oscillations that had shifted the river's outlet between the Gulf of California and the Salton Sink over the eons were picking up signals that another cycle was in the offing.

Yet Rockwood was confident that the river would behave until summer, time enough for the CDC to equip the new diversion cut with adequate control works. The river rarely flooded in winter, after all—at least not according to the twenty-seven years of records he claimed to have studied before undertaking the cut. In all that time there had occurred but three winter floods, none of them serious. As he wrote defensively much later, "I doubt as to whether anyone should be accused of negligence or carelessness in failing to foresee that which had never happened before."

His mistake was judging the Colorado by a misleadingly brief period of docility. In the winter of 1905, the river would show exactly how impulsive and cantankerous it could be. In effect, the Colorado was balanced on a geological knife edge. In his quest for an easy way to keep water flowing to his customers and so avoid bankruptcy, Charles Robinson Rockwood tipped it over.

\* \* \*

The first warning that the valley was in for an unusual winter came on February 2, with a telephone call to CDC headquarters in Calexico from Pilot Knob warning that the leading edge of a heavy flood had just passed Yuma. The surge reached Rockwood's new diversion cut within the hour, silting up the opening.

Rockwood dispatched dredges into the channel and issued a frantic order for brushwood and baling wire to erect a temporary gate. The material was still being assembled on February 19 when a second flood roared down from the Gila, filling the channel with a new load of viscous mud.

"We were not alarmed," Rockwood wrote later—at least the opening had not been eroded away, which would have been a dire event. Complacently, he figured that there would be plenty of time to upgrade the intake before the summer floods threatened it in earnest. His smugness lasted for eight days, when the river struck again.

The third flood doubled the width of the intake gap, allowing so much water to surge through that the tide destroyed the canal levees at Sharps Heading, nearly fifty miles downstream. From there, water began flowing west in sheets, threatening Mexicali and Calexico, the low-lying settler communities that straddled the international border. In desperation, the CDC shut the Sharps Heading gate. This diverted the current into a dry channel known as New River, which in turn funneled the water into the Salton Sink. That forlorn geologic basin, which had been mostly dry for four centuries, was about to be reborn as the Salton Sea.

The third flood finally awakened Rockwood to the peril created by his cut. His solution was to blockade the gap with a temporary levee made of thick mats of brush weighted down with ten thousand burlap sacks filled with sand. The levee narrowed the cut to thirty feet, a gap Rockwood prepared to close with another brush-and-sand-bag barricade.

The project was days away from completion on March 18 when the fourth flood of that remorseless winter tore downstream with breathtaking force blasting apart the barricade in seconds. Watching the debris wash down the channel, Rockwood gamely ordered one more attempt at a closure. This one had not gotten far beyond the erection of a temporary mud levee on April 18, when "a warning cry was heard at the intake." The work teams managed to scurry to safety just before another surge inundated the worksite and carried the levee off downstream.

At that moment, with the river still rising, the gap widening, the summer flood season approaching, Rockwood recognized that the CDC was at the end of its rope. Its credit was exhausted and its customers exposed to crop losses of millions of dollars attributable to its ineptitude. He concluded that his only option was to appeal for an emergency loan from the biggest commercial enterprise in the region, the Southern Pacific Railroad. The Southern Pacific, Rockwood reasoned, had a powerful interest in saving the valley from the river, for its freight revenues had grown in lockstep with the expansion of irrigation in the valley. This vision of their shared destinies gave him the courage to make a brazen appeal personally to the railroad's president, the self-made tycoon Edward H. Harriman.

Fully alive to the profits to be made in serving irrigated lands, Harriman provisionally agreed to lend the CDC $200,000. Unaware of the developing emergency, however, he believed Rockwood was seeking the money to expand the valley's irrigation channels, a misconception Rockwood did nothing to correct. In any case, Harriman insisted on stringent terms. The Southern Pacific was to control 51 percent of the CDC's stock and appoint three of its seven directors and its president. To serve as the latter, Harriman designated Epes Randolph, one of his top engineers. What the magnate could not foresee was that the deal would make him fully liable for Charles Rockwood's slipshod management, and bring him into direct conflict with a very obstinate President Theodore Roosevelt.

Loan in hand, Rockwood returned to the valley with the reduced title of chief engineer of the CDC. The situation had worsened markedly in his absence, with the diversion now more than 150 feet wide—triple its original span. That was still narrow enough to close with a conventional barricade. Most of the river, moreover, was still following its traditional path to the Gulf of California. But every day the gap grew dangerously wider. Despite this, Rockwood's attitude had turned surprisingly nonchalant. Rather than spend his newly acquired funds on an emergency barricade, he suspended all work in early June and, presuming that the current would ebb as the summer played out, decided to let nature take its course.

Six weeks later, at the beginning of August, Epes Randolph arrived for his first inspection of the canal as the CDC's president. The sight left him dumbfounded. The river was cascading through the diversion cut, dissolving the soft canal banks like sugar in warm tea. Randolph and Harold Cory, his deputy engineer, confronted Rockwood with their judgment of the peril at hand, only to hear him dismiss their concerns with bewildering sangfroid. He proposed allowing the river to continue running wild, for the current was displacing a large volume of the silt that had blocked up the channel in the first place. As Cory later recalled his attitude, it was that "considering everything, the gross benefits being worked far exceeded the damages which would be caused." A thunderstruck Cory bluntly informed Rockwood that he was "playing with fire."

Randolph hastened north to give Harriman the dismal news that his money had been sunk in one of the world's largest ratholes. The valley risked being inundated by an ungovernable river, menacing millions of dollars in crops and the livelihood of thousands. The breach could be closed, but it would take much more than the $200,000 already loaned to Rockwood. Randolph informed Harriman that the final tally might well approach $1 million.

Harriman paused to weigh this expenditure against the consequences of abandoning the valley. "Are you certain you can put that river back into the old channel?" he asked.

"It can be done," Randolph replied.

"Go ahead and do it."

The job would take seven attempts over eighteen months, and cost the railroad more than $3 million.

Through that spring and into the summer, the Imperial Valley's settlers had remained largely oblivious to the seriousness of their predicament. Then, in mid-July, the surging Alamo washed out five bridges and began to menace the homesteads on the valley's lowest-lying portions. A brigade of ranchers from the flatlands around Calexico assembled to build makeshift levees to contain the spreading flood.

The New River, a formerly dry barranca now pouring Colorado River water into the Salton Sea, soon became unfordable by conventional means. Local farmers suspended a cable over the stream to haul people, goods, and animals across the water in an undertaker's wicker basket. At least once the cable snapped in mid-journey, sending a hapless passenger to his watery death.

A few old-timers scoffed at the notion that this flood might have more staying power than the annual inundations of years past. The case was reported of Nathanial Lane, eighty, a homesteader on the valley's western fringe who spurned help from a rescue boat as the waters rose around his land. Eight days later someone remembered him and sent out another boat to see how he was faring. "The water was higher than ever," a witness recalled. "The old man had lashed his bed to the roof of his shack and had to fight all sorts of rattlesnakes, insects, etc., to keep them off. One had bitten him and his leg was swollen badly. He had had nothing to eat for three days."

Randolph and Cory frantically sought a solution to what was shaping up as the most dire engineering problem they had ever experienced. In September, Randolph settled on a scheme to use a six-hundred-foot dam of pilings, brush, and sandbags to force the river away from the breach and around the eastern shore of Disaster Island. Over the next two months the Southern Pacific spent more than $50,000 to build the structure. The job was nearly done as November drew to a close. Then the river struck again.

On the evening of November 29, the largest flood recorded on the Colorado since 1891 swept downstream from the Gila River, laden with its usual freight of uprooted trees and other debris. It washed away several miles of railroad tracks west of Yuma before slamming into Randolph's worksite. The wave left nothing of the dam but the pilings, and even carried off much of the equipment assembled for the job. Half of Disaster Island disappeared under the surface.

The river now was cascading toward the Salton Sink through a breach in its bank that yawned a quarter of a mile from end to end. Randolph devised a more elaborate plan involving a new headgate of concrete and steel at Pilot Knob and a second wooden gate near Disaster Island. Starting before Christmas, his crews worked around the clock, racing to complete the project before the beginning of flood season. In contrast to the previous winter, the river remained docile. By April, the wooden gate was nearing completion. The Pilot Knob gate was taking shape as the largest and most expensive irrigation structure in the country—the first of a series of monumental water-control works that would eventually bring the great Colorado to heel. But Randolph had spent the last of his authorization, and much work remained to be done.

Then, with a flair for timing that can only be described as elementally perverse, nature unleashed another blow. At 5:12 A.M. on Wednesday, April 18, 1906, on a clear, uncharacteristically fogless dawn, the San Andreas Fault just offshore from San Francisco snapped like an overloaded tree limb. The first shock waves struck the city less than a minute later. Within hours, much of what had been the largest metropolis on the West Coast was cut off from the outside world and engulfed in flames.

Three thousand people lost their lives and many more their livelihoods. For E. H. Harriman, the situation was catastrophic. San Francisco was the western hub of his transportation empire. From his headquarters in Oakland, he had a perfect, if dispiriting, view of the black smoke rising over San Francisco by day and flames consuming the city through the night.

It was there that Epes Randolph, who had hastened north from Calexico, tracked him down. Randolph's message was as bleak as the scene across the bay: he was on the verge of losing his battle with the river six hundred miles to the south and out of funds. Somehow, despite "the bustle and confusion of temporary offices, with the ruins of San Francisco still smoking, with the wonderful railway system which constituted Mr. Harriman's life work crippled to an unknown extent," Randolph managed to get his boss to focus, if only for a moment, on the crisis down south. Harriman listened briefly, and wrote him a check for $250,000 to bring the Colorado under control.

Returning to the river, Randolph installed Harold Cory as supervisor of the emergency program. Square-jawed and unsentimental, Cory was an accomplished engineer whose precocious résumé included his appointment at the age of twenty-six as a full professor of engineering at the University of Missouri. His grasp of the situation was all-encompassing, like a war-hardened general on the battlefield. The understanding brought him no solace. The quantity of earth washed into the Salton Sink in just nine months exceeded that excavated from the Panama Canal by a factor of four. The newly christened Salton Sea was rising seven inches a day. A change in topography that normally required eons was unfolding before his eyes, and nothing could get out of its way. "The water," he later recounted to a congressional committee, "simply tore things in the valley to pieces." Having created its new channel, the river could be rediverted only by a superhuman effort. The drop in elevation from the channel at Disaster Island to the Salton Sink was four times steeper than the route toward the Gulf of California. Nature dictated that the river would choose the steeper gradient. This it had done. As the flow toward the gulf slowed to a trickle, the flow into the Salton Sink grew into a deluge.

About a month after Cory's promotion, at the start of the summer flood season, the river unsheathed the most alarming weapon in its destructive arsenal. This was the phenomenon known as the "cutback."

In simple terms, the river was carving itself a new gorge. Rather than flowing into the Salton Sink as though down an unbroken incline, the current hurtled over a precipice at the point where the New River entered the Salton Sea. This miniature Niagara proceeded to claw its way upstream at a pace of a mile a day, leaving in its wake a canyon eighty feet deep.

For a time, the display of nature ruthlessly at work attracted curiosity seekers to the brink of the new gorge. But no one could ignore the awful consequences that would ensue if the cutback continued working its way upstream. If it managed to cleave through the main canal at the Alamo River, all the Imperial Valley's irrigation channels would drain into the gorge like unstoppered bathtubs, leaving almost all the valley's arable land sitting eighty feet above the water level. Irrigation would cease forever. "This would mean the entire depopulation of the valley in less than four days," Cory reflected later. "Every living thing would have to get out, because there would be no water at all except in the deep canyon of the New River."

The cutback soon insinuated itself into the valley's daily life. In Calexico at night it sounded like a continuous roll of thunder in the distance or, to the war veterans among the settlers, an unceasing artillery barrage. In the daytime, eruptions of dust could be seen on the horizon, thrown up by enormous masses of earth breaking off from the sides of the gorge like icebergs detaching themselves from an Arctic glacier. To peer down into the current itself was to lose faith that it could ever be brought under control—not this boiling red flood viscous with silt.

The people of Mexicali, a city that had expanded organically over the low alluvial plain at the river's edge, waged a futile battle to protect themselves from the advancing cataract. In the end there was nothing for them to do but watch stoically as the flood chewed away at the riverbanks and coursed through their streets, devouring the town house by adobe house. On June 30 the main business district collapsed into the water, a dozen brick buildings swept away in a matter of hours while the townspeople stood transfixed under clouds of spray towering forty feet in the air. Before the flood was over, four-fifths of the town would be wiped out.

Forty miles upstream, Cory was mustering his men to execute Randolph's latest plan. His task was to seal off the main canal with the iron headgate and a stone levee, forcing the river south into the bypass at Disaster Island. There it was to be corralled by the secondary gate, a solid wooden structure firmly anchored in a rock foundation. The virtue of this arrangement was that irrigation could continue to reach the valley while a permanent repair was made at the riverbank.

The staging area acquired the bustle of a military outpost, complete with platoons of female camp followers, immigrant laborers, and the idle curious. Because so many of the railroad's able-bodied men were still occupied in stricken San Francisco, Cory recruited most of his workforce from local tribes—Pimas, Papagoes, Maricopas, Yumas, Cocopahs, and Diegueños. Two thousand Indians, of whom four hundred were male laborers and the rest women and children, built themselves a makeshift camp south of the border. Mexican tax inspectors hovered nearby to ensure that the Southern Pacific paid all proper duties on the equipment and material it brought across the border. (The bill would come to $75,000.)

Dr. Heffernan, who had signed on as the camp surgeon, made the acquaintance of Frank Pollack, an opera singer whose doctors had sent him to the Western desert to cure a throat ailment. Fetching up at camp, Pollack proved himself a "most capable and efficient" general handyman. Late one night Pollack wandered out to the edge of camp and toward the Indian settlement, exercising his voice on a selection of arias. "About the time he reached O Donna E Mobile his voice was in full swing," recalled Heffernan, who then heard the camp foreman turn over in his cot and complain, "damn those Indians, they're drunk again."

Over the next several weeks, Cory succeeded in lining the channel floor with granite boulders and brush tied into bundles by iron cables, all of it pinned to the bottom by driven piles and crowned by the sturdy wooden gate. Finally, on October 10, the crews managed to steer the river into the rock-lined bypass. The Colorado had been brought to heel for the first time in over a year.

One day later, the triumphant crews watched helplessly as the foundations, which unbeknownst to them had been eroding underwater for weeks, collapsed. The gate buckled, snapped apart, and floated fifty yards downstream, where it ran aground. The river instantly resumed its thundering way toward the Salton Sea.

Cory brought the river back under control on November 4 "by exhausting the capacities of every quarry between Los Angeles and Nogales, four hundred and eighty-five miles to the east." Yet one month later, the river busted loose again. For Harry Cory, the sixth failed attempt to close the breach was the last straw. The Southern Pacific had poured more than a million dollars "into that hole" and the river had swept it all away. A sustainable repair required not only a dam, but the construction and permanent maintenance of fifteen miles of levees along the west bank, reinforced with concrete and steel to keep the river corralled even at its most violent. These would be the most expensive levees ever built over such a distance—not a job for the Southern Pacific, in his weary judgment. The railroad was the most resourceful, rich, and powerful enterprise in the Southwest, yet the river had brought it to its knees.

The solution, Cory judged, lay in the hands of the federal government. And why not? Some 350,000 of the nation's most productive irrigated acres lay in the balance, along with the fate of fifteen thousand citizens. In light of the expense already incurred by the Southern Pacific, the benefits it reaped by preserving this terrain began to look dubious—for every $1 million worth of produce it transported out of the valley, its executives later calculated, the railroad pocketed a mere $20,000 in profit. Cory informed Randolph crisply that they faced an implacable engineering problem with no immediate solution, even after unlimited expenditures. "I would not recommend any one individual nor any one corporation, no matter how strong, to try to hold that river in its bounds," he reported. "The cheapest thing would be to give it up and let it go."

But it would not be that simple.

The saga's final phase began with an exchange of testy telegrams between Edward H. Harriman and Theodore Roosevelt.

The two men had first gotten to know each other as pillars of the New York Republican Party in the 1890s—Harriman as its leading financial supporter and Roosevelt its rising flag-bearer. In 1906, Harriman and his wife were among the guests at the most outstanding social event in Washington that year, the wedding of the president's daughter Alice and Nicholas Longworth. But Roosevelt's rancorous campaign for stiff railroad regulation and his newfound habit of holding up Harriman as an exemplar of the rapacious capitalist, a ringleader of a cabal he damned in public oratory as "malefactors of great wealth," shredded the relationship between the two eminences.

This surely explained the icy formality of Harriman's telegram to Roosevelt on December 13, in which he tallied all the money the railroad had spent in its fruitless attempt to control the river—more than $1.6 million, by his reckoning—on behalf of private farmers and the federal government.

"It does not seem fair," he wrote, "that we should be called upon to do more."

Two days later Roosevelt replied to Harriman with condescending terseness: "I assume you are planning to continue work immediately on closing break in Colorado River. I should be fully informed as to how far you intend to proceed in the matter."

Harriman offered to contribute his tracks and crews and to allow the use of the Southern Pacific's quarries, but he insisted that the labor be done by men employed by the Reclamation Service. "Can you bring this about?" he asked Roosevelt.

The president refused the bait, insisting that the railroad, which he considered to be the CDC's master, complete the job. Possibly to coerce Harriman into doing his bidding, he assured the tycoon that he would ask Congress to reimburse the railroad for closing the break as soon as it reconvened in the new year. Harriman relented. On December 20 he wired Randolph: "Close that break at all cost." Forty-eight hours later, the final superhuman effort to drive the Colorado back into its old channel was launched under Harold Cory's direction.

For the next six weeks there was scarcely an asset of the Southern Pacific that Cory did not conscript to close the breach with a massive rock dam— 1,200 miles of track, three thousand flatcars, and an army of workers. Cory's demand for rolling stock was so great that passenger trains were sidetracked and rail shipments out of the Los Angeles port came to a standstill.

Cory's plan called for the construction of two railway trestles over the breach. From these it was hoped that the flatcars could dump rock into the river faster than the current could wash it away—the exact same method that would be used to seal off the river for construction of a great dam nearly thirty years later.

The river constantly molested the work; crewmen tumbled into the tumultuous waters so regularly that boats were kept anchored in midstream to haul them to safety. But after two weeks of unrelenting dumping, the submerged rock wall began to break the surface. On February 10, 1907, Cory at last declared the break closed. The Colorado, that yellow dragon, once again flowed peacefully to the Gulf of California. This time the levees held.

Charles Rockwood's flood permanently altered the landscape of the Imperial Valley. Its newest feature, the Salton Sea, was the largest lake in California, occupying five hundred square miles and boasting a maximum depth of seventy-eight feet. (The lake still holds that distinction today, although it has shrunk to 376 square miles and fifty feet in depth.)

Damage claims from the flood would clog local courthouses for years and scuttled the hopelessly insolvent CDC, which landed in receivership and was liquidated in 1909. The Southern Pacific's bill for taming the river eventually came to $3.2 million, half of it spent in the months following Roosevelt's order. Over the next eleven years, the railroad repeatedly petitioned Congress to make good on Roosevelt's promise of reimbursement. But the public had long since gained the impression that the railroad had caused the flood. Congress therefore came to view any reimbursement as "purely a gratuity, a gift of the people's money to the Southern Pacific Railroad Company," as a House committee reported in 1917. In the end, the railroad never recovered a dime from the public purse.

Harriman nonetheless felt lasting pride at having saved the Imperial Valley. "That was the best single bit of work done on my authority and responsibility," he told the financier Otto Kahn.

Shortly before his death in 1909 Harriman visited the valley, stopping to inspect the levees his crews had erected under such dire conditions. An interviewer from the *Los Angeles Examiner* asked him whether he did not regret the effort.

"This valley was worth saving, wasn't it?" he replied.

"Yes."

"Then we have the satisfaction of knowing that we saved it, haven't we?"


Theodore Roosevelt moved to exploit the great flood in his own way. On January 12, 1907—still a month before Cory closed the Colorado River breach—the president delivered to Congress his personal vision of a reclaimed and resplendent desert. It was a plan that gave the role of prime mover to the federal government, rather than lone entrepreneurs or private corporations.

Roosevelt's program conceded nothing to the grandest fancies of Oliver Wozencraft and Charles Rockwood. He embraced the concept of building a canal entirely on the American side of the border to avoid the complexities of international water management, along with a vast program of "diversion dams and distribution systems in the Colorado River Valley." He summed it all up as "a broad comprehensive scheme of development for all the irrigable land upon [the] Colorado River . . . so that none of the water of this great river which can be put to beneficial use will be allowed to go to waste."

In his conception, some 700,000 new acres of land in California and Arizona would come under irrigation. There would be permanent flood control and bounteous reservoirs—in other words, a Colorado River brought to heel once and for all under the aegis of the United States government. It was the most audacious deployment of government resources ever proposed for the continental United States, the grandest plan for an American public work since the Panama Canal.

Charles Rockwood created the opportunity, Theodore Roosevelt seized it, and his distant cousin Franklin Roosevelt would claim the political credit. But before that would happen, the U.S. Congress and seven Western states would have to spend twenty years arguing over the devilish details.

# 4

## The Lord's Dam Site

**W**hat she noticed first was the heat.

It was searing, suffocating, trapped by the steep canyon walls and radiated back into the air by the rocky, dusty flats at the edge of the river.

To Edna Jackson it was as unforgiving as an alien force. She had given up her schoolteaching job in Idaho to marry her beau, Clarence "Jack" Jackson, a surveyor who spent most of his time on the road and had finally sent for her from the Nevada desert. When she left Idaho, patches of snow still covered the ground. At her wedding ceremony two days later in Las Vegas, the thermometer read 104.

And a day after that, Jack brought her down to the canyon, where she would be sharing her living quarters with tarantulas, centipedes, and desert snakes.

> We had in the back of the Model T pickup a three-hundred pound cake of ice, enough groceries to last about a week [she recalled a half-century later]. It was a hot ride, and a slow one—a slow one because first, the Model T could not travel very fast at its best, and second, most of the way was up one dry wash and down another. I remember one narrow wash where a pick and shovel had to be used before we could get through.

As they descended the gorge, Edna spotted a herd of bighorn sheep on the hillside, gnawing on spiky desert shrubs. "One, quite close to us, was standing on a rocky pinnacle with his back arched. What a sight! We never saw so many at one time again. Maybe they were there to welcome us home."

Jack had been surveying in Boulder Canyon since December 1922, when he presented his credentials at a government office in Las Vegas and was told to report to work the next day. The job site was reached by driving north on the main highway from Las Vegas (today's Interstate 15), until it was intersected by a gravel road running east. This road ended at a borax mine, which was extracting the snowy mineral from the ancient bed of a dry lake. That was the last outpost of civilization for seventeen miles, until the journey came to an end at a riverbank where a couple of dozen tents were clustered, housing a crew of sunbaked men drilling into the river bottom from barges and clambering over the canyon walls toting measuring rods and surveyor's transits.

They were there to investigate possible locations for a high dam. The work had begun in early 1921 under the supervision of Walker Young, the thin-lipped government engineer who had inspected Jack's résumé in Las Vegas from behind a pair of round horn-rimmed glasses. Four barges were anchored in the river, each secured in place by cables driven into the canyon walls. Their wooden decks each held a derrick-mounted diamond-tipped drill that, turned by a ten horsepower gasoline motor, could bore into fifty feet of bedrock. A busy fleet of flat-bottomed skiffs ferried men and equipment back and forth.

Jack's particular job was to measure the river current. This was done from a basket suspended on a cable strung across the gorge. Every day Jack and an assistant would climb into this contraption and let gravity carry them across the canyon to the halfway point, where the cable dipped closest to the water, lowering meters into the current to read the river's flow and depth. From the midpoint they would have to haul on the cable by hand to get to the other side, before returning to base by the same method.

Home for the newlywed Edna Jackson was a place of surpassing isolation, fifty miles from the run-down rail depot where she had said her marriage vows. The camp population had peaked at about sixty men a few months before her arrival, but with the coming of summer it shrank to a skeleton staff of three, warranting Jack Jackson's decision to bring his bride into camp for companionship. Still, Edna was enthralled by the natural beauty of the place. Willows towered over the riverbank, and in spring flowers in bloom peppered the dun-colored terrain with splotches of bright color. Then there was the majesty of the gorge itself, narrow as the waist of an hourglass, with walls of solid rock towering so high on either side that she could scarcely see their summits.

Edna would later claim the distinction of being the first white woman to live in the gorge, the trailblazer for thousands of girls and women uprooted from homes in almost every state to create a semblance of domestic order in an alien and pitiless land. A hardy tolerance for self-abnegation was the one quality essential for survival in this place, as Edna quickly learned. Her food locker was a cave dug deep into the hillside, furnished with double doors to keep out the heat and the sun—the inner door a foot thick. The supplies would arrive by truck from Las Vegas accompanied by a boulder-sized block of ice that would go into the cave first, the groceries then deposited around it. Edna was warned never to leave the door even slightly ajar, for the heat would penetrate even the smallest crack. For drinking water, the camp had a barrel that would be pumped full from the river and then left to stand, for it would take at least a day for the silt to settle enough for the water to be usable.

Contact with civilization depended on two road-weary Ford Model T pickups, one of which ran on parts cannibalized from the other. Social visitors were extremely rare—the occasional carload of joyriders seeking respite from the heat of the season in the chilly river. That made it a memorable day in October 1923 when three boatloads of adventurers fresh from a U.S. Geological Survey exploration of the Grand Canyon unexpectedly emerged from upstream and pulled up at the camp. Edna served them coffee, but she failed to earn even a glancing acknowledgment in the lengthy account of their journey that appeared in the *National Geographic Magazine* the following May.

It did not take much to completely sever the link with the outside world.

One morning before dawn, Jack dispatched his assistant to Las Vegas in the working Ford for ice, food, and other supplies, with instructions to be back in camp by nightfall. When he still had not returned two days later, the marooned Jacksons packed up the last of their dwindling provisions—a canteen of water, a can of peaches, and a pair of lemons—and set off for the borax factory on foot.

The water and food ran out while they were still on the road. "We would walk five or ten minutes, then crawl under the meager shade of a mesquite bush and rest twenty minutes," Edna recalled. After a twelve-hour trek, having fended off thirst, hunger, and the occasional rattlesnake in their path, they staggered into the factory office, where they were treated for exposure and put up for the night. The next morning the plant lent them a car to drive to Las Vegas, where they eventually located their wayward driver, "who had been living it up" in the town's various dens of sin, as Edna recalled. "Needless to say, he was given two weeks notice."

Although Walker Young's camp was the first concentrated effort to survey the canyons, the search for dam sites on the river had begun almost twenty years earlier, in 1902, when the Edison Electric Company of Los Angeles dispatched its engineers to scout locations for a forty-foot rock dam capable of generating ten thousand horsepower.

Their leader was Joseph Barlow Lippincott, a veteran of John Wesley Powell's earliest irrigation survey. Lippincott returned dubious that any profitable market existed for hydroelectric generation on the Colorado. At the time, the outer limit of high-voltage electric transmission was about eighty miles. The only customers for power generated on the Colorado, therefore, were mines in Arizona and Nevada, which Lippincott disparaged as doomed to hopeless decline.

There were contradictory views, but Edison bought into its hired consultant's pessimism. Based on his recommendation, the company relinquished its options on several prospective dam sites on the lower Colorado. This rash and shortsighted act would leave the company without a bargaining chip when it attempted, a quarter-century later, to dissuade the federal government from installing a public hydroelectric station on the river, at the very location where it once held indisputable rights to the land.

Lippincott himself eventually underwent a conversion from a skeptic of power development on the Colorado into one of its chief proselytizers. Less than a decade after he maligned the Colorado to Edison Electric as a useless stream, he returned to the river as consulting engineer for the city of Los Angeles—this time delivering his extravagant description of it as an "American Nile" needing only intelligent regulation to reach its full potential in serving mankind. This latter opinion was the one that would stick.

The Reclamation Service was not as easily deterred as Edison from its impulse to build dams. Its engineers cooked up an unusual, not to say bizarre, technique for erecting a rock and concrete dam in Boulder Canyon on the cheap. Their idea was simply to blast the canyon into the river. As the proposal was described by the service's chief, Arthur Powell Davis, they would detonate a line of powder charges in the rock walls, tumbling the debris into the riverbed. Once the current carried off the finer-grained material, a rampart of granite blocks would remain. The structure would subsequently be stabilized with sheet steel and protected by a shell of reinforced concrete. The resulting dam would be remarkable for its enormous bulk—a necessity, given its crude engineering—six hundred feet tall and 3,230 feet thick, or nearly two-thirds of a mile, at its base. (Hoover Dam, which towers 726.4 feet above its foundations, is a comparatively svelte 660 feet at its thickest point.)

Despite concerns about what Davis frankly termed "the unprecedented character of the operations," the Reclamation Service toyed with this concept until 1922, when it finally concluded that corralling the Colorado behind a high dam would be hard enough without throwing an entirely novel approach at the problem. Beyond the engineering challenge, there were doubts about whether the gunpowder plot would actually save money compared to conventional construction techniques or, indeed, whether it would really be as feasible as all that. "A rock-fill structure might be cheaper, [but] we can not be sure that this will be the case," Davis acknowledged to Congress. "If some unforeseen difficulties . . . should be encountered, its expense might even be greater than that of a concrete structure." What finally tipped the scale was that "we can not be sure that it would be entirely safe." He thought it advisable, when all was said and done, to hew to orthodox engineering—raising a dam of poured concrete, resting firmly on excavated bedrock and buttressed tight against the canyon walls.

Davis reckoned it a personal victory that Congress was seriously considering a project on the scale he outlined. Bringing the lawmakers to that point had taken thirteen years.

Despite the grandeur of its vision and the urgency of its prose, Theodore Roosevelt's 1907 message about flood control on the Colorado had failed to light a fire under Congress. Not only did the lawmakers scorn the president's plea for compensation for the Southern Pacific, but through the end of the decade they moved scarcely a step closer to the "broad comprehensive scheme" he had outlined for the river.

Not that indications of the situation's urgency were lacking. The Colorado burst through its levees on several occasions, again threatening ruin for the Imperial Valley, which had doubled in population (to fifteen thousand) and tripled in assessed valuation (to nearly $10 million) since the great flood. After new flooding in 1910, the administration of William Howard Taft spent $1 million to build an emergency levee in Mexico, acting without hesitation possibly because Charley Taft, the president's half-brother, was among the investors whose Mexican landholdings were menaced. The Imperial Irrigation District, which was organized by the settlers in 1911 to acquire the original California Development Company assets from the Southern Pacific, also had to spend heavily on canal maintenance, deploying dredging crews on the Alamo twenty-four hours a day.

The canal's course through Mexican territory was at the root of the settlers' problems. The Americans complained of being fleeced mercilessly by the Mexican government through taxes and duties levied on the crews and equipment they sent across the border for canal maintenance. "They have as many different kinds [of taxes] over there as we have, and a few besides, all of which are patterned on the principle of all the traffic will bear," Philip D. Swing, the irrigation district's lawyer and later its congressman, complained at a Washington hearing. "There is the poll tax on the employees and another on the mules and horses. . . . They even charge us an import duty on the material that goes into the levees by which their own lives and property are protected."

The district was powerless to enforce rules designed to keep the canal clean and unobstructed south of the border. It was not uncommon for the settlers to find their headgates clogged by the carcasses of dead horses or cows that had tumbled into the channel on the Mexican side. As the irascible pioneer Mark Rose told a congressional committee, on one occasion "we took out the bodies of three murdered men at that one head gate."

"You have some method of filtering that water before you use it for drinking purposes, have you not?" a congressman inquired.

"There is nothing to take out the filth," Rose snapped in reply.

What the settlers found most irksome was not that Mexican peasants contaminated their water supply, noisome as conditions were. Their primary complaint concerned big landholders south of the border, who were exploiting the provision in Charles Rockwood's original right-of-way agreement mandating that up to half the irrigation water in the canal had to be made available to Mexican estates.

These landholders, as it happened, were Americans. Most of the privileged territory, 860,000 acres in Baja California, belonged to a Southern California millionaires' syndicate. Its ringleaders were General Harrison Gray Otis and his son-in-law, Harry Chandler, the proprietors of the *Los Angeles Times.*

The Ohio-born Harrison Gray Otis had seen action in fifteen Civil War battles and commanded a brigade in the Philippines during the Spanish-American War. After acquiring control of the faltering *Times* in 1886, he had established the principle by which it would be managed for the next three-quarters of a century: the newspaper's editorial judgment on any issue was to be dictated by his family's economic interests. In practice, this rule rendered the newspaper politically reactionary and ferociously anti-union. To this day the main entrance to the *Times* headquarters in downtown Los Angeles bears an etched creed handed down directly from Otis, dedicating the ediface to "the cause of true industrial freedom," transparent code for the general's violent distaste for organized labor. (The unions acknowledged the sentiment by dynamiting the *Times* building in 1910, at the cost of twenty-one lives and a life term for one of the conspirators.)

Harry Chandler, a pudgy New Hampshire farm boy, had come west to Los Angeles in 1883. Within a decade he had parlayed his entrepreneurial talents into an executive position at the *Times* and marriage to the general's daughter. In 1898, when Mexican president Porfirio Díaz threw his country open to foreign investors, Chandler promptly moved the family into the Mexican real estate business.

Before long he and his father-in-law were deeply entrenched as dependable allies of President Díaz and irritants to the settlers on the U.S. side. Judges in Díaz's courtrooms treated the magnates' Colorado River Land Company with abject deference, especially when Imperial Valley farmers filed pleas for redress on such canal matters as the payment of maintenance assessments. Unlike Chandler and Otis, groused Rose to a congressional committee, "we have no rights as American citizens down there." By 1921, the syndicate's unpaid bills had reached $4 million, forcing the irrigation district to bump up the fees on its own residents as much as tenfold to make up the difference. When one district official personally approached Harry Chandler to ask how much he would be willing to pay to settle the outstanding claims, Chandler's terse reply was: "Not one cent."

What was the syndicate's motive for refusing, a congressman asked Rose.

"To save themselves $4,000,000 that they could stick down in their jeans," he replied with characteristic brusqueness.

With the Mexican government protecting its flanks, the Colorado River Land Company was free to exploit the land like a mother lode. Arid Mexican land that Harry Chandler purchased in 1898 for as little as 60 cents an acre soared in value to as much as $280. The company leased out most of its huge estate to Japanese and Chinese tenant farmers and sharecroppers, an arrangement that aroused racist sentiments on both sides of the border—in the United States because crops farmed by cheap labor in Mexico competed in the Imperial Valley's markets, and in Mexico because the imported workers took away jobs from local peasants.

Tensions between the syndicate and the Imperial settlers rose steadily. When Mexico erupted in revolution in the autumn of 1910, the settlers lent enthusiastic support to the revolutionaries, for whom the Chandler estate presented an irresistible target. "There is an unfortunate, and, I think amazingly disloyal and stupid sympathy existing in the Imperial Valley for the insurrecto cause," Chandler wrote in high dudgeon to his father-in-law. General Otis concurred, appending his view that the revolutionaries deserved to be "exterminated in the interest of right, peace and order, and for the protection of honest citizens on both sides of the line."

Yet the Imperial settlers perceived that the armed insurrectos also posed a threat to their own precious water supply. As long as their canal lay exposed to the lawlessness raging below the border, Swing would observe, the livelihood of fifty thousand Americans was in "imminent danger."

The only suitable answer, it became clear, was to dig a new canal on American soil to permanently secure the irrigation supply for Imperial. Any such project's political course would not be smooth, however, for it would reduce the original canal serving the Otis-Chandler syndicate's estate to a dusty gulch; the family would be sure to exercise its influence in California and Washington in opposition. The conflict between the American settlers and the Mexican estate holders, with millions of dollars at stake, would play a momentous role in the battle over control of the Colorado River for the next ten years.

Indeed, power politics turned out to be a more important obstacle to the canal project than geography. Contrary to the assumptions of Rockwood and Chaffey, the ridge of sandhills on the Colorado's western bank was not a significant physical barrier. More difficult terrain had been surmounted elsewhere in the United States and, in spectacular fashion, abroad: the Suez

Canal, which had been completed in 1859, cut through one hundred miles of windblown North African desert without ever being clogged with sand. The All-American Canal, with only six miles to traverse, posed a comparatively modest technical challenge; this was demonstrated by Mark Rose, who drove a plank road through the dunes in 1918. The road was soon carrying 150 vehicles a day in both directions, unmolested by sand drifts. Rose and Phil Swing, who was elected Imperial Valley's congressman in 1920, soon joined forces to seek a federal guarantee for the $30 million bond the irrigation district needed to build the new canal. (Harry Chandler had used his influence with the California banks to dry up credit for the district, they explained.)

For Arthur Powell Davis, the valley's appeal to Congress could not have come at a more opportune moment. Davis had assumed the directorship of the Reclamation Service—a post he regarded as almost a family legacy, given his stature as the revered John Wesley Powell's nephew—in 1914. Since then he had been seeking to develop the Colorado River in accordance with the pro-irrigation precepts of his distinguished uncle. Congress's failure to respond to Theodore Roosevelt's call had caused him no end of frustration, but the Imperial Valley's plea to secure an irrigation supply free of Mexican entanglements revived his hopes.

Davis's vision of the Colorado embraced the All-American Canal as one component of a vast hydraulic machine conceived on a Rooseveltian scale. As he told Congress, building the canal made excellent sense, but only if the federal government also provided flood control dams, storage reservoirs, and hydroelectric works to fully exploit the potential of the "American Nile."

This was a shrewd pitch. It transformed a single small community's petition for financial assistance into a blueprint for a program of regional, even national, importance. Davis knew that a proposal for Colorado River development would draw interest far beyond the Imperial Valley. Arizona, Colorado, and Utah would be attracted by the opportunity to expand their irrigated acreage via a full-scale reclamation program. Veterans' advocates were already hankering after irrigated lands as a source of homesteads for thousands of soldiers demobilized after the Great War. (Among the advocates was William Ellsworth Smythe, who had parlayed his campaign against the baleful influence of the city on social values into an appointment as assistant secretary of the interior for veterans land settlement.)

Bringing these constituencies to bear on Congress, Davis soon persuaded Representative Moses Kinkaid of Nebraska, one of the House's leading promoters of Western homesteading, to introduce a bill authorizing his agency to prepare the blueprint for a comprehensive flood control program on the Colorado. Within months of the bill's passage, there would be men mapping the lower river in preparation for what would be the tallest dam in the world.

Davis had instructed his chief geologist, Homer Hamlin, to find sites with geological features that could best support the weight of a high dam while impounding the largest possible reservoir. He calculated the capacity necessary to offer Imperial Valley permanent flood control as 31 million acre-feet,* or about ten trillion gallons, which would constitute the largest man-made reservoir in the world by a huge margin. Davis contemplated paying for the dam by selling off its hydroelectric power, so he further insisted that the site be no more distant from the large electrical market of Southern California than about 350 miles—the technical limit of electrical transmission at the time.

These requirements narrowed Hamlin's search to the region around Boulder Canyon, which was roughly three hundred miles from Los Angeles and far enough downstream to create an immense reservoir without inundating the Grand Canyon. Of five possible dam sites he identified, three were in Boulder Canyon proper and the others in Black Canyon, about twenty miles further downstream. All were situated within the roughly 250-mile reach in which the river forms the boundary between Nevada and Arizona. As a result, any dam built to the Reclamation Bureau's specifications would

---

* An acre-foot is the quantity of water needed to cover one acre to a depth of one foot, equivalent to about 325,850 gallons.

have one anchorage in each of those states. This was a condition both would try to exploit to obtain special rights to the water storage and hydroelectric generation produced by Hoover Dam.

Hamlin was sufficiently intrigued by Black Canyon to pound a stake into a rock outcropping at the location he judged most suitable for a high dam. But in his initial report he unreservedly recommended Boulder, based on its apparently more robust geology; Black Canyon was merely a backup, to be considered only if further surveys in Boulder Canyon revealed unexpected complications.

In December 1920, a few months after receiving Hamlin's report, Davis stopped by Reclamation's Denver office en route from an inspection trip to the Colorado. Consumed with the excitement of his career-making enterprise, he was looking for a candidate to launch a more detailed geological and topographical study of Boulder Canyon. His engineering chief, Frank Weymouth, offered up his assistant, Walker Rollo Young. The thirty-five-year-old Young was a graduate of the University of Idaho, where he had been a star basketball player and acquired the nickname "Brig." (Although he was not a Mormon, he could not escape the handle typically bestowed in Mormon country on males with the surname Young.)

"How soon can you leave for Boulder Canyon?" Davis asked him.

"Tomorrow's Christmas," Young replied. "Why'd you have to ask at Christmas?"

Davis's impatience was palpable, so after taking the briefest of holiday sojourns with his family, Young made his way to St. Thomas, Nevada, an agricultural settlement located at the entrance to Boulder Canyon, arriving just before New Year's Day. By February, he had established his survey camp and construction shops at the upstream end of the canyon, in a narrow wash overshadowed by cliffs three thousand feet tall.

From the first it was evident that the river intended to be an uncooperative subject of study. "The Colorado was not a tame river," Young would recall with characteristic understatement. Fierce winds would erupt suddenly, roaring through the narrow canyon and transforming gentle swells into furious whitecaps. Mishaps on the water were distressingly common. Only a few weeks into the survey there were three brushes with disaster: on

February 22 a floodtide swept two men under a barge; they were recovered battered but uninjured. The next day a crewman who tumbled off a second barge avoided being carried downriver only by desperately clutching a rope until he could be hauled to safety. Then the motor on a launch carrying night shift workers gave out in midstream. One of the four men aboard was sucked under a barge and disappeared. He was all but given up for dead, but a boat sent to retrieve his body found him three hours later a few miles downstream, lying half-drowned on a rocky ledge.

Free-floating logs dislodged by flash floods upstream were a common hazard. A wayward log could broadside a barge like a battering ram, shattering the drilling tubes suspended from its keel or, worse, sending the vessel and every piece of its equipment to the bottom. Passing storms tumbled boulders off the cliffs and into the river, where they lurked just under the turbid surface as uncharted hazards to Young's rickety vessels. When a storm concentrated its fury inside the canyon the destruction could be more grievous; a violent squall in December 1921 wrecked one barge, drowned a driller, and washed out the road to St. Thomas.

Even more perilous than the work on the water were the conditions on the nearly vertical canyon walls, from which topographical engineers were mapping every square inch of the gorge. The process required teams to coordinate with each other from opposite sides of the canyon, with a rodman, or rigger, perched on one wall holding a fifteen-foot pole with a flag at one end—used to probe to the back of the caves perforating the rock—while a surveyor across the river fixed him in the crosshairs of his camera-equipped theodolite.

It was possible to reach the lowest elevations of the cliffs by ladder, but much of the gorge was inaccessible except by men lowered from the rim by rope. Sometimes the only way for a rigger to reach a measuring point beneath an overhanging ledge was to swing out on his rope over the river and back, like a pendulum. (This technique would be copied during construction a dozen years later by the legendary rope-borne high scalers, who were given the job of grooming the gorge's sheer walls for the dam's concrete abutments.)

The cliff surveyors coped with trying conditions in every season. In the spring they were beleaguered by icy winds that blinded them with sand, tore at their skin with needle-sharp flecks of rock, or bombarded them from overhead with dislodged stones. The winds died away in summer only to give way to temperatures averaging more than 107 degrees in the shade and peaking well above a punishing 120.

"In the sun, thermometers broke at 140°, rocks and metal burned the hands, and the canyon walls reflecting the sun's rays created an inferno in the canyon below," recorded Wesley R. Nelson, the project's assistant engineer, who described crews clambering over the walls stripped of every shred of clothing but shoes, trousers, and hardhats (originally made from canvas caps dipped in tar). Because the shimmer of heat waves prevented making accurate measurements across the width of the canyon at midday, in high summer the surveyors started work at two in the morning and ended their shift an hour before noon.

The surge of government activity in the canyon rippled through a river community accustomed to the nonchalant seasonal rhythms of the wilderness. The surveyors' camp attracted a clutch of civilian followers, ranging from fur traders to carpenters and rivermen. Of the latter, perhaps the most remarkable was a cheerful redheaded youth whose ease at the helm of a long, narrow motorboat transfixed Walker Young one morning as the craft navigated smoothly upstream against a stretch of violent rapids.

The helmsman was Murl Emery, who had spent almost all his seventeen years on the river. When he reappeared in his boat a few days later Young offered him a job. To his astonishment, Emery turned him down.

It was not that the boy had an objection to government work, but that he already had a job, and a good one—piloting for a nearby camp from which razor blade magnate King Gillette and headgear heir John B. Stetson were quietly exploring the feasibility of privately building a dam in partnership with Edison Electric.

The two camps made for a stark contrast. Young's outpost, Emery recalled acerbically a half-century later, was "a miserable government camp designed to be in the spot where ninety-five percent of the blowing sand was—typical government setup." The Gillette camp, as befit a bivouac for industrialists and enterpreneurs during the Roaring Twenties, was a cluster of sturdy two-story bungalows offering what Emery recalled as "the finest food in southern Nevada in just the right kind of spot."

But the private scheme soon collapsed, and Emery took Young up on his offer. Emery had learned his rivercraft from beaver trappers and bootleggers. The first group, burly, self-reliant men who turned up in St. Thomas every Christmas, showed him how to build serviceable flat-bottomed rowboats out of "two-by-fours, one-by-twelves, a bucket of tar, and a handful of nails," he recalled. The bootleggers trained him to traverse stretches of the river in all its moods and under any sky without spilling a drop of cargo. Whether opaque from its burden of silt, whitecapped from the wind, in full flood or low water, the Colorado kept no secrets from him: "I could look out on that river and tell you within two inches the depth of the water." He built his own boat in the trappers' style with a tunnel stern, meaning that the propeller turned in a channel indented in the hull, the better to keep it clear of underwater obstructions. It was this craft Emery was piloting upriver at its customary speed of about seven miles per hour the day he hove into Walker Young's view.

The redheaded "river rat," as Young called him, would become one of the most recognizable figures in the canyons. He would spend the next fifteen years ferrying workers and VIPs to the construction site and provisioning workers' families from a general store he operated largely on the principle of personal trust. After the dam's completion he continued in place as proprietor of a tourist fleet profitably plying Lake Mead.

Hundreds of visiting dignitaries got their first view of the canyon site from the thwarts of Emery's boat. There were senators and congressmen inspecting the gorge where an appropriation of unprecedented size was to be spent. There were movie stars hoping to absorb some of the glow of a project that overshadowed the grandest Hollywood production. On one occasion his passenger was a weary and defeated Herbert Hoover, visiting his colossal namesake shortly after his bitter loss to Franklin Roosevelt in the 1932 presidential election. ("No bother and easy to handle," was Emery's judgment, but "not the kind of guy you could start up a conversation with.")

On more than a dozen occasions, he carried a tall, lanky man whose pale blue eyes ranged over the canyon walls in a manner that was anything but casual. His name was Frank Crowe. A graduate of the University of Maine, by 1920 Crowe had been building dams for fifteen years. In the small fraternity of dam engineers his talent for bringing in projects under budget and ahead of schedule, even in the remotest locations and under the most merciless conditions, was a byword. For Crowe, however, everything he had achieved was but a prologue to the challenge of building the Colorado dam. Even before its final site was chosen, he felt in his bones that he had been put on earth to build it, and that it would be the capstone of his career.

In February 1922, Arthur Powell Davis presented Congress with a complete plan for taming the Colorado River. Formally entitled "Report on Problems of Imperial Valley and Vicinity," it soon became known as the Fall-Davis Report, with a formal nod to Interior Secretary Albert Fall. But it was Davis's personal manifesto.

The report assessed the irrigable acreage in the basin and estimated the volume of available water (very optimistically, as it turned out). Davis proposed that the cost of what was to be known as the Boulder Canyon Project be paid by publicly generated hydroelectricity (thereby opening a political can of worms he might more wisely have left sealed).

The Fall-Davis Report's most important contribution to the reclamation of the Colorado was its perspective. The document set forth the principle that reclamation in the Colorado basin was a federal obligation. The river could no longer be viewed as a local or regional asset to be exploited piecemeal by states or local communities jostling each other for water, but rather as a federal asset demanding broad-minded management. "The Colorado River is international," Davis observed. "The stream and many of its tributaries are interstate. . . . Its problems are of such magnitude as to be beyond the reach of other than national solution."

Inevitably, this conception reduced the All-American Canal to the status of a satellite work. The Fall-Davis Report left no doubt that, henceforth, the sun around which orbited every other component of Colorado River development would be the Boulder Canyon dam.

Davis's blueprint called for construction of a high dam "at or near Boulder Canyon," but even before the report's publication, the surveyors' enthusiasm for Boulder Canyon had drained away. Each of the three sites Walker Young's crews surveyed from the barges in the canyon turned out to have disqualifying imperfections. The site furthest upstream, initially the favorite because of its proximity to St. Thomas, was found to be bisected by a large geologic fault. The two alternative sites offered somewhat more robust bedrock, but each was wedged between sheer canyon walls that constrained the movement of men and materials; even at low flow the river washed against the cliffs on both sides, leaving not even a narrow shelf on which to safely pitch camp.

Pondering the challenge of hauling tons of gravel and concrete between the rim and the foot of the gorge with no place for storage, Walker Young decided for prudence's sake to look into Homer Hamlin's backup plan—Black Canyon. One day early in January 1922, he climbed nervously aboard a sixteen-foot rowboat for a reconnaissance trip downstream. A natural landlubber, he had hesitated at the wharf, nervous about the prospect of making it back upstream against the stiff current, particularly in a boat loaded with three other passengers—George Hammond, his two-hundred-pound drilling foreman; Harry Armistead, a burly riverman who would be manning the oars; and Armistead's dog, Baldy.

Indeed, the return trip was a trying one. The water broke over the bow like the ocean on a beach, each wave sucking up a weighty load of silt from the river bottom and dumping it onboard. When the scouting party finally landed back at camp all four were heavily encrusted with a layer of mud.

But they had also found their ideal dam site. To Young's practiced eye, Black Canyon's dimensions and geology seemed the equal of Boulder Canyon, and in many respects superior. Near the canyon's downstream outlet the group discovered the stake Homer Hamlin had pounded into the Arizona rock two years before, a weathered two-by-four adorned with a fluttering shred of white fabric. Nine years later, the eastern abutment of Hoover

Dam would be lodged against the cliffside at almost the exact spot Hamlin had staked out.

Young established a new camp on a wide wash near the mouth of Black Canyon. Nature struck back almost at once, sending a freak windstorm roaring down the gorge, stripping the camp down to the floorboards of the tents. The setback was brief, however. The camp was rebuilt within a few days and the survey continued unmolested until breaking for the summer in May.

By April the following year the survey was complete and Black Canyon's virtues were manifest. Because the new site sat at a lower elevation than Boulder Canyon and was twenty miles further downstream, it could accommodate twenty additional miles of reservoir, providing much more water storage for the same height of dam. It was twenty miles closer than Boulder Canyon to existing rail connections out of Las Vegas, which would dramatically simplify importing men and material to the worksite. Finally, its bedrock lay shallower than Boulder Canyon's, reducing the cost of excavation. Out of tradition and habit, the effort to dam the Colorado would continue to be known as the Boulder Canyon Project and its legislative mandate as the Boulder Canyon Project Act. But its location would be Black Canyon.

For Walker Young, the new site's qualities, especially its accessibility, spoke for themselves. "As I've said many times, the Lord left that dam site there," he told an interviewer forty years after its completion. "It was only up to man to discover it and to use it."

Arthur Powell Davis's report touched tangentially on one other issue that needed a solution before construction could get underway. The Colorado watershed encompassed seven states—seven squabbling entities mutually suspicious of each other's designs on the precious stream cascading down from their mountains, flowing through their pastures, and scouring gorges in their desert expanses. By declaring the Colorado to be a federal concern, Davis had evaded, rather than solved, the question of how to apportion its bounty equitably.

The states' conflicting claims already had come twice before the U.S. Supreme Court without resolution. The prospect of more protracted litigation had to be cleared away before the federal government could spend a dime on building a dam on the lower river.

With the states themselves unable to reach agreement on their own, the call rang out for something in the nature of adult supervision. The man who filled that role would place his personal stamp on the project for all time.

# PART TWO

---

# The Road to Black Canyon

# 5

# Hoover Steps In

The seven distinguished gentlemen seated inside a conference room in Washington on Thursday, January 26, 1922, listened to Commerce Secretary Herbert Hoover drone on with what must have been mixed feelings of glumness and resentment.

None was particularly happy to be thousands of miles from home in a chilly, damp city, its sky heavy with forebodings of a violent winter storm bearing down from the west. None regarded Hoover as the ideal chairman for their little group, the Colorado River Commission. But he had been appointed to the position by the only man whose opinion counted, President Warren G. Harding, so none had objected—at least not openly. Now they sat silently around the conference table—leading political figures in their own right from Wyoming, Colorado, New Mexico, Arizona, Nevada, Utah, and California—as Mr. Hoover, with his customary surfeit of formality and self-importance, told them their business. They were there, he said, to draft a compact among their seven states—in effect, an interstate treaty—to share equitably in the waters of the Colorado River. The idea was not merely to prevent the "endless litigation" that would ensue in the absence of a compact, he said; their real task was nothing less than "to secure development of the river . . . so as to give the greatest benefits to the nation."

Hoover spoke as though he had distilled all the contentious issues before them down to a few principles on which they could not fail to agree. In fact, the points he named were exactly those on which they were all in violent mutual disagreement.

When he observed that "there is little established right on the river and we have almost a clean sheet with which to begin our efforts," some of the commissioners must have shifted uneasily in their chairs. What had made this very meeting so necessary was that each state believed that it did have an "established right on the river." Furthermore, they were all deeply suspicious of each other's claims. Complicating that issue, six of the states were especially mistrustful of the seventh, California, which in economic terms was bigger than the rest of them put together. (Was it coincidence, some wondered, that California was the Iowa-born Hoover's adopted home—or had President Harding deliberately placed a Californian agent in charge of the negotiations?) The river, if anything, was the antithesis of Hoover's "clean sheet"; it more closely resembled a stained, scribbled-upon, smudged, and ink-blotted scroll, recording decades of unresolved conflict.

Hoover's view of the river as a national asset was merely wishful thinking. Were it the case, there would scarcely have been any reason to ask the seven states to negotiate a treaty; the federal government could have apportioned the waters of the river by fiat. Instead, the question of each state's claim to the Colorado was very much on the table. Hoover in his naïveté may truly have believed that the states were in agreement that the national interest should take precedence over their own, but he was to be disabused of that fantasy very quickly.

On one point, however, he was absolutely correct. "This conference is unique," he observed. The U.S. Constitution allows states to negotiate compacts among themselves subject to congressional approval, but this was the first time that as many as seven—indeed, any more than two—had attempted to do so. The whole country would be watching.

The overarching conundrum of the Colorado River basin is that, although its water is abundant and its irrigable acreage immense, the water is often separated from the nearest arable land by hundreds of miles of wilderness. Although the commission's engineering advisor, Arthur Powell Davis, assured the members that the Colorado could supply more than enough water to fulfill all the reclamation schemes they might conceive, the truth was that within no single state was there a perfect match between the potential for development and the water needed to achieve it.

Indeed, what gave the compact negotiations their urgency was the universal recognition that water without land was wasted, and land without water was worthless. The commissioners knew that a suitable compromise would have to apportion the waters so that each state was guaranteed access to as much as it needed, but not so much that it would interfere with the development of its neighbors.

How much was fair? The answer was complicated. The states could be divided roughly into two basins. The upper basin comprised Wyoming, Utah, Colorado, and New Mexico—all rural, agrarian, and underdeveloped. The lower basin states were Arizona and California—agriculturally more productive, increasingly industrial, and voraciously thirsty—and Nevada, which fit geographically with its two neighbors, but which constituted a category all its own, unpopulated, arid, and seemingly devoid of prospects for development of any kind. (That impression would be dramatically contradicted in coming decades.)

What all the states had in common was the fear that their rights to exploit the river would be constrained or blocked by the others. But as in the proverbial tale of the blind men and the elephant, each saw the Colorado in different terms. Consequently, each offered its own definition of a fair apportionment.

Rainfall and snow in the Colorado Rockies was the largest source of the river's water by volume—more than 80 percent, as Colorado's delegate, Delph Carpenter, repeated incessantly. So Colorado's position was that apportionment should be based on each state's precipitation. Arizona had the largest share of the Colorado basin lying within its boundaries—113,000 square miles, or 45 percent of the total—so it argued that the basis of apportionment should be each state's acreage within the watershed. The river's headwaters originated in Wyoming, New Mexico, and Utah, so they all argued that primacy should go to the states where the waters rose first.

California, the great unbalancing weight of the whole system, contributed the least amount of water to the river yet consumed the most, by a wide margin. So its position was that the water should be apportioned primarily to the users who employed it most productively. Did not the Imperial Valley create millions of dollars in national wealth every year through the bounty of fruits and vegetables it shipped coast to coast?

The desert state of Nevada, which contributed almost no water and consumed even less, cared little about any of these arguments, as long as it was guaranteed a share of the tax revenue and cheap power from the hydroelectric generators that would be installed on its border with Arizona.

A single consistent legal principle of water rights might have resolved their conflicts. In the West, however, there was not one principle in use, but two that were mutually incompatible. These were riparian law and the rule of prior appropriation. Unless the delegates to the compact commission could reach an agreement superseding both, the harvest would be not economic progress, but Hoover's nightmare of endless litigation.

The riparian doctrine had originated in temperate regions, where water was abundant and arable land almost always situated adjacent to a river. The rule granted the owner of land abutting a stream the right to use the water flowing past his property, on condition that his use did not interfere with the same right of landowners downstream. The river and its waters were inviolate, belonging as property to no one.

Riparian theory served agriculture particularly well, for the water sprinkled on crops eventually ran off the farm and recharged the stream. But it conflicted with the sort of industrial development that might involve damming or diverting a river, or any other practice that might diminish the volume available downstream.

Riparian law was hopelessly unsuited to the arid West, where mining, not farming, was the chief consumer of water. A mine might be many miles from the nearest stream, so miners in their rough-and-tumble way chose to ignore riparian law. Prospectors needing water for their sluice boxes simply diverted it from distant streams. Eventually this gave rise to the principle of prior appropriation, which held that water belonged to whoever first put it to use, regardless of the user's proximity to the source, and that the priority remained in force as long as the use continued. The rule of prior appropriation, in its simplest formulation, was "first in time, first in right."

While riparian law traditionally treated water as a communal resource, prior appropriation was the very model of modern capitalism, based on the idea that any resource can be converted into private property and traded in the marketplace to whoever can use it most profitably. The Western mines that first exploited the principle could not have survived without prior appropriation, but neither could the farmers of the Imperial Valley.

The evolution of water law from the riparian doctrine to prior appropriation was not destined to happen cleanly. For decades the principles coexisted uneasily in Western states, with little guidance from state and federal courts. The U.S. Supreme Court, in its major decision on the subject, *Kansas v. Colorado* (1907), ruled in effect that the division of waters of an interstate stream should be made on a case-by-case basis. The states of the upper Colorado basin viewed this nebulous decision as a sword of Damocles. It left intact existing precedents giving each state control of rivers within their borders, which afforded them some leverage over downstream states. But it gave them no assurance that the justices, ruling in a subsequent case de novo, might not uphold some downstream claim in a way that would restrict their access to their own waters. Consequently, the risk existed that Arthur Powell Davis's plan for a dam and reservoir on the lower Colorado, by spurring greater development in already fast-growing California, might give that state even greater rights to waters originating in Colorado, Utah, Wyoming, and New Mexico, strangling their economies in infancy.

Yet California could hardly view *Kansas v. Colorado* complacently. The absence of a firm precedent meant that a future Court might well curb the Imperial Valley's right to the river in deference to the upstream states, which would convert the thriving valley back into desiccated wasteland.

Hoover understood that the tension between riparian and appropriation law had been the cause of interminable courtroom battles over water in the past and could become the grounds for "probably 100 such disputes" more, as he told the compact commissioners. He believed that an effective Colorado River compact would have to repudiate both doctrines on the Colorado River, substituting a tailor-made division of water rights acceptable to all.

This was an ambitious goal. Several previous attempts at concord had failed, most notably one staged by a regional organization of civic boosters called the League of the Southwest.

The league's April 1920 convention in Los Angeles had all the atmosphere of a revival meeting, thundering with pomp and brimming with postwar optimism—"the energetic, virile Southwest . . . expressing in word and manner the courage to undertake big and promising development projects," in the less than disinterested editorial judgment of Harry Chandler's *Los Angeles Times.* The star speaker was William Jennings Bryan, the most compelling orator of the era and three-time candidate for president. In his keynote speech, the "Great Commoner" proclaimed to his audience in an immense downtown auditorium that Arthur Powell Davis's Colorado River project would turn "barren desert [into] a garden of wondrous productivity." The convention rafters rang with applause, and the delegates voted unanimously to seek $50,000 from Congress for a river survey.

But the good fellowship was an illusion. Four-fifths of the delegates were Californians, and the minority from Colorado, Utah, Wyoming, and New Mexico eyed Davis's proposal for a huge reservoir on the lower river suspiciously as a tool to enable California to steal their water.

The skepticism left over from the convention energized the upper states' search for a way to protect themselves from California's encroaching thirst. Not long afterward, the idea of apportioning the river by interstate compact was proposed by a rancher and attorney from Greeley, Colorado, who had been fairly steeped in water law for his entire legal career and also had the ear of his close friend, Colorado governor Oliver Shoup. Delph Carpenter was convinced that the solution to interstate bickering over the river lay in Article I of the U.S. Constitution, which gave Congress the authority to approve treaties among the states.

Over the years, several compacts had been negotiated to settle boundary or fishery disputes or, in a particularly noisome instance, a quarrel between New York and New Jersey over sewage dumping in New York Harbor. Carpenter believed it was the only workable alternative to endless litigation—a condition with which, as it happened, he was personally familiar; as a lawyer representing the state of Colorado he had been manacled to an intricate water dispute known as *Wyoming v. Colorado* for eleven years, during which he had suffered through thousands of hours of testimony and two frustratingly inconclusive visits to the U.S. Supreme Court.

Carpenter presented his proposal to league delegates from all seven states a few months after the Los Angeles convention. He observed that a compact would effectively take river policy out of the federal government's hands and return it to the states, where it belonged. The delegates found this logic impeccable, and without a word of debate they agreed to bring the plan to their respective capitals. By the summer of 1921, all seven governors had appointed compact commissioners, Congress had passed enabling legislation to set the negotiations in motion, and President Harding had seated Hoover as the eighth member of the body.

During the compact commission's initial round of meetings—seven sessions held in the Commerce Department building, sometimes two a day for up to four hours each—Hoover showed himself to be a prickly and insensitive leader, exasperating the commissioners with his imperious manner and his tendency to frame the issues in national, rather than regional, terms.

The negotiations got off to a poor start. On the first day Hoover proposed apportioning the water according to each state's irrigable agricultural acreage, and asked each commissioner to produce a figure for his own state. These figures were duly laid on the table and compared with Arthur Powell Davis's estimates of how much each state had under irrigation in 1920 (a total of 2,464,000 acres), and how much could be reasonably added in the future (another 3,659,000). It quickly became clear that the commissioners had flagrantly inflated their numbers, as their total exceeded Davis's projection by fully 2,800,000 acres.

Concerned that Davis's assurances of adequate water for all might be optimistic, the states had tried to build themselves healthy cushions against the chance that the river might have to be apportioned on a first-come, first-served basis. A dismayed Davis informed Hoover that the states' total claims, if accurate, would produce demand for water far outstripping even his highest projections of the streamflow—bankrupting the river, in short. Confronted by Hoover, the commissioners all admitted that they could not back up their figures with hard evidence. But none agreed to amend them.

Things deteriorated from there. In the heat of debate, personal animosities on the panel frequently bobbed to the surface, members goading each other into pungent exchanges. On at least one occasion several leaped to their feet, hands balled into fists, until cooler heads around the table persuaded the would-be combatants to stand down.

Hoover's lack of understanding of the internecine sensitivities frequently made things worse. He tried to browbeat the group into accepting the principle that flood protection for the Imperial Valley should be the most urgent item on their agenda, one that had nationwide, not merely local, implications. "I have to look at this matter from a more national point of view than some of you," he told them, tactlessly. "Here is a large community in Southern California in great jeopardy. This whole business is utterly fruitless if we cannot agree on a simple statement of an obvious fact."

What this declaration glossed over was that for the other states, flood control for California was not a simple matter—it involved precisely the thorniest issue among them, for flood control required a large reservoir on the lower Colorado, just what the upper basin feared most.

Moreover, Hoover was being disingenuous in his fixation on flood control, for the issue fed directly into a matter high on his own personal agenda—blocking the public generation of hydroelectric power on the river. Hoover, whose social milieu encompassed bankers and corporate executives, shared their view that power generation should remain the province of private utilities, not government. In his eyes, the virtue of elevating flood control as a chief goal of the compact was that the need could be addressed with a low dam—i.e., one not capable of generating hydroelectricity. It is an outstanding irony that the great power-producing dam bearing Hoover's name promoted a principle of which he vigorously disapproved.

Hoover's insistence on downstream flood protection cost him the confidence of the majority of commissioners. Their mood as they worked through the last weekend of January would have been foul in any case, darkened by the view outside the Commerce Department's windows. Hammered by its worst blizzard in more than twenty years, Washington was paralyzed. The streetcars had stopped running. Congress canceled its sessions, as did a postwar disarmament conference hosting delegates from all over the world. Hoover, undeterred, scheduled a full day of meetings for Monday, January 30, starting at ten in the morning.

On this final day of their deliberations, each state's position on its needs for water from the Colorado seemed to have solidified. Compromise looked unlikelier than ever. Finally, after several more hours of stalemate, Hoover uttered the unspoken question on everybody's minds.

"Is it worth while to have another session?" he asked. "Or shall we make the declaration now that we are so hopelessly far apart that there is no use in proceeding?"

The first words of assent came from Nevada's James G. Scrugham. "We might as well quit," he grumbled.

Yet now that Hoover's question had brought them to the brink of the abyss, the others quailed at the prospect of failure. One chastened commissioner after another allowed that they might yet be able to craft an agreement they could all live with, but only after a period of consultation and further study at home.

The Colorado River Commission then limped out of snowbound Washington. It would not reconvene for another nine months, when the setting, and the atmosphere, would be very different.

On June 5, some four months after the commission's dispirited adjournment, the U.S. Supreme Court handed down its opinion in the interminable case of *Wyoming v. Colorado*. Delph Carpenter had bragged to his fellow commissioners of Colorado's unbroken string of courthouse victories in water matters, but from almost the first paragraph of the new ruling it was evident that this string had run out.

*Wyoming v. Colorado* was a dispute over the Laramie River, which rose in Colorado and flowed north across the state line. Wyoming had filed the lawsuit in 1911, after learning that Colorado developers planned to divert

water from the river to a separate drainage basin—an act that would eliminate any possibility of its finding its way back to the main stream.

Wyoming's position was that the diversion was illegal under both riparian and appropriation law, which presupposed that water remain within the
basin where it rose. Colorado argued in opposition that a sovereign state
possessed an absolute right to divert the water within its borders.

The justices agreed that there was nothing inherently wrong with transferring water out of its native drainage basin, but they repudiated Colorado's claim to an absolute right. Instead, as Justice Willis Van Devanter
wrote, "Each state has an interest which should be respected by the other."
He held that prior appropriation, which governed water law within both
states, should apply to any cross-border stream. If appropriation was good
enough for intrastate applications, in other words, then it was "just and equitable" that it apply on an interstate basis, too.

With one stroke, the Court redefined the issue before the Colorado
River Commission. The upstream states had enticed Arizona and California to the negotiating table with the implicit threat that, were matters to
proceed to litigation, federal precedent would back their appropriation and
diversion of the Colorado, effectively giving them sovereignty over the entire river.

That threat was now nullified. It was clear that if the compact negotiations failed, the upper basin would hold an empty hand in federal court—
just as it feared it might as a consequence of the earlier ruling in *Kansas v.
Colorado*. It was now possible that the lower states, citing prior appropriation, could lay claim to a huge proportion of the Colorado's waters.

The upstream states, instantly perceiving their predicament, braced
themselves for a round of hard bargaining. "We simply must use every endeavor to bring about a compact at the next meeting," Carpenter confided
to Wyoming's commissioner, Frank C. Emerson, during the long hiatus.
"We may never again have a like opportunity."

One other development lent urgency to their labors. On April 25, Phil
Swing, representing the Imperial Valley in Congress, introduced a bill in
the House of Representatives to fund the Boulder Canyon dam and the All-
American Canal. This opened a new forum for debate on Colorado River

issues—Capitol Hill, where forty-one states with no direct interest in the outcome could have their say. If the seven squabbling sovereigns of the Colorado basin were to maintain control of their destinies, they had to reach a compromise, and quickly.

With these developments as the backdrop, Herbert Hoover called for the compact commission to reconvene in early November.

As the setting for the second round of talks, Hoover chose Bishop's Lodge, a faux adobe dude ranch located on the outskirts of Santa Fe—sufficiently isolated, in his expectation, to keep distractions to a minimum. The lodge was certainly hard to reach, more than three "exceedingly dangerous" miles from town, observed Arnold Kruckman, one of a seven-man delegation of Californians monitoring the performance of the state's compact commissioner, state engineer Wilbur McClure. "In order to get to the place," Kruckman reported, "you are obliged to wriggle in an automobile over a convolution of roads that dizzily swoop up and down like a switch-back roller coaster and hang so precariously to the steep sides of the desolate landscape that the passage of a vehicle makes you think of a fly crawling over an eyebrow."

Nevertheless, when the commissioners arrived on Thursday, November 9, the place was already teeming with advisors and lobbyists, crammed by foursomes into rooms designed for two. Hoover surveyed the mob scene with open distaste. Then he issued what Kruckman called a "ukase," evicting all but essential personnel from the lodge. To forestall special pleading, he ordered the chambermaids to remove the evictees' belongings from their quarters during breakfast the next morning and to transfer them to the lobby, packed up for their forced departure.

Among the exiles was Mark Rose, the Imperial Valley pioneer and champion of the All-American Canal, who nursed his resentment for the next few weeks in a Santa Fe rooming house with his fellows, awaiting the chance to get back at the presumptuous Hoover.

Meanwhile the talks at Bishop's Lodge proceeded smoothly. No doubt this partially reflected the pressure applied by *Wyoming v. Colorado* and Swing's bill. But the main reason was that the grounds for a workable compromise had been prepared over the summer and fall by Delph Carpenter. Reasoning that the fundamental conflict over the allocation of water was really a bilateral dispute between the four states of the upper basin and the three of the lower, Carpenter proposed simply to divide the river in half between the two basins. This handily transformed a thicket of interstate disputes among seven states into two sets of intrabasin issues that could be shoved off to the indefinite future. Only two questions would remain for the compact commission to ponder: how to calculate the total volume of water to be divided, and how to enforce the division. Carpenter's compromise was so elegant that Hoover later attempted to claim its sole parentage, writing in his memoirs that it had come to him like a lightning bolt during a sleepless night. "I scribbled it on a piece of paper and carried it into the conference next morning," he recounted. "We settled the Compact along these lines in a few hours." In truth, Carpenter's proposal had been circulating among the commissioners for weeks before the Bishop's Lodge meeting.

Calculating the volume of the river now became a major stumbling block to agreement. The problem was that no reliable data existed of the river's yield over the long term. Davis had based his own estimates on barely two decades of measurements from Reclamation's Laguna Dam, near Yuma, which had installed its first gauges in 1899. The annual measurements at Yuma between 1899 and 1921 averaged out to 16.4 million acre-feet, which suggested that each basin could be awarded a water supply of up to 8.2 million acre-feet a year. What was disquieting about these data, however, was that they also showed the annual flows to be highly variable, ranging from a low of 9.1 million acre-feet in 1902 to a peak of more than 25 million in 1909. Such inconsistency undermined the reliability of any mean flow figure based on such a brief measurement period. The upper basin states, consequently, were unwilling to promise that 8.2 million acre-feet would flow past the agreed-upon interbasin demarcation point, Lees Ferry on the Arizona-Utah border, every year. Nor would they accept Hoover's alternate proposal to calculate the guarantee as a rolling ten-year average (i.e., a total of 82 million acre-feet over any ten-year period). Even that pledge committed the upper states to giving up some of their own water in the event of an extended drought. The talks threatened to collapse until Hoover suggested they reduce the ten-year guarantee to 75 million acre-feet.

This figure, which seemed to incorporate an adequate cushion, was accepted and written into the final compact. But it still turned out to be too optimistic. Later research would establish that the 1899–1921 period was one of the wettest in the basin's history. In no ten-year period since then has the flow matched the average of 16.4 million acre-feet (including nonbasin claims) on which the compact is based; the true historic average, scientists now believe, is less than 14.7 million, insufficient to fulfill the minimum compact apportionment.

But it was in Davis's interest, and that of every state, to accept the most optimistic assumptions to get the compact drafted and approved. The commissioners all chose to believe, on scant evidence, that Davis's estimate was reasonable, even conservative. The consequences of their assumption would only emerge decades later.

Davis was plainly aware of one other important consequence of the compromise. Converting the highly variable annual volume of the Colorado into a series of ten-year averages necessarily required storage on the lower river, and lots of it. Otherwise, surpluses in wet years would flow wastefully into the Gulf of California, while downstream farms would wither from thirst in dry years. The compact was shaping up as a mandate to implement the huge Boulder Canyon dam and reservoir that Davis had proposed in the Fall-Davis Report, issued the previous February.

This implication evaded the upper basin commissioners until the fourth day of the Bishop's Lodge conference, when Hoover spilled the beans with an ill-considered aside to Davis: "Don't we predicate this whole operation," he asked, "on the creation of storage on the lower basin?" Davis artfully evaded the question, but the seed of contention had been planted. It sprouted a few days later, when California's McClure gingerly asked Hoover for the floor to "again open a matter that is considered very vital." He then proposed making the compact's implementation conditional on the construction of a dam on the lower river.

The upper states instantly rebelled. It was as though, after nearly a year of effort aimed at giving all the states equitable access to the river, California was again trying to push her interests to the head of the line. Carpenter spoke for his fellow upper basin commissioners when he warned crisply that any effort to subordinate the compact to the construction of McClure's proposed dam would mean its defeat by every state legislature outside of Arizona and California—that is, the collapse of the entire effort.

Hoover interrupted him with a strikingly undiplomatic response. "Mr. Carpenter, if you will allow me to become a Californian a minute instead of a Chairman," he began, then proceeded to explain, as the others stiffened in their seats, that the "people of the lower river" had put so much effort into cultivating their land that they deserved to be guaranteed all the water they were already using, or more.

This sounded like a replay of Hoover's plea for a flood control dam, which had provoked the collapse of the first round of talks in January. With the upper basin firmly convinced that California was already exceeding its rights to the river and was not above plotting to steal even more, this appeal could not help but provoke a new uproar. As the talks again neared collapse, Hoover hastily backed off and adjourned the meeting.

Hoover and McClure had snatched defeat from the jaws of victory. Yet the California lobbyists, who had been chafing in their Santa Fe boarding rooms, immediately set about making things worse. They drafted a condescending message to McClure, ordering him to stand his ground: "California should let it be understood that we'd never sign that compact until Congress had authorized . . . Boulder Dam and the All-American Canal." McClure showed the missive to an infuriated Hoover, who immediately summoned the entire California group to the lodge for what William J. Carr, the leader of the dispossessed Californians, later described as "a historic scene."

The encounter took place in Hoover's spacious suite, which was equipped with a grand piano and other amenities. The Californians trooped in, placed their hats on the piano, and seated themselves on stiff-backed chairs arranged in a row facing Hoover and the dour, Bible-toting McClure. Hoover "had one of his famous frowns on," Carr reported.

"Gentlemen," Hoover began, "I have just read the communication you sent to Colonel McClure. I think it was a most outrageous, scandalous thing I have ever had called to my attention. And I want to say here and now that unless you gentlemen forthwith and immediately, in writing, apologize to Colonel McClure, I'm going to disband this conference, announce that Boulder Dam project is dead, and that you are the people who killed Cock Robin."

A stunned silence fell. Suddenly Mark Rose, known to his friends as the man least likely to submit to bullying, got to his feet. He walked to the piano and grabbed his hat. "Mark was right close to Hoover, and he looked down at him with an air of supreme contempt," Carr recalled. "Looked at him as though he could almost spit in his face."

"Aw, Hell!" Rose barked, and stalked out of the room.

When the other Californians lunged for their own hats, Hoover realized that he had overplayed his hand. His carefully prepared dramatic scene devolved into slapstick as he scampered after the Californians, pleading with them to stay. But they continued walking and booked reservations for Los Angeles the next day, resigned to having lost the battle of the compact. But they had not given up the war.

On Friday, November 24, the day of the Californians' departure, the seven commissioners approved the final draft of the Colorado River Compact. Separately they approved a resolution urging "the early construction of works in the Colorado River to control the floods," hoping that this would be enough to ensure ratification by the California legislature, now thrown into doubt by the delegation's early departure. Overcome by emotion at the completion of negotiations, Hoover praised the members and thanked them for their service. "We have possibly made here, I don't know, one of the most constructive steps that has been taken in the West," he said. "It will take time to prove it, but it is possible that this will stand out as one of the landmarks of Western development." Despite all the contention that awaited the Colorado River, the decades would prove Hoover right. The Colorado River Compact would survive, in nearly unchanged form, as the founding document of what would eventually become known as the Law of the River, and the model for many interstate compacts yet to come.

That evening, in the Ben Hur Room of the Palace of the Governors in downtown Santa Fe, using the lapboard on which General Lew Wallace had finished his Christian devotional masterpiece forty years earlier while serving as New Mexico's territorial governor, they applied their signatures to the compact with a ceremonial gold pen.

Before the pact went into effect, it would have to be ratified by each of the seven states and by Congress. In seven state capitals and on Capitol Hill, special interests began sharpening their pencils to calculate how the compact might profit them. There were farm lobbies, veterans groups, electrical utility associations, and more, and they all intended to have their say.

# 6

# Battlegrounds

One February day, the newly elected congressman Philip D. Swing found himself perched on a gravel escarpment, 1,500 feet above solid ground, staring queasily down a vertical precipice at a distant ribbon of water. The tripod he cradled in his arms grew heavier by the minute. He pressed his slender frame firmly against the rock wall behind him, rooted to the spot.

Swing had only himself to blame for his predicament. Exhilarated by his first victory at the polls during the election of November 1920, he had decided to stop at Boulder Canyon on his way to Washington for the opening of Congress in March. His congressional district sprawled over seven counties from the Mexican border nearly to Lake Tahoe—49,000 square miles, almost a third of California's area. But most of the population was concentrated in San Diego and the Imperial Valley, where one issue dominated all others: the need to pry funding for the Boulder Canyon dam and the All-American Canal from the federal treasury. Swing had thought it would be a good idea to take a look at the real estate at issue so that once he reached the capital "I would know what I was talking about." Now he had a bird's-eye view, and vertigo was beginning to get the better of him.

Walker Young had picked up Swing early that morning at the train depot in Moab, Utah. Together they drove nine hours to reach the Reclamation Service's survey station at the foot of Black Canyon. The river was at low ebb in the winter calm, the spring flood surge still months away. Survey barges were out on the water, drilling for bedrock. Young led Swing up the zigzagging catwalk anchored to the Nevada cliffside, toting a camera while Swing shouldered its tripod.

A thousand feet above the river they stopped to take pictures. It was Swing who, disappointed in the view, suggested they go higher. Ascending another five hundred feet they reached an outcropping where Young pinioned the camera to its stand and panned it over the stunning landscape. Upstream, the canyon opened out against a mountain backdrop of surpassing splendor; downstream, perpendicular walls pressed in upon the gorge and the silvery river disappeared around a distant bend. The photographs Young snapped that afternoon would hang in Swing's Washington office until the end of his congressional career, ten years later.

When it was time to return to camp, Swing made the mistake of glancing down, and froze. Coaxed by Young, he slowly backed away from the precipice until he could feel his heels touch solid rock. With his backside flattened against the wall and Young's encouraging murmur in his ear, he shuffled down the catwalk, step by sideways step. Reaching solid ground at last, he let out a deep breath. Then he heard Young's guffaws from behind him.

"What are you laughing at?" Swing barked indignantly.

Still chuckling, Young pointed at Swing's rear end. Swing felt back there for the seat of his pants, only to discover that it was gone, shredded into nothing by the canyon wall.

That night back in Utah, he met the train carrying his wife and daughter and a valise containing his one spare suit. "I was lucky," he recalled, "that the train arrived at Moab after dark."

Phil Swing's law practice had sprouted, as though out of the bare earth, along with the Imperial Valley. In 1907, when he hung out his attorney's shingle in El Centro as a twenty-three-year-old stranger from San Bernardino, it was the only incorporated city in the valley. Many of the streets still were paved with sand and some businesses still operated out of tents.

The business of Imperial County revolved around water; therefore so did Swing's practice. He oversaw the creation of the Imperial Irrigation District, mediated its internal squabbles, and in 1915 negotiated its purchase of the old California Development Company assets from the Southern Pacific. On an official visit to Washington to lobby the House Irrigation Committee on behalf of the All-American Canal, he made such a strong impression on the committee chairman, Addison Smith of Idaho, that Smith buttonholed him in the hallway to offer some unsolicited advice.

No outsider could hope to put a project of that scope across in Congress, Smith told him. "Every member in there has his own pet project, and none of them is going to wetnurse someone else's baby. A project like this has to be fought for from the inside. Why don't you go home, run for Congress, and come back to fight for your own?" A few months later, the congressman who represented the valley retired. Pledging to bring home the dam and canal, Swing won the 1920 election easily on the Republican ticket.

Arriving in Washington after his junket to Boulder Canyon, Swing was let down with a thud. "I soon found out that every Congressman had projects of his own," he recalled later. "While they would listen patiently to me expound the merits of Boulder Dam, their minds were actually on their own projects."

Other conditions made the moment inauspicious to place Boulder Dam and the All-American Canal on the congressional agenda. For one thing, the Harding administration had signaled its hostility to all federal public works spending. The compact negotiations, meanwhile, would not get underway for another year.

For these reasons and others, Swing waited until April 25, 1922, in the hiatus between the January compact talks and the reconvened session at Bishop's Lodge, to introduce a bill mandating construction of the All-American Canal and a high dam in the "vicinity" of Boulder Canyon. Once California's senior senator, Hiram Johnson, became committed to carrying it in the upper chamber, the measure became known as the Swing-Johnson bill. Four versions of it would be drafted and filed in the next six years.

The first Swing-Johnson bill languished in congressional limbo while Herbert Hoover and Arthur Powell Davis labored to secure ratification of the compact by the seven basin state legislatures. In five of the state capitals, the ratification process was relatively straightforward. But the compact ran into strong headwinds in the two states that stood to gain the most from its provisions, California and Arizona.

In California, the voices of discontent were heard most stridently in the Imperial Valley, where Mark Rose led the dissenting chorus. His view of the compact had not changed since the night he had stomped out of Hoover's suite: without the firm guarantee of a dam and reservoir on the lower river, he maintained, the compact was fatally flawed. He proposed that California ratify the compact only conditionally, subject to passage of the Swing-Johnson bill in Washington. That way, there could be no compact unless there were a dam and reservoir, too.

Hoover was aghast. Any such "reservation" by one state—especially the basin's most voracious—could only provoke the others to impose conditions of their own. To save the compact he launched a round of hectic jawboning with legislative leaders in California while his assistants, Clarence Stetson and William C. Mullendore, tracked the situation in the other states via a cross-country exchange of elaborately coded telegrams. ("Michigan members Alexandria under guidance Orange and Grapefruit want Georgia as per telegram feeling camel language ambiguous Stop.") Eventually Hoover persuaded a bare majority of California lawmakers that their state would gain much more from the compact than it would lose. The California legislature narrowly approved the compact without reservations on February 1. There would be more twists and turns in the state's treatment of the measure, but for the moment, Hoover believed, the California insurrection had been suppressed.

Arizona was another matter entirely. There, anti-California demagoguery was in full cry and the fate of the compact hung by a thread.

The instigator of the Arizona revolt, as it happened, was a native Californian. George Hebard Maxwell was the son of a Forty-niner from Connecticut who had discovered, like so many others, that the lure of gold was a chimera. Abandoning his barren prospecting claim, he settled down to farm a patch of soil in Sonoma, north of San Francisco. There the young George Maxwell cut his teeth as a lawyer specializing in water law, which soon brought him under the spell of William Ellsworth Smythe. Maxwell adopted Smythe's program and emulated the older man's oratorical style. By the 1890s he reigned as the most compelling speaker and prolific pamphleteer on the nationwide water evangelism circuit.

Maxwell's proselytizing for a federal irrigation program was fundamentally anti-urban and conventionally Luddite. Like Smythe, he held that the density and squalor of the industrialized East fostered physical and moral decline. The sole solution was to groom the vast arid spaces of the West to accommodate thousands of transplanted city dwellers in a nationwide revival of self-sufficient household agriculture. As he wrote in 1906 in his newsletter, *Maxwell's Talisman,* "We believe that the Slums and Tenements and Congested Centers of population in the Cities are a savagely deteriorating social, moral and political influence, and that a great public movement should be organized . . . for the betterment of all the conditions of Rural Life."

In pursuit of this goal Maxwell made common cause with railroad magnates, manufacturers, and labor organizers. But as he aged, his talent for vitriolic debate degenerated into a febrile phobia directed at communists, anarchists, and "Asiatics"—specifically Japanese and Chinese immigrants.

In the months before the Santa Fe talks, Maxwell had crisscrossed the Southwest to sermonize about the threat of an Asiatic invasion. This, he predicted, would originate from Mexico, where the enemy were ostensibly massing, disguised as the Chandler syndicate's foreign sharecroppers. The compact and the Boulder Canyon Project, in his view, presaged an American apocalypse, for they would deliver to Mexico the water needed to develop a two-million-acre Asiatic colony south of the border. With this notion as his starting point, Maxwell typically worked himself into a hysterical rant about the peril lurking just over the horizon.

> The establishment of an Asiatic city in Mexican territory at the head of the Gulf of California [he proclaimed in a typical jeremiad] would create an

Asiatic airplane base within two hours of Los Angeles. . . . Such a project holds possibilities of future calamity so appalling as to stagger the human imagination. The urban population of that entire region, including all of southern Arizona, could be eliminated by a fleet of airplanes armed with poison gas bombs within two hours after that fleet had left its head at the Gulf of California; and a few explosive bombs, destroying the Los Angeles aqueduct and other structures necessary for the water supply would return the country to a waterless desert.

Maxwell's answer to this threat was a project called the Highline Canal, which would thread 470 miles through the Arizona desert from Boulder Canyon to Phoenix. Unfazed by expert opinion that held the canal to be an economic and geographical absurdity, he promised that it would deprive Mexico of Colorado water by diverting the entire river for irrigation in the United States.

When the compact commissioners had arrived at Bishop's Lodge for their final talks in November 1922, they found him already on the scene to hector them on the topic—a performance that earned him the undying enmity of Herbert Hoover. When he resurfaced as a foe of ratification, Hoover hastened to denounce him as a dangerous lunatic. "My recommendation is to ignore the gentleman," he advised President Harding. "He is a demagogue of the first water and has already been pretty well squelched in his own state."

Hoover underestimated his man. Far from being squelched, Maxwell had gained the ear of George W. P. Hunt, who was then serving the third of his seven two-year terms as governor of Arizona. A former prospector, Hunt had led Arizona to statehood as a member of its territorial legislature. The Arizona chauvinism in his soul was set aquiver by Maxwell's depiction of the compact as the handiwork of plutocrats and, more to the point, of Californians intent on reducing Arizonans to waterless serfdom. Following Maxwell's lead, Hunt published a screed against ratification and campaigned across the state for the compact's defeat. As proof of California's ruthless scheming, he pointed to the Swing-Johnson bill and its choir of supporters in the Golden State.

The pages of space advocating the Boulder Canyon Project by California newspapers, and the propaganda in the national magazines by the California and Mexican land interests and the insidious propaganda articles of the power trust, all bear the imprint of a desire for plunder. . . . The Colorado River is our great resource and unless we conserve it and get the maximum benefit from it, we can depend upon becoming a sort of vermiform appendix to Los Angeles, instead of becoming one of the great empire states of this nation.

Whether these were really the words of the unschooled Hunt or were dictated by Maxwell (as seems likely), his sentiment was shared by the legislature. More ominously, it appeared to be shared by the voters, who reelected Hunt to his fourth term in 1924. The compact required unanimous ratification, but with Arizona appearing to be a lost cause, its supporters began to consider how to get it enacted if one of the seven states bailed out.

For all that Hunt and Maxwell lumped in the "power trust" with Arizona's other enemies in their brief against the Swing-Johnson bill, the utility industry disliked the measure as much as they did. Flush with cash and commanding nationwide influence, the power companies wasted no time in conspiring to kill it.

In their eyes, the bill's major drawback was that it gave municipalities and other public entities preference in the purchase of hydroelectricity from the dam. The Boulder Canyon Project looked to the utilities like a sleight-of-hand trick: under the guise of flood control, it turned the government into a purveyor of tax-exempt kilowatts to public agencies, in competition with themselves.

The utilities had been at war with the advocates of public power for more than thirty years. Until recently, they had been largely successful at restricting public ownership to small rural communities they had scant interest in serving in the first place, while maintaining their grip on the big cities. But the tide had begun to turn in 1922, when Los Angeles seized Edison's electrical grid and placed it under municipal control. Other California communities soon followed L.A.'s lead.

What drove the public power movement was a nationwide consolidation of the utility industry into a small number of gargantuan holding companies with interlocking interests. The epitome was the Insull group, headquartered in Chicago but with tentacles extending into thirty states—an unsettling octopus of capital and influence. The customers most victimized by the power trust were the working class. Small residential power users paid the highest rates for the spottiest service, while big customers such as factories and refineries pocketed millions in discounts and rebates. It was not surprising that as organized labor gained strength in the first decades of the twentieth century, the unions joined with political progressives like Hiram Johnson of California to fight the utilities. Municipal-owned power companies reversed the normal pattern of electrical rates, typically reducing prices for their working-class customers by ending subsidies for industry. The Boulder Canyon Project, blessed as it would be with taxpayer-financed construction costs and federal and state tax exemptions, was almost certain to follow this pattern, becoming the benchmark against which all electricity rates would be measured.

The full scope of the utilities' covert assault on the Boulder Canyon Project would not be revealed until 1928, when their lobbying against the cause of public power would be exposed by the Federal Trade Commission. But their fingerprints appeared as early as November 1922 in the opposition campaign against the California Water and Power Act, a public referendum on the creation of a statewide hydroelectric system. Organizations later unmasked by state investigators as fronts for the utilities showered California voters with pamphlets denouncing the measure as "socialistic." (Typical title: "Shall California Be Sovietized?") In all, the utilities spent $1 million in their successful effort to defeat the California measure. This was merely a hint of what they were capable of when they believed their survival was at stake.

Conflicts over the compact and public power sharpened through 1923. Pro-dam interests, including the Imperial Irrigation District and the cities of Los Angeles and San Diego, worked to promote the Boulder Canyon Project as assiduously, if not as anonymously, as the power companies worked to scuttle it. Their Boulder Dam Association churned out tracts touting the regionwide benefits of the dam and plumping for support of the Swing-Johnson bill. The association exploited issues of economics and class, painting the power trust and utility investors like Harry Chandler as enemies of the people. "No great project was ever proposed in the interest of the great unorganized public," wrote the association's secretary, Burdett Moody, "that groups of wealth seeking special privilege do not oppose it with a desire to divert the benefits for their personal gain."

This theme proved useful in June when, in a potentially crippling blow to the project, Arthur Powell Davis was summarily fired as head of the Reclamation Service. The hatchet was wielded by Interior Secretary Hubert Work, who had recently succeeded the retired Albert Fall (soon to be disgraced in the Teapot Dome bribery scandal).

The Boulder Canyon Project's supporters lionized Davis as a martyr to the cause of reclamation on the Colorado. In single-mindedly pursuing his program, he had made numerous enemies, many of them with powerful connections. One was Eugene C. La Rue, a prominent engineer at the U.S. Geological Survey who considered himself the reigning authority on the Colorado River by virtue of the nine boat trips, totaling 1,983 miles, he had taken on the waterway since 1914. La Rue nursed a long-standing resentment of Davis, who had often treated him condescendingly and whose publicity-savvy Reclamation Service perennially overshadowed the USGS. In La Rue's view, the Boulder Canyon dam endorsed by the Fall-Davis Report was a bloated and dangerous undertaking—potentially "the most gigantic engineering blunder that has ever been made in this country," as he told Secretary Work point-blank. His counterproposal was for a network of thirteen low dams on the Colorado, including three in Boulder and Black canyons, all impounding small reservoirs to minimize evaporation.

La Rue's plan was a combination of visionary and crackpot engineering. He was correct that a chain of dams would effectively exploit the Colorado's hydroelectric potential—a principle incorporated into the government's massive Colorado River Storage Project thirty years later. It was also the case that small reservoirs would reduce evaporation losses. But La Rue's placement of three dams in Boulder and Black canyons, the hottest part of the watershed, would nullify all his evaporation gains. His expansive blueprint, moreover, would drive the cost of the project beyond the bounds of practicality, and shift a large portion of its power generation out of reach of its prime market, Southern California.

La Rue's critique of the Boulder Canyon Project was widely circulated by Arizona's Governor Hunt and other opponents during 1923. His brief period of eminence, however, would end with an appearance before the Senate Irrigation Committee in December 1925, when he proved so surly under Hiram Johnson's harsh questioning that Arizona's two senators, both of whom were on the committee, abandoned him to his fate by maintaining an embarrassed silence.

Davis's position was more effectively undermined by Herbert Hoover, his former superior at the compact commission. Hoover had strongly disagreed with Davis's plan to finance the project's construction from the sale of electricity. During House hearings on the first Swing-Johnson bill in 1922, Hoover went out of his way to torpedo the notion that a public hydroelectric plant was a necessary adjunct to a public Colorado River dam. The only urgent needs on the river, he testified, were flood control and irrigation storage; this echoed his arguments during the compact negotiations but infuriated Swing, who feared that the project's political support might evaporate unless power revenues were made available to finance its construction.

Although the project's advocates played up the idea of an anti-dam conspiracy, in fact a less sinister explanation for Davis's ouster existed: rampant fiscal mismanagement at the Reclamation Service, where projects often exceeded their cost estimates tenfold. The agency budget consistently ran in the red by tens of millions of dollars. To some extent this was an artifact of the sagging farm economy of the post–World War I years, which impoverished farmers and propelled the delinquency rate on their Reclamation Service loans as high as 60 percent. To Davis's credit, he foresaw that equipping Reclamation dams with hydroelectric generators would allow the service to end assessments on farmers who were incapable of paying them—assuming the development of public hydroelectricity could survive the ferocious opposition of the power trust. But this idea did not compensate for his agency's consistent failure to match its spending to its income. During Davis's tenure, Reclamation spent $16 million on four major dams in Montana alone. Of this sum, Work discovered, the farmers had repaid only $628,000.

In the end, the political forces arrayed against the Reclamation Service proved too strong for Davis to withstand. He was a living symbol of the dominance of engineering ambition over fiscal pragmatism at the agency. He and his predecessor, Frederick Newell, had studded the West and Midwest with grand but woefully uneconomical projects—"They have erected their own monuments," as Work observed in announcing Davis's sacking. The new interior secretary was determined to bring the agency to heel. Not only did he place it under the management of a businessman and banker, D. W. Davis (no relation to A. P. Davis), but he changed its name from the Reclamation Service to the Bureau of Reclamation, as a reminder to its self-assertive staff of their subservience to Interior Department headquarters.

Davis's ouster removed one of the most effective advocates of the Boulder Canyon Project from the corridors of power in Washington at a critical moment. The project's fate in Congress was yet uncertain, not least because the combined price tag for the dam and canal had ballooned to more than $130 million, a sum that bid fair to overwhelm a federal public works budget that had rarely exceeded $150 million in any previous year.

Johnson and Swing instantly applied pressure on Secretary Work to reassure the project's supporters that "the resignation of one or more employees need not affect the policy" favoring reclamation on the lower Colorado. Yet Work himself was not the steadfast supporter of the project that Albert Fall and Arthur Powell Davis had been. How that would affect its ability to prevail over wealthy and politically well-connected enemies no one could know.

As the important election year of 1924 dawned, national politics began to draw the Boulder Canyon Project into its magnetic field.

The previous December, Swing had reintroduced his appropriation bill, which had perished in legislative limbo at the end of his first congressional term. Hiram Johnson, who had given the measure only lukewarm and distracted support in the previous session, now became vigorously engaged. The senator's change of heart stemmed at least partially from his decision to mount a presidential primary challenge against Calvin Coolidge, who had been elevated to the White House from the vice presidency upon the sudden death of President Harding in August 1923.

Johnson was a progressive Republican with a pugnacious personality, whose tendency toward GOP apostasy was signified by his role as Theodore Roosevelt's vice presidential running mate on the Bull Moose ticket in 1912. His standard campaign photo portrayed him in a boxer's stance with his dukes up, albeit dressed incongruously in a business suit with a high collar. For all that he was taking aim at Coolidge in the 1924 election, his political bête noire was Hoover, the only other California politician casting a shadow on the national stage. Johnson had beaten Hoover in the 1920 California Republican primary for president, but he knew that would not be their last political encounter. Following the election, he had lobbied to keep Hoover out of the Harding cabinet, unsuccessfully warning the new president against appointing as commerce secretary a man he described as a "selfish, calculating, untrustworthy candidate for president . . . whom our people [i.e., California primary voters] had repudiated."

Hoover and Johnson would spend much of the postwar period trying to sabotage each other's presidential ambitions. It would be a seesaw battle, with Hoover recovering from his 1920 primary defeat to lead the Coolidge slate to victory in the 1924 California primary. Yet in the long run, this was a fight Johnson could not win, for Hoover had greater nationwide fame and more money; by the presidential election year of 1928, Johnson would no longer be considered a credible candidate in Republican circles.

In 1924, however, Johnson's presidential hopes were still alive. They were built upon an isolationist foreign policy, exemplified by his attack on the new institution of the World Court, which was supported by Coolidge. On the domestic front, he plotted out a renewed assault on the tried-and-true targets of his two triumphant California gubernatorial campaigns in 1910 and 1914: the banks, the electrical utilities, and Harry Chandler. The Boulder Canyon Project, a populist undertaking feared and detested by Southern California's moneyed interests, was an ideal vehicle for these attacks. Johnson peppered Swing with demands for background information about the Imperial Valley, "particularly . . . the hold of the banks and the tyranny of those who hold the mortgages, the newspaper ownership, the Chandler overlordship, etc."

Johnson's antipathy to Chandler, who was a close friend of Hoover's, would be an important source of tension between the two politicians. Another would be the struggle to build the Boulder Canyon Project. Although Johnson and Hoover both favored a large public project on the Colorado, their visions of its proper scale differed dramatically. Their mutual struggle to place their favored version of the project in the gorge, while maneuvering to take credit for the result and deny credit to the other, would play out as a crucial subtext in the battle to dam the river.

When the House Irrigation Committee opened hearings on the newest iteration of Swing-Johnson on February 15, 1924, the question taking center stage was whether hydroelectric sales could cover the Boulder Canyon Project's cost—indeed, whether a power market on the necessary scale even existed. No answer seemed to be in sight.

That changed with the very first witness. He was William Mulholland, who immediately offered the lawmakers a way out of their quandary. "I am here in the interest of a domestic water supply for the city of Los Angeles," he said, "and that injects a new phase into this whole matter." He could have spoken no truer words.

The Belfast-born Mulholland was an imposing figure with a walrus mustache, a piercing glare, and a domineering personality. At the city's Bureau of Water Works and Supply, where he exercised absolute authority, he was known simply as the Chief. He was a man of endless contradictions: the leading architect of public works of his day, he lacked even a basic engineering degree; a vociferous defender of the principle of municipal power ownership, he had trampled on the water rights of Owens Valley farmers to enrich the real estate tycoons of Los Angeles. It is hardly surprising that to do justice to this outsized personality, the writer Robert Towne split him into two distinct characters in his screenplay for the 1974 film *Chinatown*—the reform-minded public servant Hollis Mulwray, and the predatory land speculator Noah Cross.

Mulholland's crowning achievement, the 233-mile Los Angeles Aqueduct, had begun serving the city eleven years earlier. His dedicatory remark as the very first surge of water arrived has entered history as a classic of succinctness. "There it is," he said. "Take it."

It was more than his personality that held the committee members rapt; it was the audacity of his proposal to pump water from the Colorado River over the mountains to the distant metropolis. Mulholland delivered a vivid account of his city's suffering in the teeth of an "appalling" drought. The Southern California mountains, whose snow-capped peaks were usually seen glimmering on the horizon from downtown Los Angeles all winter long, had been brown and bare since autumn. The Owens Valley aqueduct, the city's main source of fresh water, was running dry for lack of rainfall. "This committee has got to come to our relief, or we are ruined," Mulholland warned theatrically.

The reality was not nearly so dire. The drought notwithstanding, Southern California had more than enough water for its existing needs. Mulholland was merely up to his customary trick of fabricating a water shortage to obtain a supply to fuel future growth. Just as he had scared Los Angeles voters into approving numerous bond issues for waterworks over the years, his motive for this fresh alarmism was to scare dozens of small Southern California communities into backing the construction of a regional Colorado River aqueduct. He would succeed again.

Any inclination the congressmen might have had to delve into Mulholland's claim of impending disaster disappeared once he explained its further implications: his plan would require electricity on a grand scale, and he proposed to buy it all from the Boulder Canyon Project. By his calculations, the city's power bill alone would put the project in the black. But he also held out the promise of commercial purchases. The city's own generating capacity of 130,000 horsepower was already so overstretched that it was turning away new customers—factories and refineries that would have fattened the municipal tax base. Mulholland figured that electrical demand in L.A. could grow by 20 to 25 percent a year. "The coming of the city of Los Angeles into this proposition, I think, adds amazingly, immensely, to the sureness of the return to the United States Government," he told the committee. "We promise to be very large customers."

He acknowledged that his proposal might fuel intense opposition from the utilities. By projecting such explosive demand growth from Los Angeles, after all, he was defining a huge potential market for Edison Electric. His advice to the uneasy congressmen was characteristically straightforward: they should stand up and resist the furtive corporate maneuvering of the power lobby. "All the opposition I have heard is more or less covert and on the outside," he said. "It is a good deal like a mole: You know the mole is there; you see where he has made the hole and the hump in the ground where he has crawled; but if you jab a 'snickersnee' into the hole, he may not be there."

As he wrapped up his testimony, the committee took the opportunity to solicit a nugget of professional advice: what was his opinion of the dam site and design?

Mulholland assured the members that a sounder site than Black Canyon, which had by then become the favored location, could hardly be found anywhere on the river. "I have given it the most scrutinizing inquiry as an engineer, and it is not only feasible, but it is easily feasible." If any of the congressmen harbored the slightest doubts about the site, this endorsement by a world-famous engineer with a spotless record must have quelled them.

No one could have known at the time that Mulholland's towering reputation would not survive very much longer. Only four years later, he would be a ruined man, his image as a master builder in tatters, his shoulders weighted down with blame for a prodigious catastrophe. When that time came, his cocksure guarantee of the practicality and safety of a Black Canyon dam would raise new doubts about the project, not put them to rest.

\* \* \*

After Mulholland, the committee heard from a familiar procession of engineers, utility executives, municipal officials, and farmers damning the project or pleading for its power, water, and flood control. In early spring Congress adjourned, and Swing returned home for what would be the most trying reelection campaign of his career.

Swing's labors on behalf of the Boulder Canyon Project had secured him popular support in his home district, but it also galvanized powerful political forces against him. During the run-up to the August 1924 Republican primary—his third, and the major electoral hurdle in a district with only a rudimentary Democratic organization—he was confronted with attacks on his personal character for the first time. Local newspapers aired accusations that while serving in Congress he had received illicit payments from his former employer, the Imperial Irrigation District. Details of a grand jury investigation of financial manipulations by Mark Rose and several other Swing associates were leaked to the press. To cap it all off, the Los Angeles Times reported that he had accepted the endorsement of the Ku Klux Klan, which was highly unpopular in California because of its anti-Catholic bias and its tendency to foment general civic dissension.

Swing labored to defuse the charges as false or exaggerated (the purported payoff by the Imperial Irrigation District amounted to $708.82 for an old per diem claim), not only because any legal inquiry they engendered would be costly and time-consuming, but because he feared they might be used to attack the Boulder Canyon Project in Congress. Indeed, Swing had no illusions about their source: "The allied forces of the L.A. Times crowd . . . [and] the Southern California Edison Co.," as he explained to supporters.

The Times was paying him back for more than merely his championing of the dam and canal. Harry Chandler had been ruffled by Swing during the Irrigation Committee hearings in March, to which he had been "invited"—not even Congress was so presumptuous as to summon the tycoon with a subpoena—to testify about his purported machinations against the project.

Nearing sixty, Chandler was then in the full bloom of influence and wealth. In the corridors of the Los Angeles Times building he was said to be the eleventh-richest person in the world. His authority over Southern

California politics and business was nearly absolute. He dictated votes on the Los Angeles City Council and could make or break state legislators. He served on the board of the First National Bank, the main lender to the giant utility now known as Southern California Edison, but that only hinted at his sway over banks, utilities, real estate syndicates, and other business entities statewide, most of which obediently opposed government-subsidized power generation on the Colorado.

In the hearing room Swing had accused Chandler of directing his newspaper's coverage to snuff out a public work that would improve the lives of thousands of residents and farmers, simply to augment his personal fortune. Chandler acknowledged that he opposed the All-American Canal, but denied that his opposition had anything to do with his ownership of 840,000 Mexican acres. In fact, he said, he was confident there would always be plenty of water for his holdings south of the border, even without the Mexican canal. No, his concern was for the landholders on the American side. The All-American Canal, he had concluded, was an "economic absurdity" that would render the valley "valueless for farming."

He bristled at Swing's charge that his newspaper had printed lies and propaganda against the project. "Well," he said, "I do not know that I have seen anything that smacked of propaganda. We have a very strict rule in the reportorial department. . . . We do not permit reporters or writers to do more than report facts. That is true of any well-regulated newspaper."

"You have not noticed, then, that practically every one of the articles smacked of propaganda against the proposed legislation?" Swing asked.

"No, sir," Chandler shot back. "I think we have printed the facts."

The harvest of this bickering exchange was the *Times*'s hectoring coverage of Swing's reelection campaign—"just another one of the dirty methods which this gang is disposed to use," his law partner Charles L. Childers counseled. "If you were doing nothing in Washington you would have none of this opposition." Given Swing's public efforts to explain away the smears, Childers predicted that they would have little effect at the ballot box. This proved accurate: in the August 26 primary Swing beat his nearest opponent by a three-to-one margin. The Democrats did not bother to run a candidate against him in the November election. But as an example of the ferocity with which the moneyed interests of Southern California would fight the Boulder Canyon Project, the *Times*'s treatment of his campaign left Swing with a nervous feeling.

With the election behind him, Swing returned to Washington in December to rescue the project from a political snare. His bill was in trouble and the compact ratification effort in disarray. Governor Hunt had been reelected in Arizona on an anti-compact platform, leading its supporters to despair of ever obtaining the requisite unanimous seven-state ratification. In an attempt to isolate the defiant Hunt, Delph Carpenter proposed an amendment allowing the compact to go into effect after ratification by the remaining six states. That would be better than no ratification at all, Carpenter argued, as it would bind California and the federal government to the agreed-upon apportionment of the Colorado. Carpenter hoped that Arizona, once it wearied of being the odd state out, would eventually see the benefits of joining up.

But the other states were growing restive. Leaving Arizona even temporarily outside the fold made the upper basin nervous, for an Arizona unfettered by an interstate agreement was fully capable of wrecking the balance of water rights so painstakingly crafted at Bishop's Lodge. In the Utah legislature a movement emerged to rescind its ratification vote. In California, there was renewed talk of adding a condition, or "reservation," to its ratification, allowing the compact to go into effect only after congressional approval of the Black Canyon dam.

Swing and Johnson desperately searched for a formula that would save both the compact and the bill. Their concern was rising because Hoover, the most influential figure in Colorado River politics, was becoming a negative force. Having shepherded the compact into existence, he had assumed for himself the role of arbiter on all things concerning the river—and the grandiose project envisioned by the Swing-Johnson bill was still no more to his taste than it was to the utilities or the Chandler syndicate. Rather than press for a high dam, Hoover proposed starting with a small flood control structure, perhaps built upon foundations that could support enlargement in the future. Calling this approach "taking the project at two bites," he counseled the project's supporters that a scaled-back proposal would be more palatable to Congress, and therefore more certain of passage.

To Hiram Johnson, Hoover's opposition to a high dam at Black Canyon and his preference for a modest flood control structure signaled Hoover's alliance with his old California nemeses, Chandler and the utilities. "Whenever we uncover a power trust rogue, we find Hoover," Johnson observed in one of his nearly daily letters to his two sons.

Hoover, no match for Johnson in the art of withering public rhetoric, avoided engaging him in public on the subject of the project. He would eventually strike back in his memoirs, published nearly thirty years after the fact. There he would rewrite the history of the Swing-Johnson bill to paint Johnson as a rank obstructionist and himself as the selfless hero of the project's saga. The bill, he claimed, won enactment only after "Dr. Work [Interior Secretary Hubert Work] . . . and I rewrote the whole," for it had been drafted "in such socialist terms that it could not pass the Congress." Hoover erased Phil Swing entirely from the story, the better to score off Johnson, then seven years in the grave. In his own memoirs, Swing brushed off the affront but defended his late comrade in arms, writing of his dismay that Hoover would "assail, belittle and ridicule the motives, name and character of a great American after he is dead and unable to defend himself. . . . This reveals a side of Mr. Hoover's character unknown to the public." Johnson, more dismissive of Hoover's character, would presumably not have been so shocked.

Toward the end of 1924, the Swing-Johnson bill finally began to move fitfully through Congress. One catalyst was Swing's decision to tie the bill's implementation to ratification of the Colorado River Compact. Neither measure, therefore, could go into effect without the other, an arrangement Swing and Johnson hoped would counteract the upper basin's view of the dam as a Trojan horse crafted to deprive them of their water rights. John-son, meanwhile, raised the project's profile among his Senate colleagues by scheduling a series of hearings across the West, where they heard scores of settlers describe firsthand the threat of flooding and the bounty that would come from a dependable irrigation supply.

At sixty-one, Johnson was beginning to tire of the relentless dickering over the project. He was struggling to accept Hoover's rising profile in the party, which he knew meant the end of his own presidential ambitions. He was suffering a recurrence of insomnia, an ancient complaint, and blamed it on the Boulder Canyon battle—"the most disagreeable thing that has ever come to my lot," he complained. Despite "the stupendous importance of power companies, electric trusts, and Mr. Chandler's 850,000 acres of land in Mexico," he wrote wearily to one of his sons in mid-December, "we'll continue to plug along on the matter with the result wholly problematical."

Another concern was Calvin Coolidge. In his State of the Union mes-sage in December 1925, the president exasperated Johnson by proposing a new commission to weigh the competing demands on the river before any project could be enacted. "It is the old method of stalling and destroying a bill by interminable delay," Johnson fulminated, convinced that the pro-posal was the work of a "tremendous underground opposition" whispering in Coolidge's ear. The administration seemed incapable of speaking about the project with a single voice. In March 1926, just after Interior Secretary Work unexpectedly gave the project his formal endorsement, Treasury Sec-retary Andrew Mellon weighed in with an objection to the $125 million bond issue needed to finance it.

Mellon said he preferred to pay for the dam out of current government revenues rather than through bonding, thus favoring a financing method that would strike later generations as the very antithesis of conservative fis-cal policy. But his real goal was to quash what he viewed as a fundamentally inappropriate expenditure of government funds. "I believe that, in general, sound public policy in America, as elsewhere, is to encourage private initia-tive and not to have Government ownership or operation of projects which can be handled by private capital under proper government regulations," he admonished Addison Smith, chairman of the House Irrigation Committee.

"I am loathe [sic] to have the United States embark upon enterprises not strictly governmental in their nature. It seems to me that if the project is one which can pay its way, private capital can be found."

Johnson cursed Coolidge in private for failing to keep his cabinet under control. The opening of a new Congress found him slipping into despondency about the Boulder Canyon Project's uncertain fate. He did not know that he was standing on the brink of victory.

Two events set the stage for the passage of the Swing-Johnson bill after a six-year effort. The first was the great Midwest flood of 1927, a summer deluge that killed 246 people, sweeping away bridges and breaching the levees over a thousand-mile stretch of the Mississippi River. The city of New Orleans escaped utter destruction by a hairsbreadth.

As a member of the House Flood Control Committee, Swing expressed heartfelt concern for the victims in public while taking steps behind the scenes to exploit the situation for his own constituents. Joining a congressional inspection party on a flatboat cruise down the swollen Atchafalaya tributary, he discovered the Cajun country of Longfellow's *Evangeline* to be "completely under water," with men taking to rowboats to harvest the Spanish moss hanging from the trees.

Disquietingly, he found the farmers of the region to be well versed on the details of the Boulder Canyon bill and distinctly cool to it. Cotton farmers told him they objected to irrigating a million acres for cotton in the Imperial Valley; corn farmers feared a million new acres of corn; wheat farmers a million of wheat. There could be only one explanation for this improbable unanimity of sentiment over a region of 26,000 square miles, Swing concluded: the power companies had been spreading propaganda.

The congressional debate over Mississippi flood relief gave him an opening to defuse the opposition. Whatever principle Congress settled on to justify assisting the Mississippi's flood victims plainly would apply equally to the victims of the Colorado. Accordingly, when the committee launched hearings on what would become the Flood Control Act of 1928—a levee construction program costing an unprecedented $300 million—Swing made sure that nobody overlooked the parallels. "A train load of New Orleans' leading business and civic leaders attended the hearings to plead for flood protection," he wrote later. "I took on the New Orleans men one after another . . . putting to them again and again whether they could see any difference between the Mississippi's flood threat to their people and the Colorado River flood threat to the people of the Imperial Valley. . . . The Editor of the New Orleans Picayune came up to give me warm assurances that they would all work for my bill, which they did."

This was invaluable support, if not yet quite enough to put the Swing-Johnson bill over the top. But during the early spring of 1928, ultimate deliverance arrived from an unexpected quarter. The instrument of fate was the Federal Trade Commission, which had been delegated by the Senate to investigate the utility industry's secret campaign against municipal power.

Progressives instinctively viewed this parliamentary maneuver as a victory for the power trust. The FTC was the most toothless of federal regulatory agencies; its own chairman, a renowned reactionary named William E. Humphrey, had denounced it upon his appointment by Coolidge in 1925 as a "publicity bureau to spread socialistic propaganda" and "an instrument of oppression and disturbance . . . instead of a help to business." Hiram Johnson groused to a friend that handing the probe to the FTC was tantamount to "chloroforming" the investigation.

But the commission surprised everyone, not least the utilities, with a show of unusual spine. In hearings commencing in March, the FTC exposed the power trust's clandestine propaganda campaign in damning detail. Newspaper front pages—led by an anti-utility Hearst press displaying the rabble-rousing skills it had perfected during the *Maine* affair nearly thirty years earlier—trumpeted stories of the utilities' extraordinary efforts to manipulate public opinion. College professors had been paid to develop pro-utility curricula, high school textbooks rewritten to play up the role of private utilities in modern life, and editorial pages bent to the power trust's cause. ("The article that you wrote and . . . so kindly allowed me to sign as my own has seemed to make quite a 'hit,'" a South Carolina dowager wrote to a utility executive whose words had appeared over her name in dozens of newspapers. "I feel like quite an imposter.")

In all, the utilities were revealed to have spent $1 million a year to turn public opinion against public power, and another $400,000 specifically to torpedo the Boulder Canyon bill. Some of this money was handed out to political leaders to reward their secret machinations against the project. Senator Irvine Lenroot of Wisconsin, a vehement foe of Swing-Johnson, got $20,000. Former New Mexico governor Merritt C. Mechem was paid $5,300 to report to the power companies on his closed-door meetings with other Western governors. Even two members of Hoover's compact commission, Nevada's James Scrugham and Stephen B. Davis of New Mexico, showed up on the utility payroll.

Material from the FTC's investigation would continue to flow into the public record for more than four years, eventually filling forty-four volumes. Sensing a sea change driven by nationwide revulsion over the revelations, Johnson took to the Senate floor to exhort his colleagues to "defy the power lobby" by enacting his bill. They seemed finally to be falling into line. Then fate threw up one final frightful obstacle.

Early on the morning of Monday, March 12, 1928, William Mulholland clambered over the brush-covered escarpment of San Francisquito Canyon, fifty miles north of downtown Los Angeles, straining for a closer look at the concrete abutments of the city's newest dam, the St. Francis. He had been summoned shortly after dawn by a watchman who had grown nervous about a leak in the eastern abutment. A certain amount of seepage at the sides of a dam is normal; but the watchman noticed that the leaking water had turned a muddy brown. Taking this as an indication that the flow was eating away at the dam's foundations, he sounded the alarm.

Mulholland spent a few hours on the scene. But he had no real qualms about the stability of the two-hundred-foot dam, which he had designed with an elegant downstream face tiered like the sides of an Aztec pyramid and perforated by a vertical line of outlets down the center. When these spigots were opened, water cascaded down along the terraced front wall, giving the dam the appearance more of a garden water folly than a solid bulwark holding back twelve billion gallons of water.

The structure was a showpiece for the increasingly popular arched configuration in dam architecture, which transferred to a dam's lateral anchorages some of the load exerted by its reservoir. Consequently, it could be thinner in cross section and cheaper than a conventional gravity dam, which achieved stability from its sheer weight and therefore required many times more bulk.

Of the nine dams built by the city of Los Angeles under Mulholland's leadership in the 1920s, the St. Francis Dam was the biggest and, to its builder's mind, the safest. "Of all the dams I have built and all the dams I have seen, it was the driest dam of its size I ever saw," he would later observe. It had been formally opened on March 12, 1926, two years to the day before the watchman's frantic summons.

To Mulholland that morning, the watchman's concerns seemed overwrought. The water did not strike him as particularly muddy, nor did the volume of seepage give him pause. Pronouncing the structure safe, he departed the scene around noon.

That night, at exactly two minutes and thirty seconds before midnight—the tragic moment pinpointed by the sudden short-circuiting of Southern California Edison's adjacent power line—the dam burst. The watchman, his girlfriend, and his six-year-old son were the first victims, perishing in their home a quarter-mile downstream. There would be more than 450 others.

The entire reservoir emptied in less than seventy minutes. A wall of water 140 feet high surged toward the Pacific Ocean at an estimated eighteen miles an hour. A mile and a half downstream, the wave struck a powerhouse belonging to the city, drowning sixty-four workers and family members living in the compound. At an Edison construction camp eleven miles further down, eighty-four more workmen were swept away in their sleep. A few valiant switchboard operators stayed at their posts in the flood zone, attempting to alert residents living in the fifty-four-mile path of destruction, before they were drowned themselves. Bodies were still being recovered weeks later, some washing ashore as far away as the Mexican seacoast.

In California history, the death toll of the St. Francis Dam disaster remains second only to that of the San Francisco earthquake of 1906. It still reigns as the worst failure of American civil engineering in the twentieth century. Annihilated in the catastrophe, along with $15 million in property and hundreds of lives, was William Mulholland's reputation. Ten days after the break, testifying at a coroner's inquest for sixty-five victims, he broke down in tears, asserting that he "envied those who were killed" and taking full responsibility for the toll: "If there was an error in human judgment, I was the human." After the disaster, he all but vanished from the public eye; in photographs dating from that period his arrogant glare is gone, replaced by the look of a haunted man.

To the end of his life, Mulholland nursed suspicions that the dam was destroyed by sabotage, perhaps by Owens Valley dynamiters striking back at him for the great water theft of two decades earlier. A dozen inquests and investigations proved him wrong. The dam collapsed, engineers concluded, because one end was anchored to an unstable ancient landslide, which had been coming loose for a week before it finally gave way on March 12. Later investigations further faulted the dam's design. During construction Mulholland had ordered its height raised by twenty feet without widening the base to accommodate the increased load. This made the dam so top-heavy that it became perilously unstable when its reservoir rose to within seven feet of its crest—as had happened only a few days before the collapse.

These dangers might have been alleviated had Mulholland taken steps to counter the seepage by installing drains underneath the dam and sealing faults in the foundations and abutments with grout (a fast-setting mixture of cement and water). These were novel, but widely accepted, elements of dam engineering at the time, yet he did neither. Nor did he submit his design for review by outside engineers—a procedure that was mandatory for state and federal, but not municipal, projects.

The St. Francis Dam disaster occurred at an extremely delicate moment for the Swing-Johnson bill. The House Irrigation Committee members could not help but feel queasy about the trust they had placed in Mulholland's judgment during their hearings. They had accepted as gospel his endorsement of the dam's site and its size, along with his reassurances about its safety. Now none of those judgments carried the slightest weight—if anything, they might be counted against the project.

The disquiet reached Denver, where a team of Reclamation Bureau engineers had been working on a gravity-arch design for the Black Canyon dam similar to that of the St. Francis. Aware that their projected reservoir was to be seven hundred times the size of the now drained impoundment in San Francisquito Canyon, they immediately set out to strengthen in their design all the safeguards and redundancies that Mulholland had scorned.

The rubble in the Southern California hills gave the Boulder Canyon Project's enemies a new talking point. The *Wall Street Journal* termed the St. Francis break "an indictment of municipal ownership" of electricity. Arizona governor Hunt dispatched to the scene his own investigator, who obligingly reported that the ruined dam had been the brainchild of "men of the same business intelligence" as those behind "the proposed highest water storage dam in the world" (i.e., the Boulder Canyon Project).

From Swing's standpoint, it was a stroke of luck that his bill had achieved too great a head of steam in the House to be easily derailed. But with Mulholland disgraced, Congress could hardly grant final approval without seeking the imprimatur of some unimpeachable authority, preferably a full-fledged board of engineers. Swing moved promptly to satisfy the demand. He added to the final version of the Swing-Johnson bill a mandate for a blue-ribbon board to scrutinize the Boulder Canyon project and report to Congress, specifying a deadline no later than December 1. As chairman, Congress appointed Major General William L. Sibert, whose engineering eminence stemmed from his service under General George Goethals in the building of the Panama Canal. It was a canny choice—a hero of the nation's last great engineering achievement standing in review of the next one. As Swing anticipated, the appointment of the so-called Colorado River Board calmed Congress's nerves, allowing him and Johnson to shepherd their bill to the finish line.

The measure then before Congress was the fourth Swing-Johnson bill, introduced at the start of the congressional session in late December. It bore several improvements over its predecessors, all designed to grease the path to enactment. The Interior Department was given broad latitude to manage the dam's hydroelectric potential: it could, at its discretion, build the hydroelectric plant itself, or turn that task over to any private or public contractor—whether a utility company or a municipality. That change undercut one of the objections raised by Hoover, who opposed the government's laying even the first brick of a hydropower plant while private contractors stood ready to do the job.

Swing and Johnson further addressed the mistrust of California among the other compact signatories by specifying water shares for all three lower basin states. The fourth Swing-Johnson bill provided California with an annual allocation of 4.4 million acre-feet, or a little over 58 percent of the lower basin total; Arizona with 2.8 million; and Nevada with 300,000. California's discontent with what it considered a meager share was tempered, if modestly, by a provision allowing it to consume any unused portion of Arizona's and Nevada's shares; the assumption was that it would be many decades before those states would require their full allotments. (Indeed, that point would not arrive until fifty years later.) The redrafted bill also allowed the compact to be ratified by only six states, as long as one was California—thus accommodating the compact to the reality of Arizona's obdurate opposition.

In the waning afternoon daylight of Friday, May 25, the House of Representatives passed the Boulder Canyon Project Act by voice vote. Victory was so sudden that it almost took the exhausted Swing by surprise. He mustered the strength to phone the news home, where it was greeted by the ringing of fire bells and the sounding of klaxons in the cities of the Imperial Valley.

At the opposite end of the Capitol the opposition was not quite ready to roll over. A few days after the House vote, Arizona's two senators took the floor of the upper chamber to filibuster the measure, provoking Johnson to test their endurance by forcing the Senate to stay up all night. The Arizonans held out for twenty-one and a half hours. Finally, as dawn was breaking on Tuesday, May 29, Johnson won an agreement for the bill to be brought up as the first order of business when Congress reconvened in December. With the senators as frazzled as three-year-old children, an uproar ensued over this attempt at circumventing the Arizonans' opposition. As spectators in the overhead galleries screamed encouragement, a melee broke out on the floor. Fists were on the verge of flying when the Senate leadership called an executive session and hastily adjourned for the summer.

Herbert Hoover won the Republican nomination for president on the first ballot at the party's nominating convention that June, trouncing two colorless Midwesterners. President Calvin Coolidge had announced that he did not choose to run for a second term, and Hiram Johnson had been outspent and outmaneuvered out of contention.

The fall campaign was one of smug Republican self-congratulation for the prosperous veneer of the Coolidge years and fierce religious bigotry directed at the Democratic candidate, Al Smith, the Roman Catholic governor of New York. It ended with a historic Republican landslide, Hoover taking 444 electoral votes, including New York's, to Smith's eighty-seven. The Republicans won the Midwest and the West, all of the Northeast except Massachusetts and Rhode Island, and five of the eleven traditionally Democratic states of the once "solid South."

For the Democrats the only hopeful sign in the results was Smith's majority in the nation's twelve biggest cities, which had gone for the GOP in 1924 by a solid margin. Whether that victory presaged the urban vote that would help sweep Franklin Roosevelt into office in 1932 has been widely debated, for any portents one might seek in the results of 1928 were surely outweighed by the effects of the economic calamity that was soon to engulf the nation.

When the Senate reconvened on December 3, 1928, the question of Coolidge's approval of the Swing-Johnson bill was still hanging fire. Always reluctant to spend government money, the president fretted over the dam's price tag like a working stiff beleaguered by household bills. "I am a good deal disturbed by the number of proposals that are being made for an expenditure of money," he had mentioned to a group of White House reporters in May, during one of the frequent but surreptitious press conferences

he held during his tenure. "There is this flood bill [for the Mississippi].
. . . There is the farm bill calling for $400,000,000. The Boulder Dam bill. I
think the lowest estimates on that are $125,000,000. . . . I don't know just
what will happen to the Treasury."

In his State of the Union message that December—written to be read,
not spoken aloud, and carrying on the printed page all the lilting cadence
of a telephone book—Coolidge equivocated about the bill and expressed
unease about the public ownership of hydroelectric power. "As private enterprise can very well fill this field, there is no need for the Government to
go into it," he wrote. Whether he was actually threatening a veto over the
public power preference, no one knew. But it was widely felt, as the *New
York Times* judged, that "the danger to the Boulder Canyon bill is not in
Congress but at the White House."

The Sibert board had issued its report on November 24, one week shy
of its congressional deadline. The panel endorsed the Black Canyon site selected by the Reclamation Bureau as more accessible, narrower, and capable
of impounding a larger reservoir at lower cost than any site in Boulder Canyon. With an eye toward alleviating the concerns raised by the St. Francis collapse, it pronounced the site's geology "competent to carry safely the
heavy load and abutment thrusts contemplated."

But the board also urged that the dam be engineered to "ultra-conser-
vative" specifications. "If it should fail, the flood created would probably
destroy Needles, Topock, Parker, Blythe, Yuma, and permanently destroy
the levees of the Imperial District." Invoking the Rockwood flood of nearly
a quarter-century earlier, the board projected that a flood surge would
channel a route to the Salton Sea so deep that the Colorado would probably never return to its old course. The report recommended reducing the
maximum pressure on the concrete structure to thirty tons per square foot
from the forty of the original plan, doubling the capacity of the diversion
tunnels that were to carry the river around the site during construction, and
doubling the spillway capacity to ensure that no flood could ever overtop
the dam itself. These changes would bring the estimated cost of the entire
project, including the All-American Canal and interest, to $165 million, an
increase of $35 million over previous estimates.

The project's foes and friends all found grist in the report to support their positions. Utah's Senator Reed Smoot pronounced the report the "death knell" of the project, based on Sibert's order to tighten the engineering specifications. On the other side, Hiram Johnson reminded the chamber that the Sibert board certified the dam as entirely feasible and entirely safe, once the recommended safeguards were designed in.

In this seemingly unsettled atmosphere, the Senate launched its floor debate. In a curtain-raising article on December 4, the chief Washington correspondent of the *Los Angeles Times,* Robert B. Armstrong, observed with evident satisfaction that "it now is considered improbable that any Colorado River legislation will be enacted" during the current session.

Armstrong had long been known as an indefatigable spear-carrier for Harry Chandler, but at this moment he seemed unaware that the wind had shifted at *Times* headquarters. Astonishingly, the newspaper had come out in favor of Johnson's bill, dismissing the Sibert report as "unduly pessimistic" about the cost of the engineering changes and calling for "quick action by Congress" on a measure that it had unrelentingly vilified from the day of its introduction in 1922.

What accounted for this change of heart? As a shrewd businessman, Harry Chandler had come to recognize that as spurs to the growth of Los Angeles, his corporate seat, the water and power to be supplied by the dam would easily outweigh the harm the project would cause to his industrialist cronies and his landholdings in Mexico. In any case, his syndicate's grip on events south of the border was becoming more tenuous. Chandler's finely tuned antennae had picked up signals of rising anti-Americanism in the Mexican government, and by the late 1920s he was moving to sell off his holdings in advance of their almost inevitable seizure. He was unable to fully liquidate and the Mexicans eventually expropriated hundreds of thousands of acres in the mid-1930s. (More than a decade later, the Mexican government would pay the Chandler family $5.25 million for the seizure, ten times the price Harry Chandler had paid for the land at the turn of the century.) Henceforth, the hub of the Chandler family fortune would be Southern California, a burgeoning region for which the dam was an unalloyed boon. From this point on, the

*Los Angeles Times* would be the most vociferous booster of the Boulder Canyon Project in all the West.

In the Senate, Johnson had plotted his strategy well. By maneuvering his bill to the top of the chamber's December agenda, he ensured that any renewed filibuster by the Arizona delegation would tie up dozens of anxiously awaited measures and pet projects, among them an armaments appropriation for fifteen naval cruisers and an aircraft carrier. Late on December 14, the Swing-Johnson bill came to a vote. It passed 64–11, with Arizona's two senators in opposition to the last.

One week later, on December 21, Coolidge signed the bill without comment, handing out ceremonial pens to Swing, Johnson, and George Young, editor of William Randolph Hearst's *Los Angeles Examiner,* a supporter of the project from its inception. Among the other guests Coolidge had invited to witness the signing was William Mulholland, who wisely chose to stay home.

The work authorized by the Boulder Canyon Project Act bore little resemblance to the irrigation ditch Mark Rose had proposed in his first overture to the federal government in 1912. At 726 feet, the dam would stand twice as tall as any other on earth. Its construction would require five and one half million barrels of cement, more than the total the Reclamation Bureau had poured for all previous dams in its twenty-six years of existence. Construction was expected to take seven years, with as many as one thousand workers employed on the site at any one time. Once full, its reservoir would hold 30.5 million acre-feet of water, or ten trillion gallons, inundating 227 square miles of grassed valley to an elevation of 1,229 feet above sea level.

The project confounded attempts to describe it in human terms. Elwood Mead, the Indiana-born engineer who had become reclamation commissioner in 1924 and would spend the last eight years of his life shepherding the dam to completion, tried in 1930 to communicate its scale. He wrote of a reservoir eight times larger than that of Egypt's Aswan Dam; of one million new acres to be irrigated; of the excavation of one-fourth as much earth as had been removed for the entire Panama Canal. Figuratively throwing up his hands, he finally summed it all up as "a challenge to the imagination."

At $165 million, the Boulder Canyon Project Act was the largest single appropriation bill enacted by Congress up to that time. Of that sum, the Reclamation Bureau estimated the cost of the Boulder Dam and reservoir at $70.6 million, with another $38.2 million allocated to the power plant. These funds plus interest at 4 percent per annum were to be repaid from the sale of hydroelectric power over a period of no longer than fifty years; the act mandated that not a shovel was to be turned until all necessary power contracts had been signed by municipal or utility purchasers. The bureau estimated the cost of the remaining major piece of the project, the All-American Canal, at $38.5 million, to be repaid over time by the owners of irrigated land.

Embedded in the act was congressional ratification of the Colorado River Compact, though this was not quite the same treaty as the one drafted in Santa Fe. The new version provided for the six-state ratification. This would occur on March 6, 1929, when Utah reinstated its ratification vote, rescinded two years earlier over its dissatisfaction with a six-state compact. As Carpenter and other upper basin leaders had anticipated, Arizona eventually fell into line with a ratification vote—in 1944.

To his family, Hiram Johnson spoke of the Boulder Canyon Project Act as the capstone of his political career, although he would remain in the Senate for another seventeen turbulent years. "I really think that it is enough for one man to have accomplished," he told his sons, underscoring the ordeal by citing the words uttered by an old friend after a hair-raising motorcar ride over Northern California's twisty Pacific Coast Highway—"he would not have missed the ride for a thousand dollars, but he would not undertake it again for a million. I would not have missed this great fight for very much, but I would not undertake it again for very much more."

On the evening of December 21, a curious ceremony took place on the Nevada bank of the Colorado, at the end of a lonely rutted dirt road leading down to the foot of Black Canyon. Witnessed by centipedes and scorpions of the type that had had the place to themselves for eons, about one hundred people emerged from their cars and knelt in the coarse gravel at the edge of the water. They lifted their arms in a prayer of thanksgiving adeptly choreographed by a photographer for the *Las Vegas Age,* Charles P. "Pop" Squires, proprietor.

Squires was sixty-three, a rangy, leathery figure with a protruding Adam's apple. A native Minnesotan, he had arrived in Las Vegas in 1905, convinced that there was money to be made in the development of this remote oasis bearing a name that translated, improbably, as "the meadows." As the settlement did not merit regular direct rail service, he had reached his destination via a succession of freights, transferring from train to train in a series of desolate desert sidings.

Finally, one February morning at daybreak, from the rear platform of a train that was descending into a shallow valley, Squires made out a cluster of tiny white dots "on the carpet of the pale green desert, bathed in the golden glory of the newly arisen sun."

"What is that?" he asked a conductor, who hawked out a gob of spit before answering.

"That's Las Vegas," he said. The white spots were tents, the only structures standing in Las Vegas besides a derelict passenger car serving as the railroad station.

From the moment the idea was broached of damming the lower Colorado, Squires foresaw that Las Vegas's destiny would be inextricably linked to the construction of a high dam. He became intimately involved in pushing the project along, first as a Nevada delegate to the League of the Southwest and later as an advisor to James Scrugham, Nevada's compact commissioner. He spent most of 1928 in Washington as the state's official monitor of the final debates on the Boulder Canyon bill; it was at his insistence that Nevada's 300,000 acre-foot appropriation got written into the act alongside Arizona's and California's.

The residents of Las Vegas agreed with Squires that the signing of the Boulder Canyon Project Act would open a portal to a new world. In recognition of this fact, at the very hour when the little group was paying its obeisance to the almighty at the water's edge, Las Vegas itself was erupting in more secular celebration.

Bootleg liquor flowed like river water—"There was people that got lit that never had taken a drink before," recalled one old-timer. The volunteer fire department drove its lone pump truck at a crawl down the only paved thoroughfare in town—a two-block stretch of Fremont Street—while townspeople hooked carts and baby buggies and anything else that would roll to its fenders. The revelry lasted past dawn, until the merrymakers had to go to work. But the significance of the act was lost on no one.

"People started coming in then," one resident recalled. "That was the making of Las Vegas. That made the West."

# 7

# Hurry-Up Crowe

There was no overlooking him. Not with his spare six-foot frame or the Stetson hat invariably perched on his head, or the freshly starched and ironed white shirt in which he left his house every day at the directive of his wife, Linnie. Then there was his profound knowledge of every job to be done, from the lowliest mucking out of debris piles to the pouring and working of concrete and the blasting of holes in solid rock; his majestic self-assurance; and his omnipresence.

Frank Crowe could materialize in any corner of the worksite and at any hour, midnight as likely as noon—"he was all over the job," a crewman recalled—for an instant inspection of the work being performed and the diligence of the men performing it. Encountering a slacker, he might let the man off once with an acerbic warning, but a second offense meant unceremonious exile into the cold, cruel, Depression-wracked outside world. One electrician recalled a close shave in Black Canyon on a steel scaffold thirty feet in the air, the last place one would expect to find a boss nosing about before dawn:

> Down by number nine cableway, we had a tower. I was putting the electric lining up there about half way up and Whitey, one of the signal guys, was just killing time, talking to me. I looked down and I see Mr. Crowe coming up the ladder. I said, "Psst, here comes the boss." Whitey looked up

and he saw Mr. Crowe, and the day before they had broken the records on pouring concrete, so we had to have something to say, so we said, "Oh, Mr. Crowe, we're breaking a lot of records around here these days, aren't we?" Mr. Crowe said, "Yep, including records for dead head employees." And he just kept climbing on right up the ladder. And Whitey looked at me. "You think he's talking about me?" I said, "He sure as hell isn't talking about me. Scram!"

His genius for managing men appeared early in his career. "A lanky young man with gangly arms and legs, light blue eyes, pants legs and sleeves too short, and a nasal Yankee voice from Maine," was the description offered by Elliott Paul, a laborer with a literary streak on the Yellowstone River irrigation project in Idaho in 1911. Paul marveled at how the twenty-eight-year-old Frank Crowe commanded a workforce of four hundred men with the aplomb of a seasoned general. "Bums and Bohunks, mechanics, carpenters, hard-rock men and engineers . . . I never knew what force was in Frank Crowe that made brutes fear him, but he ruled that project in the only way the roughnecks understood."

Twenty years later, the army under his command would be larger by an order of magnitude, "5,000 men jammed in a 4,000-foot canyon," Crowe recollected. Many of those men would cherish homely recollections of their encounters with Frank Crowe, yet the most telling thing about him may be how little about the inner man those anecdotes reveal. Despite decades spent placing mankind's stamp on remote wilderness rivers, he never shed his native Down East reserve. "Frank Crowe was a very truthful man" was a typical judgment. "He was a very outstanding man. Everybody liked him. Everybody had respect for his ability to make decisions." Said Marion Allen, a member of the second generation of Allens to serve on a Crowe worksite, "I only knew him for 20 or 25 years, and I didn't know him."

Frank's occasional two- or three-page handwritten letters to his mother and sister, despite their chatty veneer, project all the inner soul of a landscape photograph, as befits an unsentimental man for whom engineering and construction in the wilderness were a calling. Consider the stolid itinerary he outlined for his mother in late August 1909: "I will go with a team through the park [Yellowstone] to Gardiner hence to Helena by train then after the big day we will come back through the park. . . . I will take a camping outfit along." The "big day" mentioned, almost in passing, was his wedding day.

His opaque exterior was partially the product of design, partially shaped by events. Elliott Paul remembered spending thoroughly amiable evenings in the home of Frank and Marie Sass Crowe, even of Frank Crowe dancing a jig to the popular song "Red Wing" during the construction of Jackson Lake Dam in Wyoming, the first dam raised under his hand. But that was a very young, very green Frank Crowe. In any case, one can not be as sociable with a workforce of five thousand as with a few hundred. Nor can the doleful fact be overlooked that within a month of the completion of Jackson Lake Dam, Marie Crowe was dead at twenty-two, lost to a pregnancy-related infection that also took her unborn child.

After a remarriage there would be more losses for Crowe: an infant son and another stillborn child. If he ever blamed these tragedies on himself or on the remote hinterland life to which his career consigned his family, he left no record of it. With every loss he seemed to become more focused on his work and more aloof from his loved ones, as though determined to bond with the structures that could never be taken from him and to keep a safe emotional distance from the humans who could. He knew every man who worked for him by his first name, it was said, but his daughters could not recall ever seeing him give their mother a kiss. It became Crowe family lore that he compensated by finding the most spacious, comfortable home in every new location where they settled during his career. In Boulder City, where Hoover Dam's bosses and workers lived, the Crowe house was a landmark, a grand homestead with a 360-degree view perched upon the highest hill in town.

Over the years he assembled a cadre of top men who would join him on project after project, a permanent floating staff of deputies and foremen. He could pull them away from their farms or homes at a moment's notice with telegrams reading simply, "Come at once," or "OK for a job," signed with a terse "F T Crowe." One was Charlie Williams, a master carpenter who first met Crowe on the Guernsey Dam in Wyoming in 1925. Charlie brought along his beefy son Bernard, known as "Woody," who graduated to concrete foreman at Tieton Dam and general foreman at Deadwood, and was tapped by Crowe to be his assistant superintendent at the capstone project in Black Canyon. Anthony "Si" Bous served as master mechanic on every dam project Crowe managed, from the first at Jackson Lake to the last at Lake Shasta, California. Each loyal lieutenant recruited his brothers and sons, so that a sizable portion of the payroll could be delineated by reeling off a handful of names—"the Bous family, the Bryants, Zehnles, the Lee Cairnes, the Sasses, the Wirths, Holdens, Malans, McCabes . . ."

These were men who knew Frank Crowe's mind as well as he knew it himself, who communicated with him on an almost telepathic level. Confronted by an engineering problem on the job, they would foregather with "the old man," conversing about—well, nothing in particular, until he would get to his feet and say, "You know what to do, go ahead and do it," and walk away. And they would go ahead and do it.

Crowe himself acknowledged their loyalty to himself and the job in an unusually heartfelt letter to the widow of Floyd Bous, Si's brother, who had died in an accident on Parker Dam in 1937 following thirty years of faithful service in the Crowe brigade.

> At Jackson Lake [he wrote], our logging foreman got drunk and quit, it was Floyd that took his place until we got another. Later the Captain of the tugboat that hauled the logs across the lake got sick. It was Floyd that took over the tug until the Captain recovered. We had a dam built that required 20 gates and it was of no value without the gates. It had been impossible to get the gates before the roads were blocked with snow. It was Floyd that took 100 teams into the mountains and broke the roads and came back with the gates. . . . We construction stiffs have lost a great fellow and friend.

There were scattered naysayers, people who did not regard Frank Crowe as a genius and a paragon. Loyalists dismissed these contrarians in the usual way, as disgruntled employees—or more likely, ex-employees. "Somebody [who] got caught sleeping, I'll bet," Saul "Red" Wixson, one of the old hands, told an interviewer years later. "There's one guy that went to sleep twice in a dump truck, so he got fired. So Frank Crowe was no good, Frank Crowe was this, and Frank Crowe was that. All of that—let me be plain with you—bull shit."

Some people were clear-eyed enough to see that among Frank Crowe's virtues were nestled a few flaws. One of his secrets to keeping the men's respect and loyalty was to let others play the martinet. Throughout his career there were work stoppages to be quashed (often ruthlessly), inhuman working conditions, rampant ethnic and racial discrimination, and unnecessary deaths on his jobs. Underlying some of these conditions were the unforgiving deadlines imposed by Crowe's employers, the contractors, who thought chiefly about the bonuses they would pocket if the projects were brought in ahead of schedule, and little, if at all, about the men whose toil produced the windfalls. Crowe was the man who made sure the deadlines were met.

He had a way of absenting himself from a worksite when there was to be a strike to be put down, a shift to be laid off, or an hourly pay rate to be cut, leaving his foremen to take the heat. Sometimes he would resurface at the moment of maximum impasse, offering a compromise that required the contractors to give up very little while granting the workers just enough to let them believe they had not risked their jobs for nothing. "He of course rode herd on those who ran herd on the others," recalled Elton Garrett, who reported for the *Las Vegas Age*. "He didn't go out there and say, 'You guys get off that soapbox and come back to work.' He didn't do that. He had others. He worked out the kind of negotiation that would get the men back on the job and get the dam finished."

He portrayed himself as a sentinel of worksite safety, periodically summoning his foremen to a mass meeting to upbraid them for accidents. ("Safety Matter of Human Values, Not Money, Crowe Tells Meeting," reported the *Las Vegas Review-Journal* after one such "smoker," held in the wake of a string of maimings and deaths in Black Canyon.) The foremen dutifully relayed the lesson to the workers, but did not moderate the pace of work, the real cause of the horrific toll. It was this relentless drive that earned the boss the nickname that would stick to him his entire career: Hurry-Up Crowe.

Yet there was something more, something intangible, that endowed

Crowe with the ability to drive his crews at a clip that bowed to almost no obstacle, not a killing cold spell nor suffocating desert heat nor the boundaries of human endurance. Perhaps the secret was his ability to communicate a shared goal. Men choking on gasoline fumes in an underground tunnel nearly a mile long, or suspended on ropes two thousand feet in the air from the rim of a gorge, drills in hand, or sunk to their ankles in wet concrete under a remorseless desert sun might well question from time to time whether the work was worth the four or five dollars they earned for a punishing eight-hour shift. Frank Crowe made them understand the honor of participating in the creation of something eternal.

"I'm proud that I had a hand in it," said Tex Nunley, whose myriad jobs in Boulder Canyon included painting white crosses on solid rock walls to mark the center line of the tunnels the drillers were to drive through them. "Yes I am. I think it was a marvelous piece of work."

By 1930, when the Department of the Interior put the Boulder Canyon Project out for bid, Frank Crowe had been involved in the construction of fourteen dams, five of them as superintendent. He was widely recognized as a gifted deployer of men and materials and an audacious problem solver. When cut timber proved unattainable at Jackson Lake, he ordered an entire sawmill from Salt Lake City and had it floated to the construction site by barge. At Arrowrock Dam in Idaho he designed an intricate network of overhead cableways that could deposit concrete on the rising structure with almost pinpoint precision.

The Boulder Canyon Project preoccupied the dreams of many a Reclamation Service engineer, but for Frank Crowe the vision was freighted with destiny. As early as 1919 he had penciled out a cost estimate for the dam at the direction of Arthur Powell Davis himself. Taking a busman's holiday in 1922, he inspected Black and Boulder canyons from the deck of Murl Emery's boat and conferred quietly with Walker Young, a fellow Reclamation hand he had first met on the Arrowrock site. At 350 feet, Arrowrock had been the tallest dam in the world upon its completion in 1915. But it would be dwarfed by the colossus in Black Canyon. "I had spent my life in the river bottoms and Boulder meant a wonderful climax," Crowe recalled in 1943. "I was wild to build this dam."

So, too, were the founders of Six Companies, Inc., the unwieldy contracting consortium assembled in 1931 to make a bid on the dam project. There were originally eight companies in the group, including a paving firm, a pair of bridge and tunnel contractors from San Francisco, a partnership of two Mormon brothers who had made their fortune laying rail across the desert, and an Idaho construction firm that held the rights to the one indisputable necessity for the raising of the largest dam in the world: the services of Frank Crowe. Officially, the rationale for the consortium's creation was that it was the only way to finance the bond required for the bid. But it is perhaps more accurate to say that Six Companies was a corporate device designed to put Frank Crowe to work.

They entered the bidding as a clutch of small regional contractors, some of whom had trouble scraping together even a few hundred thousand dollars to make their required capital contribution. Afterward, they would build more dams, as well as bridges, tunnels, ships, and industrial plants of every description rising in virtually every corner of the world. But the raising of the dam on the Colorado was the crucial transformative step. Frank Crowe built the dam and turned those businessmen into tycoons.

The second son of an English mill operator and his Brooklyn-born bride, Francis Trenholm Crowe was born on October 12, 1882, in Trenholmville, Quebec, a hamlet about sixty miles east of Montreal where John Crowe briefly owned a woolen mill. By the time Frank was seventeen, the family had relocated six times, from Quebec to Iowa and back to the Eastern seaboard, finally fetching up in Byfield, Massachusetts, just north of Boston, where Frank received two years of high school education. Family tradition states that Frank's father favored a career for him in medicine or the clergy. But divinity school did not appeal to him and the cost of a medical education was out of reach. Instead, in the fall of 1901 he followed his elder brother to the University of Maine at Orono to study engineering, its specialty.

Crowe was twenty-one when he met the man who would draw him into a career of dam building. It was 1904, and he was in the third year of his engineering studies at the University of Maine.

One day in that dismal, snowy January Crowe reported to the engineering lecture hall to hear a presentation by Frank E. Weymouth, Class of 1896, who had compiled a sterling résumé during his few short years out of school. After a stint working on the Panama Canal, he had been appointed deputy to A. P. Davis, chief engineer of the U.S. Reclamation Service, which had been founded only two years earlier. Weymouth had returned to Orono to recruit young talent for the service. He painted an alluring picture of a government program transfiguring the Western wilderness, taming its rivers and crosshatching its plains with irrigation canals. In Montana, Reclamation was working to dam and divert the Yellowstone River to provide reliable irrigation to local farmers for the first time.

Crowe collared Weymouth after his speech. "If I show up on your project this spring, will you give me a job?" he asked. Armed with Weymouth's assurance, he borrowed the train fare at the end of the semester and spent the summer profitably making surveys in the wild. He returned to campus for his senior year carrying an enormous bison skull to hang in his room and boasting an improbable talent for twirling the lariat Will Rogers–style, which he demonstrated by roping fellow students from the veranda of his frat house.

Crowe's first summer in the West launched a historic partnership. Frank Weymouth mentored Crowe's rise through Reclamation's ranks, filling the service's personnel files with dispatches singing Crowe's praises and recommending promotion. "I do not know of a single man in the Reclamation Service who is as accomplished along so many lines or so versatile," he informed director Frederick H. Newell in 1911. "He is a good machinist, thoroughly understands steam engineering and a great deal about electrical engineering and is the best foreman that I have ever known and also an excellent superintendent. He is the type of man that we should endeavor to keep."

After his senior term at Orono, Crowe returned to the Yellowstone project, which had moved beyond the surveying stage and into full-scale construction. Arriving by train at Glendive, Montana, one day in mid-May, he jounced the last forty miles to the worksite in the back of a flatbed wagon. The project camp was typical of the era, operated by a private labor contractor who kept wages low and siphoned a quarter of every dollar he paid the men by charging them for tent space, meals, and purchases at an overpriced camp commissary. The men worked six days a week, resting on Sunday. This workday spanned nine stifling daylight hours from 8 A.M. to 5 P.M., with an hour for lunch.

The menu, Elliott Paul related, was "designed principally to discourage men from going too often to the can, on the bosses' time."

> Breakfast was at seven o'clock and consisted of oatmeal with condensed milk, fried sow belly or yesterday's stew meat with left-over potatoes, fried in lard, and coffee made in huge metal cans from which the grounds were seldom dumped. At noon there was stew made of meat the butchers could not dispose of elsewhere, boiled spuds with their unwashed skins on, macaroni and cheese baked in large shallow tins, or watered canned corn.... The evening meal was like the noon meal, with boiled beans instead of macaroni or corn.

The workforce comprised Central Europeans derisively labeled Bohunks, local Mormons, and itinerants disdained by their self-defined betters as hobos or bums. The bosses perpetuated a caste system by paying the immigrant workers the lowest wages—as little as $2 a day—and "American" laborers $2.25, even though the former were often better educated and skilled than their native-born counterparts. During the workweek, the sheer debilitating effect of heavy toil kept this melting pot from boiling over. Not so on the weekend, which began for the workers at the five o'clock whistle on Saturday evening. Without any provision for even marginally wholesome recreation, there was nothing for the men to do but gamble and drink and pick fights with each other in the oppressive, dusty, insect-ridden summer heat.

Thanks to the conditions they themselves created, the bosses lived in constant fear of labor unrest. The fear was justified: labor organizers prowled the West, where the dismal work camps proved to be fertile seedbeds of discontent. In June 1905—just about the time Crowe debarked from his train in Glendive—the socialist Western Federation of Miners, which had been tapping this lode for twenty years, joined with dozens of other radical groups to found the labor syndicate known as the Industrial Workers of the World. Bosses in the West would spend the next quarter-century looking under every bed in their camps for "Wobblies," as IWW members were known. It was an unwise boss who failed to develop a network of informers among his workers, another factor contributing to tensions on the worksite.

Enlightenment would come to this segment of the working world in the course of Frank Crowe's long career, but only slowly and by no means completely. The food and accommodations would be better and the pay marginally higher in Black Canyon, where the presence of workers' families would quell the search for wilder entertainments in the construction zone (if not in nearby Las Vegas). On the other hand, the scarcity of work during the depths of the Depression would keep the balance of power firmly on the employers' side, muting the workers' complaints. Accordingly, many features of the dam construction camp of 1905 would still be very much in existence on the Colorado River in 1931—including racial and ethnic discrimination, profiteering at the company store, and the flouting of health and safety regulations in the name of efficient and speedy construction. At Black Canyon, the threat of a Wobbly rebellion would still cast a shadow.

Crowe stayed on the Yellowstone project until October 1906, earning $75 a month as an engineer's aide. Then James Munn, one of the private contractors on the job, lured him away with a raise to $125 and the chance to obtain hands-on experience in a wide range of construction jobs—experience that would have required years of apprenticeship in the more bureaucratic Reclamation Service.

Munn gave Crowe a full-immersion education in construction management. But he was also heavily dependent on Reclamation contracts, so Crowe was never far from the sight of his former bosses. When Munn & Co. ran out of work in the fall of 1908, Weymouth seized the opportunity to lure Crowe back. He needed Crowe for a project at Jackson Lake, Wyoming, where plans to upgrade an existing dam had recently taken on an air of urgency. The original dam was a brush and timber contrivance built upstream on the Snake River in 1905 and floated into the lake's lone outlet, stoppering it like a cork in a bottle. The builders anchored it in place with local quarry stones and left it alone. No one noticed that its wooden footings were rotting away underwater until the damage was irreversible and its collapse only a matter of time.

Weymouth sent Crowe to scout out a site for a new dam. Characteristically, Crowe accomplished the survey quickly, although his goal was not merely to outrun the approach of winter—always early in those parts— but rather to reach Montana in time for his wedding to Marie Sass, the sister of his friend and fellow Reclamation engineer Bob Sass. Beating this deadline, he mapped a supply route for the new site by relying on an ancient trail blazed by smugglers needing to slip in and out of Jackson Hole under the nose of the law. Having been tipped to the trail by the son of one of these outlaws, Crowe traced its tortuous, overgrown path over creeks and through mountain notches. The road reached the dam site via the long way around the lake, but it did possess the virtue of skirting the gorges, forests, and a ten-thousand-foot mountain pass that made the only other access route a logistical nightmare.

When the old dam gave out on the morning after Independence Day in 1910, Crowe, with his local knowledge, was the obvious choice to build the replacement. A few weeks later he arrived in Ashton, Idaho, the Union Pacific depot nearest the old outlaw trail, on the 4 P.M. train. Along for the ride were the abstemious Arthur Powell Davis, Frank Weymouth, and— unbeknownst to the government party—six prostitutes imported to service a project-driven surge in trade. Powell, Weymouth, and Crowe were met by a clerk from the Reclamation office; the girls, more discreetly, by Ashton's lone madam and the local physician.

The Jackson Lake project would have taxed the abilities of even a seasoned dam builder, much less a youthful engineer shouldering his very first command. Nor would there be anyone he could easily turn to for advice in a crisis; Reclamation's district construction engineer, Charles Paul (Elliott's older brother), would be closest to hand, but he was headquartered in Minidoka, Idaho, 250 miles away—and come the winter snowfall, totally out of reach.

Pouring the concrete dam would be far from a routine task, but it was not the most daunting part of the project. Crowe's first challenge was to grade and pave a hundred-mile road from Ashton to the dam site in the heart of the Teton range, making sure it was robust enough to carry equipment, trucks, and provisions worth a half-million dollars, as well as hundreds of men and a herd of horses. That job had to be finished before the site got cut off from the outside world by the snow, which was capable of accumulating up to six feet overnight.

Their isolation complete, the workers would have to drain the dam site and pour four thousand cubic yards of concrete in temperatures as low as fifty degrees below zero. The dam was to be framed with slots for twenty floodgates, which would not be delivered until spring. The crews could only pray that their work was sufficiently precise to allow the steel gates to slide neatly into their portals, which by then would be set permanently in concrete.

In this snowbound fortress Crowe functioned as governor, judge, and vicar. He would be confronted that winter with the full spectrum of tribulations that can arise within an ethnically diverse camp of four hundred men. These included one murder (by knife blade, unsolved) and at least one homosexual encounter (decently hushed up). Just before the snow closed them in, a forest fire threatened to incinerate the camp and every piece of equipment in it. Crowe deployed 250 men in a three-day battle to beat it back.

Crowe maintained order through a small group of trusted foremen, not all of whom shared his scruples about using violence as an instrument of control. His most effective management technique was to keep the workforce fully occupied on three shifts around the clock. Showing a genius for logistics, he organized the myriad tasks on the site so that multiple projects proceeded in parallel, converging at just the right moment, eliminating idleness and saving weeks or even months of construction time—an early implementation of the critical path method eventually to become standard on big complex jobs.

His crews fought the ferocious winter weather to a draw. They would hack at frozen piles of gravel with pickaxes to supply aggregate to the concrete mixing plant, and pour the concrete into forms under wooden shacks heated with coal so it would set properly, protected from the cold. Come mid-January 1911, the pouring was almost complete. When the steel gates arrived a few weeks later—hauled by Floyd Bous's horse teams over the mountain road, hours ahead of a vicious blizzard—they slotted flawlessly into the concrete frames. By the spring thaw, at the point when the average project superintendent would just be emerging from months of hibernation to kick his crews into gear, Crowe's project was well on the way to completion, a dam thrown across a frigid river in record time.

Only one month before it was finished, on October 17, 1911, Marie Crowe died. Whether her husband was with her in their cabin at Jackson Lake is unrecorded. At the time, his professional attention was divided between Jackson Lake and Arrowrock, where work was just beginning under the supervision of Charles Paul and James Munn, Crowe's erstwhile partner. Four hundred miles of prairie and forested range separated the two locations. Crowe traversed the route regularly during the summer and fall of 1911 while his wife endured an increasingly painful and afflicted pregnancy. After she succumbed, the press of business prevented him from grieving for long. The day after her death he applied for six days' leave to escort her body home to Montana for burial, and on October 25 he was back at Jackson Lake, where the dam was declared completed on November 20. Crowe had brought it in for less than $465,000, nearly 20 percent below budget, earning yet another compliment from Weymouth. "I do not know of a piece of work ever done under more adverse circumstances than that at Jackson Lake," he reported to headquarters.

By then Crowe was already spending most of his time at Arrowrock. The project had become the cynosure of the engineering community. Not only was it to be the tallest dam in the world, but its site presented unique challenges, the most difficult being the diversion of the flood-prone Boise River. Because the usual solutions of earthen diversion levees and concrete aqueducts were wrong for the local topography, Charles Paul had decided to route the river directly through the solid granite gorge wall. The job of excavating what would be one of the world's longest and largest diversion tunnels—a 497-foot long, thirty-foot wide, concrete-lined behemoth—he dumped in Crowe's lap.

The tunnel proved to be an ideal dry run for Black Canyon, which would require four diversion tunnels, each ten times the length of Arrowrock's. Using a system he would replicate on the Colorado, Crowe drilled and blasted from both ends, which sped up the work but placed a premium on precise engineering, lest the converging crews blindly pass each other by, three hundred feet underground.

What made Arrowrock a milestone in Crowe's career, however, was not the tunneling but a system of overhead cableways he designed to haul concrete to the construction zone. The employment of cableways in dam work was not unprecedented, but the scale of Crowe's design was. The Arrowrock system, which cost a then astounding $73,000, comprised three cables splayed out like the ribs of a fan and extended 1,500 feet from a single fixed head tower to three tail towers on the opposite side of the river.

Each cable could position an eight-ton bucket of concrete over the pouring site and lower it four hundred feet; carry men and other materials across the gorge and down to the excavation in steel skips; and remove muck and debris that would otherwise be filling horse carts shambling out of the gorge to a dumping ground. The system's only drawback was the immobility of the towers, one of which eventually had to be dismantled and shifted downstream to cover an otherwise unreachable corner of the site. At later projects Crowe would solve this problem by placing the towers on railroad tracks so they could be moved laterally. No fewer than nine cableways would span Black Canyon, every tower but one erected on six hundred feet of rail.

The Arrowrock cable system contributed to what would become another signature of a Crowe project: the unrelenting pace of work. As at Jackson Lake the year before, Crowe attempted to keep his concreting crews deployed through the harshest weeks of winter. In this case Munn, the senior superintendent on the job, reeled in his younger colleague: thanks to his evident influence, the concrete work was suspended in February and for most of the equally frigid March.

Once the weather broke, Crowe stepped up the pace so dramatically that his demand for concrete overstretched the mixing plant's capacity. Munn was constantly sending posses into the field to find new gravel beds to feed the concrete plant's voracious appetite for all-important aggregate. In one twelve-day span that summer, Crowe's men poured 11,500 cubic yards of concrete—about as much as had been previously poured in an average month. Every record broken and every milestone was recorded for posterity, as would be done on a much larger scale at Black Canyon. There could be no doubt that two factors accounted for the speed of Arrowrock's completion: Frank Crowe's cableway and his unyielding determination.

In the decade after his triumph at Arrowrock, Crowe oversaw three more major projects for the Reclamation Service, including the creation of an extensive system of canals and reservoirs centered around the Flathead Indian Reservation in Montana and the enlargement of his own Jackson Lake dam. (The latter assignment, Weymouth reported to headquarters, Crowe found "distasteful" because it evoked distressing memories of his wife's passing, "but owing to his loyalty to the Service he accepted the position as we were strictly up against it for a first class man in the midst of the construction season.")

It was more than grief that made this an unhappy period in Crowe's life. The Flathead job was largely administrative, and its bureaucratic minutiae—such as calculating how many cement sacks could be recycled, monitoring wastage in the mess halls—made him so fidgety that he was driven to resign from the service. "I am simply marking time," he wrote to Weymouth in late 1919, adding that he was growing "as restless as an IWW."

When a federal budget crunch that February led to a severe cutback in Reclamation projects, he gave up his government seniority and joined a private road building firm. But jobs were spotty in the private sector and by the end of the year, when federal funds were again flowing, Crowe was receptive to a new offer from Weymouth. The prodigal son was welcomed back to the agency's bosom with no hard feelings, and assigned to the Tieton project in Washington state, then the agency's biggest job.

In early 1924, Weymouth offered him the post of regional engineer in

Denver, a desk from which Crowe would oversee all construction in seventeen Western states. As this was the region where Reclamation was spending most of its budget, the job was tantamount to the bureau's chief of construction. In Weymouth's view, this was the proper post for a man whose achievements at Jackson, Flathead, and Tieton included the refinement of the cableway system, the supervision of a construction camp the size of a small city (at Rimrock, the Tieton site in the Washington Cascades), and the invariable completion of construction in remote locations ahead of schedule and under budget.

For Crowe, the job seemed ideal. In 1913, just after finishing his work at Arrowrock, he had wed Linnie Korts, a Boise socialite. The union, like his marriage to Marie Sass, was touched by tragedy: the couple lost their first child, Frank Jr., just five days after his birth in 1914, while Linnie was laid up in the primitive conditions of the Jackson Lake construction camp. Eight years later they lost another son, John, to cholera, the pitiless old scourge of the Forty-niners. Attended by helpless physicians in the Yakima hospital, the five-year-old was dead within days.

The move to Denver beckoned as a chance for stability and even a taste of luxury for Linnie and the Crowes' two-year-old daughter, Patricia. Linnie was pregnant again—she would give birth to another healthy daughter, Elizabeth, early in 1925—and Crowe settled her in their first comfortable city home since she had left Boise as a newlywed twelve years earlier. Contributing to its allure, the Denver job placed Crowe at the center of planning for the Boulder Canyon Project, the dam engineer's grail, which was then making its listless way through Congress.

Still, he regarded the promotion with some trepidation. Office work and paper shuffling had never been his strong suits. "He makes no secret of the fact that he is a 'dirt' engineer with . . . no great liking for sitting in an office for long periods at a time," the Yakima newspaper wrote as he took his farewell from the Tieton project. "When persons call at Rimrock nine times out of ten they have to hunt him up in that fascinating region glibly termed 'the works.'"

The Denver job turned out to be Flathead writ large. The man who had nicknamed himself "never-my-belly-against-a-desk" (a nickname sometimes repeated derisively by field workers exasperated by his on-the-spot micromanaging) watched impotently as enticing field projects crossed his desk, reduced to memos, invoices, arid progress reports, and columns of figures on the printed page. Crowe knew he had to get out.

Almost at that very moment, a solution landed on his desk. The bids on Guernsey Dam, a Reclamation project let out to private contractors for construction, arrived in late March. Guernsey was a rockfill dam in Wyoming, near the source of the North Platte River. Other than Boulder Canyon, it was the largest dam then on Reclamation's drawing board. The winning bidder—the only qualified bidder, in fact—was a joint venture of the Utah Construction Company, which had made its name laying track for the Union Pacific Railroad, and a firm owned by Harry Morrison, a former Reclamation hand. Crowe steeled himself for his third foray out from under Reclamation's shelter. This one would last.

Crowe had first encountered Harry Winford Morrison in 1909, on the muddy bank of a canal outside Boise, where they were foremen of separate crews lining the ditch with concrete. One night, Crowe was sent to warn Morrison that an approaching flood might wash away any machinery left overnight in the excavated ditch. Arriving on the scene, he was pointed to-ward a tent in the distance, lighted from the inside by the glow of a kerosene lamp.

> About a dozen husky young fellows were seated on the beds or on pro-verbial dynamite boxes, so handy in a construction camp [Crowe recalled]. In the far corner sat a happy-looking boy with a guitar, singing one of the forty-nine verses of "Casey Jones." I asked a boy near the door flap for Mor-rison. He said: "That's Morrison singing. Don't bother him, he has a four-bit bet up that he can sing for 30 minutes without stopping or repeating, and he has only two minutes more to win." Needless to say, he won. With the finis of the songfest, Harry spent the night getting his equipment out of the river bed.

Morrison never lost his flair for the impromptu camp recital (he kept Robert W. Service's "Shooting of Dan McGrew" in his repertoire well into his seventies). A self-described backwoods boy from Illinois, he had been raised by a grandfather who served as the town miller, blacksmith, and ice man. By the age of fourteen Harry was running water for construction crews on the Illinois Central, and scarcely five years later he appeared on Reclamation's payroll out west. In the interim he had developed into a sort of mirror-image Frank Crowe: "a long, slim kid," as Crowe himself described him, ceaselessly in motion, acutely impatient with laziness or delay. The Boise canal project manager, Morris Knudsen, was impressed, even exhausted, by the bustle and enterprise of this foreman twenty-five years his junior, and also surprised when Morrison proposed that they go into business together.

The Danish-born Knudsen owned an assortment of picks and shovels and a hoard of $600 to contribute as capital.

"What have you got?" he asked Morrison.

"Just guts," Morrison replied (according to the tale he wholesaled to *Fortune* magazine a quarter-century later).

The partners pared expenses so ruthlessly that soon they were underbidding Utah Construction, cracking its stranglehold on the Union Pacific's business. This earned the upstarts a peremptory summons to their rival's corporate seat in Ogden, where W. H. Wattis, the younger of the two Mormon brothers who led Utah Construction, offered them a piece of the UP's action if only they would stop trying so hard.

The new joint venture was superbly qualified to bid on the Guernsey project. Morrison and Knudsen, after all, were both ex-Reclamation men. Utah boasted experience of dam building on a grand scale, having completed the O'Shaughnessy Dam in Yosemite National Park's Hetch Hetchy Valley in 1923 for a San Francisco municipal water project.

That $7 million project had had enough peculiarities to toughen the hide of any construction man. For one thing, it was the subject of one of the most explosive environmental battles in American history, distinguished by naturalist John Muir's impassioned protest: "Dam Hetch Hetchy! As well dam for water-tanks the people's cathedrals and churches, for no holier temple has ever been consecrated by the heart of man." (Muir's plea went unheard, and it was said that Congress's approval of the dam over his objection hastened his death from heartbreak.) Another problem was posed by the financing. San Francisco's credit was so scorned by the investment markets that the Wattis brothers had to purchase $2 million of city bonds on their own credit—advancing the city their own money, in effect, to get the project moving.

These obstacles notwithstanding, the dam was a notable engineering accomplishment, and for the Wattis brothers a profitable one, sharpening their appetite for dam building. As it happened, just as Frank Crowe was eyeing the partnership's bid and wondering if he could get in on the job, Harry Morrison's thoughts were turning to his fellow Boise foreman, whose skill as a master dam builder was a byword across the West.

Crowe accepted a job with Morrison-Knudsen at some point in April or May 1925. He would build three dams in five years for the partnership. After Guernsey came Van Giesen Dam outside Sacramento, finished in 1928 for the state of California, and Deadwood Dam in Idaho, another Reclamation project, in 1930. As always, he worked at breakneck speed, poring over the blueprints of the next dam even before he was finished with the present one. He made each project into an engineering laboratory, putting his cableways and other equipment through their paces in new settings and novel conditions. In the same way he sharpened the teamwork of his traveling brigade of underbosses. After each job they would scatter to their more or less permanent homes or ranches—Charlie Williams to Yakima, his son Woody to rural Oregon, Si Bous and Bob Sass to Boise—making sure Crowe knew where to reach them with his curt summons by wire: "Come at once." Each knew how to reach his own best workers, so that every time Crowe began a job there would be a hundred trained laborers on the site, ready to start alongside him, their first assignment often the construction of their own bunkhouses.

Linnie and the girls, uprooted from their comfortable Denver home, followed Crowe from camp to camp. Between jobs they would drop anchor in Boise, where Crowe had purchased a small home near the Morrison-Knudsen headquarters. But they would stay put only until he secured them new quarters at the worksite, whether a local bungalow or a cottage erected by his own crews.

This was true even at Deadwood, possibly the most isolated and rugged place where Frank Crowe ever raised a dam. Deadwood was a 165-foot concrete dam with a broad central spillway, nestled into a notch in a mile-high mountain ridge. It was so thoroughly hemmed in by forest and range that reaching it from the town of Cascade, twenty-five miles away as the crow flies, required traversing sixty-seven miles of dirt track and macadam and three mountain passes at elevations over seven thousand feet. Unfazed, Crowe moved his family into an onsite tent during the summer of 1929; nearly seventy years later, his older daughter, Patricia, would fondly recollect having been "raised in a large tin tub" amid the towering evergreens.

Deadwood would be the only dam site that ever stopped Crowe in his tracks. Aware that the region's heavy snowfalls could envelop the place in impenetrable seclusion, he packed the family off to Boise in the fall. If he harbored any hope of working through the winter, it was soon dashed. When the weather blocked the movement of heavy equipment on the Cascade road in early December, he was forced to halt work. Finally, one week before Christmas he surrendered to the inevitable, closing the camp for the season and sending the workforce home, leaving behind only two watchmen with enough provisions to survive up to six months in arctic isolation. Conditions were already so bad that it took days for the workers to trudge out of the valley and back to civilization, sleeping nights in shacks that Crowe's advance team had presciently erected at intervals along the trail.

Crowe returned the following March, behind a Caterpillar snowplow that required more than a week to clear the mountain road from Cascade. His first work crews arrived around the same time, some reaching the site on snowshoes or by dogsled. The road remained unserviceable for heavy equipment for another two and a half months, during which Crowe hit upon the enterprising, if expensive, stratagem of ferrying men and supplies to the dam site by airplane. (On one exceptionally taxing April day, the valiant craft and crew made nine round-trips between Cascade and the worksite.)

Yet even Deadwood ultimately yielded to Crowe. The raising of the concrete dam began in June 1930—months later than Crowe would have preferred, but still time enough to fulfill his self-imposed deadline for completion by Thanksgiving. By then Hurry-Up Crowe had a new incentive, beyond his innate drive and impatience, for making haste.

Black Canyon was waiting.

# 8

# The Silver Spike

In the teeming crowd gathered for a ceremony outside Las Vegas on the afternoon of September 17, 1930, there must have been quite a few people hoping to see the guest of honor look ridiculous. They were not disappointed.

Interior Secretary Ray Lyman Wilbur had come west for the formal launch of the Boulder Canyon Project. His role in the ritual was to drive a spike of Nevada-mined silver into a tie at the spot where the Union Pacific's Salt Lake–Los Angeles trunk line was to branch off toward the future site of Boulder City, which was to be the staging point for the project and the hometown for its workers and their families. A former president of Stanford University and a respected physician, Wilbur stood six-foot-four with a strong chin, protruding earlobes, and massive hands that all contributed to an impression of outsized clumsiness. Upon his early morning arrival at the Las Vegas train depot he had posed for a series of official photographs in a dark three-piece suit, a wool overcoat draped over one arm, towering like a circus giant over his wife, Marguerite, and his ever-present executive assistant, Northcutt Ely. He looked ungainly even in his customary habitat, the staid corridors of power in academia and Washington; in the Western desert he seemed hopelessly out of place.

Wilbur was not a popular figure in Las Vegas just then. Months earlier, he had steamed in by private railcar to judge the city's suitability as headquarters for the Boulder Canyon Project, which the community hoped would validate its self-image as the coming city of the Southwest. Aware of the secretary's bluenosed moral character, the city fathers pulled out all the stops to refashion Las Vegas as a staid, sober Christian community. The houses of prostitution on Fremont Street's notorious Block 16 were closed for the duration of his visit and Prohibition strictly enforced within the city limits, probably for the very first time. Moments after Wilbur debarked, he was whisked off for a carefully mapped tour around this Potemkin Village–for–a–day.

As it happened, Wilbur was accompanied onboard by a trainload of newspapermen and by the son of the Southern Pacific's president, who had donated the private rail car. The parched entourage quietly asked around for a drink, and John Cahlan, then the one-man news staff and later an editor of the *Las Vegas Review-Journal,* slipped them into an obliging Block 16 establishment while Wilbur was otherwise engaged. Whether one of the party let loose his tongue in a fog of intoxication, or because Las Vegas's real character could not be disguised under any quantity of municipal cosmetics, Wilbur announced the next day that the government would build a model city in the desert twenty-eight miles away to manage the project and house the dam workers. Las Vegas, he had concluded, was no place for upstanding American workers to live.

The driving of the silver spike marked Wilbur's first return to the area since rendering that disheartening verdict. The Hoover administration, perhaps desperate for some public uplift amid the deepening economic gloom, made the most of the occasion. A network radio hookup was arranged to beam Wilbur's ceremonial speech to ten million listeners in the West and Midwest. Special trains carried two hundred business and political leaders from California, and planes were hired from a local aerodrome to provide them with a bird's-eye view of the dam site.

The logistics of this complex undertaking fell to a journeyman Reclamation engineer who had taken up his post in Las Vegas only a few days before the great event. John Chatfield Page was three weeks shy of his forty-fourth birthday. A native Nebraskan and rail-thin, he stood a notch above six feet; his wrists and Adam's apple seemed to always be poking from his cuffs and collar, giving him the appearance of a dressed-up scarecrow. At rest his eyes and full lips settled into a stern glare, but in truth he was a friendly and sociable man, always primed for an evening of bridge or a Sunday morning round of golf.

His formal title was office engineer—a grandiose label for the combined roles of assistant to Walker Young, record keeper, and office manager. To reach his assignment in Las Vegas he had made a two-day drive in his green Studebaker sport coupé west across the Utah desert from Grand Junction, Colorado, his prior posting, bringing along for company only his German shepherd dog, Fritz. "Dusty trip," he wrote in his office diary with characteristic terseness. Left behind in Grand Junction were his wife, Mildred (nicknamed "Deedle"), and their two daughters, Jean and Mildred, the latter distinguished from her mother by the pet name "Baby." They were to stay in Colorado until a house could be built for them in Boulder City.

Immediately upon his arrival, Page was thrown into a whirlwind of planning for the dedication. Dozens of dignitaries had to be met at the train station, settled in rooms, and dispatched on sightseeing trips. Reclamation commissioner Elwood Mead arrived at six o'clock on the morning before the dedication with Raymond F. Walter, the bureau's chief engineer, and assorted other VIPs, all clamoring for breakfast. Afterward they drove into Black Canyon (accompanied by a crew from the Fox Movietone newsreel company), motored upriver from Murl Emery's ferry landing in two boats, and returned to Las Vegas at midday, requiring lunch.

The next day was even more hectic. Secretary Wilbur was on the move almost from the moment his train steamed into Las Vegas. From the depot he was driven directly to the dam site for a tour, then back to the city for a formal luncheon. As soon as he was done eating, he hastened to the rail spur with the rest of the official party to drive the spike.

The railroad junction, a flat patch of desert newly christened Boulder Crossing, was carpeted with thousands of onlookers baking under a 120 degree sun. Wilbur made his way to the center of the crowd, where he stood within a circle of news photographers, shoulder to shoulder with senators, congressmen, and newspaper publishers trying to get their faces into the pictures. Newsreel cameras from Fox, Pathé, and Paramount cranked away.

Swaddled in his wool suit and drenched in sweat, Wilbur gamely straddled the steel rail and grasped a heavy two-headed steel maul with his big hands. Bent double as if to focus his eyes close on the target, he resembled a buzzard inspecting a morsel in the sand. He raised the maul over his head, brought it down, and missed the spike completely.

Suppressing his embarrassment, he took two more swipes before finally driving the spike home with a clang. Etched with a ceremonial inscription, it was instantly extracted and handed to the secretary as a keepsake.

Forever after, Wilbur remained defensive about the episode: "While I had never been a track worker or wielded a maul before," he related in his memoirs, "I knew which end of the sledge to use and my aim was fairly good." Other witnesses remembered a chorus of murmured derision rising from the crowd. "Of course," one recalled, "there was a lot of miners in the background to tell him what a poor punk he was."

Ray Lyman Wilbur's appearance at Boulder Crossing was the climax of an outbreak of urgent activity in the Hoover White House commencing late in 1929. The administration's original plan had been to begin work on the Boulder Canyon Project no sooner than mid-1932, when it could be slipped into the federal public works budget. This was never going to be an easy feat, for at the close of the Roaring Twenties federal construction spending still only came to $150 million a year—less than the $165 million price tag for the whole Boulder Canyon Project, encompassing the dam and All-American Canal. Within months of Hoover's inauguration in March 1929 it had become obvious that such procrastination would not do. The intervening factor was the onset of the greatest economic crisis in modern history.

Herbert Hoover is generally excoriated for responding to the Great Depression with little more than bland utterances assuring imminent recovery. ("I am convinced we have passed the worst and with continued effort we shall rapidly recover," he told the U.S. Chamber of Commerce in May 1930, about three years before the economy actually hit bottom.) Yet he was hardly alone in expecting a brief slowdown. Informed opinion in government and economic circles generally held that the event which began in late 1929 would follow the pattern of almost every economic decline of the previous few decades by ending within a few months. Indeed, during the eleven years following the end of the Great War in 1918 there had been three recessions—starting in 1920, 1923, and 1926—each lasting less than a year and a half. It is not surprising that the global cataclysmic nature of the Great Depression eluded even sophisticated observers until mid-1931.

Hoover saw himself as forcible in addressing the slump. Within weeks of the stock market crash of October 1929, he had recognized that the economic shock demanded a response at the highest levels of government and business. In this he was the polar opposite of his most eminent cabinet member, Treasury Secretary Andrew Mellon. "Mr. Mellon had only one formula: 'Liquidate labor, liquidate stocks, liquidate the farmers, liquidate real estate,'" Hoover related in his memoirs, adding charitably that Mellon "was not hard-hearted. In fact he was generous and sympathetic with all suffering. He felt there would be less suffering if his course were pursued." Hoover, however, believed that "we should use the powers of government to cushion the situation." As he lectured a committee of business leaders on November 21, Mellon's prescription of mass unemployment would not alleviate the disease afflicting the nation: "From an economic viewpoint such action would deepen the depression by suddenly reducing purchasing power and, as a still worse consequence, it would bring about industrial strife, bitterness, disorder, and fear."

In that early stage of the Depression the question occupying President Hoover was not whether something should be done, but what. His options were constrained by several factors, not the least of which was the paltry share that federal spending contributed to the national economy. It may be tempting to think of the government's fiscal resources then in terms of the present day, when they seem virtually unlimited and states, localities, and the citizenry at large appeal routinely to Washington as the appropriator of first resort. But at the dawn of the 1930s, state and local budgets dwarfed federal outlays by a factor of ten. Limited largely to the keeping of a standing army and navy and the payment of obligations incurred in wartime (including interest on war debt and the upkeep of veterans), the federal budget amounted to a negligible 3 percent of gross national product. By the end of the twentieth century, that figure would be closer to 20 percent.

What Hoover did have in great measure was the power of moral suasion. Stepping into a role not unlike the one he had played in the compact negotiations of 1922, he summoned business executives, bankers, and leaders of state and local governments in late 1929 to a string of hortatory meetings at the White House. From the chair he tried to broker a consensus approach to the crisis in which every segment of national leadership would play an appropriate and constructive part.

To some contemporary observers this process typified Hoover's officiousness, the same unappealing trait that had provoked Mark Rose to his memorable outburst at Bishop's Lodge. It was especially irksome in the context of his failure to exercise decisive leadership over Congress and his cabinet. "He has in respect to those elements which are governmental and require his leadership—like tariffs, debts, reparations, political stabilization—been extremely disinclined to act," the political commentator Walter Lippmann wrote in 1931. Yet "scarcely a week passes but some new story comes out of Washington as to how Mr. Hoover has had somebody on the telephone and is attempting to fix this situation or that. . . . This is the reason why he has fallen under the double criticism that he is both inactive and meddlesome."

Later historians have seen the parades of economic potentates as absurd displays of complacency. John Kenneth Galbraith dismissed them as "no-business" meetings designed purely for show—"organized reassurance on a really grand scale. . . . There was a solemn session with the President, those attending had their picture taken with the President, and there was a press interview at which the conferees gave the press their opinion on the business prospect. The latter, without exception, was highly favorable."

Hoover's jawboning was not quite as feckless as all that. He did extract agreements from industrial and governmental leaders that coalesced, for a brief while, into a plausible anti-recessionary program. Among them was a pledge by business leaders to maintain wage rates, if necessary by temporarily sacrificing profits. Still, this sort of promise proved to be a flimsy bulwark against the gathering storm. Hoover would write proudly in his memoirs that the wage agreement "held up fairly well" through the end of his administration, but the truth is that it held up only until mid-1931. As the ferocious slide in economic activity continued, businesses began to slash their workforces and cut the hours of the employees who remained on the lines. In September 1931, U.S. Steel became the first big employer to abandon its pledge outright, reducing wages by 10 percent. Other major companies promptly followed suit.

Another facet of Hoover's program was to step up industrial construction and public works to fend off unemployment. On November 19, 1929, he summoned the heads of the major railroads to the White House and cadged from them an undertaking "to continue and even expand their construction and maintenance programs over the next year." During the next few days, utility presidents and manufacturing executives were seen taking the same pledge. On November 23, Hoover wired governors and mayors around the land urging them to expand their public works programs. "They responded with full assurances," he said.

Hoover had been contemplating a stimulative federal public works program on a major scale even before the stock market crash. Shortly after the 1928 election he unveiled a proposal for a $3 billion public works fund. This idea would never advance much beyond the rhetorical, in part because the meager federal construction budget was a hopelessly shallow foundation on which to erect a program of such magnitude. (Peacetime construction spending by the federal government would not exceed $2 billion until after 1950.) Although state and local governments spent a combined $2.3 billion on infrastructure in 1929, the three levels of government together managed to pump up public works spending only by about $400 million the next year, to a total of $2.86 billion.

The industrialists' construction promises were doomed to be abandoned even faster than their wage commitments. Private construction spending fell from $9 billion in 1929 to $6.3 billion one year later, a collapse that nullified the modest increase in public works. In the years to come, that trend line would head even more precipitously down.

The deterioration in business activity mocked Hoover's confidence in the dual approach of delivering public reassurances and ramping up public construction to battle the economic cycle. He had put all his eggs into those two baskets in his first State of the Union message, delivered on December 3, 1929, scarcely six weeks after the Great Crash, proclaiming that he had

> instituted systematic, voluntary measures of cooperation with the business institutions and with State and municipal authorities to make certain that fundamental businesses of the country shall continue as usual, that wages and therefore consuming power shall not be reduced, and that a special effort shall be made to expand construction work in order to assist in equalizing other deficits in employment. . . . I am convinced that through these measures we have reestablished confidence. Wages should remain stable. A very large degree of industrial unemployment and suffering which would otherwise have occurred has been prevented.

Perhaps more than the phrase "prosperity is just around the corner" (which he always denied having uttered), Hoover's reputation for having stared blindly into the oncoming storm rests on these words.

In the panicky months following the 1929 crash, Hoover's grandiose talk of a $3 billion public works program inflamed the public imagination. Proposals for even larger programs—$5 billion, $7 billion, $8.5 billion—poured into Washington from local chambers of commerce and committees of economists and engineers. William Randolph Hearst collected endorsements from thirty-one prominent economists for his own $5 billion plan, which was publicized coast to coast by his chain of newspapers.

Leaving aside the impossibility of funding all this activity from the public purse, the main problem with these programs was the dearth of construction plans to absorb even a fraction of the phantom billions—there were almost no surveys, no feasibility studies, no blueprints, and no prospect for drafting them in time to budge the unemployment rolls in the near term. The lone exception was the Bureau of Reclamation, which had one enormous project already mapped out, with years of engineering and architectural studies behind it, all tied up neatly with the ribbon of congressional approval and bow of a presidential signature. This was, of course, the Boulder Canyon Project.

Still, the White House's order in late 1929 to place the project on the front burner caught Reclamation's designers short. At the bureau's Denver regional headquarters, chief designing engineer John L. "Jack" Savage was still coming to grips with its sheer magnitude. More than twice the height of Arrowrock, then the tallest dam in existence, the dam in Black Canyon required a quantum leap in engineering and construction technique. Savage had compiled the most advanced technical information available on hydraulic pressure, the characteristics of mass concrete, and metal stress, and had built a handful of test models, but he had not answered most of the questions posed by the wedging of a 726-foot-tall slab of solid concrete into a narrow V-shaped gorge in the desert. Some of these questions would not be answered until the dam was already rising in the canyon. Some, with potentially grave consequences, would not be answered until it was finished and already straining to hold back trillions of gallons of water.

Of more immediate concern to the White House was a provision in the Boulder Canyon Project Act forbidding the spending of even a dime on construction until the Interior Department had reached agreements with electricity buyers sufficient to pay off the project within fifty years, interest included. The responsible official, Interior Secretary Wilbur, had failed to pursue this task with any urgency. Upon taking office, he had set a deadline of October 1, 1929, for the submission of bids for the power. But progress on the contracts soon slowed to a crawl.

Apportioning the power was a dauntingly complicated job. Applications had arrived from twenty-seven bidders—cities, counties, private utilities, even a handful of ambitious individuals—seeking a total of two and one-half times the dam's projected generating capacity. The three most serious applicants were the city of Los Angeles, Southern California Edison, and the Metropolitan Water District of Southern California (a municipal consortium founded by Mulholland in 1926). Los Angeles and Edison each applied to purchase the entire capacity of 3.6 billion kilowatts and the Metropolitan Water District about half, which it said would be needed to pump water from the river to its customers. Among other bidders, the state of Nevada applied for about a third of the capacity; this was vastly more than it could use within its borders, but it hoped to sell the excess to other states for a tidy profit.

Wilbur's post placed him at the uneasy center of the most contentious battle involving the Colorado River since the compact negotiations seven years earlier. All the old arguments over public vs. private power generation were again on the table, with millions of dollars in potential profit hanging in the balance. There were countless municipal feuds to contend with, not to mention political pressures swirling about the highest-profile construction project in the land. It all amounted to "an invitation into a spider's web," Northcutt Ely recollected.

Wilbur, who detested confrontation, was temperamentally unsuited to mediating this raucous conflict. At one point he tried to squelch the quarreling by delivering a sermon to the combatants on the virtues of compromise and consensus: "Start miserable little squabbling over little political units and you can't win. . . . Give and take—take your turn—do your share,— these are communal laws." His anodyne words were ignored, if not ridiculed, by his listeners, who had been passionately brawling over the river for twenty years.

He was also indifferent to the Boulder Canyon Project Act's mandate that preference in the allocation of the hydroelectric supply go to public entities. Whether the power was delivered "from a stock company with trained men and group under government regulation, or from a government unit operating with government bonds . . . always seemed of secondary interest to me," he said later. "Whichever plan could offer the most to the consumer at the light socket seemed the better one to me." Of course, this presupposed that Wilbur would be able to penetrate the jungle of utility accounting to identify the "better" plan, public or private, a goal that had eluded trained economists for decades.

In any case, Wilbur viewed the dam chiefly as a waterworks, with power generation an incidental benefit. While this position echoed that of his mentor, Herbert Hoover, it was contradicted by the explicit language of the statute, which treated the dam's hydroelectric capacity as an important bounty. It also attracted the skeptical attention of the progressive press, ever vigilant for signs that President Hoover—"champion and propagandist of the utility interests," in the words of *The Nation*—was plotting to hand out surreptitious favors to the power trust.

With the power debate certain to turn ugly, Wilbur withdrew from the fray. He dumped the matter on Ely and Elwood Mead, the professorial Reclamation commissioner, with instructions to meet with all the bidders and report back when the matter was settled.

On their first pass, Ely and Mead opted for simplicity. Their proposal, announced on October 21, awarded the Metropolitan Water District half the dam's hydroelectric capacity, and Edison and the city of Los Angeles each half of the remainder. These allotments were subject only to pro rata reductions to accommodate deliveries to the states of Nevada and Arizona, which could claim up to 18 percent each (provided they could use the electricity within their borders) and to small cities in Southern California, which could claim up to a combined 4 percent.

This formula achieved the remarkable feat of satisfying no one. The Metropolitan Water District fretted that it would not have enough power to pump its water over the mountains. Los Angeles officials complained that any allocation to Edison affronted the public preference provision. Edison complained that two million householders—themselves members of the public, after all—had been prejudiced simply because they happened to be customers of a private utility. Pasadena, Burbank, and other small cities groused that overbearing Los Angeles had swindled them out of their share of the Colorado's largesse. And Nevada and Arizona, in whose cliffsides the power-generating dam would be anchored, sounded their usual complaints about California's rapacious appetite for their natural resources. Wilbur had little choice but to air everyone's grievances at a disagreeable public hearing in Washington.

The hearing attracted several figures familiar from the Colorado River battles of the early 1920s. Representative Phil Swing was present to safeguard the interests of Anaheim, Riverside, San Bernardino, and other communities in his district. W. C. Mullendore, who had been Hoover's assistant at Santa Fe, surfaced as an attorney for Southern California Edison. "By coincidence," the *Los Angeles Times* observed, Mullendore had been spotted visiting the White House, stoking suspicions that President Hoover was prepared to intervene on Edison's behalf. Mullendore "was calling merely to pay his respects," the newspaper stated, adding skeptically, "or so it was reported."

Once the hearing convened on November 12, Wilbur sat by, bored and impatient, as the speakers rehearsed their ancient disputes for two long days. Edison reigned as the common target of all the other parties, excoriated relentlessly for its supposed profiteering. At length Wilbur testily adjourned the proceedings, snapping, "We simply can't keep on interminably chewing the same gum over and over." The hearing, as he might have anticipated, brought the controversies no closer to resolution.

It was another five months before the final apportionment was completed and the contracts signed, again thanks to the tireless Ely and Mead. They cut the Metropolitan Water District's base allocation to 36 percent from the original 50 percent, although it was still to receive the largest share, along with the right of first refusal on any power unclaimed by Arizona and Nevada. In practical terms, this guaranteed it about as much power as it would have had under the original formula. Los Angeles got a guaranteed minimum 15 percent, plus any Nevada and Arizona shares not needed by the MWD. These could bring the city's share to a maximum of 33 percent. The small Southern California cities were awarded up to 6 percent, although only Burbank, Pasadena, and Glendale ultimately decided to sign power contracts.

Edison was the biggest loser, its original 25 percent share cut to 9 percent. Conceding that further objection would be fruitless, the utility comforted itself with a consolation prize: the right to share direct operation of the power plant with Los Angeles. Each was to run its own generators with its own staff, an arrangement each felt would prevent any manipulation or sabotage by the other. (Suspicions bred of a decade-long war between these two power-generating behemoths plainly ran deep.)

On April 26, signed contracts for $327 million in power sales—the largest power transaction to that date—were flown from Los Angeles to Washington and placed before Congress, which promptly voted approval. On July 3, Hoover signed an appropriation of $10,660,000 to begin construction, and four days later Wilbur wired Mead: "You are directed to commence construction on Boulder Dam to-day." Before the sun had set on the dam site 2,430 miles from Washington, Walker Young's crews were staking out the route of a supply railroad.

Wilbur's entanglement in the hydropower donnybrook may have been mere misfortune, but for his role in a more enduring controversy he had no one to blame but himself. This was the profoundly fraught question of the dam's name.

With the clang of his mallet on the silver spike still echoing over the desert flats, the interior secretary sprang the issue on an unsuspecting public at the Boulder Crossing dedication. Citing a purported tradition of naming great dams after great presidents—"we have the Roosevelt Dam, the Wilson Dam, the Coolidge Dam"—he proclaimed his intention to name the Boulder Canyon dam after "the great engineer whose vision and persistence, first as chairman of the Colorado River Commission in 1922, and on many occasions since, has done much to make it possible," Herbert Hoover.

Wilbur had so effectively concealed his intention that nary a hint of it had leaked in advance. From his standpoint this was fortunate, for it might have been squelched by premature public disclosure. His audience in the desert certainly was taken by surprise. Although he wrote in his memoirs that "the great crowd gave a gasp, then broke into cheers," contemporary accounts fail to document such a spontaneous celebration. John Page recorded the event in his diary with dutiful circumspection, noting simply that Wilbur drove the silver spike but not that he missed it twice, and adding without comment that the secretary "dedicated the work as 'Hoover' dam."

The christening failed to win universal plaudits. By circumventing a national discussion about renaming what had always been known as the Boulder Canyon Project, Wilbur effectively ambushed a large constituency of interested citizens. Although it is doubtful that this diverse and historically contentious group would have agreed easily on a single honoree, Wilbur slighted a dozen appropriate candidates, ranging from Hiram Johnson and Phil Swing to Arthur Powell Davis and his illustrious uncle, John Wesley Powell. (The names of the latter two would eventually adorn other Colorado River works.) Johnson felt the affront keenly. His discovery of Wilbur's announcement, from a newsboy aboard a westbound train taking him from Washington home to San Francisco, left him "plainly indignant," a witness reported. Swing, who was also on board, tried to salve Johnson's hurt feelings by belittling the significance of Wilbur's action, but "there was no other topic of conversation on the rest of the ride."

Wilbur's attempt to rationalize his decision by conjuring a "tradition" from the naming of dams after Theodore Roosevelt, Woodrow Wilson, and Calvin Coolidge was specious. None of them had been president when they were so honored; Wilson, indeed, had died just before his name went on a Tennessee Valley Authority dam in 1924. To place a sitting president's name on a major federal project at the very outset of his term was unprecedented.

Many of those intimately involved in bringing the project to realization, moreover, regarded Hoover's role in the process equivocally. The dam that was to rise from the floor of Black Canyon did not resemble anything that he had ever favored, and it encompassed features, such as the government-owned power plant, that he had actively opposed. Others who had chafed at Hoover's involvement in river affairs going back to the compact negotiations in 1922 thought his appropriation of credit unpardonably high-handed. William J. Carr, who had assisted the California delegation in Santa Fe and helped Swing draft the Boulder Canyon Project Act, later maintained that if they had foreseen Wilbur's move they would have written the name "Boulder Dam" into the bill. "Everybody would have accepted it as entirely appropriate," he wrote, "because everybody assumed that it was too big to name after any one individual, as it was."

Hoover would always maintain that Wilbur's announcement was an entirely proper acknowledgment of his own preeminent role in the dam's creation, which included, as he wrote in his memoirs, "the chairmanship of the Colorado River Commission which had paved the way for its construction . . . my personal guidance of its engineering . . . [and] the legislation authorizing it, which had been largely prepared by me"—inflating his real role almost beyond recognition.

Wilbur's act launched a political tit-for-tat that lasted for seventeen years, through the entire Roosevelt presidency and into the administration of Harry Truman, at which point a Republican Congress permanently affixed Hoover's name to the dam. Across that time span "Hoover Dam" and "Boulder Dam" were used interchangeably, the preference often depending on the political leanings of the speaker. The matter generated so much confusion and acrimony that in the *Las Vegas Review-Journal* in 1947 a letter writer named Frank Romano Sr. was provoked to propose that the structure in Black Canyon be named "Hoogivza Dam."

"Now," he pleaded, "let's hear no more about it."

In 1930, however, there was no way to dismiss the magnitude of the project that was about to be launched in the canyon. There was money at stake—big money—and careers to be made.

# 9

# The Big Six

D enver in March is a city trapped in the change of seasons, caught
between winter slow to relinquish its icy grip and spring heralding its
arrival with weeks of sleet and frigid rain. Such was the Denver that
greeted Frank Crowe as his train pulled into Union Station on Tuesday,
March 3, 1931.

In a downtown storefront at ten o'clock the following morning the U.S.
Bureau of Reclamation was to open construction bids on Hoover Dam. The
ritual would crown two hectic months for Crowe, endless hours spent tor-
turing figures and weighing uncertainties to arrive at a single number that
might secure victory. He was a master at the black art of paring costs so that
the final bid would be low yet not too low: the basic idea was to win the job
without undercutting the runner-up by too much, lest a big chunk of potential profit lie unclaimed on the table. But he was not the only such wizard in
the land. How many of his rivals had spent January and February hunched
over their own books, trying to conjure up their own magic number?

Crowe worked late into the night in his room at Denver's newest and
most stylish hotel, the Cosmopolitan, leafing through his pages of notes
and formulas, and searching out a few last pennies to prune, then caught a
few hours sleep. At 9:45 Wednesday morning he presented himself at 1437
Welton Street, a few blocks from City Hall and the U.S. Mint. The address
belonged to a vacant storefront Reclamation had rented for the occasion,

knowing that its own cramped offices nearby would not accommodate the throng of builders, suppliers, journalists, and curiosity seekers hoping to witness the launch of a historic enterprise. Despite the blustery weather outdoors the narrow room was close and humid under a hazy nimbus of pipe and cigar smoke. More than one hundred anxious businessmen and engineers sat wedged cheek by jowl on folding chairs or clustered in a dense mass in the rear, fidgeting uncomfortably in wool suits and stiff collars; scores of others, too tardy or unimportant to secure a space indoors, milled about on the sidewalk.

Crowe shouldered his way to the front of the room, where a huge American flag was tacked to the wall. He added his buff government-issued bid envelope to a pile lying on a wooden table. Inside was a proposal to build Hoover Dam for $48,890,995.50.

Before him was unmistakable evidence of the Darwinian process that had winnowed out those contractors who lacked the money, strength of character, or vision to raise the tallest dam in the world from the bed of the intransigent Colorado. The number of firms that had ordered the bid documents upon their release on the tenth of January was 107. The number of envelopes on the table was five.

The contract for Hoover Dam, officially estimated by Reclamation's engineering staff to be worth $48,866,254, would be the largest the federal government had ever issued. Even contractors who had honed their skills for years building bridges, tunnels, and railroads to span the continent and dams corralling its wildest rivers saw it as a job of surpassing magnitude. It tantalized them as a potential source of glory and profit but also, quite possibly, of financial ruin. It was big enough to commandeer their dreams and risky enough to give them nightmares.

For more than a year consultants had been returning from the Colorado River with nightmarish reports about the engineering challenges, the remoteness of the site, and the murderous heat. As one wrote to his East Coast banking clients:

> I consider it almost impossible to build. The hazard is much greater than in any construction contract I have ever known. It is a super-project which

calls for a super-organization having super-financial strength and I know of no super-organization that may bid on it.

This was not an extreme viewpoint. The government specifications were of uncommon complexity, listing 119 individual items ranging from the grand (3,400,000 cubic yards of concrete to be poured for the dam itself) to the picayune (a three-quarter-inch lacquer finish to be applied to the concrete floors of the hydroelectric station). In recognition of the job's scale, the government mandated that a $2 million bond accompany every bid and that the victor post a $5 million construction surety bond, the largest ever written on a single contract.

The winning bidder would have to shoulder enormous risks. Although the government was to furnish at its own expense all the raw materials and equipment for the dam's permanent structure, the contractor would bear responsibility for all construction equipment, labor, and temporary materials such as bracing timber. The builder would also be held to a string of exacting deadlines, among them driving four diversion tunnels through solid rock by October 1, 1933, and raising the dam to 427 feet (the height at which it could begin generating electricity) by August 1, 1936. The penalty for missing any of the interim targets was $3,000 a day.

The specifications required the entire project to be completed in 2,565 days (i.e., seven years), with the same $3,000 daily penalty lurking on the horizon. This period seemed at once too short for such a gargantuan job and uncomfortably long for an insurer to be on the hook for a $5 million bond, especially given a clause in the specifications absolving the government of any liability for losses if Congress withdrew its funding prior to the project's completion. "Who could tell what Congress would or would not do over a seven year period and a probable change of administration?" wondered Leland W. Cutler, the San Francisco insurance man who was to assemble the bonding syndicate for Crowe's employers.

Adding to the contractor's risk were the project's unique features, which were manifestly difficult to cost out. These included the unprecedented specification of a network of pipes to be laid throughout the dam to carry cooling water from a dedicated refrigeration plant, the only way to carry off the heat generated by the record-breaking mass of concrete as it cured. The design and consequently the cost of this scheme, which would ultimately require 662 miles of piping, would have to be worked out as construction proceeded.

On the plus side, the contractors were given a free hand in managing their labor force, save for two mandates. They were to give hiring preference "so far as practicable" to veterans of the Spanish-American War, the Philippine "insurrection" of 1899–1902, and the Great War; and they were forbidden to employ "Mongolian labor." The former provision reflected the familiar concerns about unemployment among veterans that had animated the development schemes of William Ellsworth Smythe and George Maxwell. The latter was an artifact of the Chinese Exclusion Act of 1882, enacted when American paranoia over imported Asian labor had been at its peak. The exclusion was written in the Newlands Act of 1902, which had established the Reclamation Service. It applied to every government-financed dam project until 1943, when it was finally repealed by Congress.

The very size of the Boulder Canyon contract was what made a consortium approach necessary. Customarily, Reclamation divided its dam projects into individual jobs and put the contracts out to bid separately, so that a half-dozen contractors might be involved on a single project. Boulder Dam was plainly too complex a job for such a system, for any conflict between contractors or missteps in coordination could bring the massive project to a halt. Accordingly, the bureau required that the dam be bid as a single job. The winner would need to call on skills in excavation, tunnel building, underwater construction, and surface paving, under conditions in which organizational talent and financial strength would be crucial. Instead of letting the Boulder Dam contracts piecemeal and managing the coordination on the ground, in other words, the government was mandating that individual contractors—blasters, tunnelers, concrete men, and road builders—come together as a unit in advance.

Despite these challenges, there were men who thought of the dam contract as something akin to their birthright. Preeminent among them were the owners of Utah Construction Company and Morrison-Knudsen, who had formed their joint venture to take on jobs just like this one. The Wattis brothers and Harry Morrison put their faith in their chief superintendents: in Morrison-Knudsen's case Frank Crowe, and on Utah's side Henry Lawler, whom the Wattises believed, rather optimistically, to be Crowe's match in the field. "Frank and Hank will build that dam," William H. Wattis boasted.

The partners had been eyeing the Boulder Canyon Project since the mid-1920s, while the Swing-Johnson bill was still wending its way through Congress. In those days the project seemed easily within the partnership's engineering capabilities as well as its capital resources. If worse came to worst, Will Wattis reassured himself and his brother Edmund, "we can raise what we need on the ranch." This was a reference to one hundred square miles of pastureland, supporting 100,000 head of cattle, that the company owned in Utah, Nevada, and Idaho. The ranch produced little in annual income, but the land was a readily marketable asset.

Fatefully, in the course of the next few years time and circumstance caught up to the Wattis brothers. By 1930, they no longer resembled the imperious pair who had summoned the upstart Harry Morrison to Ogden with a curt command. Will, or W.H., was seventy-two, racked with pain from bone cancer, which shortened his temper and sapped his self-confidence. Edmund, seventy-six, who served as vice chairman under his younger brother, was in scarcely better health, so afflicted with Parkinson's that his palsied hand could barely inscribe a legible signature on a sheet of paper.

To the dismay of Edmund and Harry Morrison, W.H. had begun to waver on the dam contract just as the bid deadline approached. Habitually reluctant to do business with strangers—"Is he our kind?" was his characteristic query whenever a joint venture was proposed with a new partner—he was even more tetchy now about a project that could bring Utah down. "If we can't do the job alone," he told his brother, "to hell with it."

His two partners despaired of budging W.H. by themselves. There was only one man on earth capable of bullying Will Wattis into action, and as the deadline to submit bids drew near they turned to him with a desperate appeal. His name was Marriner Eccles, and he held Utah Construction's purse strings in his hands.

Within a few short years Marriner Stoddard Eccles would come into his own as the most eminent economic policymaker in the country, Franklin Roosevelt's appointee as chairman of the Federal Reserve Board. His origins were less august. Born in 1890 in Logan, Utah, he was the eldest of nine children of his father's second polygamous marriage. The senior Eccles, David, was Utah's leading industrialist and the leading tithe payer to the Mormon church, and his second marriage had been negotiated principally as a business alliance with his new bride's father. But he treated his second family as subordinate to his first in nearly every way: they lived in harsher circumstances, saw less of him, and had fewer legal rights—a point that was driven home in 1912, when the sixty-three-year-old patriarch died intestate.

Because plural marriages were then no longer recognized by Utah law, Marriner's mother was cut out of her husband's estate, while David's first wife received a mandatory one-third share. The children of both marriages each inherited equal portions of the remainder, but the first marriage had produced twelve children, so the senior clan ended up with a commanding 70 percent control of the Eccles fortune. Marriner's older half-brothers, who now controlled the boards of seventeen corporations with holdings in lumber, sugar, railroads, construction, and banking, looked down on him as an undereducated poor relation and shut him out of all family councils.

This was a fatal misjudgment. In contrast to his half-brothers, who would prove to be inept stewards of their legacy, Marriner had a natural aptitude for business. By the end of the decade he had built up the value of his own clan's interests to the point where he was able to force a breakup of the Eccles holdings on highly advantageous terms. Among the spoils he received were controlling shares in the Eccles banks and a seat on the board of the contracting company David Eccles had cofounded at the turn of the century, Utah Construction.

Years of condescending treatment by incompetent elders had invested Marriner with a cynical view of the older generation's claims to superior enlightenment, along with a certain tactlessness of expression. He wasted little time before displaying these traits to W. H. Wattis, who called meetings of the board when the spirit moved him and withheld basic financial information from the directors. After witnessing Wattis in action for a few months, Marriner confronted him in a memorable scene, insisting that Utah Construction's governance be placed on a professional footing, including a fixed schedule for board meetings and the regular dissemination of financial statements to every director. Old Will Wattis predictably kicked up a storm, accusing his junior of ingratitude, greed, arrogance, and a host of other sins.

To the astonishment of the other directors, Marriner stood his ground. Aided by the fact that his proposals were grounded in a compelling logic, he forced W.H. to back down and submit to reform. Due in part to the layering on of professional managerial standards, Utah Construction thrived in the following years. The tension between Wattis and Eccles never entirely disappeared, but Wattis eventually came to terms with the incontestable talent of the young interloper. In September 1931, he summoned his two daughters to his deathbed and made a surprising request. "I want you girls to promise me that after I'm gone, you will do everything you can to put Marriner into the presidency of Utah," he said. "Ed can't handle the job. He's too old. But Marriner can."

So it is unsurprising that Edmund Wattis and Harry Morrison called for Eccles at this critical juncture. W.H. had moved into a two-room suite at St. Francis Hospital in San Francisco, there to submit to a fashionable cancer therapy involving injections of an extract from the adrenal glands of sheep. Its originators, Drs. Walter B. Coffey and John Davis Humber, claimed that the injections first eliminated the pain of cancer and then the tumor itself. In Wattis's case the treatment achieved neither goal. (Coffey and Humber would parlay their treatment into an appearance on the cover of *Time*, the hallmark of contemporary celebrity, only to be discredited shortly afterward by the American medical establishment.)

Eccles reached Wattis on a long-distance telephone line as the others listened in at Utah's office. The task before him required every ounce of his power to withstand Wattis's volleys of cranky abuse. Yet bit by bit he drove home the point that Boulder Canyon was too important a project for Utah to spurn, even if it meant taking on a boatload of new partners. The construction industry of the future would be inherited by the builders of Boulder Dam, he told Wattis. All others would be left behind.

W.H. finally capitulated to Eccles's relentless badgering. "If you feel as strongly as that about the Boulder project," he said, "come to San Francisco and see me in the hospital." The agreement to form the construction giant Six Companies was sealed there; bowing to Will Wattis's infirmity, the new partners would hold their first seven board meetings there, too, at the bedside of the terminally ill old man, well into the spring.

Just as the Boulder Canyon Project gripped the Wattis brothers and Harry Morrison, its siren call reached clear across the continent to torment a man sweating through the night on a camp bed in Cuba's torrid interior.

Henry J. Kaiser was just completing a $20 million contract to push a paved road two hundred miles across Camagüey province, in an area accessible only by an interminable ride on a soot-spewing train followed by a full day on horseback. It was the most grueling job Kaiser had ever taken, involving the raising of five hundred bridges over flood-prone streambeds splayed across Camagüey like strands of a spiderweb. His workforce consisted of six thousand Cuban laborers whose remedy for any vehicle's malfunction was to whack at its carburetor with a wrench.

But Kaiser knew that raising the world's tallest dam in the American desert would be a staggeringly more complex job. "I lay awake nights in my sweltering tent and thought about it," he recollected. "I knew it was too big for me, yet I figured there must be some way to get in on it."

Kaiser had been born in 1882 in upstate New York to a father who scratched out a penurious living making gloves and boots by hand, at a time when the mechanization of the leather trade had already rendered his craft an anachronism. By the age of sixteen, Henry, on the run from his father's obsolescent lifestyle, was working as a traveling salesman of photography supplies, tapping into the surging mass market created by George Eastman's Kodak cameras. In the Adirondack resort town of Lake Placid he offered the owner of a photography shop a year's worth of his enterprising skills in exchange for a share of the business. A natural salesman with a taste for the motivational bromide ("There's only one time to do anything, and that's today"), he presently bought out his employer and expanded the shop into a chain that sold equipment and offered portrait photography to the social elite in their holiday haunts from Lake Placid to Daytona Beach.

Then, like thousands of men of his generation, he headed west in search of the main chance. He found it peddling heavy equipment to road builders in Washington state. By 1913, just entering his thirties, he had acquired his own building firm and was taking jobs away from his former customers by ruthless underbidding. Come the 1920s, Kaiser crews were building roads from California to the Mississippi. At the time he accepted the subcontract to build the Camagüey highway, he considered himself the top paving man in North America.

But Camagüey was to be the last highway he ever built. In mid-1930, he spent several of those stifling nights in Cuba straining his powers of persuasion to sell his mentor and best friend, Warren A. Bechtel, on the idea of forming a partnership to build the big dam. The project would be a turning point in both their lives.

Like Kaiser, Bechtel was a huge, hulking individual, another product of a rural upbringing invested with a desperate desire to get off the farm—in his case in Peabody, Kansas. His first attempt at independence was a flop: in 1891, aged nineteen, he joined a mostly female dance band on trombone, an instrument he had practiced obsessively through long nights on the featureless plain. But the band went bust during a tour of downstate Illinois, and a marooned and deflated Warren returned home on train fare wired by his father.

In 1899 he tried again, laying track in Oklahoma with his own mule team, bringing along his bride and their two-year-old son. For four years they chased railroad jobs, living in tents and boxcars on the worksites. They had a second son, and the Bechtel brood became a familiar sight in camps across the Midwest, so that the senior Bechtel acquired the nickname that would stay with him to the end of his days. He was known as "Dad."

They wound up stranded in Nevada, where they discovered that the contractor who had promised Dad a job had gone bust before their arrival. "I landed in Reno with a wife, two babies, a slide trombone, and a ten-dollar bill," he would recall. Presently he landed a position with the Southern Pacific, where he displayed a natural talent for coordinating heavy equipment on a big job. Striking out on his own, he gained an enviable reputation for integrity and efficiency. By 1906 he had made enough money to buy his own steam shovel. The track-mounted Marion Model 20 had been one of the workhorses of the Panama Canal, a behemoth with a towering steam boiler housed inside an iconic red wooden cab. Not one to hide his ambition, Dad painted the legend "W. A. Bechtel Co." across the side of the cab in tall white letters. In fact his company would not be incorporated for another sixteen years.

The first encounter between these two equally brash, overbearing men took place one day in 1921 on a Kaiser road building job in rural Northern California. "I was standing alone surveying thirty miles of paving which we were constructing," Henry recalled, "when suddenly in a whirl of dust up rolled an automobile and out of it jumped a stranger. 'Your name Kaiser?' he asked."

Bechtel complimented the younger man on the orderliness of his worksite. Then he prodded Kaiser to join the contractors association he had founded to lobby the government for work. Kaiser had built his firm by playing cut-throat with other contractors, not by joining with them, but as a new entrant in the California market he recognized that the time had come to seek shelter in the shade of an influential mentor. Bechtel, who had been a leader in the local construction industry for nearly fifteen years and whose reputation for fair dealing was unimpeachable, seemed the right man. Bechtel, in his turn, valued Kaiser's salesmanship and ingenuity. By the end of their conversation Kaiser had joined Bechtel's group, the Associated General Contractors. A business alliance sealed with a handshake would follow, with millions of dollars' worth of joint construction jobs in the offing.

Yet despite his skill at wheedling, Kaiser discovered that the Boulder Canyon job was not easy to sell to Bechtel. Experience had made Dad wary of dam building as a calling. Two years earlier he had finished Bowman Dam in the California Sierras, in a region of steep gorges served only by wagon trails and cut off from the outside world for six months of the year. It was a grand achievement, one of the largest rockfill dams in the world, but it had taxed even Dad's peerless talent for logistics. The job had required building a camp with a field hospital, maintaining one hundred head of cattle and a slaughterhouse to feed the crew through the winter—and in the end the irrigation district that had ordered the job ran out of money to pay for it. To Bechtel, Boulder Canyon looked like Bowman inflated to gargantuan dimensions. He tried to let his protégé down gently. "Henry," he said, "it sounds a little ambitious."

"Dad," Kaiser replied, dipping into his storehouse of inspirational aphorisms, "problems are only opportunities in work clothes."

Kaiser labored unrelentingly to wear Bechtel down for the rest of their stay together in Cuba, much as Marriner Eccles would work on the ailing W. H. Wattis (though with rather less friction). He compared Boulder Dam to such wonders of the world as the Pyramids and the Great Wall of China. He promised that when the dam was completed the name of W. A. Bechtel Co. would be etched on a bronze plaque at its crest, validating for all eternity the optimistic legend Dad had painted on the side of his Marion steam shovel.

Eventually Bechtel threw in the towel. Within a few months of their return from Cuba he and Kaiser were preparing a joint bid on the dam with a big Boston contracting firm named Warren Bros., with which Kaiser had partnered on the Camagüey job. But almost as soon as they set out to find further partners, they tripped over the trail of Morrison-Knudsen and Utah Construction. It was not long before both ventures accepted the inescapable logic of joining forces.

Utah and Morrison-Knudsen had already formed the seed of an alliance. The partnership had started with $1.5 million in capital, two-thirds of it pledged by Utah. That this sum was not remotely sufficient for the Boulder Canyon Project became clear as soon as Crowe delivered his rough estimate of its cost—$50 million. With that much at stake, the banks committing to bond the project were insisting that the builders show that they had $5 million in working capital.

Finding more partners did not promise to be easy. Morrison appealed for suggestions to Leland Cutler, his insurance broker at the Fidelity & Deposit Co. Together they narrowed the roll of candidates to a tiny handful. High on the list was Charles A. Shea, the leading tunnel and sewer builder in the region.

Charlie Shea was the son of a college-educated contractor who had bequeathed each of his nine children shares of the family plumbing firm, J. F. Shea Company, sufficient to sustain them into adulthood. Yet Charlie preferred to project the image of a workingman who had raised himself by his own bootstraps: shaped like a fire hydrant, he was foul-mouthed and unkempt, a hard drinker, a brawler, and a gambler. He had long since left his wife and family in Portland and decamped to San Francisco, where his hotel suite doubled as residence and office and where, as would be discovered belatedly at the reading of his will, he had long maintained an unmarried domestic arrangement with another woman.

At the Boulder Canyon dam site he would become a familiar and beloved figure, indistinguishable in appearance from the hundreds of muckers and puddlers on the job, holding court seated on an upturned bucket, the only Six Companies board member with an empathetic understanding of the backbreaking rigors of the job.

More relevant to Morrison's quest, Shea was willing to contribute $500,000 toward the consortium's capital. As an added dividend, he brought along another Portland firm, Pacific Bridge Company, with which he customarily bid bridge and tunnel jobs. The relationship between J. F. Shea and Pacific Bridge was based on absolute mutual trust—"we never had a written contract," recalled Gorrill Swigert, Pacific's president—which could not help but impress W. H. Wattis, concerned as the old man was about venturing with unfamiliar partners. Pacific also agreed to post $500,000, bringing the total in the till to $2.5 million.

Another candidate for partnership was MacDonald & Kahn, a San Francisco construction firm that was a Cutler insurance client. The firm "not only had an enviable reputation as successful contractors but . . . a great deal of available money and practically unlimited credit," Cutler told Morrison pointedly. It had prospered in San Francisco's post-earthquake construction boom, erecting such signature buildings as the Mark Hopkins Hotel.

Alan MacDonald and Felix Kahn were the quintessential odd couple. The former was a short-fused Scot with a Cornell degree who boasted of having been fired from fifteen jobs in a row before landing one he could keep, at Pittsburgh's Truscon Steel. There he met Kahn, the son of an immigrant rabbi who had sold fruit on Detroit street corners to make ends meet and raised five sons who went on to distinguished careers in architecture and engineering. If there was any doubt in W. H. Wattis's mind that the short, urbane, Jewish Kahn was "our kind," it was dispelled when Kahn wrote out a check for $1 million. "That made me one of the family right away," Kahn recounted later.

Bechtel and Kaiser recognized that the Morrison-Utah group had gathered critical momentum. Fortuitously, Dad Bechtel and the Wattis brothers were old associates and occasional partners, leaving no question that Dad was one of "our kind." Bechtel, Kaiser, and Warren Bros. threw in their lot with Utah and Morrison, jointly pledging the last $1.5 million needed to reach the $5 million goal.

At that point, another obstacle emerged to the bid: Cutler's bonding syndicate began to come apart. Unnerved by the morbid engineering reports, banks in New York and Boston were bailing out. Cutler was compelled to travel back east, where he went virtually door-to-door, begging friends in the business to take pieces of the syndication, even if it were as little as a quarter- or half-percent. Eventually he cajoled twenty-seven surety companies into participating ("It takes a great many halves to make 100 percent," he observed), but on unforgiving terms: they insisted that the builders put up not $5 million in capital, but $8 million.

This was almost certainly a deal-breaker, since some of the contractors were already falling short on their original pledges. Warren Bros. had come up completely empty-handed, possibly because $12 million in Cuban bonds it had accepted as payment for its share of the Camagüey project proved to be unmarketable. Bechtel and Kaiser cut Warren Bros. loose from their partnership and covered its contribution themselves. Pacific Bridge had raised $200,000, or 40 percent of its note, from its lawyer. Morrison-Knudsen had borrowed $100,000 from Alan MacDonald's brother Graeme and raised another $45,000 by cashing in a nest egg belonging to Ann Morrison, Harry's wife. (She was repaid in Morrison-Knudsen shares, which made her the firm's biggest stockholder.)

Cutler's saving solution was to capitalize the consortium at $8 million, but to require only $5 million to be paid in at the outset, with the remaining

$3 million pledged in principle to cover any unforeseen emergency. It was a largely illusory commitment, given that the builders would probably be unable to raise the additional sum if the project faltered. But it was enough to persuade the financiers that their risks were covered.

On a fog-shrouded morning in February 1931, the principals of the bidding group, absent the ailing Wattis brothers, assembled at the Engineers Club of San Francisco, a grandly named banquet room in an office building around the corner from the hotel where Charlie Shea kept house.

Some of the participants were freshly returned from the Colorado, where they had journeyed to see what they were letting themselves in for. One inspection party of eighteen executives spent two weeks at the site trying to gin up a rough estimate of the construction cost. They emerged with not much more confidence than had the bankers' consulting engineers. Just to reach the canyon they had endured an eighty-mile automobile trip, followed by a five-mile trek on foot and a motorboat ride up the muddy river. The only signs of life they reported seeing were two owls on a rock on the Nevada side and five jackasses on the Arizona side. Then they entered the canyon, only to be overwhelmed by its glowering walls. It was lost on no one that as many as five thousand men would have to be transported to the top of these cliffs and then 1,800 feet down to the riverbed every day. "It hit us all the same," recalled B. Frank Modglin, the general manager of MacDonald & Kahn, "and candidly we were all scared stiff."

But there was no turning back now. At the Engineers Club they cobbled together a preliminary bid from among the estimates prepared separately by three trusted underlings: Utah's chief engineer, J. Q. Barlow, Chad Calhoun of MacDonald & Kahn, and Frank Crowe, each of whom had been working with harried urgency since the Reclamation Bureau released the bid specifications on January 10.

Part of the challenge was that the government specifications incorporated a fair amount of guesswork by Jack Savage and his team at Reclamation's Denver office. The dam design was still very much in flux, largely because Savage was having trouble meeting the tightened standards mandated by the Sibert board following the St. Francis Dam disaster. A particular problem was the board's reduction of the maximum allowable pressure on the upstream face from the original specification of 41.3 tons, which it considered insufficiently conservative for "a structure of this unprecedented magnitude and importance, failure of which would result in . . . an overwhelming disaster." The board ratcheted the permissible load down to thirty tons.

Despite running through nearly three dozen tentative designs, Savage was unable to get his test stresses down below thirty-three tons. He was still searching for a solution when Hoover's order to commence construction deprived him of eighteen months of further testing and study. Instead he had to put the design process on hold and publish the specifications without delay, using the data at hand. Changes would have to be made in practically every feature of the dam, some of them years after the contract was signed.

For all that, the three estimates laid on the table at the Engineers Club were in astonishingly close agreement, a gratifying indication that once broken down into its component pieces the project would be manageable: the difference between the high and low figures of $40 million and $40.7 million amounted to less than 1.75 percent, with the third estimate landing smack in the middle.

There was less concord among the personalities in the room, however. Largely this was the fault of Henry Kaiser, who took advantage of the Wattis brothers' absence to appropriate the role of chairman. His high-handedness led to an embarrassing faux pas when he called a break for lunch. Leading the other bosses out the door, he overlooked Marriner Eccles, who was on hand to represent Utah Construction but had uncharacteristically held his brusque tongue all morning long. Eccles was left behind with the junior accountants whom Kaiser had instructed to refine the bid figures over sandwiches, while the senior members filed out to lunch in style. Dad Bechtel soon realized the oversight and dispatched one of his sons to retrieve the marooned Eccles. Whether because he was already exasperated with the bluster of his seniors or because he genuinely felt greater affinity with the junior number crunchers, Eccles declined the honor.

The board members duly returned after lunch to complete a few formalities, including the choice of a name for their venture, which was about to file its incorporation papers in Delaware. Several generic names, such as Continental Construction and Western Construction, were considered and dismissed before Felix Kahn proposed Six Companies.

"The name just came to me," he recollected, but in actuality it was an inside joke among the San Franciscans in the room. The Six Companies was well known in the city as a benevolent association of Chinese businesses that served as a communal welfare organization in counterweight to the Chinese tongs, which were criminal gangs. Kahn may have hoped that the name would project the same aura of steadfastness and fellowship in the Anglo business world that it did in Chinatown. His suggestion won immediate approval. The sole catch was that, despite the withdrawal of Warren Bros., there were still seven companies in the joint venture, not six. But if the Bechtel-Kaiser partnership was taken as a single unit—as well it might—the arithmetic worked out nicely. Indeed, on the formal Six Companies letterhead the two would be listed together, as "Bechtel & Kaiser," among the six constituent partners.

On February 25, the board members met again in Will Wattis's hospital suite—for the first time as Six Companies, Inc.—to elect officers. Wattis was named president, in recognition of his craggy seniority and also, quite likely, the running out of his mortal string; he would succumb to his cancer six months later, to be succeeded as president by Dad Bechtel. In the meantime, Bechtel was designated as first vice president, E. O. Wattis as second vice president, Kahn as treasurer, and Shea as secretary.

As though to rebuke Kaiser for his overbearing performance at the Engineers Club meeting, his partners left him off the officers roll. They did, however, give him a special brief as liaison with government officials in Washington. This was a canny move, for it exploited his exceptional persuasive skills while keeping him tied down three thousand miles away and out of his partners' hair. In the fullness of time, however, it would have the unintended consequence of boosting Kaiser to national prominence as the public face of the preeminent construction project in the land, a role into which he would slip as though into a tailored suit: it would not be long before he would be referring to the project in the press as "my dam."

The Six Companies partners met once more on March 2, two days before the bid opening. Gathered around Wattis's hospital bed, they listened as Crowe paged through the bid items one last time. At his side was a scale model of the dam, with breakaway parts to illustrate the various stages of construction. Finally they voted to approve Crowe's estimates and add 25 percent for profit and contingencies, a decision they had left for the very end so that no one would let slip the ultimate figure. Then, leaving Will and Ed Wattis behind, the others boarded a train for Denver.

At ten o'clock sharp on March 4, Raymond F. Walter, who had succeeded Crowe as the Bureau of Reclamation's chief engineer, positioned himself behind a table in the Welton Street storefront and began reading the bids. One, from the John Bernard Simon Construction Co. of New York, was for "$200,000,000 or cost plus 10 per cent." The other, for "$88,000 less than the lowest bid you get," generated "considerable humor" (as a newspaper report put it) at the expense of the bidder, Edwin A. Smith of Louisville, Kentucky, who had appended "a family history and references of good character." But because neither bid was accompanied by the requisite $2 million bond, Walter rejected them out of hand.

Bids from three construction consortiums remained to be opened. The Woods Bros. Corporation of Lincoln, Nebraska, bid $58,653,107.50. A group headed by the Arundel Corporation of Baltimore bid $53,893,878.70. Crowe's bid for Six Companies, therefore, came in more than $5 million below his nearest rival, an enormous amount of potential profit to leave on the table. If it were any consolation to his bosses, however, his bid was a masterpiece of the estimator's art: it exceeded the official government figure by a mere $24,741.50, or five-hundredths of a percent—an achievement akin to hitting the center of a dartboard from the far side of town.

Crowe's bid bespoke his skill and experience. For one thing, it was heavily front-loaded—that is, he overbid on the first stages of work to generate an early profit, which could be used to finance the rest of the work. For example, he bid $8.50 per cubic yard, or a total of $13,285,500, to excavate the diversion tunnels, by far the biggest piece of the first phase. This compared to the bureau's estimate of $10,159,000 for the same job. Combined with overbids on other major elements of the diversion tunnel phase, the tactic would place a profit of more than $4.4 million in Six Companies' hands by the time the tunnels were completed, a mere two and one-half years into the project.

It bears noting that it was not unusual for contractors to submit such "unbalanced" bids on multistage projects. Indeed, Arundel, the runner-up, matched Crowe's bid for the diversion tunnels penny for penny, and Wood Bros. was only a hair behind. All three firms compensated for the front-end overestimation by low-balling the later phases, including the pouring of concrete for the dam. But Crowe's figure for that job, $9,180,000, was nearly $2 million below the government estimate and a full $5 million below Arundel's. It is there that Six Companies won the bid, and likely that Crowe's unique experience in pouring concrete fast and cheaply from overhead cableways gave him the knowledge and self-assurance needed to cut the price perilously close to the bone.

Within hours of the bid opening, the victorious contractors found themselves catapulted onto the national stage, pestered by newspapermen for every detail of the big job ahead, their names bandied far and wide in the first frenzied glimmerings of fame. Crowe wired his siblings and his mother back east at noontime. ("WE ARE THE SUCCESSFUL BIDDERS ON HOOVER DAM AT FORTY NINE MILLION DOLLARS. FRANK.") Dad Bechtel, cornered by journalists on Welton Street, established the signature corporate tone of Six Companies as one of studied, if slightly supercilious, nonchalance. He told the newsmen that the Big Six, as the company came to be known in shorthand, was prepared to put one thousand men to work in the canyon "at once." "We do not consider this a hazardous job," he added jauntily. "It does not involve unusual difficulties, although the magnitude of the project has given the public that firm impression."

A few days later Will Wattis seconded Dad's viewpoint with a further seasoning of braggadocio. Tracked down in his hospital room by a reporter for *Time*, the "small, spry, white-haired" builder held forth, brandishing a big black victory cigar, as his "jolly blue eyes snapped with delight."

"Now this dam is just a dam but it's a damn big dam," he said. "Otherwise it's no different than others we've thrown up in a dozen places. It involves a lot of money—more money than any one contractor has a right to have."

As for his own role, Six Companies had been putting it about that he was suffering only a "mild form of cancer" and was fully up to the challenge of managing the greatest construction job ever launched within the continental United States. "I don't know when I'll get out of here," he told *Time*. "I think I am improving but don't worry, I'll be on the job." He would not live to visit the worksite.

Crowe was anxious to visit his family in Boise, however briefly, before moving to the dam site. But early on the morning after the bid ceremony he stopped to take care of a few things that could not wait, such as summoning his loyal crew to work; when the Western Union office in Denver opened for business at 8 A.M. he was already at the door, clutching a sheaf of telegrams for his scattered lieutenants. ("OK FOR A JOB ON HOOVER DAM . . . FT CROWE.") The next day he was in Boise, and only five days after that, on March 11, on his way south to Las Vegas to set up his temporary offices. He left Linnie and the children behind with a promise to send for them as soon as a house was raised for them in the glorified work camp to be known as Boulder City, as yet a vacant, windswept waste eight miles west of the river.

Dad Bechtel's promise to launch the project with an inaugural workforce of one thousand workers was wildly premature. In truth, the project would not be ready to deploy that many men for several months; at mid-April, a few weeks after the contract was signed, the Six Companies payroll listed only 312 laborers, earning an average of $5 a day. There was as yet no housing or provisioning for the workforce. Reclamation officials, panicky over what was certain to be an onslaught of unemployed men, admonished job seekers to avoid Las Vegas unless they had a job offer in hand or the resources to support themselves indefinitely. When he arrived on March 12,

Crowe tried to reinforce the message by issuing a public warning via the newspapers that "we must have a place to eat and sleep before we can put men to work."

No one was listening. Since early January, men and their families had been packing their meager possessions and leaving their homes, joining a new migration west not unlike that of the fortune seekers of 1849. In the first months of 1931 they were already converging by the thousands on the knife-pointed southern tip of Nevada, drawn to the inhospitable gorge of the Colorado River by rumors, so rarely heard in those dispiriting days, of work.

# 10

# Ragtown

**D**epression winter, 1931. The last hope for a brief downturn was draining away. From the corridors of the Hoover White House to the boardrooms of Wall Street, from crippled Midwestern farms to the shuttered mining camps of the West, the realization dawned that the nation faced not a passing lull in the economic cycle, but elemental disaster. Before the end of 1930, four million persons had become unemployed. Come 1933 the figure would more than triple.

By late spring the nation's agony would be in full cry. The banking sector, the financial spine of the economy, was in tatters. Its collapse had begun to accelerate at a sickening rate in late 1930. Six hundred banks failed in November and December alone—as many as in the ten months before. The toll included the biggest failure of all, the Bank of the United States; the fortunes of its 450,000 depositors, mostly Jewish small merchants, were vaporized while J. P. Morgan and the rest of gentile Wall Street coolly rebuffed entreaties by the Federal Reserve Bank for a rescue plan. Their rejection stank of anti-Semitism. It was surely ill-advised. "You are making the most colossal mistake in the banking history of New York," the state banking commissioner warned them.

His outlook was too narrow. The failure of the Bank of the United States rattled more than New York banking; it destroyed trust in the financial system from the lowliest penny depositors to the most eminent Wall Street grandees. The idea that the nation's economic leadership was unable or unwilling to keep the bank from slipping beneath the waves dealt a "serious shock . . . to confidence not only in commercial banks but also in the Federal Reserve System," the monetary historians Milton Friedman and Anna Jacobson Schwartz later observed. The loss of faith in the nation's institutions and in its very future spread fast.

Of those drawn to Black Canyon during those forlorn months, only a few laborers possessed prearranged jobs or much ready money. They were the lucky ones, who could afford to put themselves up in rooming houses in Las Vegas, twenty-eight miles from the river, where government bureaucrats also found their lodging. For the rest there were no options but to pitch camp alongside the others who in their desperation had answered the same siren call.

The largest camp occupied Hemenway Wash, a fan-shaped alluvial incline at a bend of the Colorado just where it entered Black Canyon. As the wash filled up with refugees, Walker Young placed it under the jurisdiction of Claude Williams, a government ranger in his late twenties. Young had earlier employed Williams as the boss of a fifty-man squad evicting bootleggers from nearby canyons and caves, where they had set up stills in anticipation of a surge of custom from thirsty laborers. Now he hoped that the ranger's authoritative yet polite manner would keep a burgeoning community of querulous job seekers pacified—"he was a rather cocky individual," Young recalled, but "well-dressed, neat, very courteous to everyone, an easy man to talk with."

By appointing Williams, Young also hoped to appease his increasingly edgy superiors. Reclamation commissioner Elwood Mead advocated simply running the squatters off, lest Hemenway Wash become an unhygienic hive of vagrancy and crime. Young had been fighting this narrow-minded policy since February, when he warned Mead that it would inflict needless pain on the ejected families, many of them headed by ex-servicemen and union members, and blacken the bureau's image as a benevolent source of employment in a time of want. Having sent Williams to the camp one day to check on the residents' condition, Young was able to reassure his superiors that "they all seem to be a fairly good class of people."

> Certainly, at least, they could not be classed as undesirable. . . . None of the campers there on that day had the appearance of being entirely destitute, and all seemed to be clean and comfortably dressed. Several of the families had children, and all of the children looked clean and healthy. The heads of the families now there are evidently in good faith looking for work. . . . While those who are at present camping upon withdrawn land [that is, land the government had closed to visitors and industry] are doing so without permission they are doing no particular harm and bothering no one.

Young reminded Mead that once work got underway, the construction contractors might well need to tap this handy supply of labor. But his main goal was to persuade his boss to consider "the human side, and also the general effect such policy might have with the public at large." Mead briefly toyed with issuing squatting permits limited to seven days but soon relented, even ratifying Young's request to install four latrines, two for women and two for men, at the site.

Yet Mead's concerns were not unjustified. The first time Young sent Claude Williams to investigate, there were twenty-five families in residence, or fewer than a hundred persons. Within a few weeks there were 1,500. A population that size required at least a modicum of policing.

Claude Williams presided over his "empire of squatters" from a big framed tent with a shaded veranda nestled against the cliffside, the words *U.S. Marshal* spelled out in whitewashed stones in the front yard. At the outset he attempted to impose a sort of order on the site, which he christened Williamsville, by arranging the campsites in rows to simulate the street grid of a suburban hamlet; his wife, Dorothy, even contributed a weekly column to the *Las Vegas Review-Journal* optimistically entitled "Williamsville Town Topics." But he could not prevent the settlement from acquiring the same bedraggled appearance as the Hoovervilles springing up all over the country to contain the Depression's poor and dispossessed. Nor could he keep the residents from giving it a name much more suggestive of the conditions in which they subsisted. They called it Ragtown.

"That's what it looked like," recalled Erma Godbey. "It looked like anyplace that is just built out of pasteboard cartons or anything else. Everybody had come in just a car with no furniture or anything."

The Godbeys were quintessential Ragtown squatters. Tom Godbey had been fired from a gold mine in Oatman, Arizona, for mouthing off about a cut in the $5.50 daily wage the workers received to slave away in a sweltering mine while scalding water dripped down their backs, raising welts and boils. His outburst ran afoul of a state law punishing "criminal syndicalism." He had spoken his mind at noon and was out of a job before sunset.

There was no going back to Silverton, Colorado, their hometown, where the mines had all closed. The only option was to move forward. With the Boulder Canyon Project opening a mere hundred miles up the river, Erma enlisted her parents to drive them north from Oatman in their aging seven-passenger Dodge Brothers touring car: Erma, Tom, and their four children, the youngest only five months old.

Everything they owned was roped to the car's fabric roof—a mattress, two cribs, two baby mattresses, their clothes, and a bucketful of cooking utensils. The route led them over unpaved roads through a swirl of grit and dust in merciless heat. Not a leaf of greenery nor scarcely any sign of human habitation could be seen from horizon to horizon, until they reached Railroad Pass, a notch in the salmon-tinted crags overlooking Black Canyon. The Nevada legislature had legalized gambling in March and a casino was already rising in the pass, just beyond the boundary of the government reservation staked out around the dam site. On the far side of the pass was a broad, bare plain dotted with mesquite and dwarf cactus and scores of canvas tents. These were reserved for the workingmen, the Godbeys were told. No job? "Then you'll have to go down to the river bottom."

The landscape at Hemenway Wash looked like the last way station to the end of the world. On a large rock overlooking the rutted trail someone had painted the words "HELL HOLE." Erma's mother, casting a tearful look around at the tatters and rags that passed for housing, became consumed by a vision of her daughter sucked into the vortex of economic catastrophe.

"Well, I'll never see you again, I'll never see you again," she moaned in despair.

Erma, shaken, reminded her mother of the hardships she had prevailed over in her own time. Hadn't she regaled her family with tales of driving cattle from Texas to Colorado on horseback when she was eleven years old? "I said, 'Oh, Mom, we're tough. Remember, we're from pioneer stock, we'll last,'" Erma recalled. "But she cried, and she left us."

Yet there were signs of human resourcefulness in the face of abject destitution permeating Ragtown. No debris that could be reconfigured into a patch of shelter went to waste. Some people had made domiciles out of the cars that had expended their last breaths carrying them to the river. "Packing boxes were mesmerized into lumber, cardboard cartons made beautiful walls," a witness recalled. "Tarred roofing paper was used as a luxury, flattened gasoline tins were a sign of 20th century extravagance, and burlap served a dozen purposes from doors and window curtains to walls and tablecloths."

Erma Godbey lost no time accommodating herself to the imperatives of survival. The first was to repel the heat. From a distance, the gorge might have seemed like a cool haven in the desert bisected by the glistening silver ribbon of the Colorado; but the walls of Black Canyon concentrated the heat like the lining of a furnace and held it until well after dusk, so that in the summer the thermometer read 120 degrees from nine in the morning to nine at night. To make a tiny bit of shade, Erma sacrificed a treasured set of woolen bed blankets that had cost her $32 a pair (eight days of Tom's wages), rigging them to a clothesline with safety pins. The adults swaddled themselves in wet sheets at night so they could sleep and draped wet sheets over the baby's crib to cool the oppressive air. Even so, the child would become dehydrated overnight and drink prodigious volumes of water in the morning—from a cup, to Erma's amazement.

After a week of living in the open they acquired a proper tent. The seller was the widow of a mucker, whose lowly job had consisted of cleaning out the debris from the dynamite blasts driving tunnels into the canyon wall.

This man was so anxious to get in to work to earn his wages [Erma recalled], that he went in a little ahead of the other men, and the blast hadn't finished going off. Just as he put his shovel down to muck out, a delayed blast went off and the handle of his shovel disemboweled him. His wife, the only thing she could do was to have the body sent back home to her relatives, what was left of it. Then she'd just have to move on. So we bought her tent . . . I think we paid something like six bucks. It was a very fine tent.

Owning a tent jumped the Godbeys up in Ragtown's social scale, ranked below only the tiny elite whose tents were furnished with plank floors. Most other residents existed under makeshift lean-tos or under the stars.

Still, the range of class in Ragtown was narrow. Conditions at the riverbank were a shared experience. The children learned not to walk barefoot on the sand and to shake out their clothing in the morning to roust scorpions, which skittered across the tamped-down ground like mice. A dog barking at the shadows under a floorboard likely as not had run a Gila monster to ground.

Meanwhile the heat inflicted sunstroke and sunburn as deadly as the vermin-borne diseases that afflicted impoverished communities in other places and times. There was no electricity and no ice. Butter could not be kept firm, so it was sold in glass jars; all other provisioning was done as canned goods, for nothing else could be kept fresh for more than a few hours.

The leading purveyor of food and supplies was the ubiquitous Murl Emery, who expanded a boathouse he had erected at Hemenway Wash into a proper general store, complete with a soda pop shack. Emery had been surprised and appalled by the sudden influx of pauperized families to his outpost on the riverbank. "They'd come with their kids," he recalled.

They came with everything on their backs. And their cars had broke down before they got here, and they walked. No one helped them. I was the only person they had access to. The government would have nothing to do with them. So we began to feed these people. All of a sudden this lousy store came to the point that we had two trucks on the road hauling supplies.

The boom in his business soon outpaced his ability to manage inventory. Even in normal times he kept an irregular set of books, and these were not normal times. The goods arrived by truck days ahead of the invoices, and Emery soon gave up matching the prices at which he sold with those he paid. Instead he instituted an honor system, charging his customers whatever they said they had paid at home and bestowing liberal credit. By some mysterious functioning of human nature, the arrangement worked. "I wound up with two checks I never collected," he recalled. "I'm satisfied that they were two men who were lost and not accounted for."

The community that bore the brunt of the population explosion was Las Vegas. A railroad depot of five thousand souls in 1930, the city saw its population nearly quadruple in the first months of 1931, the newcomers almost all unemployed job seekers. Every municipal service was strained beyond the breaking point, from the school system, which comprised a single grammar school and high school, to the police department, which had fewer than twenty men in uniform. Everyone entering town for the first time was shocked and moved by the sight of men massed in quest of work. Thomas Cave Wilson, a twenty-four-year-old newspaper reporter with a job offer from Pop Squires at the *Age*, arrived from Reno late one afternoon in a nine-passenger jitney. As they cruised down Fremont Street, he tapped the driver on the shoulder.

"Is there going to be a parade or something?"

"Why do you ask?" the driver replied.

"Well, all these crowds," Wilson said. "The streets are just black with people standing on the sidewalk."

"Those are men waiting for jobs on the dam."

The city's release valve for the rising tide of vagrancy and petty crime was the back room of its tiny police station. Fifteen feet by forty, the room's only concession to sanitation was its tilted concrete floor, which slanted down into a cesspool and was hosed down every two or three days. The room could comfortably hold no more than twenty-five men, which did not

stop the authorities from filling it with as many as 150 on a rowdy night—
"stacked up like cordwood," recalled John Cahlan of the *Review-Journal*,
who moonlighted as a judge. "It was called the Blue Room, and anybody
who was incarcerated more than a day or two never wanted to see it again."

The great migration brought other consequences less amenable to such
crude justice. Pop Squires, pondering the Dickensian state of children hunkered down with their families in the streets and alleys of the city, became
tormented by the thought that the dam project he had championed might
turn out to be something of a curse. On February 10, following a nocturnal
tour of his overwhelmed city, he set down his findings in a front-page editorial in the *Age*, right next to a lead article trumpeting a huge rally on the
New York Stock Exchange. (It was the start of a false spring for the stock
market, which would presently resume its historic slide.)

### A PITIFUL AND PATHETIC SIGHT.

While the county, assisted by the Salvation Army, are feeding hundreds
of big, strong, able-bodied men, little children are actually and without any
reservation STARVING TO DEATH. . . . Here we heard a story of hunger,
cold, and poverty. There we heard a mother tell us that the first food they
had had in two days was purchased with a dollar given her that afternoon
by one of our city police officers. . . . Our next stop brought us in front of a
one-room shack. There, seated on a box, wrapped in an old blanket, sat a
young woman, the mother of three small children. There was no light in the
place, no stove—just a bare small room, just large enough for the small bed.
A little curly headed girl woke up at the sound of voices, she must have been
about three, she wanted something to eat.

Squires demanded that aid be distributed to women and children first,
ahead of the "big, husky men" he seemed to think had been shouldering
their way to the front of the bread lines. But the truth was that the local
Salvation Army was hard pressed to serve even a fraction of the hungry, no
matter their age or sex. Tom Wilson, who had been so shocked by his first
glimpse of the unemployed, grew more dismayed to realize that his new
hometown had never acquired the knowledge or the inclination to respond

to need on such a scale. "Everybody was starving," he recalled. "There was no Red Cross, there was no charity, no nothin'."

Having witnessed not a few job-seeking males collapse on the street from hunger, Wilson enlisted friends to make the rounds of downtown shops, scrounging day-old bread from the bakeries, wilted vegetables from the farmers' market, and odds and ends from the grocers. Then he hired two short-order cooks from a Fremont Street greasy spoon to turn it all into soup. They fed 1,500 men every morning for two weeks.

> They'd line up before daybreak in an alley that was parallel to Fremont Street, and they'd police themselves. They'd form a committee, and somebody'd wash the dishes and pans, and somebody'd hand out food. You had to be there about five, and the guys would already be lined up, two or three blocks or more long. They'd all get something to eat—pretty simple, whatever it was, but at least it kept them alive. And then every day we'd run a page one editorial on "Where's the Red Cross?" After ten days or so of this, we got it hot enough so the Red Cross, nationally, sent people in. They organized and set up a soup kitchen. Our deal was over with. But nobody gave a damn about anybody. It was a real, rough, tough little town then.

Like Young, Squires, and Wilson, Frank Crowe was unable to evade the reality of the economic climate. Wherever he set foot in town he was enveloped in a cloud of "panic-stricken" men badgering him with "hoarse queries": "When you gonna get going, chief? How about a job? Sorry to bother you, mister, but I'm pretty hard up." With his six-foot-two frame and signature Stetson, he was an easy target for importuning, but in the first weeks after his arrival in Las Vegas there was little he could do for job seekers. The Six Companies board had dispatched him to Nevada with only $50,000 to start construction of two temporary work camps near the river's edge. The money would cover six weeks' pay for a workforce of about three hundred men who were initially engaged building a half-dozen wooden structures, perched uneasily on a steep hillside overlooking the river, as dormitories for themselves.

Crowe was vexed by more than the logistics of launching the project.

He was also having difficulties with his Six Companies bosses. The partners normally got along well with each other, sharing as they did the life experience of "ordinary American boys" forged into men by hard work, risk taking, and luck. The Wattis brothers had grown up on a dismal family farm, Kahn pocketed his first pennies as a Detroit newsboy, Shea had started looking after his eight orphaned siblings at the age of thirteen, and Morrison, Bechtel, and Kaiser had each left home as youths to find their fortune.

The similarities ended there. Crowe, whose blessing and curse it was to work with them in close quarters for a decade, never had any trouble telling them apart.

> Kaiser and Morrison always thought of a job in terms of draglines and steam shovels. Kahn figured in terms of money and an organization chart. Charlie Shea always thought in terms of men. Charlie Shea hated to write letters. But Morrison, on the other hand, thought nothing of dictating a hundred letters in a morning. Morrison never drank, never smoked, never gambled; he was a puritan. Charlie Shea didn't drink either, but he was crazy about gambling.

Such a group might well have disintegrated from the collision of egos, and indeed some of their closest advisors braced themselves for a fracture: "Isn't it wonderful how the boys have stuck together?" Felix Kahn remarked one day to Guy Stevick, Leland Cutler's astute senior partner. "Yes, it's wonderful," Stevick replied, "but how will it be when you start losing money?"

As it happened, the profits kept rolling in, and the board coalesced into a handful of personal alliances—Morrison and the Wattises; Bechtel and Kaiser; and, most improbably, Shea and Kahn. These sons of a plumber and a rabbi indulged their shared passion for games of chance during five-hour car trips across the desert, Crowe at the wheel, by shooting craps on the floor of their Lincoln coach. One time they enticed Dad into another game: Crowe was driving them down Montgomery Street in San Francisco when Kahn spotted Bechtel on the sidewalk. "Drive over!" he ordered. From the curb he shouted, "Dad, I'm matching you a double eagle." (According to the rules of coin matching, the challenger wins if both coins come up heads or tails, and loses if they do not match.) "Dad didn't even say good morning," Crowe said. "He just gave Felix a quick disapproving look, dug into his vest pocket for a coin, and slapped it on the car window. He took his hand off and said to Felix 'you lose' and walked off without another word."

Shea and Kahn also shared a preference for living near the dam site rather than the metropolis, though for different reasons. Shea was escaping a family situation in Portland he found unutterably drab, and in any case relished rubbing shoulders with the workmen. Kahn's sojourn may have had a more devious purpose. MacDonald & Kahn had come under investigation for bribing a Los Angeles city official to secure a million-dollar settlement in a municipal construction dispute. Investigators discovered that $80,000 had been withdrawn from the firm's bank account on the same day that the official, Sidney T. Graves, deposited a nearly identical sum in cash at his own bank. To make the case, the investigators demanded access to MacDonald & Kahn's books, which mysteriously disappeared from the firm's San Francisco office. It was lost on nobody that as long as they were cached in another state—Nevada, perhaps—they were out of reach of California authorities. In the event, the only person ever indicted and punished for the crime was the hapless Graves, who was sentenced to three years in San Quentin.

Crowe soon discovered that the main drawback of working for a consortium of strong-willed self-made men was that the management was all chiefs, and they did not speak with anything like a single voice. Indeed, for a time the one irresolvable management issue at Big Six headquarters—their "first hot argument," one unidentified partner told a writer from *Fortune*— was how to organize the project. "Kaiser thought the job should be run like an army, with a general in supreme charge. That idea got nowhere because no one, least of all Henry himself, wanted to be a private."

The upshot was that with the exception of the ailing Will Wattis the partners each spent long sojourns at the site, serially volunteering to Crowe their opinions—or in their view, directives—about how to run the job. Accustomed to working in the wilderness, far from the reach of interfering superiors, Crowe discovered himself beset, in what should have been one of the remotest spots on earth, by a half-dozen high-powered busybodies at cross-purposes with one another.

After three months of such kibitzing, he was at his wits' end. Asked one day by Guy Stevick how he could best help the job proceed, Crowe growled, "Have your directors' meetings in San Francisco, not on the job."

Fortunately, he had an ally on the board: Charlie Shea, who had reserved for himself the role of onsite supervisor and resented the intrusions of his colleagues. Shea tactfully persuaded the others to consign the direct supervision of Crowe to a committee of three: himself; Kahn, whom he could trust to stay in the background; and Henry Kaiser, who was granted the title of committee chairman, but whom Shea expected to remain safely at his lobbying post in Washington for the duration of construction.

Through this arrangement Shea also effectively emasculated another meddler—Hank Lawler, the Utah Construction chief engineer who was functioning as the Wattis brothers' eyes and ears. Lawler, a hidebound and unimaginative engineer of the old school, had interposed himself between the field office and the board so that every message passing from one to the other crossed his desk. By leaving Lawler's name off the executive committee, Shea cemented his own position as project supervisor and Crowe's as field general. Kahn was placed in charge of budgeting as well as feeding and housing the workers. Steve Bechtel, Dad's second son, was handed responsibility for purchasing, a post in which he soon became overrun with armies of "peddlers," but in which he ably oversaw nearly $10 million in material orders over the next five years. The rest of the board was expected to keep away, except for rare ceremonial visits during which they would be sequestered in a guesthouse built for the purpose in Boulder City. From then on, the work proceeded unmolested.

On March 16, 1931, a team of government surveyors assembled by a granite outcropping at the crown of Hemenway Wash and drove a whitewashed stake into the ground. Forever after, the citizens of Boulder City would celebrate that day as the town's anniversary.

# Ragtown

Elwood Mead had spoken well of this site's suitability to house the dam workers and their families. "Here there is fertile soil; here winds have an unimpeded sweep from every direction; here there is also an inspiring view of deserts and lonesome gorges and lofty mountains. The view from Boulder City will be so inspiring and wonderful as to be worth traveling around the world to see."

This was Mead, the reclamation visionary, at his most fanciful. In truth, a less prepossessing site could scarcely have been imagined. The sandy flatland was home to scrub brush and the lowest orders of wildlife: scorpions, centipedes, and black widow spiders jolted from their nests by the bustle and scrape of the survey party. The wind that Mead so ardently praised varied from wan breezes flitting over the ground to arid gusts bearing cinders that stung like needles—though, to be fair, it did generally succeed in lowering the temperature a few degrees below that of stifling Las Vegas, the nearest human settlement.

To the government planners, the site's chief virtue was not its ostensibly salubrious climate, but the barren territory separating it like a cordon sanitaire from that unruly city twenty-eight miles to the northwest. From Ray Lyman Wilbur to Walker Young, the overseers of Hoover Dam shared a determination to provide a pristine and sober cloister for the workers. The dam specifications required the contractors to house 80 percent of their employees in a government-controlled municipality where it was intended that Prohibition, among other moral constraints, would be strictly enforced. Wilbur and Mead took the mandate so seriously that they earmarked nearly $2 million in government funds to build the workers a literal version of the Pilgrim leader John Winthrop's symbolic "city upon a hill."

As the spring of 1931 turned to summer, the townsite taking shape at the crown of the wash looked to the residents occupying its base in Ragtown like a mirage. In Boulder City there would be cozy little bungalows, graded streets, parks, stores, and churches. In Ragtown, there was heat and squalor to addle the mind. One day in June, as the thermometer hit 130 degrees, Claude Williams was summoned to the riverfront to rescue an undeserving soul from his outraged neighbors. He was J. R. Smeal, who had punished his two young sons for a domestic infraction by staking them out naked on the scalding gravel. The neighbors had hauled Smeal from his automobile and beaten him to within an inch of his life, and they were fixing to finish the job with a lynching when Williams interrupted the grim party. He sent Smeal off in his car with orders never to return and handed the boys over to child welfare authorities in Las Vegas.

The incident exemplified the dislocated psychology of Ragtown's residents, marooned under a copper-colored sun in a no-man's-land where illness and death were all too familiar acquaintances. Erma Godbey felt herself losing her grip on reality. A combination of sunburn, windburn, campfire burn, and, for all she knew, a disease she had picked up from the river had turned her face into a seared and desiccated mask. Terrified that she might infect the children, she had been self-medicating with a facial bath of pure Listerine, which was then marketed as a topical disinfectant.

Finally, she prevailed on her husband to drive her into Las Vegas to see a doctor. This involved first setting their car in the river for three days to swell its weather-beaten wooden spokes, lest the wheels shake themselves into matchsticks on the gullied road. They stopped at the first doctor's shingle they encountered and presented themselves to an appalled physician.

"My God, woman, you've got the worst case of desert sunburn I've ever seen in my life," he exclaimed, shuddering with dismay when she described her homegrown treatment. "What you've been doing is just cooking your face over and over again." He made her swear off the Listerine, then sent her off with a prescription for a soothing ointment.

Back at Ragtown, things were going from bad to worse. Four women died on a single day, the twenty-sixth of July. They ranged in age from sixty to sixteen, as though the death angel of the wash was determined to show off his impartiality. One victim, a twenty-eight-year-old bride from New York, lived just three tents down from the Godbeys.

> She was sick. [Her husband] had done the best he could. He left her with a thermos bottle with ice. . . . She just got to feeling terribly bad, so she tied a note on her dog's collar, and told him to go get the ranger. . . . In the note she asked Mr. Williams to come and get her and take her to the river so she

could get in the water to get cooled off. By the time Mr. Williams got to her she was just lying across a folding cot and she was dead.

Claude Williams asked Erma to straighten up the corpse in the name of modesty and had the husband retrieved from the worksite. The husband arrived about an hour later, so befogged with grief that he attempted to revive his wife with artificial respiration. Then, staring at the women hovering in attendance, he asked, "Anybody going to Alaska? Anybody want to buy a fur coat?"

At first Erma thought he had lost his mind in the sun. Then she realized that he was just trying to raise enough money to bury his poor wife. Back in her tent, Erma confronted her husband, who had found a job with a highway crew. "We've just absolutely got to get out of here," she said. "I've got to get somewhere I can get the babies to a doctor, and also myself." Three days later they pulled up stakes and moved to a campground outside Las Vegas. Although the tents were pitched so close together that no family could keep its homely secrets from its neighbors, at least there was bubbling fresh water from an artesian well.

As Six Companies launched construction in Black Canyon, the tide of financial catastrophe lapped at the feet of one of the consortium's principals. Marriner Eccles, whose inheritance included several of Utah's leading financial institutions, was facing a run on his banks.

Eccles's bookish youth as a member of an outcast clan had given him an introspective cast of mind, and the worsening crisis had driven him to a spell of anguished soul-searching. "The pit grew deeper and I found myself in it," he would write later. "I saw for the first time that though I had been active in the world of finance and production for seventeen years and knew its techniques, I knew less than nothing about its economic and social effects. . . . Night after night . . . I would return home exhausted by the pretensions of knowledge I was forced to wear in a daytime masquerade."

On a Sunday in June, Eccles received word that the Ogden State Bank, one of Utah's grandest, would fail to open the next day. Ogden State was not an Eccles bank but the harvest would be just as grim as if it were: come Monday morning his own panicky depositors were sure to be clamoring for their money.

An hour before his own Ogden bank opened that day, he delivered precise instructions to his employees. "We can't break this run today," he said. "The best we can do is slow it down." When depositors came to close out their accounts, the tellers were to pay out every cent—but at a snail's pace. Every signature card was to be checked against the records, even for their oldest customers. "Take your time about it. And one other thing: when you pay out, don't use any big bills. Pay out in fives and tens, and count slowly."

These tactics enabled the bank to husband its currency supply until late that afternoon, when a Federal Reserve Bank official arrived from Salt Lake City in an armored car filled with cash. Eccles hauled the man by the collar to a marble countertop and ordered him to address the crowd. "I want to assure you we have brought up a lot of currency," the Fed official said, "and there's a lot more where that came from."

As Eccles hoped, the run exhausted itself that day. But it had greater repercussions. Heretofore a provincial businessman casting nary a shadow on the national scene, Eccles's assertiveness brought national attention to his blunt views about "the failure of financial and political leadership in the world" that had helped bring on what was now commonly referred to as the "Depression," with a capital "D." By 1933 he was advising President Roosevelt on banking policy, and in November 1934, FDR appointed him chairman of the Federal Reserve, which he and many others had condemned for its ineffectual response to the crisis. His first assignment would be to implement historic reforms he had drafted himself to turn the central bank into a genuinely effective guardian of sound banking and of the American economy.

Meanwhile, the crisis continued to bite at home. A collapse in commodity prices produced a comeuppance for the elder Eccles clan, which, in a testament to Marriner's character, brought him more pain than schadenfreude. In 1932, he received a call from his half-brother David, who had lost everything and was appealing for a helping hand. Marriner, then struggling to keep his own holdings from going under, simply did not have the resources.

"I would if I could," he replied mournfully. "But I can't." He later confided in his memoirs, "Living with yourself under the circumstances was a daily ordeal."

As it happened, virtually the only Eccles enterprise that would record a profit for 1932 was Utah Construction, "a welcome relief from the banking atmosphere in which I had been living," he recalled. In Black Canyon that year, Six Companies, of which Utah was the largest partner, would put more than three thousand men to work and record a profit of more than $2 million on a job not even halfway done. Its method of reaching that mark would eventually place it under an embarassing spotlight.

# Rush Job

In contrast to the uncertainties facing the families of laborers who had come to Black Canyon with nothing but the thin hope for backbreaking, underpaid employment, Reclamation staff members had almost unimaginable job security, not to mention the higher pay of government scale.

Yet in those days the lot of a reclamation engineer's family was scarcely the epitome of comfort. Stella Warfield Carmody had learned this from bitter experience. Reassuring as it was to have a husband with a secure job as the clouds of Depression darkened, there was still something spiritually crushing in the life of a nomad. For too many years Stella had been dragged from job site to job site, uprooted from one home after another after a scant few months in place, bidding farewell to friends made in the crucible of shared hardship, not sure if or when they would ever encounter each other again in their random travels. Taking stock one day, she came to the depressing conclusion that she had spent half her life packing up her cherished household goods for shipment and the other half "assembling and mending what [was] left of them."

Then the project to end all projects beckoned. The construction of Hoover Dam was to last five or six years. The Reclamation families were to be housed in tidy bungalows in a neat and trim planned community complete with stores, schools, and churches, not tents in the wilderness or mean apartments isolated far from the worksite. For Reclamation's long-suffering wives, a husband's assignment to Hoover Dam offered the gift of domestic stability and a solid foundation for family life. Even if Boulder City was being thrown together in a place that had never before supported a human population, for the first time a dam project meant home.

The Reclamation women were an intrepid breed and Stella Carmody more intrepid than most. Kentuckian by birth, she had already followed her husband, Dominick, to postings in Montana, Oregon, and Washington when Walker Young personally requested his assignment to Black Canyon in October 1930. Stella arrived dreaming of "the calls from ladies of the various churches and clubs, the invitations to join in things; altogether the usual small-town procedure," only to discover that Boulder City would not be built for another year and her domicile in the meantime was again to be an overpriced apartment, this time in a rustic desert town named Las Vegas. With the survey camp located thirty miles away she would see her husband only once a week, on Sunday. "Sunk in a sea of boredom," she decided one day to take herself on an automobile jaunt across the open gray desert to visit the dam site.

For much of the way the only signs of human existence were surveyor's flags hanging limply on wooden posts along the trail and mounds of rocks marking prospectors' claims. Near the crest of Hemenway Wash, at the future site of Boulder City, a wag had erected a placard reading "City Limits of Los Angeles." Stella noticed that a solitary service station had sprouted in the wasteland "like a big yellow mushroom," as she described the sight in an essay for *New Reclamation Era*, the bureau's monthly newsletter. After passing the cluster of army tents huddled around a flagpole that served as the survey camp, she turned onto a winding trail that led down to the riverbed. There she discovered the Colorado in its decidedly underwhelming late autumn ebb—"a broad and apparently stagnant stream crawling between the sands on the Nevada side and a low bare 'bench' on the Arizona shore." A pack of burros for hire shuffled about next to a weather-beaten curio shop, where Stella examined a desiccated tarantula displayed under glass.

The surveyors had knocked off for the day, but had left signs of their labor all around. There were 150-foot ladders bolted to the cliffside and a cable strung across the gorge to carry the men to the Arizona shore in a suspended wooden skip. Equipment stowed on ledges high in the sheer rock face glinted in the sun. She was struck, as so many had been before her, by the apparent futility of a human assault on "those strange mountains, that oily river, those masses of black rock." Heading home, she felt weighed down by a foreboding of "depression and danger."

Seven months later, in May, she made a second pilgrimage to the river, only to find the landscape entirely transformed. The once desolate trail marked by surveyors' posts was now lined with service stations, food shacks, and lunch stands, and jammed with traffic:

> Large, powerful cars carrying tourists to view the dam site, smaller cars speeding into Las Vegas, old fashioned touring cars filled with camping paraphernalia, Government-owned cars, depot wagons, trucks loaded with everything imaginable from intricate-looking machinery to thriving families with their household goods surrounding them.

The riverfront where she had been overwhelmed by a vision of man's puniness had since morphed into Ragtown. The curio shop seemed to have been elbowed out of existence by tents and shacks occupied by teeming humanity—Stella called them "prisoners of hope" (rather condescendingly), living "in cars, in dog tents, in portable houses, and even camping frankly out in the open, their beds neatly made and their week's wash swinging on a line."

Further along were the precariously anchored bunkhouses, mess tents, and machine shops of what was now known as River Camp. The job site itself was distinguished by a blur of constant motion: "Men climbing perpendicular ladders five or six hundred feet to the top; men clustered about the mouths of embryo tunnels; men swinging across the turgid stream in little cars attached to strong cables; men and machinery going into places where even a mountain goat would hesitate to climb."

Suddenly her ears were assaulted by a shrill whistle seeming to emanate from a hollow in the mountain on the Arizona side, followed by "a thud like distant thunder," a flash of light, and a blood-chilling roar as "masses of rock and sand shot out as if from a cannon's mouth . . . rolling, pitching, tearing, beating down everything in their path." The blasts kept coming until the mountains themselves seemed to ring with the reverberating cannonades. "Long after the last rock had buried itself in the water I could hear shrieks and cries like the tumult of a battlefield; could feel the canyon shudder . . . and this is only the beginning."

Actually the eruption of activity on the high desert had started months earlier, even before Frank Crowe's arrival as superintendent in late March. Indeed, the bustle could properly be dated back to the afternoon of September 17, 1930, when Secretary Wilbur's driving of the silver spike launched the Union Pacific on the construction of a 22.7-mile branch line from its main track to the future site of Boulder City. Three months later, on December 16, Southern Sierras Power Co., a subsidiary of Southern California Edison, began stringing a 90,000 volt, two-hundred-mile power line from Victorville, California, to Boulder City on a right of way that would eventually carry electricity generated at the river in the opposite direction, back to Los Angeles.

On January 7—three days before the dam specifications were released to the public—Walker Young and John Page opened bids at the Las Vegas courthouse for an eight-mile gravel highway connecting Boulder City to the canyon rim and for a ten-and-a-half-mile railroad spur from Union Pacific's Boulder City terminus to the canyon rim. (The remaining legs of the construction railroad, from the rim to gravel and concrete plants and to the dam site, were part of the main dam contract.)

Thus, by the time Crowe took up his role as general superintendent, the three lifelines of his project—railroad, highway, and power line—were all under construction, and one, the Union Pacific branch, was already nearing completion. The advanced state of preliminary construction encouraged Crowe to get a head start on the first major task at the river, the driving of four immense tunnels to divert the Colorado around the construction zone. The government designers regarded the tunnels as the most important element of the project next to the raising of the concrete dam itself. They called for two on each side of the river, each fifty-six feet in diameter and averaging four thousand feet in length—a feat of solid rock excavation equaled by only one other project on earth, the 4.5-mile Rove Tunnel outside Marseilles, which had opened to canal traffic in 1927. Once holed through, the tunnels were to be lined with concrete three feet thick, creating smooth fifty-foot bores. After the river had been returned to its natural bed, the tunnels would become permanent adjuncts to the dam: the two outer diversions, Nos. 1 (on the Nevada side) and 4 (on the Arizona side), would be converted into outlets for the two reservoir spillways, while portions of Tunnels Nos. 2 and 3 would be relined with steel plate to feed water from intake towers in the reservoir to the powerhouse's seventeen gargantuan turbines.

The contract required Six Companies to complete the excavation and concrete lining by October 1, 1933. Based on existing construction experience, this was an extremely ambitious two-and-a-half-year time frame, with the $3,000-per-day penalty for missing the deadline looming on the horizon. The Rove Tunnel had taken fifteen years to build, a disconcerting standard even if one accounted for its larger dimensions—one-third wider than the Colorado diversions and half again as long as all four combined—and for advances in excavation technology in the years since its inception. Crowe faced a multitude of uncertainties, including the prospect of encountering faults, hot springs, or other obstacles underground, not to mention the unsolved riddle of how to efficiently drill and blast a cylindrical bore more than five stories high out of solid rock.

Compounding the headache was the worksite's limited access. Only the Union Pacific railroad job was moving along on schedule. Lewis Construction of Los Angeles, which had won the $455,000 contract to build the government railroad, had underestimated the difficulty of traversing a route that dropped a dizzying 1,100 feet over slightly more than ten miles. Five tunnels had to be bored through the rock on a single one-mile stretch. The tunnel site crossed a section of the canyon so steep that the only way to get fuel and supplies to the blasting crews was by burro. Lewis would need to strain every resource it had to meet its contractual deadline of late September.

Even worse travails confronted the contractor on the thoroughfare most important to Crowe at this stage of work—the highway to carry trucks and other heavy equipment from Boulder City to the site. High on the Nevada cliffs, Robert G. LeTourneau, perhaps the most inventive and resourceful road builder in the country, was stymied. The obstacle in LeTourneau's way was an outcropping of andesite lava that had thus far resisted all his efforts to demolish it. A man whose Christian faith was a byword in the construction business, R.G. was tormented by the thought that his difficulties might be a judgment from God. A year earlier he had forsworn his usual annual gift to charity, diverting the money to build a new factory and pledging to the Lord a redoubled share of the profits to come in its stead. "God does not do business that way," he reflected later. "Start to hedge, and He knows you as a man of little faith. He sure spotted my false reasoning in a hurry."

The volcanic breccia in his way was as hard and unforgiving as steel, and it was chewing his men's drill bits into filings. Not even the technique known as "springing a pocket" had worked: normally you drilled a hole fifteen feet deep, rammed a stick of dynamite into it, and blew out a cavity that in turn could be packed with enough explosive to pulverize the obstruction. In this case the pilot blasts barely left scorch marks.

Eventually, LeTourneau solved the problem by hollowing out a thin layer of soft rock underlying the surface tier of lava.

> Even with power drills it was a long, arduous job through a layer that at times was not more than three feet thick [he recounted]. . . . The noise in the tunnel was deafening, the dust-filled air practically unbreathable, and in some places the rock drilled out ahead had to be scooped up by hand, passed under the stomach, and kicked back with the feet to men with buckets who, in turn, had to squirm back to the face of the cliff to dump their loads.

Finally a void was created big enough to accept a carload of dynamite. LeTourneau watched tensely as the fuse was lit. "Came the zero hour. A rock bubble bulged out of the ground, and then the bubble burst. The whole sky was flame, smoke, and rock. We were back in business again."

The job almost bankrupted LeTourneau, who had to shut down work-sites all over the West Coast to free crews and equipment to help finish the roadway. He would never reveal how much he lost on the job, beyond calling the sum "too horrible to contemplate." In his memoirs, however, he did disclose that the job left him more than $50,000 in debt, making him quite likely the only contractor to lose money on Hoover Dam.

In one respect, LeTourneau's struggle with the unyielding rock was good news for Crowe, who concluded from his subcontractor's travails that the regional geology was so sound his diversion tunnels would need minimal timber bracing underground. On the other hand, it was also plain that there could be no skimping on dynamite. Crowe's blasting scheme would call for filling 174 drill holes with dynamite for every advance of eight to ten feet through the rock.

LeTourneau's delay cost Crowe weeks of progress. Until equipment could be driven by road down to the riverbank, men and machines had to be floated to the location by barges secured to cables played out from the shoreline of Hemenway Wash two miles upstream. Their only suitable land-fall was a boulder-strewn shelf on the Arizona bank barely wide enough to accommodate two diesel compressors and blacksmith equipment for sharpening the drilling steels. Consequently, not until May 12 could the first blasting begin, starting on the Arizona side—most likely the explosions Mrs. Carmody heard on her second visit to the site. A suspension footbridge was soon thrown across the river so that crews debarking from the barges on the eastern bank could cross the river to commence drilling into the Nevada cliffs.

Crowe started the tunnels by driving adits, shafts eight by ten feet in cross-section, horizontally from the cliffsides to intersect with the planned routes of the main tunnels. This meant penetrating as far as 850 feet on the Arizona side and 630 feet on the Nevada side. Deep inside the rock, the adits were to branch into two perpendicular "pioneer" tunnels twelve feet by twelve feet leading off in either direction along the paths of the main diversion tunnels. The pioneers served several purposes: they established the headings of the main tunnels so that once crews began excavating from opposite portals toward each other they would be sure to meet in the middle; they allowed for cross-ventilation in the main cut; and they provided the tunneling crews with useful clues to the geological conditions ahead. Once the pioneer shafts were holed through, they would be widened out and become the crowns of the main tunnels. By that point, Crowe hoped, his handpicked cadre of foremen and field engineers would have solved the riddle of how to gouge a fifty-six-foot hole out of solid rock.

Around the time that the blasting began, two men who would be instrumental in turning the dam into an icon of 1930s art deco style appeared on the scene.

The first was the architect Gordon B. Kaufmann. British-born and German-trained, the forty-two-year-old Kaufmann had made his reputation during the 1920s with designs for hotels and mansions across Southern California. In late 1930 (the exact date is not recorded) he received a commission to oversee the architectural presentation of Hoover Dam. The appointment seemed somewhat superfluous at the time, as Reclamation designers had already produced an architectural plan, if a busy and conventional one. In retrospect, it seems likely that Kaufmann was recruited by Harry Chandler, who was now taking a personal interest in the Colorado River project. As the leading voice of conservative Republicanism on the West Coast, Chandler wielded substantial influence inside the Hoover White House. He had just awarded Kaufmann a handsome commission to design a new headquarters for his newspaper in downtown Los Angeles—one whose majestic concrete lines would be seen to echo those of the dam when the two structures were dedicated within weeks of each other in 1935. For Chandler, there could scarcely be a better way to impose his personal stamp on his pet project in the desert than to place his pet architect in charge.

Whatever its genesis, the choice of Kaufmann as the architect of Hoover Dam was a fortuitous one. Kaufmann was already abandoning the Spanish colonial style cherished by his society patrons in favor of a stripped-down art deco aesthetic inspired by such avant-garde architects as Raymond Hood and the Vienna-born Richard Neutra, whom Kaufmann had briefly employed. It would be precisely the right approach to bring the dam's monumental scale and machine-age gracefulness into high relief.

Early in 1931, Kaufmann began hacking away at Reclamation's architectural scheme, which was burdened with such neoclassical gingerbread as pediments, elaborate balustrades on the dam crest, and columns capped with bronze eagles. The facade of the powerhouse at the dam's toe was cross-hatched with dozens of small square windows reminiscent of the front of a New England textile factory. Altogether the dam gave the impression of a powerful structure concealed behind clutter. This was the antithesis of the principle of simplicity newly influential in contemporary architecture, and it offended Kaufmann's conviction that the dam's architecture should be "a complementary treatment rather than a dominant phase of the whole design."

Kaufmann's revised blueprint pared away all excess ornamentation. He distilled the powerhouse's busy factory-style fenestration into five narrow windowed columns manifesting solidity and strength. At the crest, he cut back the observation balconies and molded them to the downstream face, creating a dramatic interplay of surface and shadow, especially under the nighttime lighting he mandated. The only pure ornamentation he permitted was a pair of concrete panels by the Norwegian-born Chicago sculptor Oskar J. W. Hansen, to be placed over the doors to the passenger elevators at the crest of the dam, one portraying "Irrigation, Navigation, Power Development, Flood Control and Water Supply" (a roll of the dam's purposes dating back to Arthur Powell Davis), the other comprising the seals of the seven basin states.

Kaufmann explained that his changes would emphasize the dam's character as "pure engineering," underscoring its "superlative dimensions, its awe-inspiring site and the comprehension of its useful purposes." He succeeded brilliantly. In another architect's hands, the quest for simplification might have produced a repellent severity. For all that Hoover Dam stands as a peerless feat of utilitarian engineering carried out by a cast of thousands, credit for its unique projection of beauty, grace, and power belongs to Gordon Kaufmann alone.

The second important new recruit to the Reclamation team in early 1931 was a lantern-jawed thirty-two-year-old draftsman, musician, and self-taught photographer from Kansas City named Bernard Dean Glaha.

Ben Glaha had first joined Reclamation in 1925 as a lowly timekeeper on a Wyoming survey team. Within a few years he came to Walker Young's attention as a cartographer of exceptional skill—"more ... an artist than the average," as Young reported to Mead late in 1931. Young was eager to document on film the construction of his grandest project, one that he knew would bring glory to the name of Reclamation. Glaha seemed to have the proper qualifications for the task—familiarity with photographic equipment, an artistic eye, and a modicum of engineering knowledge. Initially unsure that the photography job could "consume the entire time of one man," Young simply appended the new assignment to Glaha's regular draftsman's duties. By the end of 1932, however, Glaha was shooting full-time, compiling a record of men employed on a monumental task that would equal the best work of recognized documentarians like Lewis Hine and inspire eminent contemporaries like Ansel Adams and Margaret Bourke-White (whom he would personally escort around the dam site in March 1935).

That said, Glaha's sojourn at the dam site began inauspiciously. He wilted in the stifling heat of the canyon, possibly because he had been transferred directly from the bureau's Owyhee Dam project in southwest Idaho, where the outstanding meteorological enemy was not summer but the frigid and snowbound winter. A monster heat wave in early July so sapped Glaha's energy that John Page, finding him "scarcely able to work," packed him off for a month to the Sierra resort of Mount Charleston fifty miles away.

He seems to have returned invigorated. As his photographic responsibilities moved to the forefront, Glaha dispelled any impression of his physical frailty by taking, literally, to the skies. No "coddled artist-photographer," he shot pictures from Crowe's cableways seven hundred feet in the air and from bosun's chairs hanging from ropes two hundred feet below the canyon's rim. He built aeries in the cliffs high above the river, the better to capture panoramic views of the advancing work. He shot day and night, in the remorseless summer heat and the biting winds of spring, struggling to protect his equipment from seeping water in the tunnels and his photographic plates from the dust ever-present in the air. He experimented successfully with an innovative smokeless flash powder to illuminate the work inside the gloomy diversion tunnels, where flashbulbs were inadequate and the haze created by ordinary flash powder obscured his images.

Nor was his apparatus designed for traveling light. His workhorse still cameras were a 5" x 7" Speed Graphic (the iconic apparatus carried by period newspapermen) and a 5" x 7" view camera, a large wooden box with a bellows focus. Both were fitted with anastigmat lenses, which eliminated distortion and preserved the perpendicular lines even of off-center images, making them especially well suited for architectural photography. He used large glass plates so the negatives would retain their crystalline sharpness when enlarged in his hand-built darkroom.

Reclamation headquarters in Washington was slow to recognize the virtues of Glaha's work. Mead repeatedly vetoed Young's requisition orders for photographic equipment; on one occasion in 1931 the commissioner, plainly ignorant of photographic technique, rejected a request for a telephoto lens on the grounds that "any enlarging you wish can readily be made in the Washington office." He overruled Young's plan to purchase a movie camera, with which Glaha hoped to record the progress of construction day by day from a permanent platform high above the gorge. Instead he proposed to send a bureau cameraman out from Washington a couple of times a year. "This I feel sure will be sufficient to show . . . the progress being made," he wrote Young.

Glaha countered Mead's stinginess by subordinating his personal safety to the quest for the telling shot, clambering over catwalks with his boxy cameras, tripods, and plates. He and Young eventually won the commissioner over by showering him with photographs of surpassing beauty and drama and promising him even better results with the right equipment. In early 1933 Mead capitulated to Young's argument that the lack of a tele-photo lens had deprived the world of shots of the dam's fabled high scalers, the rope-borne acrobats drilling the canyon walls to prepare them for the dam abutments: "This work is highly spectacular and if properly photo-graphed would make interesting subjects," Young assured his boss. He was correct. The photograph of a crew of seven captured by Glaha's lens on April 10, 1933, framed by the canyon wall among their bundles of cables and ropes, would become one of the project's signature images. Mead soon relented on the purchase of a movie camera, one of which presently was anchored to a steel and concrete platform high above the riverbed, where Glaha would shoot ten feet of film every other day, compressing more than three years of construction into an arresting forty-five-minute motion picture reel.

Glaha eventually produced some four thousand negatives and thirty thousand feet of movie film at the dam site. Aesthetes, critics, and the general public all thrilled to the astonishing variety of this body of work, depicting everything from intricate webs of girders and power lines to solitary laborers outlined in minuscule fragility against their monumental handiwork. Under Ben Glaha's practiced eye, even staged ceremonial portraits achieved a timeless drama, as when the pouring of the millionth cubic yard of concrete in the dam on January 7, 1934, brought Shea, Kahn, Crowe, Young, and Page together to pose, rather precariously, on a timber slat laid over the wet concrete next to a sixteen-ton concrete bucket.

"Compositionally perfect, his work never loses sight of the more important human thing back of the steel and concrete," effused the pioneering photographer and filmmaker Willard Van Dyke in a 1935 critique. "His prints are living documents of the heat, the sweat, the effort, and the pain endured by the workers that the dam may be built."

In 1931 the engineering details of the structure that Kaufmann would clean up on the drawing board and Glaha would memorialize on film were still gestating on Reclamation's drafting tables.

Jack Savage, grappling with the Sibert board's mandate to reduce the maximum stress on the dam from forty tons to thirty, concluded that the only way to do so would be to immensely augment the dam's mass. This would not only increase the project's cost appreciably, he calculated, but would actually compromise its strength, for the enlarged base would span two significant faults in the canyon floor. In the end Savage dodged the issue by tweaking his mathematical formulas to show that the existing specifications would hold the stresses to thirty-four tons. Mead certified those results as sufficient to meet the Sibert board's standard, and the board obligingly concurred, possibly without realizing that Savage had not actually modified his original design one bit to meet their mandate.

But other design issues could not be so easily finessed. The dam's size posed novel questions about the transmission of stresses and strains to the foundation and the canyon walls. More than for any other dam ever built, the engineers had to consider not only the strains the environment would impose on Hoover Dam, but those the dam would impose on its environment. The dam would splay the canyon walls apart while loading underground faults with the weight of millions of cubic feet of concrete, tons of steel, and more than 10 trillion gallons of impounded water, possibly straining them to the point of fracture and, consequently, earthquake.

Conventional metrics of shear, twist, tension, and compression could not easily be applied in Black Canyon because of the dynamic interactions between the dam and the canyon—as the dam deformed the canyon, the tension and compression applied to the structure by the cliffsides would themselves change. These conditions would somehow have to be field-tested to determine whether any threatened to bring the dam to the threshold of failure. In practice, the engineers' concerns focused on two issues: the formulation of the concrete of the dam, and its shape.

The Reclamation Bureau had accumulated two decades of experience in working with concrete, but never at the volume or density required by Hoover Dam. To fill in the blanks, the bureau embarked on a research program of unprecedented scale.

Concrete consists of water, Portland cement (a mixture of mineral oxides, clay, and limestone), and aggregate (sand, gravel, and rock). The proportions of these ingredients are infinitely variable, producing in turn infinite variations in strength, durability, curing time, and resistance to compression or tension (i.e., strength). The goal of concrete engineering is to find exactly the right mixture of fine and coarse aggregate, and the right ratio of aggregate, cement, and water, to produce the desired workability, durability, strength, and appearance.

Existing research from around the world generally pertained to ordinary concrete for ordinary applications. Hoover Dam was no ordinary structure. To take just one aspect of the job, conventional concrete almost never used aggregate larger than one and a half inches in diameter. The designers calculated that to withstand the compressive stresses deep within the concrete mass, the internal concrete would require aggregate as large as nine inches. But no one knew much about the behavior in field conditions of concrete of such novel formulation—one of many riddles of materials science that "have not heretofore been satisfactorily solved," as Mead observed in a classic example of an engineer's understatement. Given Hoover Dam's magnitude and the requirement for "absolute safety," guesswork would not serve.

Between 1931 and 1933 the bureau tested fifteen thousand concrete samples in ninety-four different formulations. This work was farmed out to three universities and two specialized government labs, one of which was equipped with a hydraulic press capable of delivering four million tons of pressure, sufficient to reduce a solid concrete cylinder three feet in diameter and six feet tall to dust. The results of these studies would take up four hefty volumes of the seven-part compilation of technical reports the bureau published in 1938, a hoard of data that advanced the science of concrete manufacture by a quantum leap and would be mined assiduously by dam builders and others in the construction trades for years to come.

While the dam's concrete was developed according to the most up-to-date science, its shape was not. Indeed, for all that Hoover Dam set a new standard for materials science, in engineering terms it was conservative throwback.

Theories of dam design had evolved rapidly in the 1920s. In a groundbreaking paper in 1921, the Swiss engineer Fred Noetzli had expressed contempt for traditional "gravity" dams, so-called because they achieved stability by posing their brute weight against the weight of the water in their reservoirs—in engineering terms, they transferred the load in one direction, down to the foundation. Typically built on a straight line, gravity dams looked and performed like massive ramparts, projecting a comforting impression of bulky strength.

Noetzli calculated that, despite their appearance, the safety margin of gravity dams was much lower than had been previously suspected. Among other flaws, they were prone to seepage, which allowed water permeating their foundations to press up against their bulk, a condition known as "uplift." This reduced the effective weight of gravity dams and left them vulnerable to being pushed over by the weight of water behind them. (Uplift certainly was a factor in the 1928 St. Francis collapse.) As an alternative, Noetzli proposed the arched dam, the curved shape of which would transfer stress not only vertically down to its foundation but horizontally across to its abutments. This, he argued, vastly increased the margin of safety and rendered uplift a negligible, if not irrelevant, factor. Indeed, an arched dam could be much thinner than a gravity dam (and therefore much cheaper) without compromising its reliability.

The Bureau of Reclamation, with a massive program of dam construction on the drawing board, was strongly attracted to the principle of cheaper construction through improved design, and developed steadily more sophisticated theoretical analyses of curved dams during the early 1920s. But mathematical modeling was a poor substitute for field testing, especially when applied to dams that looked too flimsy to stand. In 1925, Reclamation joined with Southern California Edison, another entity with an abiding interest in building hydroelectric dams, to erect a $110,000 experimental arched dam with only one purpose: to be stressed and strained to the point of disintegration while engineers monitored every shudder.

The Stevenson Creek Test Dam rose over a quiet tributary of the San Joaquin River about fifty miles from Fresno. The sixty-foot dam was an alarmingly slender wall of concrete, like the false front on a movie set, seven and a half feet wide at the base and only two feet wide at its crest. Weblike scaffolding hung from its downstream face bearing hundreds of gauges to measure deflections in the concrete wall as the water level crept up the opposite side. The dam sat in a symmetrical V-shaped notch at the head of a canyon so compact it could be filled and emptied in a single night. (Measurements were typically taken between midnight and dawn to minimize distortions from temperature changes produced by sunlight.)

Stevenson Creek's data validated the leading analytical method for arch dams, a process known as trial-load analysis, which involved calculating the deflection of concrete along a dam's arches (that is, horizontally) and cantilevers (vertically) under the pressure of a filled reservoir. In a properly designed dam, the deflections would be equal in both vectors at any given point; discrepancies indicated points where the structure would have to be strengthened.

The findings, along with data from several scale models of Hoover Dam assembled by Savage, suggested that Hoover was not merely well designed, but substantially overdesigned. At 726.4 feet in height and 660 feet wide at its base, the dam would be so resistant to overturning that the arch, its most distinctive design feature, was rendered unnecessary for stability: Hoover Dam could be built either on a straight line or, if the curve were retained, with two-thirds less concrete.

Reclamation stood at a crossroads. The knowledge it acquired on Stevenson Creek and its development of trial-load methodology could have allowed it to build the world's preeminent arched dam, a symbol not only of America's resilient spirit but its faith in technology—saving tens of millions of dollars in the process. But in the end it quailed at making a radical departure from traditional construction in Black Canyon. Reconfiguring Hoover as a pure arched dam would not be seriously considered.

There were several reasons for this. One was certainly the failure of the arched St. Francis Dam, still fresh in public memory. Another was Hoover Dam's stature as a showpiece project, which argued against too much experimentation beyond what was strictly necessary to solve the problems of its site and size. With Reclamation's practical experience in building thin arched dams limited to Owyhee Dam in Idaho, designed in 1926, the Black Canyon project did not seem the right candidate to test the limits of the engineering. Finally, Hoover Dam's fundamental design was already well advanced and regarded as rock-stable. The Reclamation Bureau would not build a thin arch dam of significant height until twenty-five years later, when it would raise the Glen Canyon Dam on the Colorado three hundred miles upstream of Black Canyon. Despite Fred Noetzli's conviction that the gravity dam was "a thing of the past" and "an economic crime," Hoover Dam's bulk remained integral to its design and, indeed, essential to its image of power and strength.

This underscores the aesthetic and psychological aspects of the American dam building style of the 1930s, a "celebration of mass" in which weightiness and grandeur were seen as counterbalancing the meanness and constraints of the Great Depression. It was indicative of the potency of this idea that the very first cover of Henry Luce's *Life* magazine in November 1936 featured not a contemporary film star like Charlie Chaplin or a political leader like Franklin Roosevelt, but the gargantuan concrete spillway gates of Montana's Fort Peck Dam, photographed by Margaret Bourke-White. By then the great project on the Colorado River had already set the standard for the dam as an expression of monumental power sculpted in concrete.

Another issue drawing Reclamation's attention in the spring of 1931 was the acquisition of land for the reservoir, which would inundate 115 miles of valley along the Colorado and a tributary, the Virgin River. Spreading over 247 square miles when filled, the reservoir would rank as the largest man-made body of water in the world. The human consequences of the inundation seemed modest enough—about 375 persons would be directly affected, mostly residents of the Moapa Valley village of St. Thomas which would be subsumed beneath the reservoir, and the owners of about 12,600 acres of farmland and salt and gypsum mines. The balance of the 158,000 acres that would end up underwater, mostly barren desert and unpopulated woodland, was already under government title.

Still, tiny as it was, St. Thomas was not a place to be trifled with. It was one of the oldest settlements in Nevada, having been established in 1865 by Mormon pioneers dispatched from Salt Lake City personally by Brigham Young. Named after the expedition's leader, Thomas Sasson Smith, the town evolved into the hub of the agricultural community farming the bottomland of the Muddy River valley, virtually the only arable land in the southern half of Nevada. In 1931, St. Thomas was also known for its historic Mormon cemetery, which contained seventy-nine graves the government would have to exhume and relocate (with appropriate solicitude) ahead of the inundation. Walker Young himself felt a sentimental attachment to St. Thomas. He had moved into the town with his wife and young daughter, Jane, in 1922 during the first Reclamation surveys of Boulder Canyon, pitching the family tent on the property of the Chadburns, a Mormon family with six children who supplied the Youngs with fresh vegetables and milk.

Commissioner Mead had allocated a maximum of a half-million dollars for the acquisition of private land in the reservoir zone, but the St. Thomas landowners were disinclined to accept a peremptory offer. After the bureau appointed two outside experts as an appraisal board—Harry Crain, a real estate appraiser from Wyoming, and Cecil Creel, a professor of agriculture from the University of Nevada—the townspeople insisted on the inclusion of one of their own. Their choice was Levi Syphus, a retired Nevada state senator and descendant of one of the original Mormon settlers. In his favor, as Young reported, he was "intimately acquainted with land in the reservoir site." From Reclamation's standpoint, this intimacy proved to be more a curse than a virtue, for Syphus promptly began to make a nuisance of himself.

Crain and Creel had expected their task to be routine—merely verifying property assessments and designating a nominal rate for farmland they considered to be only marginally productive. Young and Mead regarded them as instruments of the Reclamation's quest to acquire property for the reservoir at the lowest possible price.

Syphus arrived for the inaugural meeting of the three-man board on February 3 fresh from consultations with Mormon elders in Salt Lake. He made it clear that he had no intention of rubber-stamping the low-ball valuations favored by Reclamation. He proposed instead that the board consider the value of the farmland at issue not as it was—isolated and watered only intermittently by overflow from the Muddy River—but as if it were generously irrigated. That, he suggested, would warrant increasing the existing assessments as much as fourfold.

Syphus introduced other issues his co-appraisers considered irrelevant. These included the claim of John F. Perkins, a well-connected local prospector. Perkins demanded compensation for the many "ornamental and fruit trees, shrubs, vines, tropical trees, etc." he had planted on his property and on which he had lavished "years of patient toil." He argued that their shade was of tangible value—pointing out that on one occasion when Wilbur and Mead visited St. Thomas "they stopped for a conference in the shade of these trees and commented favorably on the industry and care which had made them possible."

Even Young was tempted to concede that Perkins might have a point, given the insufferable climate. But Mead, whose ambitious dam construction program would look to Black Canyon for precedents on a wide range of technical and legal issues, was not about to endorse new property rights involving ornamental beauty, shade, or other intangibles that could only handcuff the bureau later. Coming west to impose his will on the appraisal board in person, he dismissed Perkins's claim out of hand and ordered the board to set land values according to conventional standards and, if necessary, by a 2–1 vote. No doubt he foresaw the result. The three members issued unanimous appraisals for only forty-eight of the 266 private tracts under consideration, all low-value parcels to which they assigned a total value of $16,389. On each of the more valuable remaining parcels Syphus dissented, voting for higher prices on every one. He was outvoted every time. Crain and Creel voted to appraise those for a total of $484,864, bringing the grand total of land acquisition for the reservoir to $501,253, hitting Mead's half-million-dollar target virtually on the nose.

The impending inundation of the Moapa Valley was to have one other consequence that received even less attention from Mead: the destruction of a potentially rich Native American archaeological record.

In 1924, a curator from the Museum of the American Indian in New York named Mark Harrington had excavated a line of sand dunes along the Muddy River just south of St. Thomas, where a couple of local prospectors had found shards of painted pottery amid some adobe ruins. Harrington had spent years excavating old cave dwellings around the Southwest and recognized the pottery as Pueblo Indian in origin—an important find, given that the Pueblos were thought never to have settled west of the Colorado.

He eventually identified seventy-seven sites in the lower Moapa Valley near the Muddy's confluence with the Virgin—"an almost unbroken line of ancient villages" ranging from temporary camps of nomadic hunters to permanent settlements of subsistence farmers, some dating to as far back as A.D. 500. The most important was a "long straggling" collection of forty-six structures, including one with ninety-five rooms, that ranged along five miles of the Muddy. He dubbed this the "Lost City," as it was located where an early explorer had reported seeing a settlement that later dropped from sight.

After a single season in the field, Harrington's money ran out. He shut down the site, hoping to return soon. He would not get back for more than five years. That was in 1930, when he learned to his alarm that the entire Moapa Valley was to be flooded. With the backing of ex-governor James Scrugham, he hastily raised funds for new excavations. These began at the Lost City with crews from the New Deal's Civilian Conservation Corps and the National Park Service in 1933 and continued until 1935, when the encroaching waters of Lake Mead were all but "lapping at their feet." Meanwhile he supervised the building of a museum for the remains near the town of Overton, an old Mormon settlement perched at the edge of the new waterline. There they remain on display to this day.

The concept of salvage archaeology was virtually unknown when Harrington began his fevered efforts to rescue the Lost City from the encroaching Lake Mead; it would not become an integral part of government planning until the Tennessee Valley Authority began its vast dam building program in the late 1930s. In time the very idea of planning a dam and filling its reservoir without investigating and organizing the recovery of archaeological artifacts would become unimaginable—one more precedent established at Hoover Dam.

By the late spring of 1931, Frank Crowe's worksite resembled a battlefield on the eve of the clash of armies. Adits had been driven into both cliffsides and the first pioneer tunnels were being excavated. At the canyon rim, crews were laying twenty-six miles of track from the terminus of the government railroad at Boulder City to a location upriver, where Six Companies would build a plant to prepare concrete aggregate. Very little heavy construction could be done until mid-June, when LeTourneau expected to finish his highway and Southern Sierras Power Co. its power line. Meanwhile Crowe could only wait, like a fretful general praying for fair weather. Early in April, Six Companies had laid out $79,285 for heavy equipment, explosives, and timber. With no room yet to park it at the riverbank, the equipment and supplies sat idle at the crest of Hemenway Wash.

Three hundred men were on the payroll, taking down $1,600 a day, or an average of about $5 each. By July, their ranks would more than quadruple in preparation for full-scale construction. A mess tent capable of feeding 350 men at a sitting had been erected near the site of Boulder City by Anderson Brothers, a catering firm best known for feeding Hollywood location crews in the chaparral-covered hills of Southern California. A cluster of seventy-five-bed bunkhouses and a second mess hall with three hundred seats stood at River Camp, the spot two miles upstream of the dam site from which the work barges departed.

Work may have barely begun, but the schedule that would prevail throughout the construction period was already established: three shifts were working around the clock, seven days a week, driving adits, erecting railroad trestles, and carving roadbeds into the rocks.

The elemental battle with the Colorado was about to be joined; but nature still had a few unpleasant surprises in store.

# The Wobblies' Last Stand

Harry Large and Andrew Lane were not the first men to lose their lives on the Boulder Canyon Project. That baleful distinction belongs to J. Gregory Tierney, a Reclamation Bureau driller who fell from an upturned survey barge on the Colorado and drowned on December 20, 1922. His body was never recovered, although parties scoured the riverbanks as far as Blythe, California, twenty miles downstream, where they found only the barge's splintered remains. Thirteen years later to the day, Tierney's son Patrick, a Reclamation electrician, would fall to his death from an intake tower. Patrick Tierney would be the last man to die during the construction phase, he and his father representing mordant bookends of the project's record of human loss.

But Large and Lane—the former a journeyman miner, the latter an experienced tunnel foreman—were the first to die during construction. On May 17, 1931, they were clearing a ledge of rock at the entrance to a diversion tunnel on the Arizona side when the cliffside gave way, burying them so deeply under twenty thousand square yards of boulders and gravel that it took hours for crews to recover their hopelessly mangled bodies. A third worker, Henry Ludwig, tried frantically to scurry out from under the cascading debris, only to be caught by the leg and knocked unconscious. He survived, but his shattered limb had to be amputated.

The incident was one in a string of mishaps suggesting that safety had taken a back seat to the unsparing pace of work, a pattern familiar from Hurry-Up Crowe's previous jobs. The first accident in the series had occurred late on the afternoon of May 8, when a gang building a track bed for the construction railroad halfway up the cliff set off thirty simultaneous blasts of dynamite, showering loose boulders onto eleven men still working two hundred yards below them. The most grievously injured man, P. L. Lezie, was flattened by a careening boulder. Herman Schmitts, a co-worker, received a fractured skull, among other injuries. "His ear was almost severed from his head," the *Age* reported gruesomely.

The blast and its aftermath underscored how slipshod safety provisions had become in the canyon. As there was no first-aid or medical service on the job site, the injured men had to be taken by motorboat to River Camp, where co-workers summoned an ambulance from Las Vegas Hospital by telephone. On its way down the rutted gravel track into the canyon this overworked vehicle blew a tire. Having no spare, the driver continued rolling on the wheel rim, an act which soon immobilized the ambulance completely. Lezie and Schmitts were finally transferred to the hospital in the bed of a pickup truck. Although neither was expected to live through the night, both miraculously survived, as did six other seriously injured men. Unnerved by the narrowness of their escape, the survivors were unanimous in asserting that, as John Page noted in his diary, they had been given "no warning . . . and no chance to get cover."

The next day, a furious Nevada mine official appeared in Walker Young's office, demanding a copy of the government's incident report. His arrival was a vivid reminder of a controversy Young had been trying to suppress for months. The issue was whether the laws of Nevada or those of the U.S. government would prevail inside the 115-square-mile federal reservation encompassing the job site, nine miles of Black Canyon gorge, and the site of Boulder City.

In practical terms, the dispute boiled down to two issues: workplace safety and taxation. The Nevada legislature had fired the first shot in March, when it voted to extend the state mining safety code to tunnel work. The vote was manifestly aimed at Six Companies, which had been issuing broad hints that as a federal contractor it considered itself exempt from the prying attentions of state mining inspectors. Meanwhile the Nevada tax assessor, Frank De Vinney, was preparing a hefty tax appraisal of the equipment Six Companies had assembled in the canyon. These steps would launch a two-year bout of litigation in federal court.

The visiting Nevada official informed Young that the state blamed the Big Six for the blasting accident. Anxious to keep clear of the developing ruckus, Young handed over his preliminary report, on the understanding that the United States government would be held harmless in the case. Under the government contract, he pointed out, Six Companies bore contractual responsibility for all construction activity at the river.

Six Companies itself was far from unruffled. A few days after the accident Dad Bechtel himself showed up in Las Vegas with a corporate attorney bobbing in his wake. The Big Six did not carry liability insurance, Bechtel confided to Page; therefore he hoped to settle all accident claims quickly, quietly, and privately. Page, as leery as his boss of being drawn into an ugly legal snarl, kept his counsel. "Gave them no information re accident," he confided to his journal. Months later, the company would pay off Lezie, the most critically injured victim, with $5,000 in cash plus the cost of his hospitalization.

Conditions on the worksite were about to get worse. Nine days after the errant blast came the rock slide that took the lives of Large and Lane. The day after that brought the death of Fred Olsen, an employee of Lewis Construction Company, the railroad contractor, from another premature detonation.

The toll of injury and death ebbed for several weeks. Then, in the middle of June, the weather changed and the folly of putting hundreds of men to work in a narrow desert canyon without adequate living facilities became inescapable.

The summer of 1931 was a record scorcher, running about twelve degrees hotter than normal. In July, Charlie Shea reported to his fellow Six Companies directors, the maximum temperature in the canyon averaged 119.9 degrees Fahrenheit and the minimum, generally touched briefly only an hour or two before dawn, was 94.9. But the weather conditions in the gorge had become a byword months earlier. Soon after the first work crews arrived in April, they began to encounter the frequent heat spells, interspersed with ferocious windstorms and relieved only sporadically by rain, characteristic of the climate for most of the year.

The experience of Arleigh Meredith Beals, a Penn State graduate who had landed a job as a shovel operator, was typical. Corresponding with Marion Riblet, his inconstant fiancée back home in Harborcreek, Pennsylvania, he described a springtime climate going from bad to worse: "It's getting hot here. Temp 120 degrees today. Is it any wonder that I am losing weight? (April 7). . . . Remember what you said about the 'ends of the earth'? Do you still feel that way? I guess you don't as you would be here now. Well darling I must close now. It's too damn hot to write even. (April 21). . . . It's just as hot as ever out here. Hotter than that in fact! It makes me homesick to think of the blossoming flowers and such things back home. . . . (May 10)." Soon after writing this last letter, he gave up and returned to Harborcreek.

These conditions were hardly surprising; the very point of building Boulder City was to shelter the workforce from the desert climate. Reclamation commissioner Mead, whose experience of construction in harsh environments stretched from the deserts of the American West to the Australian outback, seemed to take a perverse delight in regaling audiences with the details of life in Black Canyon, as though the torments to which he was exposing thousands of desperate men were somehow good for their souls:

> The summer wind which sweeps over the gorge from the desert feels like a blast from a furnace. At the rim of the gorge, where much of the work must be done, there is neither soil, grass, nor trees. The sun beats down on a broken surface of lava rocks. At midday they cannot be touched with the naked hand. It is bad enough as a place for men at work. It is no place for a boarding house or a sleeping porch.

Mead's apparent indifference to the dam workers' comfort should be understood in the context of his professional vision. At Black Canyon, anything that interfered with the project's ultimate realization, whether it was squatters in Ragtown or grousing laborers at the dam site, earned his enmity. An Indiana farm boy born in 1858 and raised in an era when America was transitioning from a rural to an urban society, he was sentimental about the agrarian lifestyle. His views about the resulting erosion of social values closely paralleled those of his contemporaries William Ellsworth Smythe and George Maxwell. What he added to their water evangelism was a rigorous understanding of irrigation engineering; indeed, with a faculty appointment at Colorado State Agricultural College in 1883 he had become the first professor of that technical discipline in the nation.

Given his record, which included leadership of the movement to settle returning veterans of the First World War on irrigated farmland, he was the obvious choice for Reclamation commissioner, effectively succeeding the ousted Arthur Powell Davis, when the job opened up again in 1924. Yet he was not so much a humanitarian as a technocrat. Steeped in the economics and mechanics of irrigation, he understood perfectly how to convert plans on paper into projects on the ground. But he was a poor judge of humankind, and therefore was often disappointed to find that public he wished to guide to a better life preferred to seek its opportunities elsewhere and on its own terms—as when soldiers returning home in 1918 shunned the rural resettlement programs he had fought to establish while they were still Over There.

In any case, there was no easy way to prepare men for conditions in Black Canyon. The problem was not merely that Boulder City was yet unbuilt, but that Six Companies had selected the worst possible location for the bivouac it dubbed River Camp, that cluster of wooden dormitories hammered together in March and April.

River Camp stood at a bend in the Colorado known as Cape Horn. It was wedged between the river and the cliffside on a barren forty-five-degree slope where the gorge narrowed into Black Canyon. The camp was open to the beating sun yet shut off from cross-breezes, an airless, stupefying place where the stench of the latrines settled in the bunkhouses like a miasma. On occasion boulders would break loose from the steep slope and come crashing through the bunkhouse walls. (No one was ever reported injured in these incidents, although the lingering menace surely lent uneasiness to the men's slumber.)

The beds at River Camp were crude cots with filthy blankets—not that sleep would have been easier in a feather bed with spotless linens. "I tried to sleep between 7.30 [p.m.], when I quit, and 5.30 when I went to work again, but it was simply impossible," wrote Victor Castle to a friend in Los Angeles. "I was tired but with a temperature which never dropped below 130 during the night sleep was out of the question. By morning I felt burned to a crisp." Castle soon abandoned his job as a waiter in the Anderson Brothers mess hall, forgoing $2 a day.

There was no running water for showering and no cool water to drink. The men bathed in the turbid river, dousing themselves in water colored "an opaque yellow like coffee with too much cream," as it was described by the author Edmund Wilson. Their drinking water was pumped from the river into a tank hung on the Nevada cliffside, where it simmered in the sun while the silt settled out, eventually yielding what an employee described as a "consommé" marginally suitable for human consumption.

As the heat rose, the health of the men in River Camp sank. The bacteria-infested river water gave them ceaseless diarrhea. The Anderson Brothers' efforts to keep their provisions cooled to forty degrees in an ice locker regularly failed; one batch of sandwiches made from rotted pork in early July poisoned twenty men.

The ferocious heat was too much even for veterans of such sweltering climes as the Philippines or Panama. One man who had spent five years working on the Panama Canal lasted all of three days on the dam site before collapsing with uncontrollable vomiting and cramps. Anderson Brothers laid out copious spreads to feed entire shifts who were too exhausted or cramped to down a single forkful. "It was quite a sight to see a hundred or more men trying to eat, all stripped to their waists, with rivulets of sweat running down their faces and backs," Castle reported.

The emergency remedy for heat stroke was a dousing with buckets of ice from the Anderson Brothers cooler. "We had what we called the ice brigade," recalled Robert Parker, a seventeen-year-old kitchen mop hand during that killing summer. "When somebody in the canyon became overcome with the heat, we dashed out there with these ice buckets and we'd pack them in ice. If their heart took it and they survived, okay. But if their heart stopped, that was it. We sent for the undertaker."

The fundamental problem, as a medical research team from Harvard University determined the following summer, was that the bodies of men existing twenty-four hours a day in the punishing heat—sleeping as well as working in the gorge—were unable to adjust to the climate. "What we demonstrated was that you can give men who work eight hours a day in temperatures up to a hundred and five or ten, and then provide comfortable comfort for them for the other sixteen hours, and they can fully recuperate during that time," recalled Dr. David Bruce Dill, who led the team. "So the body reserves go downhill during eight hours of work, but they are fully restored within sixteen hours of recovery. That's the main thing."

He also noticed that the men, while drinking plenty of water, were skimping on salt. This may have been because the meat they were served, salted to keep it from spoiling, was already too heavily seasoned for their taste. But the consequence was a chronic salt deficiency that contributed to the incidence of heatstroke and cramps.

Dill's findings were not novel; salt tablets had been part of the medical arsenal in hot climates for years. The knowledge simply had not reached Black Canyon in 1931—another example of how Reclamation and its principal contractor were unprepared for the work schedule.

The toll was horrific during that merciless summer. Sixteen deaths from heatstroke among the dam workers and other residents of the riverbank were recorded between June 25 and July 26, 1931. Seven were Six Companies employees and four worked in the Anderson Brothers mess tent, where the strain of bending over a bank of stoves in an enclosed gallery could only have exacerbated the climate's effect. On July 20, John Page morbidly noted in his diary, the heat claimed Charles Allen, a Six Companies employee, as well as Edna Grace Mitchell, the fifteen-year-old daughter of a dam worker squatting in Ragtown. After learning that her family was too destitute to call for an undertaker, Page dispatched one from Las Vegas on the government's account. That did not end the parade of tragedy. Page recorded that five other workers were brought to

Las Vegas Hospital that same day, all comatose from sunstroke. He did not mention that on its way out of Boulder City their ambulance sideswiped an automobile driven by Jack O'Keefe of San Francisco, who then veered into an oncoming car and received fatal chest injuries. This was one of the earliest mishaps that would give the new Boulder Highway, linking well-liquored Las Vegas with dry Boulder City, its reputation as the region's worst deathtrap.

Reclamation officials and the Six Companies directors concealed any concerns they might have had about the deaths behind a scrim of bureaucratic euphemism. Shea, reporting to his board about conditions at the river in late July, acknowledged "very trying conditions at that place. Several of the employees have died or had to leave and this naturally has lowered the morale of the other employees to some extent." Page, writing for the 1931 *Annual Project History*, observed even more dispassionately that many of the workers "were unused to living under desert conditions, and the consequent number of fatalities due to heat prostration were to some extent alarming."

Nor could the employees expect much help from local officials, who had little authority to investigate conditions at the worksite and scant success at gathering objective information from Six Companies even when they had clear legal jurisdiction, as in the event of a fatality. The Las Vegas coroner's jury looking into the deaths of two Six Companies tunnel workers, James P. Sweezy and William Bryant, from a premature blast on June 20, had little choice but to absolve the company of responsibility after hearing from four witnesses: a Six Companies doctor, two Six Companies insurance men, and Frank Crowe.

Mead was unapologetic about putting hundreds of men to work without adequate shelter and under the indulgent oversight of government inspectors. "There is no question that the work of the engineers of the Reclamation Bureau and the work of the contractors thus far has been carried out under very difficult and often very dangerous conditions," he wrote to *The New Republic*, responding to a series of muckraking articles about labor conditions at the dam. "These are inseparable from the location."

The August 26 letter showed Mead at his most insensitive. He argued that the deaths thus far, while "deplored by all," were not excessive given the location. "There were forty deaths from heat recently reported in one day in the Imperial Valley, and only one death reported in the same day on the Boulder Canyon work," he wrote, attributing the disparity to "the very large expenditures to mitigate climatic conditions and protect the workers" in the canyon, rather than to the fact that the Imperial Valley encompassed 525,000 acres of cultivated farmland and a population of 61,000, and Boulder Canyon was a single confined worksite one mile in length, with fewer than 1,400 workers in place. The truth is that during the summer of 1931 the government and the contractors were taking virtually no steps to mitigate the climate or protect the workers.

Mead demanded credit for at least staking out Boulder City as a wholesome and comfortable refuge, even if it was as yet no more than an expanse of raw desert. "The plans of both the Bureau and the contractor provide for the planting of shade trees and the seeding of large areas to grass as soon as water is available for irrigation and the summer heat is over." Next year, he promised, "there will be an entirely different story."

That was true. But by the time his letter appeared in print, the workers' fury at their treatment had already boiled over, stoked by outside agitation.

Even before the arrival of high summer, conditions in Black Canyon had seized the attention of a down-at-the-heels labor organization headquartered in Chicago, more than 1,700 miles away.

The Industrial Workers of the World, the Wobblies, still carried a fearsome reputation in the industrial and mining zones of the West and Midwest. The union had been founded in 1905 at a secret conference in Chicago by a group of twenty-five labor radicals, including William D. "Big Bill" Haywood, a dispossessed miner and rancher whose burly physique, perpetual scowl, and black cowlick became iconic IWW images, and Mary "Mother" Jones, the tireless advocate for miners' rights. Eugene V. Debs, the five-time Socialist candidate for president, was too sick to attend in person but very much present in spirit.

The union drew its philosophical principles from the anarcho-syndicalist labor movement of nineteenth-century revolutionary Europe. This birthright animated the preamble to the IWW constitution, which was filled with expressions of utopian aspiration ("We are forming the structure of the new society within the shell of the old") and the Marxian rhetoric of the class struggle ("It is the historic mission of the working class to do away with capitalism"). In the United States, the Wobblies waged battle against capitalism in general and the American Federation of Labor specifically. The two organizations differed strategically and tactically: Where the AF of L favored collective bargaining to secure immediate, tangible gains such as wage increases and shorter work days, the IWW aimed to foment political change through the general strike, a quintessentially European approach. There is reason to doubt whether the IWW membership ever exceeded 100,000 at any given time. Its resonance in American labor culture is much greater, however—due in part to its militancy, the disproportionate and violent reaction it often provoked from the authorities, and the martyrdom of popular, seminal IWW figures like Joe Hill and Frank Little.

The Wobblies experienced their greatest successes—and first crushing defeats—in the violent and vermin-infested mining camps of the West. In 1906 they moved into Goldfield, Nevada, an archetypal mining town where a boomtime veneer concealed a core of ruthless exploitation. By drawing into a single union all the wage workers in the community—"miners, engineers, clerks, stenographers, teamsters, dishwashers, waiters, and all sorts of what are called 'common laborers,'" a Wobbly organizer recalled—the IWW extracted a dollar-a-day wage increase and improved working conditions for all.

But solidarity in Goldfield soon collapsed, undermined by internal squabbles, an influx of scab labor, and worker desperation born of the severe depression known as the Panic of 1907. The Wobblies were also the target of concerted official repression: President Theodore Roosevelt sent federal troops into the region under the misapprehension, fostered by the mine owners and Nevada governor John Sparks, that union-inspired violence was in the offing. The breaking of the union and the restoration of the old pay scale in Goldfield underscored the IWW's tenuous hold on the loyalty of the rank and file. Its revolutionary credo and its tendency to attract violent official countermeasures scared off the average worker, who came to view Wobblies stereotypically as "a bunch of bums with bombs in hip pockets, advocating violent sabotage," lamented the union's official historian, Fred Thompson. It was not unusual for the IWW to successfully identify and publicize an abusive condition and call for a strike, only to watch from the sidelines as the workers reorganized themselves under non-Wobbly leadership. This very pattern would reappear at Hoover Dam.

The repression of the IWW peaked in 1918 with the trial in federal court of 101 leaders, including Haywood, for antiwar activities. The judge was Kenesaw Mountain Landis, a forbidding jurist who would shortly leave the bench to become baseball commissioner in the wake of the 1919 Black Sox scandal. After weeks of testimony the jury deliberated for less than an hour before finding all 101 defendants guilty. Landis promptly imposed sentences of up to twenty years and fines totaling $2.5 million. When a federal Court of Appeals upheld the sentences, Haywood, who was out on bail, fled to Russia rather than return to prison. His exit cost the union $80,000 in forfeited bond—much of it drawn from the dues of working-class members—and invested the entire movement with the stench of cowardice and hypocrisy. Haywood remained the object of vituperation by IWW loyalists to the end of his days, reached finally in a fog of alcoholism and loneliness in Moscow in 1928. The IWW's credibility never fully recovered. By 1931 its membership had dwindled to a few thousand. A new general secretary taking office that year found $29 in the cash box to pay printing bills and the staff's back wages.

Yet in the first days of the Depression the IWW stirred back to life. Hoover Dam, which was luring the dispossessed and unemployed from all over the country to a single woebegone spot in the Nevada desert, loomed as an irresistible strategic objective. The union had first proclaimed its intention to organize the Boulder Canyon project in late 1930, but markedly stepped up its rhetoric after the bid openings. The Seattle-based IWW organ *Industrial Worker* marked the occasion by describing the leadership of Six Companies as "the U.C. [Utah Construction] Co. and its two pimps, Morrison & Knudsen and Betchel & Keyser [sic] . . . notorious for their low wages, rotten camp conditions and belly-robbing cookhouses; not to mention unsafe equipment and an unequaled collection of petty slave drivers."

This language sounded a generic Wobbly note, but the union could claim to be speaking from experience: in 1923 it had struck Utah Construction's Hetch Hetchy project. The job action ended in a typical Wobbly denouement, fizzling after the company imported hundreds of unemployed strikebreakers "with wrinkles in their bellies and flat broke," as an official IWW history put it.

*Industrial Worker* and the union's Chicago-based weekly, *Industrial Solidarity*, vigilantly followed developments in Black Canyon. The latter reported the injuries of Lezie and Schmitts under the front-page headline, "SIX COMPANIES THREATEN WORKERS' LIVES." "The man-killing on Boulder Dam has begun," the article read. "[U]nless the workers on this job unite in a militant union, it will be a record of bloody murder." Two Sundays later, on May 30, *Industrial Worker* announced the deaths of Large and Lane with the headline, "LIFE HELD CHEAP at Boulder Dam."

By then, eleven IWW organizers were in Las Vegas. Their leader was Frank Desmond Anderson, a twenty-eight-year-old mineworker who had been organizing for the union since the age of nineteen. The writer Edmund Wilson described Anderson in terms that evoked a youthful Bill Haywood: "a short strong-knit man with a dark glaring purposeful eye." Anderson had hired on at the dam as a chuck tender, which meant he helped tunnel drillers manually position their drill bits in the rock wall. This was a dangerous and by no means unskilled job, suggesting that Anderson, who had recently been employed on a J. F. Shea Company job in Oregon, possessed a journeyman's experience in the mining crafts. That would explain how he found employment within days of his arrival in Las Vegas.

As a chuck tender Anderson was paid 62 1/2 cents an hour, a notch above the minimum wage in the gorge. He spent his nonworking hours peddling the Wobbly weeklies for a nickel a copy and engaging his co-workers in discussions about conditions at the dam site. Sensitive to the IWW's undeserved reputation for violence, he regularly searched his associates to keep them clean of firearms. But he encouraged them to move freely among the other workers with what Wilson described as "Wobbly jauntiness," and soon was claiming that the Wobbly unit at the dam, I.U. (for "Industrial Union") No. 310, had signed up four hundred members. Given the events of the coming weeks, this figure must be considered a gross exaggeration. Although their influence would be felt greatly at least for a brief time, the Wobblies' core membership on the site probably never exceeded a few dozen men.

For all that, they found plenty of simmering discontent on the workforce. Six Companies had wide latitude to establish its own hiring and wage policies. It also benefited from the enormous quantity of idle labor at hand, which kept its employees suitably docile. Since late 1930, more than ten thousand unemployed men had registered with the U.S. Department of Labor in Las Vegas. Many had taken up quasi-permanent residence on the Las Vegas courthouse lawn, where the city fathers did them a modest favor by running the sprinklers on hot nights to keep them cool, if soaked to the skin.

The contractors also made the most of their exemption from wage regulations imposed by the federal Davis-Bacon Act, which President Hoover had signed on March 3. Davis-Bacon required contractors on federal projects to pay workers the locally prevailing wages, which in practice meant union scale. But because the law went into effect on March 31, six days after the official signing of the Hoover Dam contract, the Labor Department had ruled that it did not apply at the dam site.

Whether Big Six's wage scale—which initially ranged from $3.50 per day for the humblest muckers in the diversion tunnels to $6 for truck drivers, welders, and skilled machine operators—would have met the prevailing-wage test is hard to gauge. Reclamation commissioner Mead, taking umbrage at an assertion by *The New Republic* that the contractors were shortchanging workers under the government's nose, wrote back in August 1931 to argue that "exactly the contrary is the truth"—that Six Companies was voluntarily paying workers more than other employers in the region. In contrast, the Central Labor Council of Las Vegas complained that the Big Six was undercutting the regional wage scale for skilled mechanics by 25 to 50 percent.

Six Companies also flouted the mandate in its contract—derived directly from the Boulder Canyon Project Act—that it favor ex-servicemen and American citizens in hiring. Crowe, reminded of this provision by Leonard Blood, the Las Vegas representative of the Department of Labor, responded that he intended to give his old crews first preference whether they met the statutory qualifications or not. A frustrated Blood complained to Washington that the only requests for labor he ever received from the Big Six were for clerical or temporary help; when it came to construction workers, who commanded higher wages, "foremen were sending for their relatives from all parts of the United States." His examination of the Six Companies payroll records in mid-1931 revealed that fewer than one in three men employed on the dam were ex-servicemen and that eighty men, or more than 10 percent of the workers, were foreigners. Blood informed Charlie Shea that by ignoring the registration rolls his office painstakingly compiled from job seekers in Las Vegas, Six Companies was in violation of its government contract. But his demands for compliance were simply ignored by Shea, Crowe, and Mead, and for that matter by Hoover's shiftless secretary of labor, William Doak.

Organized labor got the same brush-off. In early May, the AF of L had asked for a meeting with the Six Companies board, citing its solid record of lobbying for the Swing-Johnson bill. The directors replied truculently that "the labor policy of this corporation will be that policy which is required by the plans and specifications governing labor as indicated by contract between the United States Government and the Six Companies Inc." Around the same time, an agent from the International Brotherhood of Electrical Workers tracked down Crowe on the worksite to press him on wage rates, only to be ejected with the message that there was "nothing to discuss."

Taking a page from traditional mining company practice and operating comfortably outside the oversight of the federal and state governments, the Big Six subjected its humbled workers to what Edmund Wilson described, justifiably, as "systematic skimping [and] petty swindling." The company paid the men only for the hours they actually spent on the site, although hundreds were commuting from Las Vegas—a trip that could easily consume three hours a day—for want of suitable quarters closer in. The Big Six charged the men $1.50 a day for meals at the company mess hall but paid only $1.125 per man to its catering firm, Anderson Brothers, thus skimming a tidy profit from its own payroll. Upstairs from the mess hall, Six Companies operated a commissary that accepted only company scrip, the private currency in which it handed out wage advances. Its practice of paying the men their cash wages only once a month—a violation of Nevada law, which mandated semimonthly pay envelopes—guaranteed that the demand for scrip would remain robust and thus that the company store would continue to do "exceptionally good business with very gratifying profits," as the Big Six board was informed that summer. So gratifying, indeed, that the company tried to maintain this stranglehold on its employees' custom once Boulder City opened for occupancy. Only after vehement protests from the city's suffering private merchants reached the Roosevelt administration did the Interior Department outlaw the company's scrip trade, in 1933.

Friday night, July 10, found Frank Anderson in downtown Las Vegas, hawking week-old copies of *Industrial Worker* prominently featuring an article about back-to-back fatalities in the canyon ("THREE MORE MEN ARE KILLED AT BOULDER DAM"), along with a call to action by the workers: "Wake up and organize . . ."

Anderson had chosen a provocative section of sidewalk—directly in front of the Boulder Club, a Fremont Street casino and bar part-owned by Glenn "Bud" Bodell, a deputy sheriff known for his hostility to labor organizers. Anderson could hardly have been surprised, therefore, to be accosted by Eddie Johnson, a cauliflower-eared tough on Bodell's payroll. Brandishing a sheriff's badge, Johnson slapped Anderson with a vagrancy charge and shipped him off to the Blue Room. There the prisoner chatted volubly with his keepers, claiming to have enrolled hundreds of River Camp workers in the IWW, and to be well on the way to establishing Wobbly control of the entire Boulder Canyon Project.

His boasts produced an immediate sensation. "I.W.W. GROUP AT DAM REVEALED; CITY PRISON IS GUARDED AS BREAK IS FEARED," blared the *Age*. Yet the threat of a "break" was wholly imaginary: Anderson's strategy, as it happened, was to stay in jail, using it as a political soapbox, not to burst out to freedom.

He was joined in the Blue Room the next morning by his colleagues Louis Gracey and C. E. Setzer, who had been wiring IWW headquarters in Chicago with the news of Anderson's arrest when they were collared by a police squad alerted by a nosy telegraph office manager. At his fingerprinting, Gracey proved to be as brimful of Wobbly brio as Anderson. "Yes, I've been fingerprinted before," he allowed to a group of reporters. "I've been in plenty of jails."

The Wobblies' chattiness perplexed the police, who plainly expected their prisoners to maintain the stoic silence of a revolutionary cell. Instead the unionists talked freely, even giving up the names of seven other IWW organizers at camp without prompting.

The Las Vegas cops did not recognize a classic Wobbly strategy derived from the "free speech" campaigns of the union's early days. Between 1906 and 1916 the IWW had conducted dozens of these pioneering nonviolent protests, which involved staging public demonstrations of anticapitalist propaganda to goad police into making mass arrests. The union would then summon sympathizers from across the country to continue the speechifying, eventually so overcrowding the local jail that the authorities had to back down. Meanwhile, the union's cause would have gained free publicity, sometimes nationwide.

The Las Vegas campaign followed the same script, at first. The Blue Room soon contained eight Wobbly organizers, all charged as vagrants, the city's all-purpose legal designation of undesirable outsiders. But rather than agreeing to be shipped quietly out of town in the unspoken compact between cops and vagabonds, they insisted on their constitutional right to trial by their peers. This demand sent startled city attorneys scurrying to their statute books to find a precedent for empaneling a jury to hear a municipal ordinance violation, normally disposed of with a hearing, a fine, and a stern word from the bench.

Over the next couple of days three more union members were arrested. They, too, were tossed into the holding pen, which they shared with drunks of both sexes. At mealtime the agitators were herded to one side of the room and left unfed while the other prisoners received their rations. Sympathizers attempting to bring them food were turned away at the jailhouse door.

Their frustration was matched by the city's, for no sympathy or support was forthcoming from the federal government, whose big project in the canyon was the root of all the disorder. Assistant U.S. Attorney George Montrose refused to take over the case, observing pointedly that the defendants had neither committed a crime on federal property nor taken any steps to interfere with the work. Walker Young, who had witnessed the IWW's free speech strategy in action while supervising Reclamation projects in the Northwest, reasoned that the city's hysterical reaction merely abetted the union's goals and counseled calm. "The whole thing, so far as I can see, is just another attempt on the part of the agitators to gain the publicity so necessary to their cause," he told the *Review-Journal* in a clearheaded interview. "Most of the I.W.W. disturbances are in the newspapers, and while we are taking no chances, it is not nearly so bad as it has been painted."

Asked about rumors that two thousand Wobblies were streaming from all corners of the country toward the reservation to "force the tenets of the order on the Boulder Dam workmen," he smiled complacently. "We'll take care of that situation when it arises," he said. He would soon change his tune.

On Wednesday, July 15, Municipal Judge W. G. Morse convened the vagrancy hearing, having rejected the jury demand. T. Alonzo Wells, a Las Vegas lawyer who viewed the Wobblies as a welcome break from his usual clientele of small-time criminals and Saturday night drunks, made short work of the charge. He proved that although Anderson had been laid off from the dam, he had remained on the IWW payroll for $28 a week plus the use of a car. This was rather better pay than he had earned as a chuck tender; indeed, as Wells later joshed to an acquaintance passing through town, the Wobbly prisoners actually had more money in their pockets than most of the unemployed men swarming into Las Vegas. City Attorney Frank Stevens, his vagrancy case in tatters, tried to argue that Anderson's role as an IWW organizer was sufficient by itself to warrant his deportation from the city limits. Judge Morse was having none of it. The next morning he ordered Anderson released. Stevens, bowing to reality, dropped the charges against the others.

The elated Wobbly press compared the outcome to the great Goldfield organizing victory of 1906 and the free speech crusades of bygone days. It was somewhat less than that. Anderson and his cohort had won too quickly for their cases to develop into the cause célèbre the union had been angling for. A much bigger explosion would be needed to focus nationwide attention on working conditions at the dam site. Conveniently enough, the Big Six itself was about to light the fuse.

Following the Anderson acquittals, Six Companies made several improvements in camp. They shipped in clean drinking water from Las Vegas, although not enough of it. They installed a water cooler at the Anderson mess hall, although one too small to satisfy demand. A powder storeroom that had been located unnervingly close to a spark-producing blacksmithing shop on the Nevada worksite was relocated across the river.

Yet whatever goodwill the company gained with these modest improvements it abruptly and inexplicably squandered on August 7. That afternoon at four o'clock, as the swing shift debarked from the barges dropping them off at the worksite, they were greeted by a notice stating that pay for all tunnel workers was to be cut.

The blow fell most heavily on the lowliest laborers. A reduction from $5 to $4 a day was imposed on muckers, who shoveled out the debris from the dynamite blasts, and nippers, who hauled heavy supplies into the tunnels and packed the drill holes with explosives. Cable tenders, who worked the tow lines for barges and other equipment, were to be cut from $5.60 to $4; and motormen and brakemen from $5.60 to $5.

The shift workers instantly perceived the new pay scale as a bloodthirsty expression of the law of supply and demand. As long as platoons of jobless men remained camped on the Las Vegas courthouse lawn, there was no limit to how low Six Companies could push wages. As the day crew emerged from the tunnels they discovered the swing shift in full cry. Goaded by two Wobbly speakers, four hundred workers from both shifts repaired to the Anderson Brothers mess hall, where they voted to strike, elected a committee to draw up a list of demands, and dispatched a delegation to pass the word to the work camps situated around the Boulder City townsite.

At seven that evening, six hundred men crowded the square in front of the Boulder City mess hall to hear the men from River Camp. They elected their own committee and also voted to strike. Work at the dam was shut down for the night—the first break in construction since Frank Crowe had summoned his loyal troops to the river in March.

As it had on countless other occasions, the IWW now became caught in a vise of its own manufacture. It had articulated the men's grievances effectively but failed to organize the rank and file into a cohesive force. Yet it had become so closely associated with the complaints about working conditions that Six Companies had no trouble blaming the strike on "radical agitators." From the bosses' standpoint this had the dual virtue of discrediting the strikers' cause and exaggerating the prospect of violence.

Fully alive to the Wobblies' equivocal reputation, the workers promptly disassociated themselves from the radical union. "We're not wobblies, and don't want to be classed as such," the committee announced through its chairman, L. L. "Red" Williams. "There is no organization or anything else. Just a committee of eleven, six from the tunnel workers and five from the surface men."

The IWW organizers were swiftly ushered away from the front. Workers and residents who lived through the affair would refer to it forever after as the "Wobbly strike" of 1931, but like so many revolts the union had incited, this one developed as a Wobbly strike without Wobblies. Whether the IWW, a derelict union with little money and scarcely any national organization to speak of, could have managed the strike to a successful conclusion is impossible to say. But with the experienced agitator Frank Anderson on their side to remind them of the larger issues at stake and to encourage solidarity, the workers might have prevailed. Instead, thrown back on their own resources, they were about to find themselves hopelessly overmatched by Six Companies and Frank Crowe.

Late on the night of Friday, August 7, the joint workers committee finished drafting a list of seven demands, to be presented to Crowe in person the next morning at ten. In addition to a minimum daily wage of $5 for surface workers, $5.50 for tunnel laborers, and $6 for skilled workmen, the committee demanded improved living conditions in the camps; a reliable supply of cold or iced water at the job site; an eight-hour day "camp to camp" (that is, paid travel time); strict enforcement of Arizona and Nevada mining laws by a safety inspector stationed at every tunnel portal; a flat rate of $1.50 a day for meals (graveyard shift workers took four meals at the mess hall, resulting in a $2 deduction from their pay packet); and amnesty for the strikers. None of these demands qualified as "radical." The workers sought only to restore wages to the levels of two days earlier, and most of the other demands, such as cold water and a safe working environment, were already mandated by the government contract, but thus far honored in the breach.

The workers assumed that if Crowe's vaunted fellowship with the men meant anything, it was that he would give them a fair, even benevolent, hearing. They quickly discovered the limits of his empathy. At his office the next morning Crowe greeted the committee with icy formality. A stenographer was on hand to transcribe the visitors' words, as though they were giving testimony in court. Crowe listened quietly but was exasperatingly coy in response. He told them he would need twenty-four hours to think things over and that all work would remain suspended in the meantime, and ordered them to wait until the stenographer had finished her transcription. Then, in another stilted gesture, he handed them each a typed copy.

Returned to camp, Red Williams briefed the rank and file from atop a water tank in the dormitory yard. He predicted optimistically that Crowe would at worst submit their demands to arbitration, and added that he was looking forward to further discussions with the boss. Plainly, despite Crowe's manifest coolness, he believed he had launched a lasting dialogue between workforce and management.

This assumption was hopelessly naive. Although Crowe had given himself a full day to consider their demands, he made his position clear only a few hours later with a scathing newspaper interview in which he condemned the strikers' complaints as the grousing of malcontents stirred up by radical elements. He denied that any man spent more than thirty minutes on a truck reaching the worksite. Reforms in the living conditions at River Camp had been stalled, he observed acidly, by the walkout itself: "If this strike hadn't been called, we would have had electricity in the river dormitories by tonight, which means fans, lights, and all the rest. The Frigidaires are already furnishing the cold water demanded, and we are going just as fast as we can to clear up all complaint." As evidence that the worksite's safety record was adequate and improving, he pointed out that not a single accident had been recorded during the entire month of July. Finally, he ascribed the tumult over the pay cut to a simple misunderstanding. Only thirty men were affected, he explained, muckers whose jobs had been rendered superfluous by mechanized equipment. Six Companies had made every effort to find them new work outside the tunnels but, regrettably, their new assignments paid less than work underground. Their wages were adjusted accordingly.

The press swallowed this spiel uncritically, but the workers must have seen that it bristled with falsehoods. They knew it was not uncommon for the truck trip between the worksite and the camps in the flats above Hemenway Wash to take an hour or even two each way—and some men were still commuting from Las Vegas. The bunkhouses that Crowe claimed were only hours from being equipped with fans, lights, and coolers had not yet been wired for electricity, and the appliances themselves had not been delivered.

Crowe's description of the accident record in July was crafty, to say the least. While in the strict definition of the term no construction accidents had occurred, five workers had died at work that month—four from heat prostration and one from drowning. Another succumbed to appendicitis, possibly due to the lack of medical staff at the riverfront. Heat prostration had also claimed four employees of Anderson Brothers, a Big Six subcontractor whose workers arguably fell within Crowe's jurisdiction.

"Pretty thin, Crowe," *Industrial Solidarity* lectured the superintendent, noting that the workmen's compensation funds in Nevada and Arizona were paying off six injury claims from a less than perfect month on the job. "If they aren't accident cases why are Nevada and Arizona paying compensation?" the paper asked. The pay cut affected at least 180 workers, not thirty, according to the strike committee.

Crowe's public comments presaged the verdict he delivered to the committee the next morning. There would be no pay raise for the workers and no concession on any other demand, he told them. All work was to be suspended indefinitely. The entire workforce was laid off and all employees were expected to vacate the Six Companies camps by 5 P.M. that day. Final paychecks had already been prepared and distribution would begin before noon.

Crowe had effectively turned a strike by a few hundred men into a lockout of 1,400. In hindsight, the strikers had no reason to expect any other response. From the outset Frank Crowe had run the Boulder Canyon job along the lines that had long since earned him the nickname of Hurry-Up: relentlessly paced work and a bulldozer's approach to all obstacles, manmade or natural. The man who had faced down blizzards, deep freezes, and even a forest fire to raise dams across the Western wilderness was not about to brook a work stoppage by laborers—certainly not when a robust supply of replacement labor remained near at hand and his bosses faced stiff financial penalties for every day they missed their contractual deadlines.

Crowe told reporters that the lockout might last "a month or longer," but expressed confidence that even at such length it would pay off in dollars and cents. "We are six months ahead of schedule on the work now," he said, "and we can afford to refuse concessions which would cost $2,000 daily or $3,000,000 during the seven years we are allowed to finish the work." His estimate of the progress of the tunnels was seconded by W. H. Wattis, who asserted from his San Francisco hospital suite that "we are several months ahead of schedule" and "can easily afford to wait for better conditions." The absurdity of this claim was promptly pointed out by the IWW, which noted that construction had been underway only for four months. If it were true that the contractor already had created a six-month cushion, "then the men have been forced to do about double the work usually required in eight hours . . . in the midst of HEAT THAT RANGES FROM 100 to 123."

The claim was, indeed, fiction. The tunnels were not ahead of schedule, but seriously behind, hampered by delays in construction of the access road and railroad and by the difficulty of developing new excavation methods to manage their towering dimensions. Power lines had only reached the riverfront on June 25; until then, drilling and ventilation equipment ran on air compressors powered by a pair of two hundred horsepower diesel engines. Work on the main tunnels would not even begin until September 21, still six weeks away. Charlie Shea would reveal to John Page a few weeks later that the progress of excavation had been so "unsatisfactory" in May and June that the company had considered shutting down completely to reorganize the work. The Big Six was saved from having to take that embarrassing step in public view by the men's fortuitous decision to walk off the job, allowing Crowe and Shea to redesign the work plan under cover of the labor stoppage.

Crowe and his superiors may well have had one other reason to welcome a temporary halt, if not a lengthy one. By demonstrating their firm resolve against organized action of any sort, they would cement their command over the labor force for good. As Wattis put it from his sickbed, "They will have to work under our conditions or not at all."

Crowe's decisive actions during the first days of the walkout created an awkward situation for Walker Young. The senior government officer on the reservation, Young had maintained a laissez-faire stance toward Six Companies' labor practices, partially in recognition that the company possessed near-total autonomy on wages and conditions under the construction contract. Still, the wage provision had been designed chiefly to force the contractor to bear the risk that wages would creep upward as the Depression ebbed—not provide it with an opportunity for the ruthless exploitation of a labor surplus.

Six Companies had evidently thought it unnecessary to inform Young that it was poised to cut wages prior to doing so on August 7. The walkout and the company's counterstrike therefore took him completely by surprise; not until he arrived at the Anderson mess hall on the morning of August 8 did he learn that all work on Hoover Dam had ceased the night before.

Young spent the day in frantic telephone calls with Ray Walter, the Reclamation chief engineer in Denver, and with Mead in Washington. The only immediate result of these conversations was a request Mead relayed to the army to place soldiers on alert at Fort Douglas, Utah, in case they were needed to keep order—a dramatic change from Young's lighthearted dismissal of the Wobbly threat the month before.

Sunday morning brought further signs that Young intended to take charge of the situation. At 3 A.M., Deputy U.S. Attorney George Montrose and U.S. Marshal Jacob Fulmer, summoned from Reno, arrived by train in Las Vegas, where they were immediately ushered into a predawn meeting with Young, John Page, and Charlie Shea. The four federal officials then drove together to Boulder City to establish a situation room in one of the few finished buildings in town, a government warehouse. From that point until work resumed five days later, Frank Crowe melted into the background and Walker Young stepped forward. Young projected a more circumspect and seemingly more conciliatory image than the hard-driving Crowe, which encouraged the workers to believe that the government might favor their cause or at least remain neutral. But Young, too, had plans to turn the walkout to his advantage.

The suspension of work threw hundreds of men and their families back on the mercy of the Depression. For some men the layoff paychecks seemed hardly worth collecting. R. P. Norton, a tunnel worker who had put in only a few days on the job before the lockout commenced, was the bemused recipient of a check for 70 cents, scarcely more than an hour's gross wage, after Six Companies' deductions for room and board at River Camp. He never bothered to cash it.

Others took their money and hared off to Las Vegas, where alarmed city officials braced themselves for a sudden invasion of furloughed men with money in their pockets and simmering resentments to uncork. Police Chief Clay Williams supplemented his twenty-man police force with as many trustworthy able-bodied men as he could deputize and tried to prevail upon saloonkeepers and liquor store owners to shut down at least for a few days. This request could not have been widely honored, for drunken brawls erupted all along the casino and whorehouse strip on Fremont Street. At least one gambling hall, worried that disaffected dam workers might storm the money cage, stationed guards with machine guns next to the cashiers. The sale of guns and ammunition to the public was barred. Rumors of Wobbly sabotage took wing, fueled by the discovery of powder, caps, and fuses in a truck trying to enter the reservation on August 11. The supplies were confiscated from the driver, who claimed he was only trying to sell the matériel to a construction crew at the dam. Clark County Sheriff Joe Keate seized several sawed-off shotguns from cars prowling the road into the reservation from Las Vegas, although it was never revealed whether the firearms belonged to workers or company agents. Taking a reasonable precaution, U.S. Marshal Fulmer deputized and armed six Reclamation Bureau employees and ordered them to move all the dynamite cached in depositories around the job site into one central magazine, which they were to keep under guard.

Yet as was often the case with Wobbly job actions, the fear of violence and sabotage was grossly exaggerated. The Las Vegas police soon succeeded in sweeping most drunken workers off Fremont Street before they could build up a head of steam. Page scribbled the words "no disturbances" or "all quiet" in his diary almost every day of the stoppage. When U.S. Labor Secretary Doak phoned his local representative, Leonard Blood, in a lather asking whether to call for "the marines to put down an insurrection in the Boulder Dam reservation," Blood assured him that there was "no trouble and no need for the marines."

The flight of laid-off workers to Las Vegas left a hardy core of fewer than two hundred strikers hunkered down on the reservation as of Monday night, August 10—about half at River Camp and the rest in a tent settlement atop Hemenway Wash, about a mile outside the still skeletal Boulder City. They stayed in communication with one another, pooling funds to buy the beans, bread, and coffee kept heated over open fires. The nights they spent buffeted by winds that covered their food and bedding with pebbly gray sand, consumed with speculation about the government's next step, rumored to be a forced evacuation of the entire reservation.

Their only basis for hope that the federal government would remain neutral came from an incident over the weekend, when Six Companies sent a truck convoy into River Camp. The trucks were manned by guards who forced the strikers to board at gunpoint, assaulting IWW organizer Fred Fuglevik with the stock of a shotgun when he resisted. The loaded convoy was about to pull out when it was halted by the timely arrival of a U.S. deputy marshal, who ordered the trucks unloaded and disarmed the guards. He instructed the Six Companies agents that they could not forcibly move the men without a government order. In fact, Montrose had earlier informed Shea that any dispossession of men by Six Companies would have to comply with Nevada state law, which required three days' notice.

But the federal government's neutrality was an illusion. The interests of Six Companies and the Reclamation Bureau were, at their core, identical: both sought rapid completion of the dam at the lowest cost. Walker Young had no more intention of letting the workforce dictate wages and conditions than had Frank Crowe. On the morning of August 11, while the local newspapers were still trying to guess at Young's plans—the *Review-Journal* described him as "silent as the Egyptian sphinx since the start of the trouble"—he was already drafting an order for federal marshals to clear the last strikers off the reservation so Six Companies could resume work.

Commissioner Mead, for his part, left no doubt where his sympathies lay. He repeated to reporters in Washington his oft-expressed position that "the present wage rate is considerably above that of the surrounding region, and it will undoubtedly be maintained." He blamed the disturbance on the heat—to which, he said, the workers had been exposed only because Six Companies had kept the job operating through the summer out of concern for "the number of men who would be thrown out of work" if the project were shut down until fall.

Mead's view of the strike as a symptom of temporary insanity among the head-addled rank and file rapidly became received wisdom in the press and among government officials. As an editorialist at the *New York Times* wrote in late August, "what [the strikers] really wanted was a modified climate. It was not working conditions but a thermometer which boiled over that caused the trouble. . . . As a matter of fact, the Six Companies is providing for the workers about as well as could be expected in a country probably never intended for human habitation by a beneficent Creator."

This argument glossed over the government's role in imposing hardships on the labor force by accelerating construction. President Hoover's order had necessitated that construction in the canyon precede what originally was to be the preliminary phase, the preparation of living quarters. None of the key government officials involved in the decision—Mead, Wilbur, and Hoover—could have been unaware of the deadly conditions facing the men in the gorge. Inexcusably, the government colluded with Six Companies in belittling the workers' legitimate complaints, breaking the strike, and punishing the strike leaders.

Not everyone lined up with Mead to congratulate Six Companies for its altruism and forbearance. One expression of support for the strikers came from an unexpected, but not unwelcome, source. This was Minnie "Ma" Kennedy, the mother of the flamboyant tent evangelist Aimee Semple McPherson. Ma Kennedy was herself an evangelist and at that moment in time a newsmaker on the national stage. Early that summer, she had married a Seattle preacher named Guy Edward Hudson, a tall, gaunt specimen with a receding hairline, soulful dark eyes, and, it transpired, two other wives, both determined to sue him for bigamy. The press diligently followed the saga of Ma Kennedy and the lover she addressed as "Whataman"—for newspaper writers an irresistible nickname—as she scurried between Los Angeles, where Hudson was fighting his wives in court, and Las Vegas, where she was given to Sunday preaching in casinos, declaiming from atop the blackjack tables.

On August 8, just as the walkout was beginning, Ma Kennedy made a pilgrimage to the dam site and told the newsmen following her like a dust cloud that she had met with the workers. "You know where my sympathies lie," she said. On a more substantial level, she set up a soup kitchen where her simple price was a crack at her clients' souls. "All these poor men who were sleeping on the Union Pacific lawn and the courthouse lawn, and hadn't maybe had a meal in three days, went to hear Ma Kennedy preach," recalled Erma Godbey. "If they would walk up and kneel down, she would pat them on the head and pray with them. Then she'd kiss them on the head and give them a little slip of paper which entitled them to a free meal."

\* \* \*

Las Vegas labor leaders had been watching resentfully as the influx of job seekers drove local wages relentlessly down. Late on August 11, the AF of L–dominated Las Vegas Central Labor Council passed a resolution giving the strikers its explicit support—perhaps the only time the AF of L openly backed a job action launched by its nemesis, the IWW. "We know that the conditions complained of by the employees of the Six Companies are the true conditions existing there," the resolution stated, "notwithstanding the fact that the officials of the Six Companies make denial of these charges." The contractor is "simply taking advantage of the depression throughout the country and the mob of broke and hungry men to establish a wage scale which is entirely unreasonable. . . . We feel that it is a crime against humanity to ask men to work in that Hell-hole of heat that they encounter at Boulder dam and to do it for a pittance."

But for the strikers time was already running out. At 6 P.M. that very day, Walker Young summoned the strike committee to the Boulder City warehouse and ordered the last die-hard pickets to clear off the reservation. The government would send two trucks at 8 A.M. sharp, he told them, adding, a bit nervously, "I hope that I may count on your continued good behavior."

Edmund Wilson spent that night at River Camp, the better to witness the evacuation. The thirty-six-year-old writer had made his name as a literary critic with his recently published book *Axel's Castle,* a survey of Symbolist writing. But he fashioned himself a journalist and social commentator, and in that guise had spent the better part of a year visiting such hot spots of Depression America as the mill towns of New England and the coal mining districts of Kentucky.

The Wobblies held a definite fascination for the progressive Wilson, who believed they occupied an anticapitalist middle ground between the AF of L, which was too inclined to collaborate with management, and the communists, who were too freighted with dour ideological rhetoric about class warfare. In his telling, the Wobblies of Black Canyon were free spirits, engaging and even "rakish" in demeanor during that tense night of waiting for the government trucks. "Some people wouldn't believe that a fellow can get a kick out of this kind of work," he quoted one organizer. "But you get a kick out of pulling off a strike—get sent to San Quentin and get a kick out of it!"

Still, Wilson was too keen an observer not to notice a rising disaffection in camp with the IWW, which yet again had called workingmen out on strike against long odds, asking them to risk the starvation of their wives and children for uncertain gain.

Dawn broke, overcast and suddenly cooler. The holdouts on the reservation stirred, cooked eggs they had bartered, and boiled and reboiled the last dregs of coffee grounds to supply everyone with a cupful of wan brown liquid. The government arrived at eight, Walker Young driving his own car with Marshal Fulmer in the passenger seat. Two open trucks and an empty bus brought up the rear.

Young stepped out of the car, edgy and drawn, wearing a pair of leather puttees like an aging doughboy. He and Fulmer, an older man in a string tie, were the only two figures of authority on the spot, unarmed federal bureaucrats confronting a band of resentful men who could have overwhelmed them instantly, given the inclination. But the committee had pledged its word that there would be no violence, and in any case everyone in camp knew the strike was effectively over.

At that moment, as though to signal the sodden end of the walkout, the heavens opened up. Everybody, Young and Fulmer included, took refuge from the downpour under the overhanging mess hall roof for the reading of the formal order of eviction. From somewhere in the crowd came one last voice of braggadocio: What if the men refuse to go—will the government use force?

Young hesitated, as if trying to summon a bit of Crowe's bravura. "We ask you to go and we depend on you to go," he replied at length. "There's been no question at all of force."

"But if we don't go, you'll make us?"

"Yes, if you refuse to go . . ." Young paused again. "We'll . . . make you."

Suddenly there was a rumble from up the hill, and cries of "Look out!" A small avalanche of rocks and boulders—"either loosened by the rain or launched by a strategic hand," wrote Wilson—swept down the slope and across the camp. Regaining his perch atop a wooden bench, Young tried to bring the discussion to a rapid close. His idea was to clear the reservation and "make a clean start."

Bring in scabs, in other words, a worker called out.

"I hate to call any man a scab," Young said.

Finally, Red Williams ended the dialogue. The wind went out of the crowd. It was time to hold up their end of the bargain and go quietly. The men gathered their belongings and piled into the government vehicles to be driven toward Railroad Pass and off the reservation.

Even as Young and Fulmer were conferring with the River Camp holdouts, deputy marshals were swarming over the rest of the reservation, enforcing Young's evacuation edict against anyone without an actual job. In Young's words that meant "all past employees of Six Companies, job seekers, tourists, campers, and other visitors"—in practice, all but a few Reclamation office personnel. The hardest blow, naturally, fell on Ragtown, where about one hundred families were again dispossessed and trucked off, like refugees, to the reservation's periphery.

The relocation was witnessed by the ever-present Murl Emery, whose cynicism mounted when he noticed that Six Companies, proclaiming its reluctance to let the uprooted families starve, sent a couple of trucks loaded with provisions to the boundary line where the residents were left to squat. "They did give it to them," Emery recalled, "but they had motion pictures of it, taking pictures of feeding those families. I had those same trucks going back and forth to Vegas for days and days while all this was going on. But I forgot the motion picture."

The next day brought more tangible changes to the reservation. A cattle gate was thrown across the main road from Las Vegas, manned by a dozen armed Reclamation Bureau guards backed up by a squad of sheriff's deputies. A hand-painted sign soon appeared, warning against the possession of "intoxicating liquors, narcotics, explosives or fire arms" on government property.

Walker Young's indulgence toward campers and squatters on the federal reservation had ended. Mead's concerns about the dangers of impromptu settlements like Ragtown had been proven right, in a sense; as construction advanced, the need for security and order left no room for half-measures. Complete control was exercised, or none at all. That meant guardhouses at the reservation portals and strict rules governing behavior, strictly enforced. Those with jobs at the dam were to be given credentials allowing them to pass through the gate; everyone else would need a pass personally signed by Young. These were to be issued "rather sparingly."

With the reservation secured on August 13, Young instructed Six Companies to resume work, an event the *Review-Journal* marked with two-inch headlines like those that might announce the end of a war. A new hiring procedure was established. Leonard Blood, whose federal hiring hall had been consistently bypassed by Six Companies, moved into a one-room wooden shack at the main gate where all job applicants, new or old, were to report. Blood announced that the Boulder Canyon Project Act's statutory preference for veterans and American citizens would be "rigidly adhered to" and that the sub-rosa favoritism and nepotism of the past had ended. The shift bosses who had been doing most of the hiring for the Big Six henceforth would have "nothing whatsoever to do with this end of the work," he said.

Almost immediately he was undercut by Frank Crowe, who issued his own directive that "no new men would be hired until all the old worthy employees who desire, are back on the job"—a policy that would obviously preserve the old inequities. He stationed shift bosses inside Blood's shack with instructions to reject any applicant they suspected of complicity in the strike. Blood was unwilling or powerless to overrule what the Wobblies characterized as a "blacklist." ("The Six Companies had their bosses standing there and unless they said that a man was a good, faithful and spineless slave, they were turned down," reported the embittered *Industrial Solidarity*.)

Crowe never acknowledged that wage rates or working conditions had anything to do with the walkout. "So you saw in the paper that we had a strike," he wrote tersely to his mother, Emma, on August 22. "It wasn't much we just canned a bunch of bums." Yet despite being vilified by the Wobbly press as the agent of Six Companies' detestable labor policies, Crowe emerged from the strike with his reputation among the workers intact, even enhanced. In part this reflected his withdrawal from the fray after his rejection of the strike demands on August 8, leaving Walker Young to execute the harsher antilabor steps. In any event, his distaste for radical labor organizers was undoubtedly shared by most workers. Furthermore, by articulating the policy of giving hiring preference to "old worthies" ahead of outsiders, he established himself as their rescuer from a frightening brush with renewed joblessness. Once Boulder City opened for occupancy and living standards rose even for those with the most menial jobs, Crowe's stature as the dispenser of employment rose along with it.

Not until 1932 was Blood able to end what he called "the friend and relative system of employment" and change the composition of the workforce. By June that year, he reported, ex-servicemen comprised 47 percent of the payroll, compared to 29 percent before the strike, and there were no longer any foreigners on the site without final citizenship papers. "All workmen were sent to the job on their ability to perform the duties required of them and not their ability to form 'connections,'" Blood reported to Washington.

Despite Crowe's stringent vetting procedures, the rehiring proceeded quickly. Some 730 men out of the pre-strike contingent of 1,400 were rehired within twenty-four hours of the resumption order. Many had spent the intervening time milling around Blood's shack, sweltering in the hundred-degree heat miles from shelter, water, or food, waiting for foremen to pick out their old teams and pass them through the gate. Once inside, they were informed that the lower pay scale introduced on August 7, with minimums set at $4 a day, would remain in effect for the duration of construction.

At Railroad Pass, a mile or so over the horizon, a dwindling group of die-hard pickets tried to keep the strike alive with hand-lettered banners. Their cause was hopeless. On Friday afternoon, August 14, they gathered at the Las Vegas Airdome, an open-air movie theater on Fremont Street. Reports were that eight hundred persons attended, but three-quarters of these were almost certainly spectators looking to satisfy their curiosity or hoping to scare up a few hours' idle entertainment. The rhetoric from the podium was appreciably more belligerent than before, reflecting the strikers' increased desperation, and possibly their increased realism. Among other things, they condemned the federal government as a collaborator of Six Companies, rather than a neutral party. What was left of the strike committee wired Nevada governor Fred Balzar that night with a message of pure bluster: "Boulder Dam strike still on. One dollar wage cut still in effect for forty percent tunnel crews. Six Companies employing strike breakers. Is the state of Nevada going to uphold Six Companies cutting wages in this time of depression?"

Balzar responded by telegram the next day: "State of Nevada absolutely neutral in all labor disputes."

That Sunday, the last 126 strikers voted at their campsite near Railroad Pass to end the strike—or as they preferred to put it, "transfer the strike back to the job." Most employees on the site could be forgiven for wondering what the week-long work stoppage had gained them. The reduced wage scale remained in effect. Work conditions improved modestly, but much of the improvement would be due to the change of seasons and, more significantly, to progress on the construction of Boulder City, which would welcome its first residents in early October. Before the end of the year, Six Companies relocated the mess hall, commissary, and dormitories to the new town and demolished River Camp, that distasteful reminder of the killing summer of 1931.

The short-lived strike at Hoover Dam was a reminder of the IWW's habitual shortcoming: an inability to build a solid organization with a sound strategic plan that could hold the loyalty of the men against pressure from the bosses. It was a wildcat strike, not a strategic action, and therefore doomed to fail. By claiming credit for the walkout, the IWW inherited popular blame for its failure, a blow to its reputation it could ill afford. The Depression could have been the union's heyday; instead it was another way station to its ultimate marginalization. By the end of 1931 it could no longer afford to keep two weekly newspapers operating, and *Industrial Solidarity* was closed.

The true beneficiary of the 1931 strike was Six Companies, which solidified its authority over wages and working conditions in the canyon. The company would find itself at loggerheads with the government over many issues in the next few years, but its treatment of the workers would not be among them—at least not until very late in the project, when a new administration governed in Washington.

The Wobblies did not entirely vanish from the canyon after the strike of 1931. Frank Anderson remained in the area, managing to keep a tiny cadre of members together for the next two years. When, in August 1933, he tried again to call the men out on strike, the effort would unfold as farce.

Toward the end of August, Young, seeking to enhance security in his enclosed and fenced 115-square-mile domain, found the ideal man to serve as his chief ranger: Bud Bodell, the Clark County deputy sheriff and club owner who had issued the original order to arrest Frank Anderson in July. A former daredevil auto racer from Ely, Nevada, Bodell had shown himself to be a fearless nemesis of bootleggers, radicals, and strikers. His approach was to bust heads as a quick and efficient way to maintain civic order, bypassing the courthouse altogether. A photograph from the period shows him standing in front of Boulder City's first police station, sandy-haired and defiant, decked out in jodhpurs with an enormous ivory-handled revolver hanging menacingly from the waist, hands clasped behind his back in a pose of fearless invulnerability. As the law in Boulder City, serving the interests of both the government and Six Companies, he would become a ubiquitous, feared, and detested figure all over town.

But he would serve an even more imperious master. Boulder City was poised to become a thriving community under the authority of a man whose view of unionists and other disturbers of the peace was even more uncompromising than Crowe's, Young's, or Bodell's. His name was Sims Ely.

# Ely's Kingdom

He was a severe, wizened old man, with the censorious personality of an Old Testament prophet and the humorless expression of the pitchfork-wielding farmer in Grant Wood's *American Gothic*. He disapproved of drink, gambling, adultery, and unionism, every trace of which he was determined to eradicate from Boulder City, where his position embraced the roles of mayor, judge, jury, prosecutor, and schoolmaster, keeper of order and defender of public morality. Sims Ely reported for duty as city manager of Boulder City (his official title) on October 3, 1931. A few months shy of his seventieth birthday, he had come to take charge of a community that was not yet quite born.

Outdoors, he could be glimpsed walking the streets head down, never engaging a soul, his ever-present Norfolk jacket and knickerbocker trousers accentuating his air of the antique. But inside his City Hall office there was no doubt about his authority, the heart of which was the power of eviction: he could bar any man from entering the federal reservation—for a day, a week, a lifetime—and consequently deprive him of his job at the dam. A condemnation from Sims Ely could mean the loss of a man's living, domicile, even family.

Ely was born in 1862, in the heat of the Civil War, in rural Overton County, Tennessee, which mustered for the Confederate side in that deeply divided state. He told his children that he struck his first blow for the South at the age of three by kicking the shin of a Yankee officer who had invaded the house looking for Sims's father, a Confederate soldier. "This was typical of him," reflected a family member, searching for a moral in this yarn from the era of the Lost Cause: "He stood up for his principles all his life."

In 1895 he moved to the Arizona territory, where he worked in banking and acquired a part interest in the *Phoenix Republican* (now the *Arizona Republic*), which had been founded five years earlier to promote a decidedly anti-Mexican political platform. His subsequent career embraced the full range of professions open to an intelligent and determined man in the frontier period; when Interior Secretary Wilbur tapped him to run Boulder City he was serving as a director and treasurer of the Federal Land Bank of Berkeley, California, which provided farm credit in the Southwest as one of twelve federally chartered regional agricultural banks.

Wilbur wanted a city manager who "would have full control and would keep off the reservation those who socially misbehaved in any way." Ely, he reckoned, "could handle the problem well, for he was familiar with Western life." Wilbur downplayed another possible qualification: his own personal assistant, Northcutt Ely, was Sims Ely's son.

Sims Ely wielded absolute power with absolute confidence, even relish. One day, according to a story Northcutt told, he gave a tour of Boulder City to Colorado governor Edwin "Big Ed" Johnson, who was known for his own straitlaced views about public morality. Ely showed Johnson to the city jail, where a dam worker had been deposited for beating his wife. There had been no trial.

"We threw him in there for three days," Ely said. "If he doesn't like it, he can give up his job—there are plenty of people waiting to take his place."

"Sims," the governor observed admiringly, "you run this place without a taint of legality."

Not that Ely's approach was necessarily unwelcome to the citizens of Boulder City. His iron discipline reassured many in this desert community inhabited by a diverse population including not a few roughnecks. Northcutt Ely tried to summon that reality with a tetchy rebuke to a Las Vegas newspaper that criticized, a half-century after the fact, his father's tendency to use "coercion, blackmail, and harassment to keep people in line."

It is quite true that my father was not liked by the would-be brothel operators, the wife beaters, the child molesters, the bootleggers, the deadbeats who failed to pay alimony, and others whom he expelled from the reservation for cause, but . . . he was esteemed and supported by the moral elements of the town.

John Page put the situation more concisely, if indelicately, in a letter to Ely in 1947, when Page was reclamation commissioner and the eighty-five-year-old Ely had finally been forced into retirement. "You know," he wrote, "you were the first Hitler when it came to governing Boulder City. And the strange thing was that the people generally liked it."

He was the first authority figure Boulderites ever knew. Many of them, adults and children alike, were under the impression that he had always been there and always would be. It was his job to ensure that all the standard virtues of American society were imported into Boulder City, a showplace work camp for the showiest public project of the era. Perhaps inevitably, he imported a few of society's subtler vices, too, such as racism, class discrimination, and political favoritism.

The construction of Boulder City started in April 1931 with the erection of a giant water tank—to this day the outstanding municipal landmark—on a rocky outcropping atop Hemenway Wash. From there the city was to spread out in a wide fan mapped to the contours of the land by a Dutch-born urban planner named Saco Rienk DeBoer.

DeBoer, then working in Denver, was a disciple of the visionary landscape designer Frederick Law Olmsted. He jumped at Reclamation's offer to plan a model town from the ground up—"an oasis in the desert," as the government put it—to be managed in accordance with the most modern principles of municipal administration. He divided the city into industrial, commercial, and residential zones to minimize traffic congestion and arranged the commercial blocks around open squares to "create store groups of unusual beauty"—clothing shops in one square, groceries in another, and so on. One zone was to consist exclusively of houses of worship, in the expectation that the godly cluster would "stimulate religious consciousness."

DeBoer laid out the city's residential district just as meticulously. He banished vehicular thoroughfares from the zone and arranged the single-family homes on open V-shaped plats of eighteen units each, every house with its own tiny front yard and each giving onto a communal backyard playground "which is absolutely safe, close to all homes, and attractive." Most distinctively, the residential zone was sequestered from the rest of the city by a wide forest belt winding sinuously from a community recreation field on the western edge of town, past the site of a grand resort hotel, and east and north to the administration building, neighboring the water tank and majestically overlooking a broad, perfectly groomed public lawn.

It was an ambitious and idealistic scheme that fully honored Reclamation's ambition to promote moral and civic uplift. But much of it was destined to go unrealized. Reclamation had appropriated a generous $2 million to build Boulder City, yet DeBoer's plan would have busted the budget. Therefore Elwood Mead and Walker Young reshaped his design along much more conventional lines. They eliminated his pride, the forest belt, as well as the grand hotel and recreation field. The residential playgrounds were rubbed out, as were the elementary and secondary schools—a stroke of shortsightedness that would bedevil the town administration within a few short months.

Cumulatively these alterations eradicated the most important element of DeBoer's plan, its egalitarian spirit. While DeBoer had placed all the residences into one district without regard to the status or income of the occupants, the new city plan underscored the social and economic divide between Reclamation's staff and the Six Companies laborers. DeBoer's idealized American hamlet was transformed into a quintessential company town, with management perched at the top of the pyramid not only socially, but geographically.

DeBoer found these changes highly objectionable, but the bureau's budgetary utilitarianism prevailed. So did its class consciousness. The bureau and Six Companies both thought of the Reclamation engineers and construction superintendents as members of a permanent professional elite and of the dam workers as a caste of itinerant laborers. The new plan, accordingly, clustered the bureau employees' homes around Reclamation's hacienda-style administration building, at the highest point in town most exposed to the cooling breezes. There the lawns were seeded and flower beds tended by a landscape gardener on the government payroll. On a sandy flatland down the hill, past the central business district, were found the homes for the working class.

The government families had the pick of their lots, as well as a choice among blueprints personally vetted by Gordon Kaufmann, the bureau's outside architect. Their homes were built for comfort and durability, with double walls and attics to absorb the heat. They had neat stucco exteriors, which encouraged the addition of the personal touches that made a house a home, such as window treatments and flower boxes—"all of them different," Stella Carmody reported, "all of them harmonious." They were equipped with modern conveniences like telephones, spacious refrigerators, electric ranges, and electric cooling systems. Joining the Reclamation hands in their hilltop district was Frank Crowe, for whom Six Companies built a "substantial villa." Nicknamed "Crowe's Nest" for its 360-degree view, it was very likely the most lavish family residence in Boulder City.

Unlike the Reclamation families, the workers waited up to a year to lease a Six Companies house with unfinished wood floors that tended to fill the palms and knees of crawling babies with splinters. Cracks in the plywood-sheathed walls let in windblown sand by the shovelful. Six Companies threw up row after row of these indistinguishable two- and three-room bungalows designed so simply that a two-man carpentering crew could assemble three of them in two days. There were no phones or refrigerators, but simple gas ranges and water heaters fueled by bottled propane; for comfort the inhabitants resorted to "swamp coolers," water-soaked blankets or linens hung over open windows to catch the occasional breeze. For landscaping they were on their own; spurred on by a monthly prize for the best-decorated yard, they swarmed into the desert and came back with cactus, Joshua trees, and purple sage, which they planted in beds of sand trimmed with stones.

Utilities and other basic amenities were spotty, at first. The homes were equipped with indoor toilets but no running water, so behind every other home stood a two-hole outhouse. "I have rented one of the new houses," a young Six Companies engineer wrote his bride in October 1931. "So far there is electricity only; no running water, no sewers, no streets, nothing but sand. Bring complete camping equipment and a week's supply of food."

Ultimately the Big Six erected 658 of these determinedly temporary structures, which were expected to be bulldozed out of existence once the dam was finished and the workforce dispersed. The smallest, comprising a bedroom and bathroom, rented for $15 a month; $4 more got the tenant a living room as well. A two-bedroom home rented for $30. Unmarried laborers were accommodated in eight two-story H-shaped dormitories located on the west side of town, each with 172 private rooms measuring eight feet by ten and furnished with a steel frame bed, mattress, blanket, bed linens, and a chair. For this room, with board and transport to the worksite thrown in, the Boulder City Company, a Six Companies subsidiary headed by Felix Kahn, deducted $1.60 a day from a worker's paycheck. Six Companies' unmarried male office workers had their own dormitory of fifty-three rooms, reflecting perhaps a certain corporate skittishness about mixing blue collars with white.

Charging rent on this scale for the modest single family homes was pure profiteering. Six Companies records indicate that it spent an average of $260 to build each home. It told the Reclamation Bureau, however, that they cost a total of $477,331, which works out to an average $725 each; a separate estimate prepared by John Page for bureau headquarters in late 1931 put the cost of the largest two- and three-bedroom homes at $800 and $1,150, respectively.

The discrepancy cannot fully be accounted for by the cost of the gas appliances, which cost less than $130, or by the ground rent of $5,000 a month the company paid the government for all its Boulder City facilities (encompassing its homes, offices, and warehouses). The company stated that the rent it charged workers was calculated to amortize the cost of the cottages over five years at 6 percent a year, but that only underscores its excessiveness. Even if one were to give the company the benefit of the doubt and estimate the average cost of the homes including appliances at $550, that would justify an average rent of about $9.60 per month, or about half of what the company charged.

Such "petty swindling," to recall Edmund Wilson's phrase, extended to the company's other transactions with its employees. Page, who at the end of 1931 conducted a three-month investigation of post-strike labor conditions on the reservation, reported to Young that the workers' "principal complaint" was the company's nickel-and-diming deductions for housing, food, and transport. He concluded that the contractor turned a profit in every category. Adding to the workers' discontent was the company's transfer of these services to the Boulder City Company, transparently its own subsidiary. This maneuver had an "undesirable psychological effect" on morale, Page found, as the employees viewed it as merely "an attempt to shift the obligations and responsibility of the employer" to an ostensibly independent operation. Page's investigation notwithstanding, federal officials did not lift a finger to interfere with the company's fleecing of its own employees.

Boulder City took a long time to shed its embryonic appearance. At first even the more substantial Reclamation neighborhood resembled a construction zone; John Page's elder daughter, Jean, recalled him laying a pair of wide boards over their front yard so she and her sister could walk from the porch to the street without sinking up to their ankles in sand. She and her friends learned never to touch a garden hose after dark without first checking it with a flashlight, as that was when the community's robust population of black widow spiders came out for water. ("In the beginning we had the feeling that we were intruding on the insect population," she reckoned. "After all, it had been their home for a long time.")

The town made a disconcerting first impression. With its rows upon rows of identical bungalows and its sparse greenery, "it was the weirdest place I'd ever seen," related Dorothy Nunley, the wife of veteran tunnel man Tex Nunley. Then there was its around-the-clock heartbeat—a rarity in those days even in a major metropolis, let alone an isolated camp town.

Coming from staid Long Beach, California, where the sidewalks were rolled up at nine in the evening, Dorothy said, "I was used to people going to bed at night and not seeing anything until the next day." Instead, Boulder City stayed open all night to serve the men on all three shifts—the movie theater, for example, scheduled a swing shift matinee in the morning, another show in the afternoon, and two at night.

In the working-class precincts, families eked out a few extra dollars a month by renting out extra space until enough houses and dormitories were built to fill demand, an equilibrium that was not reached until early 1933. "[We] had three beds on our sleeping porch that were occupied twenty-four hours a day," recalled Ann Stebens, the daughter of a motor pool mechanic who was eight when her family moved to Boulder City in September 1932.

> A man would pay two dollars a week, for lunches and a bed. My mother made lunches for all of them. One man would get off at 7:00 in the morning, the man that was going to work at 7:00 would get up, fold his sheets, put them on the shelf. The next man coming in would take his sheets off the shelf, make up the bed and go to bed. At 3:00 he got up, another one came in, put his sheets on the bed, and we had three beds that were occupied that way for months.

For all that the site had been selected for its comparatively benign conditions, the bureau planners understood that without the amelioration of plant cover the beating sun would make the town "almost unendurable" in the summer, especially once the desert sand was layered over with heat-retaining pavement and concrete sidewalks.

The assignment to turn the raw desert green was handed to a thirty-one-year-old landscape designer from Oregon with the comically inappropriate name of Wilbur W. Weed. The difference in climate between Weed's rainy native Northwest and his barren new home must have made a strong impression, for his first instinct was to dress Boulder City with cactus and other native flora on the principle that the most practical approach to desert horticulture was "cooperating with nature rather than opposing it." This plan was vetoed by his Reclamation bosses, who informed him that "we have enough desert, glaring sand, and cacti in the surrounding area without having to be further reminded of it." Their preference was for "normal development," by which they meant importing trees, shrubs, and grasses from temperate climes into the desert ecology by the thousands. The bureau had promised the dam workers a healthful settlement, and it regarded the shade trees and parklike greens of an idealized small-town America as a covenant of that promise.

Weed turned his efforts to identifying exogenous plants that might thrive in this hostile environment. By the end of January he had placed orders for 9,150 trees and shrubs and 1,200 rosebushes—eleven carloads of flora costing a total of $4,205. Most of these were destined to perish.

Nature constantly confounded Weed's judgments about which species would survive best in the alien environment. He had figured that evergreen shrubs with small, thick, leathery leaves would fare well because they would retain the most moisture in hot, dry conditions; instead, these "took the shortest period to oblivion." He found that irrigation cycles had to be timed rigorously, for too much water could be every bit as lethal as too little. The sandy ground of Boulder City was easily windblown and almost entirely devoid of the decayed biological matter that sustains plant life. Weed had no trouble understanding why the would-be gardener in Boulder City might be driven to the expedient of "planting a concrete lawn and painting it green."

Yet by the late spring of 1932, his work had largely consigned to history the dust storms that had tormented residents by turning the white linens on their clotheslines brown. Weed had initiated a transformation of the desert outpost into a garden whose winds carried not clouds of sand but the scents of flowering plants. That July, the residents celebrated a milestone for their young city when the lawn in front of the administration building was mowed for the very first time.

There were other occasions for outpourings of civic pride. "Every time there was a public building completed—the government garage, the Veteran's Hall, the P.O.—there was a dance to 'initiate' it," Jean Page recollected. The first church services were held in a multidenominational worship house that had been conceived as a temporary expedient by a delegation of fourteen Las Vegas pastors who met with Page in March 1931 to look over church blueprints. Page recorded that all Christian denominations were represented, except the Mormons, who solved the problem of accommodations for themselves by transporting a clapboard church building in its entirety, all the way from Las Vegas, by truck.

Six Companies built a hospital for its workers and bureau employees on the hill where DeBoer had originally decreed a resort hotel. Employees paid a $1.50 monthly fee entitling them to comprehensive treatment—the earliest expression of Henry Kaiser's concept of employer-provided prepaid medical care, which would ultimately flower into the nonprofit Kaiser Permanente Health Plan. Their family members, however, were still required to drive into Las Vegas for treatment.

Ely's initial task as city manager was to fill up Boulder City's commercial center. The groundwork had been laid before his arrival by bureau officials who had spent months pondering the best method of apportioning permits for businesses ranging from barbershops to department stores.

The one path they rejected from the outset was trusting to free enterprise. They feared that Boulder City would acquire the image of a boom town, attracting inexperienced and unwary entrepreneurs whose inevitable failure would leave vacant storefronts behind. The bureau attempted to nip this phenomenon in the bud by warning publicly that "the probable population of Boulder City is more limited than is popularly imagined," that new businesses would face potent competition from the Six Companies commissary, and that there was no certainty that the town would even survive beyond the completion of the dam, then forecast for 1938.

The planners fixed the number of permits in every business category at one, two, or three—the actual number chosen "largely by guesswork," Ely conceded. These would be parceled out to applicants of suitable "character, personality, age, physical condition" and financial resources, picked from among the three thousand inquiries that arrived on Ely's desk before the end of 1931.

Ely layered his own personal standards over the bureau's guidelines. He rejected an application for a dance hall despite the would-be proprietor's pledge to employ "respectable girls on salary . . . [as] dance partners for men customers," because he was convinced that the scheme could not be otherwise than a front for prostitution. Proposals to sell what he considered "undesirable literature"—it is unclear whether the offense was politics or prurience—were similarly rejected. Ely granted a permit for a taxicab service, then hastily revoked it after discovering that the owner was being paid by a casino and brothel at Railroad Pass, a few miles up the road from the Boulder City gate, to ferry customers from town for free.

By mid-1932 Ely had licensed 113 businesses in Boulder City without suffering, as he proudly remarked, a single failure. Among them were a department store, a grocery, two drugstores, two menswear stores (and one for ladies), two butcher shops, two beauty salons, four restaurants, a movie theater, mortuary, and tailor. "Of course, [they] are not doing so well as they would like," Ely reported, "but all are probably doing better than they could do anywhere else just now, for here is one of the few unimpaired pay rolls of the country."

Ely exercised an especially profound influence over the town's social character. There was scarcely a corner of Boulder City life that he would not stick his nose into. A resident could be haled before the city manager for beating his wife, allowing his property to run down, or having books overdue at the city library. ("I had to take a day off to go up and see Sims about this," recalled a dam worker charged with the latter offense. "Each book was worth about 50¢, but he fined me a couple of dollars for each, which I paid.")

Ely aimed his fiercest enforcement efforts at the iniquity of liquor. Cars entering the federal reservation were searched for bootleg alcohol (and, after the repeal of Prohibition in 1933, brand-name brews). Vehicles discovered to be carrying contraband were often impounded. Public drunkenness was grounds for permanent banishment from the city. Yet the vice stubbornly resisted eradication. Three days after Christmas 1932, Ely felt compelled to publish an emphatic reminder of the municipal regulations. "Because the rule forbidding intoxication was apparently not known by all, we were lenient in dealing with several cases of 'Christmas Drunks.' Ignorance of this regulation will not be accepted as an excuse hereafter and no leniency can be expected."

He proceeded to deliver a rather menacing sermon of the sort that would earn him the nickname "Deacon":

> Most bootleg liquor is poisonous. . . . [W]hen a man with a hang-over returns to a hazardous work he is not able to guard his own life properly, and he is a menace to his fellow workers. It is unfortunate that some of the men working here have very short memories concerning the terrible conditions of unemployment which prevail elsewhere. Within a short time after getting their jobs they forget all about the privations, hardships, and despair they underwent before they secured employment, and they proceed to blow their money with bootleggers. It is a matter of choosing between drink and the job.

He was equally unyielding in his insistence on public modesty, in which he crossed well over the line into priggishness. When the American Legion initiated a series of moonlight dances for young adults, he forbid their dimming the lights, relenting only when the chaperones, all local matrons, pleaded that the boys could not otherwise summon the courage to ask the girls to dance. Children under sixteen were subject to a nine o'clock curfew, marked by a siren sounded from the fire house.

The root of his bluenosed morality was a patently Victorian notion of feminine frailty. "I always think of the woman as at a disadvantage, and of having a right to my protection," he once told his son a propos of a financial scam perpetrated on a dowager of his acquaintance. "Women never seem to have that general understanding of the proper approach to an investment, they are natural gamblers, with great reluctance to taking losses, always bringing personal equations into the problem."

This may explain his uncompromising approach to domestic relations. He forcibly removed one young girl from her home following an allegation of paternal abuse, transferred her to a neighbor's family, and evicted the alleged abuser from his household and work. Wife beaters faced similar penalties; although in such cases the husband's eviction often was followed by that of his unfortunate spouse, as her right to continue living within the city limits disappeared along with her husband's employment.

Some residents learned to use his solicitude to their advantage: it became an open secret in Boulder City that the best way for a man to extract a favorable ruling from Ely was to send his wife to plead his case. There were even snickers that his stringency on sexual matters reflected suppressed urges of his own. Some noticed his unfailing attendance at the games of the schoolgirls' baseball team. ("He loved to see those girls in their shorts getting skinned up," one resident observed.) There was even an unverified rumor that he had gotten his own secretary "in trouble." The child was given up for adoption, according to the story.

The interest Ely shared with Reclamation and Six Companies in keeping Boulder City tranquil, safe, and free from labor dissension—along with his familial connection to the Interior Department's senior management—made his job security unassailable. Residents assumed that any complaints about his performance sent up the departmental chain of command would only be short-circuited by his son Northcutt, still occupying his perch at Secretary Wilbur's right hand.

Ely's regime acquired a noxious edge from his partnership with Bud Bodell, who became the reservation's chief ranger shortly after the 1931 strike. Bodell's enthusiastic strikebreaking that summer had brought him to Walker Young's attention, even as it earned him the curses of the Wobbly press, which called him "Mussolini" Bodell and "Boss-herder of the reservation." ("Efficient? Sure!" remarked *Industrial Worker*. "A Mussolini must always be efficient for the Boss's dollars or he wouldn't be Mussolini for long.") Ely and Bodell, the one a stern Midwestern farmer's son and the other a roughhousing daredevil from rural Nevada, developed an uneasy symbiosis. It would not last long.

Bodell was given to grossly exaggerating the scale of the criminal threat in town, the better to rationalize his shows of force. During the strike he had claimed to have identified a cadre of two thousand Wobblies at the dam. This was a wildly improbable estimate, but one he used to justify arming dozens of citizens to guard the Six Companies truck fleet, which he claimed the strikers were planning to sabotage. No such plot ever surfaced. Within the reservation, his swagger was vastly disproportionate to the actual level of wrongdoing. He would later acknowledge that only a single felony had occurred during his entire tenure in Boulder City, which lasted to the end of the construction period in 1936. This was the robbing of an evening's receipts from Earl Brothers, the theater owner, by thieves who bound and gagged his wife and absconded with his car.

But the city management's main target was not street crime. Of much greater concern to Ely and Young were bootlegging and labor organizing. Bodell's squad of ten reservation rangers made regular forays onto the Boulder City–Las Vegas highway to drive off bootleggers, whose rickety booze shacks on the highway proved harder to eradicate than scorpions' nests. There was no denying that this was a legitimate public safety issue, even if it involved the rangers' straying outside their jurisdiction. For the highway was infamous for the slaughter wreaked by drunk drivers. Bodell claimed that twenty-seven lives had been lost on the two-lane stretch between the reservation limits and Railroad Pass, a distance of less than five miles, from 1931 to 1932, amid many more injuries. For once his figures did not smack of exaggeration. Alarmed by the carnage, the local U.S. attorney authorized him late in 1932 to rub out five dozen bootleg joints. In one raid he made thirty-two arrests, followed a few nights later by seventeen more. On their third foray the rangers simply burned all the remaining shacks to the ground.

It is harder to rationalize Bodell's policing of putative "radicalism" at the dam site. There his role was manifestly designed to keep the men in line, as a reporter from the Scripps-Howard newspaper chain observed in January 1932. Bodell "rules the morals and manners of the dam workers with a breezy confidence that he knows what is good for his wards," the correspondent wrote. "He works on a double theory—give the men something to do; crush out radicalism at the first whisper." To monitor loose talk, he bragged, he employed thirty officers working undercover as laborers on the job. He even supervised the workmen's illicit poker games, which he claimed had been infiltrated by card sharps until he moved them inside the Six Companies recreation hall "where we can watch them." Bodell's force, the newsman concluded, "considers its business to see the gambling laws are broken in the proper manner; that liquor is kept from the workers; that wobblies who talk too much are run off the reservation."

Any resident's opinion of the Ely regime depended not only on whether and how often one got brought before him, but also on which end of the town one lived in. Among the conditions of life in Boulder City that Ely enforced was its social stratification. The Reclamation and Six Companies families almost never mixed. They shopped in different stores—the Reclamation families in the independent Manix and Vaughn Department Store; the workers, living paycheck to paycheck or on scrip, in the Six Companies commissary. "If they had bridge parties, we were never invited," one Six Companies wife recalled of the snooty Reclamation women. It was widely noted among the Six Companies families that Ely and Bodell went easy on Reclamation kids caught misbehaving and, for that matter, on their parents. At a certain level this was unsurprising, as Ely's authority over an individual's employment did not extend to staff of the Reclamation Bureau. But it certainly contributed to his image among the working-class families as a capricious autocrat with an ornery streak.

This may have explained Ely's attempt to make an example of Woody Williams, one of Frank Crowe's most trusted lieutenants, after Williams showed up drunk at a Legion dance with a flask peeking from his hip pocket. For this flagrant offense against public order Ely ordered Williams off the reservation for thirty days. The very next morning Ely was confronted by Crowe, the only Six Companies employee who matched him in rank and who insisted Williams be readmitted at the gate. The matter had to be resolved by Walker Young, who threw his weight behind his city manager. "He's off for thirty days," Young told Crowe. (Young later claimed that Williams eventually thanked him for standing his ground, saying that the public humiliation helped steer him away from liquor.)

To Six Companies families, the resolution still smacked of favoritism. Were the offender any other working stiff, "Ely would have said, 'Off the reservation. Don't come back,'" one worker observed years later. "They made an exception for the assistant superintendent. That's why it pays to be a big shot sometimes."

The Big Six, however, consistently ranked as Ely's toughest adversary. No issue illustrated that like the battle waged over Boulder City's schools.

Considering how much care went into planning the city, the government's failure to provide for schooling its children verges on the inexplicable. Nothing was more predictable than the need for school buildings, in light of the community's unusual demographics. The city's birth rate was "much higher than in any other town in the United States," Ely reported in 1932, ascribing the phenomenon to its position as "the only community in the whole country in which substantially all the families are young." That spring a municipal census counted 513 children of primary and high school age inside the city limits. As an indication of the demand for school facilities these figures were undoubtedly conservative, for scores of dam worker families still occupied Hoovervilles outside town and new families were arriving every week. The children soon became pawns in a three-way imbroglio involving the state of Nevada, the federal government, and Six Companies.

Inevitably, the issue was money—specifically Clark County assessor De Vinney's attempt to levy an excise tax on Six Companies' equipment. The county would gain handsomely if it could make the levy stick; De Vinney calculated the bill at $182,500 for 1931, even before the project ramped up to full strength. But Six Companies was not about to relinquish its claimed exemption from local and state taxes without a fight. Reclamation supported the company's position, fearing that ceding taxing powers to local jurisdictions would set the stage for a far broader erosion of its authority—including the loss of its ability to ban from its work camp gambling and prostitution, those vices for which Nevada law famously provided a safe haven.

No one was more horrified by the prospect of a Boulder City contaminated by drinking, gambling, and whoring than Sims Ely. But Ely, who had served as president of the Phoenix school board for sixteen years, also harbored an ambition to create a strong educational system in Boulder City. This condemned him to a conflict of interest, as the state was unwilling to fund Boulder City schools unless it could also levy taxes within the city limits. "This matter of high class schools for Boulder City is close to my heart,"

Ely told Mead. "Equally close is the matter of so fortifying the government's position that we may protect life and property and enforce law and order according to the policies we have adopted. . . . Once the state of Nevada is permitted to enter the reservation for the purpose of assessing and taxing property the camel will follow its nose into the tent."

His preference was to obtain money for schools and teachers from Congress or Six Companies, the better to safeguard his municipal prerogatives from the state's encroachment. But Six Companies refused to donate any money for the education of its employees' children, which it insisted was the government's responsibility. Federal officials, having failed to appropriate the needed funds in the first place, pleaded that they had no money to spend. And neither the state nor the county would agree to expend public funds to educate children living on property they could not tax.

Each party's position hardened as Boulder City's first school year loomed in the fall of 1931. Las Vegas was willing to accept only thirty-five grade school pupils and ten high-schoolers from Boulder City, and then only on payment of $15 a month tuition. This would be an insupportable burden for families whose breadwinners earned as little as $4 a day.

Desperation for a solution rose, as dozens of Boulder City schoolchildren (or parents writing in their names) observed in letters to Washington. "This dam is to be built, and we are doing our part towards it, and I think that the US should do something towards making Boulder City a model city by having adequate means of schooling," Donald Stiess, an improbably eloquent Boulder City eighth-grader, informed President Hoover. "It doesn't seem right that we, living in the United States, should be without schools."

Young eventually shamed Las Vegas into waiving the tuition for 1931–1932 by citing the boon to Las Vegas represented by the construction of the dam. Still, the Las Vegas city fathers could now add the cost of educating the government's wards (as well as cleaning up after homeless dam workers and feeding the unemployed) as one of the burdens imposed on its budget by the dam project.

Nevada's congressional delegation finally pushed through a $70,000 appropriation in the spring of 1932 (up from the $57,000 requested by the parsimonious Mead). This was sufficient to build an eight-room schoolhouse, but not to hire teachers for it. Ely again appealed to Six Companies, whose dependents counted for 80 percent of the school-age population. Through Dad Bechtel, he asked the Big Six for $30,000 to cover salaries for fifteen elementary school teachers at $2,000 each, the minimum pay he judged necessary to attract "college graduates of the highest type."

The company's response showed it at its most callous. At first the board refused to put up a dime unless it was indemnified against the local tax bill. This obviously was a promise Ely had no authority to make. The company's fallback position was to offer a mere $18,800, guaranteed for a single year only.

Ely's initial reaction to the company's cheeseparing was fury. "It is to the interest of the Six Companies not to take a position that the public could regard as niggardly . . . as compared to the great sum which popular imagination has figured as obtainable from taxation," he fumed to Mead. But he accepted the offer with a public show of graciousness, praising Six Companies, presumably through clenched teeth, for its "fine public spirit."

A few months later Ely returned to the Six Companies well, this time seeking money for high school teachers. But the board had reached the limit of its public spirit. Charlie Shea delivered their unanimous verdict to Ely personally, explaining that the "board felt poor." Only two weeks earlier, as it happened, the directors had pocketed the government's initial installment payment on the construction contract by voting a cash dividend for themselves of $30 a share, or $1.2 million.

Comeuppance of a sort was in the offing. On February 15, 1933, U.S. District Judge Frank Norcross upheld Nevada's taxing authority on the reservation. Norcross rejected the company's argument that the Boulder Canyon Project Act gave the government the right to seize the 115 square miles of the reservation. Instead, he held, the government could condemn only what was needed for the dam's "permanent" structures. In practical terms, that meant a slice of the Nevada riverbank "one mile in length and not exceeding one-fourth of a mile in width." For tax purposes, the rest of the vast reservation was placed under the jurisdiction of Nevada authorities.

Clark County immediately presented the company with a bill for $330,000, covering 1931 through 1933. The Big Six dodged the assessor for another six months, during which it continued to hold the schoolchildren hostage by refusing to pay for elementary school teachers for a second year unless a compromise settlement was reached. (The board meanwhile declared another dividend of $35 a share, or $1.4 million.) The two sides finally reached a settlement on August 7—for a reduced payment of $182,000 to cover 1931–1933 and a formula for assessments of its equipment and property going forward. The deal transferred responsibility for school budgets to the state, and just in time, for the start of the new academic year was less than a month away. Even so, the situation improved only slowly. The burgeoning population of grammar school children quickly burst the seams of the original schoolhouse, requiring them to attend in half-day shifts. High-schoolers would continue to travel to Las Vegas, a fifty-six-mile round-trip every school day, until a permanent high school was opened in Boulder City in 1941.

Wednesday, November 25, 1931:

On Thanksgiving Eve a dance was given in the Six Companies' mess hall by the volunteer firemen, at which was present a crowd of merrymakers variously estimated at 1,500 to 2,000. Dancing was almost impossible on account of the crowd that packed the 62 by 135 foot dining room, but everyone was there for a good time and had it. With all the merrymaking, there was no drinking or evidence of disorder. The Federal Rangers were successfully on the job to stop the flow of liquor into the reservation.

—*The Reclamation Era*

The following day, Boulder City's first Thanksgiving, Six Companies threw the mess hall open to employees and their families for a "bountiful repast," charging a discounted price of 75 cents for adults, children free. (The Reclamation families, typically, marked the holiday with a separate feast at the government survey camp near the river's edge.)

On any normal workday the Anderson Brothers mess was a prodigious operation, with seating for 1,200 men at a time and shifts turning over around the clock, provisioned by truck and rail from California and Utah, and from a 160-acre dairy farm the Andersons established in Logandale, eighty miles away. But this Thanksgiving was special. There were crisp white linens on the tables and china plates for 2,500 employees and their families. "Did they eat, and how! . . . 2,400 pounds of turkey, 300 gallons of oyster soup, half a ton of candied sweet potatoes, a case of olives, 10 crates of celery, 5 crates of lettuce, 300 pounds of cranberries, 760 pies, half a ton of plum pudding with hard sauce, 500 pounds of candy, and the same amount of nuts."

The people had come from all over the country and every segment of the economy. They had been farmers, miners, carpenters, even a few doctors and business executives, all down on their luck. They had camped in the desert or on the Las Vegas courthouse lawn, huddled under tattered shelters in Ragtown, slept in their cars. Now they were in the one refuge in America with an "unimpaired pay roll," as Mr. Ely would remind them (over and over). For a precious moment their existence seemed secure.

It is hardly surprising that they saw their half-built hometown as idyllic, notwithstanding the blowing sand and the rickety houses and the vaguely menacing ranger force garbed in khaki. Those first residents would never forget the sense of community of those years. The evenings spent on the lawn fronting the administration building, where you could lie on blankets with your family and visit with your neighbors. Sidewalks where children could gather safely (until the siren sounded at nine). Shops, churches, a recreation hall and, eventually, schools. The kids remembered that in the theater, the only air-conditioned building in town, 10 cents would buy a seat you could hold all afternoon on a Saturday to watch the serials, if your gang did not become rowdy enough to be thrown out. "You couldn't have a flat tire, cause there would be fifteen people there lifting the car," remembered Vivian Russell, who came with her parents in 1932. "It was just, take care of each other."

That Thanksgiving dinner in 1931 marked the birth of Boulder City as a living community and launched its first tradition; for as long as the project down in the gorge employed enough men to keep the mess hall filled, every Thanksgiving and Christmas Day would be observed the same way.

The project's inexorable clock had been wound and set to ticking. Before the next Thanksgiving rolled around, the work would pass its first important milestone by subjecting a great river to a manhandling like none ever attempted in history. An unprecedented engineering challenge would have been met and overcome, and the stage set for the next one.

# PART THREE

---

# The Arch

# 14

# The Jumbos

I n mid-August 1931, Crowe was impatient to begin the first and most challenging phase of construction: the driving of the diversion tunnels.

The Wobblies' strike and LeTourneau's painfully slow progress on the construction highway had imposed a nearly intolerable delay. But the obstacles had been cleared at last. The workforce was again docile. A paved highway snaked its way from Boulder City to the canyon rim, where it connected with a road Six Companies had built along the Nevada cliffside to reach the lower tunnel portals. Its completion had enabled Crowe to move his fleet of trucks and electric shovels to the riverbank at last. There they were marshaled alongside a collection of compressors, blacksmithing equipment, and electrical transformers, the last of which were ready to be wired to the heavy-duty power line that Southern Sierras Power Company had finished stringing east from the California border in June. A wooden trestle bridge had been thrown across the river, allowing men to pass to the Arizona job site by foot.

Squinting into the sun-bleached sky from the riverbank Crowe could see, high above, dozens of men suspended six or seven hundred feet off the ground, seated precariously on wooden bosun's chairs suspended from the rim by inch-thick hemp ropes. These were the high scalers, the project's certified daredevils, who were grooming the canyon walls by shaving outcroppings with jackhammers or drills, lest a stone or boulder come loose and turn into a projectile lethal to unsuspecting workers on the ground. The high scalers would write themselves into Hoover Dam legend with acrobatic stunts that grew in the telling. Already, with the work only just launched, they were developing a distinctive swagger. "It was a job that only youths relished," reported a Six Companies official, "for it involved the operating of drills and crowbars, and the handling of dynamite, while dangling at the end of thin ropes hundreds of feet above the jagged rocks of the canyon bottom."

The first cadres of high scalers were Indian tribesmen accustomed to clambering over mountain crags, or "ex-sailors or circus performers." The unemployment lines were filled with less hardy men who came to the canyon thinking they were suited to the work, only to take one look down from the rim and change their minds. "A lot of these guys were pretty hungry that came to work," recalled one member of the elect. "But they weren't *that* hungry."

It would not be long before the first high scaler lost his life falling from the canyon wall. He was Jack "Salty" Russell, who was perched with his jackhammer four hundred feet off the ground on September 21, 1931, when a sling full of steel drilling rods came loose above him. One bar hit him full on the head, sending him plummeting to the ground and leaving "brains and blood with pieces of torn flesh and tattered clothing scattered over the jagged rock," *Industrial Worker* reported, not without a certain grim censoriousness.

For all the high scalers' aerial activity in those first months following the strike, work on the ground still proceeded at a crawl. The hang-up was the basic engineering problem that had perplexed Crowe since he first surveyed the site in March: how to get drills to the loftier elevations of the fifty-six-foot diameter tunnels. Crowe wanted the drill holes on the rock face to be driven horizontally, so that each round of blasting would leave a vertical wall, the better to keep the tunnels on accurate headings. That meant somehow drilling directly into the rock from forty or fifty feet aloft, which in turn meant contriving a system that would allow crews and equipment to be shifted quickly—withdrawn a safe distance before the drilled bores were blasted and returned just as speedily to resume drilling at the new face. It would take so much time to repeatedly erect and dismantle conventional scaffolding that Crowe despaired of getting the four tunnels driven and concreted in the twenty-four months allotted by the contract.

The solution to this dilemma is commonly credited to Bernard "Woody" Williams, Crowe's deputy superintendent and the son of his chief carpenter, Charlie Williams. Woody had started working with Crowe ten years earlier, as a burly nineteen-year-old college dropout recruited by his father to work on Rimrock Dam in Washington state. Following Rimrock he stuck with the team, moving up the ranks with each new project. Now, on their fifth collaboration, Williams was again to demonstrate his resourcefulness and imagination.

Initially Williams toyed with the idea of modular scaffolds fitted permanently with pneumatic drills. The structures could be raised and removed with minimal disassembly, but the process would still demand inordinate effort and consume precious time. One day the sight of one of the company's 1916-vintage five-ton International trucks, acquired in almost mint condition as war surplus, gave Williams a brainstorm. Why not mount the scaffolds on the truck, so they could be wheeled into position for drilling and simply driven away before blasting?

The first "Williams jumbo" was a rickety timber prototype bolted onto the bed of a spare International. It declared its value instantly. The scaffold on wheels was the kind of innovation that seems in retrospect to have been inevitable. Its one shortcoming was that the vibration of all the drills working simultaneously tended to shake the frame apart, so as soon as the principle of mobile scaffolding was proved in field testing, the Six Companies machine shops in Boulder City geared up to replicate it in steel. There would be eight in all.

The steel jumbo was studded with heavy equipment. Up to thirty drills hung by swivels from horizontal bars on three levels, allowing three teams of drillers at once to assault the rock face, two on raised platforms and the third standing on solid ground. Two more platforms served as racks for the more than five tons of hollow one-and-a-quarter-inch sharpened steel rods the drills drove into the rock. The drills were fed by water and air lines permanently affixed to the jumbo frame. In turn, these were attached via manifolds to water and air pipelines laid along the tunnel floor or hung on its side walls; an arrangement that allowed them to be disconnected easily at the manifolds when the jumbo was to be pulled away for blasting, and promptly reconnected for the next round of drilling. Crowning the structure was a canted roof of sheet steel to shield the men from falling rock. The machine was designed to be no more than half the width of the tunnel so crews could drill one side of the rock face while power shovels mucked out debris next to them, and to leave enough lateral clearance for jumbos and dump trucks to pass each other inside the tunnel bores. Even so, the quarters were so tight that vehicles often scraped against each other while passing in the dark, sending off metallic sparks.

With the invention of the jumbo the driving of the bypass tunnels kicked into high gear. For the rest of the construction period Black Canyon would experience silence only on Christmas and the Fourth of July, the sole days of rest on the Six Companies calendar. At all other times, activity continued around the clock, three shifts a day, seven days a week. Crowe was in his element as the ubiquitous master of unceasing activity, his old habit revived of popping up anywhere on the site and at any hour to bedevil the unsuspecting slacker or shirker. One day toward the end of a shift, he encountered a laborer leaning on his shovel, idly waiting for the whistle to blow.

"What are you waiting for?" Crowe snapped.

"I'm just waiting for 3:30," replied the worker, unaware of who was interrupting his leisure. "It's payday."

Crowe retorted that he couldn't help the time to pass. "But I sure as hell can help you with payday—go get it!" The worker found his pay and his pink slip in the same envelope.

The first operational jumbo was wheeled up to the lower portal face of Tunnel No. 4, the further from the river on the Arizona side, on September 21. A painted circle delineated the specified fifty-six-foot diameter of the finished bore, with a whitewashed cross marking its dead center. With a roar of compressors, the scream of drills, and the hiss of water under high pressure, more than twenty men began driving holes in a hemisphere of rock twelve feet deep at one side of the painted cross. When they were done, they yielded their places to powdermen laden with primers, sticks of dynamite, and twenty-foot-long wooden rods—"powder sticks"—used to seat the dynamite deep within the drilled bores. The truck was backed away, shifted into position before the other hemisphere of the painted ring, and the process repeated. By late that afternoon the fuses left dangling from the filled holes all had been wired to a single electrical cable, the equipment and men moved a safe distance away, and the charges blown. When the dust cleared, an indentation sixteen feet deep was left in the rock face, over a mound of smoking rubble.

Initially, progress was poor. Only three or four more blasts, removing only sixty feet of rock, were set off over the last nine days of September. The problem may have been the wooden jumbo, whose struts had to be hammered back together after every round of drilling. Meanwhile, the steel jumbo frames were coming off the assembly line in Boulder City at a snail's pace: only three would be built by the end of October. The full complement of eight—one for each end of all four tunnels—would not be ready until the very end of the year. During October, 625 feet of tunnel would be drilled and blasted—ten times September's total but still painfully meager. The pace would have to pick up smartly if all four tunnels, totaling sixteen thousand feet, were to be excavated and lined with concrete to meet the contractual deadline of October 1, 1933, and beat the penalty.

Crowe and Shea need not have fretted. Three more jumbos were outfitted and brought down to the riverbank in November, making six in all and allowing work to proceed simultaneously on all four tunnels, two of which were being drilled from both the upstream and downstream ends. More important, the tunnel crews, now comprising more than 1,800 miners, were developing the efficiency and coordination of circus roustabouts. The average jumbo team numbered twenty-two drillers, twenty-one chuck tenders (who positioned the points of the steel bits on the rock), and five nippers, the lowly menials assigned to feeding fresh steel to the drillers and tenders. As the crews found their rhythm, the average time needed to back a jumbo to the rock face, pound chucks under its wheels, and connect the spaghetti strands of air, water, and power lines to the drills was twenty minutes. An especially able crew could do it in ten.

The crews' efficiency was undoubtedly enhanced by the convenience of having the men all living in one place. Although Six Companies would continue building new homes for another year, by early 1932 it was close to fulfilling its contractual commitment to domicile 80 percent of its workforce in Boulder City.

Three times a day, as early as 5:40 A.M., the entire town was jolted awake by the mess hall whistle announcing breakfast for the upcoming shift. The men would crowd under the Anderson Brothers' steel-trussed roof, up to 1,200 at a time, to partake of a copious bill of fare: oatmeal, sausages, ham, omelets, pancakes, biscuits, doughnuts, and torrents of coffee and juice. Then they lined up to pack their lunches—as much as they could carry, selected from three menus posted at the hall or from baskets of sandwiches individually wrapped in wax paper by a staff that had worked through the night. "It was nothing to see some of these guys stuff their shirts, pants legs etc. with a couple of dozen oranges, half a dozen or so nice grapefruits, and load up with a couple of dozen sandwiches," recalled laborer W. A. Whynn. In due course this gravy train caught the attention of the Six Companies board, which had already begun to gripe about the cost of subsidizing the mess hall. An order promptly came down requiring the kitchen staff henceforth to pack the men's lunches themselves, and leave them on a counter marked with each worker's number to control wastage. ("Judas Priest, these same wasteful men put up an awful squack," Whynn commented.)

From the mess hall it was a short stroll to the trucks waiting to transport the men seven miles to the river. The strikers' objections notwithstanding, this transfer, which yet took as much as an hour, was still on the workers' clock. In the early days it was accomplished by loading fifty men at a time into the open beds of dump trucks. Late in 1932 the company fitted three of its versatile Internationals with seats for 150 men in double decks, creating transports the crews promptly dubbed "Big Berthas." Many riders preferred the top deck, which caught the cooling breezes. Riding upstairs also demanded superior sangfroid, as the deck extended so far over the front of the truck that on one particular hairpin turn the passengers got the momentary sensation of hanging directly over the river, as though riding a roller coaster on which the descending track has suddenly dropped out of sight.

Once the trucks reached the riverbank, the job's unforgiving rhythm took over. It was filthy, hot, dangerous work with an established pecking order. The least privileged workers were assigned to the lowest line of drills, which got bombarded by rock from above and drenched with hot water sprayed at the wall to control dust. Their steels were laid out next to the jumbo wheels, so their nippers had to lie prone under the trucks, contorting themselves painfully to deliver every new rod. The nippers' lone consolation (so it was supposed) was that the crawlspace under the trucks was "a good safe place—if something caved in, it might get the ones above you, but not you," as an ex-nipper recalled years later.

A novice worker's first impression of the tunnel's interior evoked Dante's seventh circle of hell, the air filled with fumes and smoke amid an indescribable clamor while the very ground shuddered from the drilling. Marion Allen found his first day on the job—December 13, 1931—to be a profoundly disorienting experience. Allen was twenty-five and down to his last 17 cents when he snagged a position on the dam site through his father, a Crowe veteran. Assigned to the lower Arizona portal under Red McCabe, a legendary foreman "so tough he could bite a nail in two," he managed to wriggle into his work clothes in the change room just as McCabe signaled the start of the shift with a barked "Let's go!" The room emptied in about thirty seconds.

"I was swept along with a hundred or more men, all headed into a huge tunnel. Suddenly a deafening roar started and the farther into the tunnel we got the louder it became. Under the brilliant floodlight I saw this monstrosity about three stories high and covered with pipes and what looked like jackhammers, except they were bigger. As more and more men climbed up on this rig the noise became louder." Spotting his father nearby, Allen called out to him, but his words were swallowed up in the din. "He just grinned and shook his head for there was no way one could hear another even with the mouth against the ear." Communication in this circle of hell was by sign language alone.

McCabe assigned Marion to a crew of nippers standing by with their eyes fixed on the jumbo, waiting to be signaled for fresh steel (three fingers meant a six-foot length, four fingers meant eight feet, and so on—progressively longer steels ordered as the drills probed deeper). Hypnotized by the incessant vibration, the noise, and the glare of floodlights, Allen was overcome by a dreamlike sensation that the jumbo was hovering in the air before him. He was jolted out of his reverie by the arrival of a screeching truck laden with crates of dynamite, which were promptly, and (it seemed to him) all too cavalierly tossed from the truck bed into the arms of the waiting powdermen.

Suddenly the lights flickered out. The power was always cut before explosives were packed into the bores, to remove the opportunity for a stray electrical spark to ignite the notoriously tetchy mercury fulminate primers. The onset of gloom was a signal for the powder crews to clamber onto the jumbo and start filling the holes with dynamite, gingerly shoving them home with their long sticks. The trailing primer wires were braided together and connected to a cable running out to an electrician safely sheltered in an adit, detonator at the ready. The primers were set to fire in a sixteen-step sequence starting at the top center of the face and radiating out toward the sides and base, a pattern designed to collapse the rock into a tidy mound.

As a newly minted tunnel hand Allen soon got caught up in the natural competitiveness of the jumbo crews: "The main thing was this challenge. You had to beat the other crew. You had to get more footage—'We got two more feet than you did!' This was the whole conversation. Those miners would run into that tunnel, drill all these holes, and run back out again so they could shoot, just to beat the other crew."

The competitive frenzy, openly encouraged by Crowe and his foremen, had its dark side. Deaths on the job soared to their highest level since that summer's epidemic of heatstroke. From early September through November 1932, when the tunnels were completed, the official toll listed thirty-three men killed in premature blasts, rock slides, falls, truck accidents, or cave-ins (including one disastrous collapse that killed three men on October 17), marking the tunneling as the most perilous phase of the construction period.

Slipshod handling of explosives produced numerous injuries, particularly in the early stages of the excavation when the men were still being schooled in the unruly personalities of primers and dynamite. The first tunnel workers killed by a premature explosion were M. J. Sidmore and Frank Manning, thirty-seven-year-old miners who were dismembered on December 15, 1931, by a blast that also blew Forest Weathers, their foreman, clear out of the tunnel and into the river.

The grunts—electricians' aides who strung the wires connecting the loads to the detonator—got ringside views of the gruesome consequence of a powderman's shoving dynamite too hard with his stick. They learned to keep clear of the rock face during the loading process. Even when a prematurely detonating primer failed to set off dynamite the result could be horrific, for the drilled holes concentrated the primer's explosive force like a rifle bore, powerful enough to rip a body in two. That fate befell Gus Enberg, a thirty-six-year-old miner, one January morning when three sticks of dynamite and a primer got hung up on a fault fifteen feet deep in a drilled hole. Frustrated beyond the bounds of common sense, Enberg gave the pack one last sharp jab with his stick. The detonating primer blasted a column of rock into Enberg's body point-blank, pulverizing his right arm, blowing off his left at the elbow, and shattering one leg. He died in agony that afternoon. Miraculously, the primer left the three sticks of dynamite crammed inside the bore intact, averting an even more catastrophic explosion.

The miners also lived in terror of "missed holes." These were drilled bores whose loads had somehow failed to fire. After a blast they lay buried within the debris mound like dormant bombs, requiring only the strike of a shovel to set off a blast imperiling every mucker in the vicinity—muckers like Howard Cornelius, twenty-three, of Glendo, Wyoming, whose skull was stove in by a boulder when a latent load showered his crew with airborne rubble.

But the greatest fear inside the tunnels was of cave-ins, which could instantly reduce an entire shift to anarchy. Rules were in place to avert such a disaster, including a prohibition against allowing jumbos back into a tunnel after a blast until a safety officer had inspected the heading for loose rock. But identifying weak spots in the smoky darkness was more an art than a science. There were men who could "smell loose rock," as Allen put it, but the skill was a rare one.

The roof fell in during one of Allen's shifts when a novice safety man failed to spy a vein of fractured rock directly over the work zone. Allen's jumbo had just backed up to the rock face when half of the tunnel suddenly collapsed. Most of the drillers were shielded by the steel canopy and the jumbo frame, but several on the lowest level were hit by the rockfall and a crew of nippers was pinned under the truck.

The screams of injured men and the cries of the trapped nippers mingled with the roar of compressed air escaping from severed lines, the groaning of truck engines, and the sirens of approaching ambulances. Red McCabe took charge, deploying a team to dig the trapped men out by hand. Suddenly, to his horror, he heard the jumbo's engine rumble to life. A miner had taken the initiative to move the truck out of the way, unaware that by budging the vehicle he risked dumping tons of loosened rock onto the men trapped underneath. McCabe scrambled up to the cab and bodily hauled the driver out of his seat, averting a dozen deaths but taking a slug on the chin from the would-be hero. Eventually the men were dug out, bruised and scraped but otherwise unhurt. Most of them refused to report to the hospital, lest they lose hours and fall behind the drilling pace of a rival crew. Allen reported that McCabe and the driver later settled their differences over drinks in Las Vegas.

The Six Companies public relations office, which invariably depicted the workers as cold-blooded in the face of danger, characterized the tide of casualties as the inevitable by-product of heavy construction in perilous Black Canyon. Under the circumstances, the company maintained, safety regulations, no matter how rigorously enforced, could do only so much to stave off injury and death. This shifted the blame for injuries and deaths from its own policies onto the shoulders of nature and fate.

Coroner's juries on both sides of the river customarily accepted this argument at face value, ignoring often clear evidence of negligence by management. The case of A. O. George, a mechanic crushed to death between two trucks on March 10, 1932, was typical. George was on his very first shift—he had clocked a mere thirty-five minutes of work for Six Companies—when he was crushed to death between two trucks, suffering "a fractured skull, fractured ribs . . . a severed right arm, [and] the breaking and crushing of both legs." Testimony established that a truck driver backing up without checking behind him had pinned George against the vehicle he was repairing. The jury ruled the accident "unavoidable."

The publicity department that worked so hard to foster the impression of Big Six's blamelessness was Henry Kaiser's brainchild. Kaiser had settled comfortably into his role as the partnership's principal spokesman and glad-hander in Washington—a position undoubtedly enhanced by the marriage of his son Edgar to Elwood Mead's daughter, Susan, in August 1932. (The couple left directly from their wedding breakfast for Boulder City, where Edgar was employed as a Six Companies office supervisor.) Kaiser had demonstrated his instinct for public relations at the outset of the project by persuading his partners to build a deluxe guesthouse in Boulder City. The board members initially balked at this unprecedented $25,000 frill for what was, after all, a glorified construction camp. But they were steamrollered by Kaiser, who predicted that as the world's preeminent public work the dam would attract a parade of VIPs, many of whom would be in a position to do Six Companies good if properly coddled. He got his way. The guesthouse was superbly appointed, big enough to accommodate six visitors at a time, air-conditioned, and staffed with a butler, liveried servants, and a top-notch chef. It proved so popular that the board members soon were squabbling with each other to secure vacancies for their invited guests. They even considered charging visitors a fee.

Smarting from the drubbing Six Companies had taken in the press during the 1931 strike, Kaiser hired an ex-newspaperman named Norman Gallison to make sure that "the facts are truthfully presented to both newspapers and magazines"—that is, to ensure that Six Companies was presented in the best light. Gallison's shop issued a prodigious flood of press kits, briefs, and prefabricated news items to keep the national media filled with colorful yarns about the project's intrepid miners and high scalers. His efforts soon got under the skin of Walker Young, who complained to Mead that unless Reclamation mounted a publicity campaign of its own "the public will not know that we have anything to do with the Boulder Canyon project." Mead, who feared that the press's incessant harping on "the disgraceful conditions that are alleged to prevail" at the dam might inspire a congressional investigation, concurred. "If you have an opportunity to show what is being done to provide a water supply, or the plans for sowing grass and planting trees, it is good to get it out," he counseled Young, suggesting further that Young solicit complimentary letters from prominent visitors to the dam, for display to newspaper reporters and congressmen. "We have made good use of two such letters recently," he noted.

Both PR drives got geared up none too soon. For early in 1932, a new threat to the workers' health developed: the men were succumbing to carbon monoxide poisoning at an alarming rate.

The cause was the Big Six's deployment of gasoline-powered rather than electrical trucks and bulldozers in the underground excavations. This caused few problems during the early stage of blasting, when the tunnels were shallow and the exhaust fumes could be dispersed by a slight breeze. But by January, when the tunnels reached as far as a quarter-mile underground, ventilation became a critical issue. After every blast, a Caterpillar bulldozer would lead a parade of as many as eighteen dump trucks into the tunnels. There they would idle, belching exhaust into the stagnant air, waiting to be loaded with debris for hauling to the waste pits. The men developed their own rules of thumb for gauging the concentration of carbon monoxide. If the electric lights in the tunnel acquired a bluish halo "we would know the gas was getting pretty rough in there," one recalled. Others resorted to the time-honored miners' practice of bringing caged canaries into the tunnels to warn them of oxygen depletion.

It was not uncommon for crews to be overcome without warning by monoxide clouds carried on the unpredictable currents inside the long, curving, debris-strewn tunnels or released from a niche in the rock by a power shovel's swipe. If a man was lucky, the effect would be limited to a passing wave of nausea and a splitting headache. If not, the result could be unconsciousness or death.

One night the gassing of an entire shift was witnessed by an appalled Murl Emery. "I was called out to go down to the boats. A major catastrophe—go down to the boats. So I dashed down and jumped on the first boat that left and got down to the upper portals. They were hauling men out of those tunnels like cordwood."

There were too many to count; in the frenzy the only fact that registered in Emery's mind was that the men weren't dead—yet—but were barely drawing breath. He laid a half-dozen in the keel of his boat and motored them upriver to the camp landing, where they were transferred to ambulances for the desperate dash to the Big Six hospital in Boulder City.

There, like other gas victims, they were treated for what company doctors recorded as pneumonia. This diagnosis was openly derided by workers and their families as a subterfuge concocted by the Big Six to deny workmen's compensation to the injured men. A man fairly had to leave his corpse in the canyon, it was said, to be judged a victim of an industrial accident for which the company could be held liable. "If they ever got you in the hospital, [they said] you didn't get killed on the job, you just died," a miner observed.

During the five years of major construction in Black Canyon, not a single worker was recorded as having died from carbon monoxide exposure. On the other hand, deaths from pneumonia and other cardiopulmonary ailments surged, beginning with the death from "bronchial pneumonia" of F. H. Wolff, a Six Companies miner, on October 8, a few weeks after blasting began. Wolff's death was filed by the Reclamation Bureau under the general category of "natural causes."

Four more Six Companies men died of pneumonia and one of a coronary occlusion in 1931. Over the following three years, a period in which underground work shifted from the main tunnels to the spillway tunnels and subterranean penstocks that were to carry water from the reservoir to the power turbines, thirty-seven more working men died of pneumonia or coronary problems. They often succumbed in clusters, as in the first two weeks of December 1932, when five died from "pneumonia" and two from "heart trouble," as recorded in official Reclamation files. During this time the bureau, which tracked all civilian deaths on the reservation, including those of premature infants, recorded no other pneumonia deaths in Boulder City. Although pneumonia was by no means an uncommon medical complaint in Depression America, the concentration of so many cases among the tunnel workers strongly suggests that pneumonia, and to a lesser extent coronary problems, were proxies for gas poisoning. This was the universal assumption among Boulder City residents. "If you said they died of gasses in the tunnels, they were obligated to compensate you, to compensate the family," recalled the wife of one tunnel inspector. "So they'd say just 'pneumonia,' and they'd get by with that. We never felt that was fair."

Despite horrific incidents like the one Emery witnessed, Six Companies promulgated the fiction that the air in the tunnels was positively salubrious. Gallison fed newspapers and wire services with highly technical explanations of how the "natural air currents" and "natural convection" within the tunnels, assisted by high-pressure fans, "maintained a cool, clean, and pleasant working condition" for the muckers. "Under working conditions," he asserted, "activities could be resumed in five minutes after blasting with perfect safety and comfort."

This was an ambitious schedule, to say the least. Experienced mining hands believed that fifteen to twenty-five minutes was the minimum needed to disperse the smoke and dust of a powder blast so the men could work safely, leaving aside the exhaust fumes of idling trucks. After stone cofferdams were erected at the upper portals to protect the tunnels from spring floods, whatever natural ventilation might have existed was further stifled, warranting a longer pause before men were permitted to reenter the tunnels. But Six Companies policy did not change. The five-minute turnaround cited by Gallison was likely more a reflection of Frank Crowe's "hurry-up" mentality than of any calculated margin of safety.

Six Companies was not above blaming the outbreak of pulmonary disease on the men's overindulgence. The eminent syndicated columnist Arthur Brisbane, whom Henry Kaiser brought to Boulder City for a VIP tour in November 1931, reported obligingly, and pejoratively, on the copious quantities of food shoveled down by the workers at the Anderson mess hall. "The food is excellent and too abundant, in the opinion of this writer," he observed. "It is sad to hear that numbers of the men, when they first came, long out of work and ill fed, ate to excess and were made ill in spite of warnings." Sims Ely made a similar point in his 1932 Yuletide warning about the evils of alcohol, which he blamed for the outbreak of pulmonary disease among other evils. "Physicians say that many of the cases of pneumonia we have had here this winter were doubtless attributable to a low resistance brought about by drinking bootleg liquor," he wrote.

In truth, the use of gasoline engines underground was an anachronism in mining and tunneling by 1931, except in Black Canyon. As early as 1905 the Reclamation Bureau relied on electricity to power earthmoving equipment on its Gunnison Tunnel in western Colorado, keeping diesel trucks on hand only as temporary backups in case a power line went down. The most celebrated tunnel project of the 1920s, the Cascade Tunnel in Washington state (1929), also relied on electric-powered equipment. Nevada, which claimed jurisdiction over the two tunnels on the western side of Black Canyon, had outlawed the use of gasoline engines in underground mining in 1929 and extended the ban to all underground excavations in March 1931. Even U.S. Bureau of Mines regulations barred the underground operation of gasoline engines, although there was never any effort by Reclamation inspectors or other federal personnel in Black Canyon to enforce those rules.

Six Companies' rationale for disregarding the regulations and industry standards appears to be entirely economic. The company made no secret of its intention to save money by using the same fleet of earthmovers for the underground boring of the tunnels and the open-air excavation of the riverbed. It later calculated that bringing in a separate electrified fleet to drive the tunnels would have cost $300,000 and delayed the work for weeks, if not months.

Nevada inspector of mines Andy J. Stinson launched an attack on the Big Six's gasoline fleet on November 7, 1931, ordering the company to withdraw its trucks and shovels from the tunnels in compliance with state law. Six days later, company lawyers swarmed into federal court in San Francisco, demanding that a three-judge panel enjoin the state from interfering with the work.

Much was at stake in the company's motion. The tunnel excavation was due for completion by the end of May 1932. The longer Stinson could be held at bay by legal maneuvering, the more likely it was that the blasting and mucking would end before the lawsuit did. Raising that very point, the state urged the court to rule speedily so Six Companies could not profit by flouting the law. Instead, the judges took their time, granting the company's request for a preliminary injunction until a hearing on January 3. When that day arrived, they asked for more information and set a new deadline for mid-April.

Over the following weeks the two sides engaged in a duel of experts. In mid-January Nevada sent two chemical engineers, Fred L. Lowell and S. C. Dinsmore, into the tunnels for air samples. They were met by a squadron of Six Companies engineers, who performed shadow tests at every stop. Six Companies also tampered with the evidence: at several sampling points, Lowell and Dinsmore found the usual complement of ten to twelve trucks idling; but in each case the vehicles cleared out, as if by a silent command, before the engineers could get their gas meters set up.

The expert teams unsurprisingly came to dramatically different conclusions. Lowell declared that the workers in the tunnels "are laboring under conditions of danger." By contrast, the Six Companies engineers found the atmosphere underground to be "cool, clean, and pleasant . . . [showing] only traces of carbon monoxide or no carbon monoxide at all." One had even queried "various workmen for their impressions of the air": A few allowed that they sometimes "had a little headache," he reported, but for the most part their "replies were uniform to the effect that air was good and that no discomfort had been experienced. . . . The replies appeared to be freely and frankly given," the Six Companies engineer reported.

Satisfied that a health emergency that might mandate a rapid resolution of the case was "extremely remote," the judges extended the temporary restraining order on April 28, pending a final decision. This afforded Crowe an unmolested opportunity to finish drilling and blasting the tunnels. The bodies carried out of the tunnels were not of much interest to the judges; they reserved their scrutiny for the dry testimony of scientific experts reaching contradictory conclusions and the reassuring words of cowed workmen interrogated by agents of their employer.

U.S. District Judge Frank Norcross, who led the three-judge panel in the gas case while hearing the tax dispute between Clark County and Six Companies solo, delivered a split decision in both matters on February 15, 1933. He ruled that Six Companies was indeed subject to state and local taxation. But writing for the majority in the gas case, he exempted the contractor from the state mining code, finding that Nevada's law applied only to mining tunnels, rather than to "tunnels not in mines." Therefore Six Companies was in the clear. By then it hardly mattered, as the tunnels had been completed three months earlier and the Colorado was already flowing underground.

The gas issue was not yet resolved, however. Six Companies had fought off the state of Nevada, but many of its victims were yet to have their day in court. When that day came, the company would display its basest instincts.

# 15

# Turning Points

A t the dawn of the New Year 1932, work on the bypass tunnels acceler-
ated to breakneck speed. Now drilling all four tunnels from both ends,
Crowe's men had blasted through 3,848 linear feet of rock in December, more than double the volume of the month before. In January progress
nearly doubled again to a spectacular 6,773 feet, leaving less than a mile to
be drilled before all four channels were holed through.

The progress was partially due to the miners' extraordinary good luck.
They had driven through three miles of solid rock without striking a single
fault or suffering a single major cave-in (though minor cave-ins were too
numerous to count). As Crowe had divined from the experience of R. G.
LeTourneau, not a single yard of roof had required bracing with timber.

The crews were now working with almost military precision. In late fall
the average time required for a complete round of demolition and mucking
out in a single heading had been fourteen and a half hours, allowing fewer
than two full rounds to be set every twenty-four hours. Come late January
the pace picked up to as many as three rounds a day. The men's rapidly increasing expertise, to be sure, was not proof against the occasional horren-
dous mishap: during the first three months of 1932, eleven fatalities marred
the work record, including deaths by drowning, rock slides, one plunge
from the Nevada cliffside, three truck collisions, and two more mysterious
cases of cardiopulmonary failure.

Indeed, there were indications that familiarity with routine was breeding carelessness. One night in early January, just before the 11:30 night shift whistle, Marion Allen was finishing up a clerical task on the Arizona side and contemplating an early dash across the canyon footbridge to beat the rush for a seat in a homebound Big Bertha. Instead, Red McCabe handed him a message to deliver to the shift workers in Tunnel No. 3. With a flickering hope that he could yet make the first bus, Allen took off at a sprint. He got a few hundred yards into the tunnel when he realized that the vast space was uncannily quiet. With the magnitude of his frightful predicament dawning on him, he spun on his heels in panic and bolted for the portal, desperate to outrun the blast he knew was coming. But it was too late. "Something hit me in the back and carried me down the tunnel. I fell on my face but caught myself as I hit the ground and I laid there for a few minutes. Rock was all around me." He pulled himself upright and checked for broken bones. Then he staggered from the smoking tunnel, an apparition covered in dust and muck, startling an electrician waiting near the entrance for the all-clear siren. Allen hurried on, his head ringing, not pausing to wonder why the guard who was always supposed to be posted at the mouth of a tunnel about to be blown had left his station untended. At home he spent two days sleeping off a severe concussion. About ten years later a doctor performing a routine physical asked him if he had ever had any ear trouble. "Not that I can remember, why?" he replied. "Because both your eardrums have been cracked," the doctor said.

The one-day record for excavation on the job site was set on January 20, when the four tunnels advanced a combined 256 feet. The crews of Tunnel No. 4, furthest from the river on the Arizona side, claimed the title for the best week's work by setting sixteen rounds of explosive that removed 280 linear feet of rock, or 17.5 feet per round, from February 1 to February 8. By then two of the shafts had been holed through, their jumbos meeting halfway: Tunnel No. 3, next to the river on the Arizona side, on January 30, and Tunnel No. 2, its counterpart on the Nevada side, four days later.

But that was the last progress to be made for weeks in the diversion bores. The river was about to remind Frank Crowe and his men, as in decades past it had reminded such would-be masters as Charles Rockwood and Epes Randolph, that only a fool would trust it to stay tame for long.

On Tuesday, February 9, John Page eyed the gray skies from his comfortable perch in Boulder City and scribbled a terse meteorological note in his daily journal: "Rainy & river rising."

Miles away in the canyon, Frank Crowe could scarcely have contemplated conditions with the same detachment. The tunnel portals were protected from flash flooding only by low dikes. No one had thought it necessary to take more drastic measures, for the Colorado had flooded in February only once in the previous twenty years. "It was a nineteen to one bet there would not be a flood in February," Henry Kaiser observed ruefully a few weeks later. "We took the bet and lost a quarter of a million dollars."

The river had started rising the night before, swollen by twenty-four hours of steady rain upstream. Then the heavens opened up over St. Thomas, the downpour transforming the sleepy Virgin River into a rampaging torrent barreling toward Black Canyon, twenty-five miles away. It struck the worksite at 3:30 that afternoon, blasting the trestle bridge across the gorge to smithereens and scattering hundreds of men just arriving for the swing shift. To Crowe it looked like "a wall of yellow mud" fixing to wash his men clear out of the canyon.

Frantically he redeployed three hundred men to throw sandbag dikes across the upstream tunnel portals. The river swept away the bags like a dragon flicking its tail and surged into the tunnels, driving marooned workers onto rock ledges or to the roofs of their swamped vehicles. Electrician George Carr, seeking refuge in the scoop of a power shovel, received a 2,300-volt shock when the rising water short-circuited its electrical wiring. His fellow crewmen managed to sling a rope around his prostrate form and used it to pull him free and onto dry land.

For three days the Colorado rampaged, pounding the canyon with wave after wave. In one three-hour span the river rose more than sixteen feet, receded by a few inches, then delivered another blitz. Crowe, conceding a rare defeat at the hands of nature, withdrew his forces to wait for the water to recede. He laid off five hundred workers for the duration, keeping the rest on hand to muck out from the flood. Fifteen to twenty feet of standing water would have to be pumped from the lower ends of the tunnels; the upstream ends were drier, but covered by a layer of gooey, stinking mud into which the men sank up to their waists. "Typical Colorado water," Marion Allen griped: "Too thick to pump . . . too thin to shovel." The viscous slop so thoroughly clogged their pumps that the only way to clear it was to dynamite the "inverts"—the tunnels' unexcavated bottom sections—and mix the rubble with the mud, forming a rank slurry the shovels could load into dump trucks. It was more than three weeks before the tunnels were sufficiently cleaned out for normal operations to resume.

The flood left its mark on the monthly figures: a mere 1,958 feet excavated in February, less than a third as much as in January and the lowest tally since November, back when the crews were still learning to handle the jumbos. Nevertheless, the blasting inched nearer to completion. Miners were already swarming through three holed-out tunnels to begin trimming operations, which entailed checking for rock projecting into the fifty-six-foot circle, marking the outcroppings with a splash of white paint, and blowing them loose with well-placed charges.

A gallery of giant forms taking shape on the beach hinted at what was next in store. They were gantries constructed from lattices of structural steel, the tallest ones looming fifty feet overhead, the largest pieces of equipment in the canyon. Their role was to support the steel bulkheads that would shape poured concrete into three-foot-thick cylindrical shells to line the tunnels.

There were three sets of these innovative machines. The smallest, the invert jumbos, would be wheeled into the tunnels first on rails laid along the floor from portal to portal. Each twenty-foot gantry carried two concrete buckets to pour the tunnels' concave floor.

They would be followed close behind by sidewall jumbos, which were fitted with curved quarter-inch steel bulkheads forty-two feet tall and eighty feet long. Each bulkhead was perforated by eight vertical rows of gated portholes. The design allowed the bulkhead to be positioned against the tunnel sides with a three-foot-wide gap, which would be filled with concrete pumped through the holes, starting with the lowest ones. The pour continued until the concrete reached forty-two feet above the invert. Then pneumatic jacks would pull the steel forms away from the walls and the jumbo would roll down the tunnel to the next section to be concreted.

The most elaborate jumbo carried eighty-foot-long forms to shape concrete for the arched ceiling. This job presented a special challenge: the sides and the invert could be poured by gravity, but the ceiling was high overhead. Crowe and Williams solved the problem by feeding concrete into the void with pneumatic guns, mounted on gantries trailing behind the arch jumbos like dinghies.

To produce the 400,000 cubic yards of concrete required for the tunnel linings, Crowe erected an entire manufacturing plant on a rocky Nevada ledge about a mile upstream from the upper portals. Designated Lomix, it would be the source of all concrete for the tunnels, spillways, and the first 430 feet of the dam's elevation. Once the dam exceeded that height, Lomix would be cannibalized and partially reassembled high on the canyon rim, where it would be rechristened Himix and used to supply concrete for the rest of the work.

The tunnel pour was the first test of Reclamation's extensive research on mass concrete. The initial results were not auspicious. The bureau had developed a special quick-setting concrete to speed the work, but its scientists had overshot the mark: before the concrete could be poured at the worksite, it had already begun to set in the buckets filled at Lomix. The doors of the buckets swung open—and nothing flowed out. The concrete had hardened into solid blocks that had to be jackhammered free or, in especially stubborn cases, drilled out.

The recipe was soon adjusted, but another surprise awaited the work crews: the setting concrete generated immense heat. Even experienced concrete men were unaccustomed to working with three-foot-thick slabs in confined, stifling quarters like the tunnels. Some first learned this fundamental principle of concrete chemistry from trying to sit on the surface of the pour during a meal break. The finishers and puddlers—the latter assigned to trample imperfections and air pockets out of the wet concrete in heavy boots, like rustic winemakers crushing grapes—worked stripped to the waist, stopping periodically to unlace their boots, pour out streams of sweat, and wring out their socks.

Once the invert was poured, troweled smooth, and cured for two weeks under a spray of water, it was covered over with a layer of dirt to provide a roadway for trucks delivering concrete for the sidewalls. This produced another unforeseen problem, for the water sprayed on the sidewalls drained into the roadbed, turning it into a swamp of slippery mud and shallow pools.

The water posed a special hazard, as Allen witnessed one day while helping to finish the side walls. Two workers carrying a plank had passed him on their way down the tunnel, but he thought no more of it until he heard a sudden cry and a splash. Running to investigate, he came upon one of the men standing dazed over a motionless body half-submerged in a puddle. Allen's nose wrinkled at the sharp smell of ozone, the sign of an electrical discharge. The victim died later that night. A short in a jumbo's electrical system, it was determined, had conducted electricity to the pooled water just as the unfortunate laborer set his foot in it. The accident led the crews to abandon water curing inside the tunnels in favor of keeping the concrete damp with a coat of mixed asphalt and oil.

For all that the remarkable pace of progress in the bypass tunnels measured up as a new career triumph for Hurry-Up Crowe, it created political problems for the Boulder Canyon Project in Washington. Crowe's headlong rush to finish the tunnels by mid-1932 required a workforce much larger than Reclamation had budgeted for. As a result, the available funds for the fiscal year were nearly exhausted months ahead of schedule. The timing of the shortfall was inopportune: the dam's construction budget for 1931–1932 provided little money for contingencies. Congress, already coping with coast-to-coast economic disaster and cost overruns in other public works projects, was disinclined to appropriate new millions to Boulder Canyon where, for all the lawmakers knew, money was being spent as imprudently as in other government worksites. As the deadline for a new appropriation drew near, the prospect arose of a complete shutdown of the project.

Some blame for the predicament belonged to Congress, and some to the Reclamation Bureau. Congress, in its desperation to balance the federal budget, had taken a sharp axe to the Interior Department's budget, slashing the Hoover Dam appropriation for the fiscal year to $6 million from $10 million. (The folly of budget balancing during a severe economic downturn would not be fully appreciated in the United States until later in the 1930s.)

Ray Lyman Wilbur, who nursed the conviction that congressional Democrats had cut the dam appropriation merely to embarrass Hoover ahead of the 1932 presidential election, described the action as "cruel, foolish, actually wasteful, and pushed through in the hope of partisan advantage." The truth was more complicated. It was Reclamation Commissioner Mead himself who had lulled the lawmakers into complacency about the construction budget, assuring both houses early in 1932 that $6 million was enough to carry the project through December. At that point, he assumed, the funding could be topped off via the customary device of a supplemental appropriation, if necessary. Now, with the project facing a critical shortfall, Mead had to return to Capitol Hill to admit sheepishly that his projections had been wrong. Unless it received an immediate emergency infusion of $7 million, he informed Congress in May, the nation's showcase dam project might have to be suspended before the end of summer.

As skeptical Democrats on the House Appropriations Committee subjected Mead to five days of merciless grilling, he struggled to make the straightforward point that money spent now would yield greater savings later. The facts were these: almost from the beginning of work in the canyon, Crowe had understood that the entire construction schedule hung on the fulcrum of the 1933 spring flood season. If the draining of the river and the sealing of the canyon with cofferdams could not be completed before then, the unfinished work would be washed away by the rising waters. The only options, therefore, were to complete the cofferdams before the floods arrived, or to hold off all work until the summer. Because the latter choice meant pushing back the construction calendar by as much as a year, Crowe (with Mead's evident assent) opted for the former, which meant performing much of the work well ahead of schedule.

Although accelerating the excavation and construction of the cofferdams to beat the floods required expanding the workforce to 3,800 men from 1,400, the number on which Mead had based his original budget request, the avoidance of delay meant that the government would pocket revenues from an extra year of power generation ($6 million), and incur one fewer year of interest charges ($1 million)—a huge gain in return for a comparatively modest short-term investment.

Mead seemed unable to explain the situation without raising the suspicion that he was covering up cost overruns. He made matters worse by answering the lawmakers' questions truculently, as though nettled by their lack of trust in his judgment. "If we put the situation before you as to what we need," he snapped at the committee chairman, Joseph W. Byrns of Tennessee, "what difference does it make?"

"You may be as wrong now as you were in February," Byrns replied coldly.

With the owlish irrigation bureaucrat proving his own worst enemy at the witness table, it fell to Henry Kaiser to extricate his future in-law from the firing line. Kaiser's instincts told him that the fate of the project might hinge on his ability to smooth the ruffled feathers of the lawmakers, who were seriously considering accepting a one-year moratorium on the work to bring its spending into line with the appropriation. The loss of momentum, he feared, would be calamitous. Who could say whether the project would ever get started again, considering the uncertainties still lurking on the economic horizon? Given that the government contract stated that Six Companies would have no right to recover its investment if Congress opted to cancel the dam, a break in the work might plunge him and every one of his partners into bankruptcy. On the other hand, Kaiser knew that once the cofferdams were finished and the great dam started rising majestically from the riverbed, it would take superhuman determination, always in short supply in the capital, for Congress to interfere with its progress. It was crucial to get to that point without a break.

Taking his turn behind the witness table, the burly Kaiser addressed the committee with the combination of charm, bluster, and guile he had honed lobbying Washington from a suite in the tony Shoreham Hotel. After dutifully complimenting the committee on its "patience, tolerance, and kindness," he launched a cunning defense of the $7 million emergency request:

The failure to appropriate it will have the following results. It will kill the opportunity of the Government to continue the work of building this project. It will kill the possibility of the Government [continuing] to employ the 3,000 men who are now employed. . . . It will kill the possibility of the Government to profit from the extent of six or more millions of dollars through a 1-year earlier completion. . . . It will kill the opportunity of the Government to remove the hazard to life and property for one whole year of the thousands and thousands of people living in the Imperial Valley.

Starkly he laid out the human consequences of suspending the work. Nearly four thousand families would have to abandon Boulder City.

You will force about 7,000 citizens of the United States out on that desert . . . in the most terrific heat of the year, estimated at 120° of temperature. . . . Now, what will happen when all of these men are turned out of their homes with their children? It will be equal to death to them. I do not want to be at Boulder City when that happens. . . . I do not want to visualize the serious results. It is the most serious thing I have ever confronted in my history.

Having conjured up the image of more Hoovervilles teeming with parched and sunstroked refugees, Kaiser turned over his trump card. Hoover Dam was more than a regional boon for California and the West. "The men that we employ and the materials that we purchase," he reminded his audience, "come from every State in the Union." Stop the work, he warned, and orders will cease for parts from the East and provisions from the South and the Midwest, spreading unemployment. Referring to the steel pipelines that would carry water to the generating turbines, he said, "Under this $7,000,000 contract provision for penstock pipe, all of that work would probably be purchased east of the Mississippi River"—much of it in Pennsylvania, Ohio, New York, and Illinois, he noted, mentioning four extremely populous states rich in votes.

Even before he had finished, the committee members were falling over themselves to disavow any intention of suspending the work temporarily, much less abandoning the project outright. "Who started that propaganda?" one snapped.

Six weeks later a $10 million appropriation for the dam, restoring all the money that Congress had lopped off the Interior Department's original request and adding more, passed as part of a mammoth $2.1 billion relief measure. Never again would Congress or the White House allow funding for the dam to run dry.

Kaiser's presentation established Hoover Dam as a national undertaking. From that moment on, public interest in the monumental project rising in the distant Western desert would grow exponentially, as would Henry Kaiser's repute as its builder and driving force. Foreign dignitaries on visits of state would demand a tour of the Colorado worksite, movie stars would hasten from Hollywood to be photographed with the immense work as the backdrop; politicians would scurry westward to bask in its majestic glow. Not least among the latter would be Franklin D. Roosevelt, who derided Hoover during the 1932 campaign for his wasteful spending on public works, but as president would redefine the project as a prototypical achievement of the New Deal.

Almost at the very moment when Kaiser was defending the project he had begun to refer to as "my dam," a pivotal event of that historic election year was taking place nearby. This was the entry into Washington of the Bonus Army, which would do so much to hammer into public consciousness the desperate straits of the ordinary worker and the fundamental heartlessness of Herbert Hoover's economic policy.

The Bonus Expeditionary Force, as it was formally known, was the brainchild of Walter W. Waters, an unemployed veteran of the Great War. At a meeting in his hometown of Portland, Oregon, Waters had proposed that every man present take to the rails to demand immediate payment of the veterans' bonus Congress had enacted in 1924. The bonus had been pegged at a dollar a day of stateside service during the war plus another 25 cents for every day spent overseas, but redemption was deferred for two decades, until 1945. As the nation sank into Depression and pressure mounted to accelerate the redemption, a heedless Congress tabled almost every proposal. The one bill that reached President Hoover's desk earned his prompt veto in 1931 as a "wasteful expenditure."

On May 11, Waters began his march on Washington accompanied by three hundred fellow jobless veterans and their families. Roused every morning by a bugler's reveille, they maintained military discipline and hewed strictly to the principles of temperance and nonviolence that Waters laid down. Swelling into a throng of thousands, they drew the attention of the entire nation.

On May 31, the morning after Memorial Day, just as Mead and Kaiser were preparing to face Byrns's committee, Waters's force reached its bivouac, Anacostia Park on the southern outskirts of Washington, D.C. By July 28, the park hosted twenty thousand protesters, for the most part in civil and patient humor. That afternoon they were suddenly overrun by army cavalry and tanks under the command of General Douglas MacArthur, while his staff aide, Major Dwight D. Eisenhower, looked on in dismay.

News of the burning of the Anacostia campground and the gassing and bayoneting of civilians—an infant born during the march was listed among the slain—screamed from the front pages of newspapers all over the country, as did President Hoover's initial endorsement of MacArthur's sally as a blow against "mob rule."

In Albany, New York, listening to reports from the front, the Democratic presidential candidate, Franklin Roosevelt, turned to his advisor Felix Frankfurter. "Well, Felix," he said, "this elects me." It was a fair conclusion, if a bit premature. Months of increasingly bitter campaigning yet lay ahead.

For Herbert Hoover, 1932 had opened under an evil cloud. Great Britain had abandoned the gold standard the previous fall, provoking several other European countries to follow suit. This threatened a drain on U.S. gold reserves staved off only by the Federal Reserve Board's decision to raise interest rates, which temporarily encouraged foreigners to continue to hold dollars. But the hike further throttled a domestic economy already gasping for breath thanks to a shrinking demand for goods. Confidence in the nation's banks reached such a low ebb that citizens were hoarding more than a billion dollars, drying up the river of liquid credit needed to support industrial activity.

Hoover's renomination at the Republican National Convention that June was preordained, if only because no one else wanted his job. The Grand Old Party emerged from the convention hall in Chicago profoundly dispirited. Hoover estimated his odds of reelection at less than one in ten, and announced that he would do no personal campaigning to improve them.

The Republicans were yoked to a conception of federal power that the Depression had rendered irredeemably outdated and that placed hard limits on Hoover's range of action. One of the most outspoken opponents of federal "overcentralization" was Interior Secretary Wilbur, who preached that the expansion of the federal role in the economy demanded by Hoover's critics would be "quack medicine" for what was at heart "a transient phenomenon in American life." Yet Wilbur's position condemned him to hopeless self-contradiction. It was he, after all, who had delivered the order to jump-start the Boulder Canyon Project, the largest federal public project since the days of Theodore Roosevelt, precisely because no one could think of a way to relieve unemployment other than priming the pump with $100 million in federal spending. And it was he who had forever linked his mentor's name to the concept of grand federal public works by calling the project Hoover Dam.

Wilbur never seemed to comprehend the contradiction in his campaigning against greater federal spending at the very moment when he was promoting the grandest federal expenditure of the era. Then again, he was oblivious to the scale of the disaster enveloping the country, which he believed to be a hiccup inflated to look like a cataclysm by Hoover's enemies. "I have no wish to minimize in any way the seriousness of the depression," he wrote years later, "but the fact remains that the gloom dispensers and those 'playing politics at the expense of human misery' (as Mr. Hoover described them) pictured it as much worse than it was"—an astonishing misjudgment that underscores the Hoover administration's fundamental blindness to the need for innovative federal action.

In early fall, goaded by Roosevelt's dismissal of his economic policies as hidebound and ineffectual, Hoover emerged from his White House cloister and embarked on a punishing schedule of speeches and radio addresses, each one explicating his policies in numbing detail. (The first speech, delivered October 4 in Des Moines, took up seventy-one printed pages.) Meanwhile the GOP establishment, which had gone into hibernation after the convention, rearmed for battle. Calvin Coolidge, Henry Ford, and Alice Roosevelt Longworth delivered radio homilies on Hoover's behalf. The president seemed energized, thundering in New York's Madison Square Garden one week before election day that Roosevelt's so-called "new deal," nebulous as it then was, would "destroy the foundations of our American system."

But in the end, the return to public view of the stiff, sober Hoover only underscored the contrast between him and his opponent, a charming upstart who seemed to be crafting his own legend before the nation's eyes. As the candidates withdrew to their homes to await the electorate's judgment— the president to Palo Alto, California, the challenger to his family estate on the Hudson River—Hoover already seemed defeated and disillusioned, the atmosphere on his westbound train funereal. The Hoovervilles, the assault on the Bonus Army, and the grinding weight of the Depression were obstacles too great to overcome. On election day, November 8, Hoover won only six of the forty-eight states and less than 40 percent of the popular vote.

The rejected president put a brave face on his defeat. Receiving newspapermen in his home on the Stanford campus the morning after election day, he announced that he had spent his "best night's sleep in years." But the historic landslide clearly left its mark, for he veered into a dispirited monologue about retiring to California and withdrawing entirely from public life. By the end of the day he had mapped out a train route for what looked to be his last return trip to Washington: other than a brief detour to Southern California, where his son, Herbert Jr., was raising a family, there would be only one other stop along the way—at Black Canyon, which he had not seen since he had toured it as the chairman of the compact commission in 1922 . . . ten years, and an eternity, before.

Although it had been founded by a Republican administration, the Boulder City that Hoover was about to visit for the first time had been solidly

Democratic from its inception, that party boasting a three-to-one margin in registrations over the GOP. Sims Ely, perhaps sensitive to the embarrassing implications of a Democratic landslide on the federal reservation, had hung pro-Hoover bunting all over the commercial district and, more significantly, tried to bar polling places from the city. This apparent effort to suppress the Democratic vote was attacked as "un-American" by, among others, Nevada's lone congressman, Republican Sam Arentz. Ely hastily backed down, explaining lamely that he merely had been trying to protect Boulderites' votes from invalidation based on the continuing dispute over state and federal jurisdiction on the reservation. Boulder City was duly assigned two polling places, where Roosevelt handily defeated Hoover 1,620 votes to 454 on election day.

Young, Page, and Crowe met Hoover's train when it pulled into Boulder City depot at 8:35 P.M. on Saturday, November 12. An hour behind schedule, it disgorged a traveling party of sixty. The president and first lady received the standard VIP tour of the time—a breakneck drive through the concreted diversion Tunnel No. 2, with Walker Young at the wheel. Then they hastened back to town.

If Hoover had been unaware that the dam workers had delivered an overwhelming majority to his opponent, he got the message upon entering the Anderson mess hall, filled at that evening hour with the swing shift at dinner and the night shift sitting down to breakfast. A smattering of boos rose from the tables. But it was perhaps a more stinging affront that most of the workers coldly refused even to acknowledge his presence. Hoover had launched the project that provided them with their paychecks, but he had also presided over the disaster that had forced them onto the government payroll in the first place. One onlooker recalled: "They wouldn't stand up. They kept on eating."

Twenty minutes later Young escorted Hoover to the administration building lawn for a short speech, broadcast nationally over a coast-to-coast radio hookup. He spent most of the allotted fifteen minutes reliving the 1922 compact commission, the congressional debates, the power contract negotiations—ancient events irrelevant to most of his listeners or dim in their memory. As if to return the insult of the silent men at the Anderson mess, he paid fulsome homage to the members of the compact commission and to the legislators who voted to build the dam, but only a glancing acknowledgment to the laborers on "this magnificent construction." Finally, plainly aware that the dam might well keep his name alive for posterity long after all other memories of his ill-starred presidency had faded, he closed with what was certainly a heartfelt request: "I hope to be present at its final completion as a bystander." In the Roosevelt White House this plea would go unheard.

Then it was over. On his drive back to the train Hoover was accompanied by Pop Squires and his daughter Florence Boyer, who was shocked by the honored guest's appearance—"I never in my life saw a man look so worn out and so completely defeated," she recounted later. The presidential train pulled out at 10:15, one hour and forty minutes after its arrival.

Overlooked in Hoover's haste to get back to Washington, where he was to preside as a lame duck over an intractable domestic crisis for four more months, was that he missed by only a few hours the most momentous event yet in the history of Black Canyon and Hoover Dam. At 11:30 the next morning, the Colorado River would be diverted totally from its path by the hand of man for the first time.

Armed with the $10 million appropriation Henry Kaiser had secured from Congress, Crowe had pressed on with the tunneling, pouring nine thousand linear feet of concrete over the summer. When the river's level fell again in early September, he got a jump start on the permanent cofferdams—the huge mounds of rock, compacted earth, and concrete that would keep the riverbed dry as Hoover Dam was raised. Starting from the Nevada bank about two hundred feet downstream of the tunnel portals, trucks dumped enormous quantities of tunnel muck into the water, forming a dike that inched out toward the midpoint of the river about 250 feet away. There it turned downstream along the center line of the riverbed for about seven hundred feet before curving back to shore. The goal was to enclose the Nevada half of the upper cofferdam site so it could be pumped dry, while corralling the river into a 190-foot-wide channel along the Arizona bank. This enabled workers to start excavating a foundation for the crucial upper cofferdam a month before the river was diverted.

It was now the moment for the main event. In the twilight of November 12, as President Hoover's train was still chugging its way toward the Boulder City depot, every truck in the Six Companies fleet capable of hauling rock was directed to the canyon. They parked at the riverbank and along the cliffside road, each one already freighted with a full load of gravel and rock. A trestle bridge spanned the river about one hundred feet downstream of the tunnel portals.

The river, though at a low ebb, seemed restive during what were to be its last hours of pure liberty. Only that afternoon it had capsized a barge carrying an enormous dragline apparatus—a first cousin to a power shovel—devouring the two-hundred-ton dredging machine "like a horse taking a pill" and leaving no trace of it except a ripple on the water where the tip of its towering boom peeked above the surface.

As noon approached on Sunday, the drivers climbed behind their wheels, set their engines throbbing, and positioned their feet over their clutches as though awaiting the crack of a starter's pistol. At the given signal they were to proceed over the bridge, dump their loads over the side, and circle back to the riverbank for reloading. The strategy was to build up a makeshift levee by filling the river with rock and spoil faster than the current could wash it downstream, just as Charles Rockwood had done to try to close his breach twenty-seven years before.

It was a holiday weekend—Armistice Day—and cars full of tourists streamed through the reservation gates. Except for a handful of VIPs and newsreel cameramen, visitors were barred from the river and from Lookout Point on the Nevada rim, where it was feared that a record throng of sightseers might breach the low protective fencing. But thousands found their own vantage points to witness the historic turning of the river.

They were not disappointed. At 11:30 precisely the canyon shook with an enormous roar as the low concrete cofferdam sealing Tunnel No. 4 was blasted apart with dynamite. There was a grinding of gears, and the column of trucks made its way onto the trestle bridge to begin dumping. For fifteen hours the procession continued, dropping as many as four loads, a prodigious fifty tons of earth and rock, into the swirling current every sixty seconds.

That was not the full extent of the spectacle. Possibly hoping to give the onlookers a sight they would never forget, Crowe arranged for the blast at Tunnel No. 4 to be followed almost immediately by a sequence of explosions along both canyon walls, some 3,500 charges in all, to shake from the cliffsides every shard of loose rock that might imperil the excavation crews who would soon be working in the dry riverbed. For a full ten minutes, titanic jets of debris shot out from both cliffsides and thudded into the water, filling the gorge with a thick cloud of dust in what the *Review-Journal* judged to be "an amazing celebration of the triumph of diversion."

Beneath the smoky haze the frenzied dumping continued from the trestle bridge. The underwater dike rose hour by hour and foot by foot, until in the early evening of November 13 it finally poked its top above the surface and the Colorado gave in. As though finally accepting that the path of least resistance led it out of its primordial bed, its waters poured into Tunnel No. 4, thundering past crews that had been frantically clearing rubble from the portal opening. The successful diversion was marked by an anonymous cry piercing the din: "She's taking it, boys, she's taking it!"

The dumping would continue through the night. By dawn the Colorado River was flowing entirely into the two Arizona bypass tunnels, which carried the torrent three-quarters of a mile downstream before returning it to the riverbed. (The Nevada tunnels were held in reserve for the high water of flood season.) At the downstream end of the canyon, just above the tunnels' outlets, crews were building a second cofferdam to complete the sealing off of the worksite.

That morning, Frank Crowe might have paused to reflect on how much his crews had achieved. The hardest part of the project was now behind them. Crowe had built dams like this one, if much smaller, many times over. But he had never diverted a river like the Colorado.

Yet even that task had scarcely slowed him down. He had been at work for scarcely twenty-two months, and he was now a year ahead of schedule.

1

Black Canyon, 1858: As seen in Baron von Egloffstein's gothic imagination and published in J. C. Ives's report of his exploration of the Colorado River.

Imperial Valley and the Salton Sink, c. 1904, in a rendering by the U.S. Bureau of Reclamation. Rockwood's ill-fated canal tracked the bed of the Alamo River, visible just south of the California/Mexico line.

3

C. R. ROCKWOOD
Undaunted Promoter of Imperial
Valley Project

A. H. HEBER
First President of the California
Development Company

GEORGE CHAFFEY
Who watered and named the
Imperial Valley, 1900-1902

EPES RANDOLPH
Representative of the Harriman interests from June, 1905, to date

The founders of Imperial Valley and its savior, as portrayed in Harold Cory's 1915 history of the valley: Rockwood and Heber of the California Development Company partnered with the brilliant water engineer George Chaffey to build the first canal. But it took Epes Randolph of the Southern Pacific Rail Road, with Cory as his chief engineer, to end the devastating flood caused by the project's flaws.

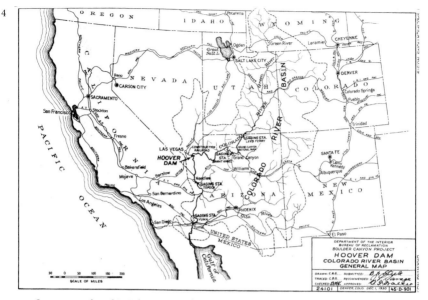

Seven states shared jurisdiction over the Colorado River basin, provoking a contentious negotiation over water rights chaired by then–Commerce Secretary Herbert Hoover.

5

Interior Secretary Ray Lyman Wilbur wielding a two-headed maul at the silver spike ceremony launching the Boulder Canyon Project, September 17, 1930. At the close of his dedicatory speech he surprised the crowd by christening the project "Hoover Dam."

6

The first visionary: Oliver M. Wozencraft, early in his twenty-eight-year campaign to irrigate the California desert with waters from the Colorado.

7

Arthur Powell Davis, nephew of the great explorer John Wesley Powell, conceived the Boulder Canyon Project and as Reclamation Commissioner moved it forward.

8

Philip D. Swing, Imperial Valley's
first congressman, was sent to
Washington with one principal
task: obtain federal approval for the
Boulder Canyon Project.

9

Sen. Hiram W. Johnson of California,
scourge of corporate interests and the
dam project's champion in the upper
house, in a characteristic campaign pose.

10

Murl Emery, lifelong "river rat" and
ubiquitous figure on the Colorado throughout
the construction era.

11

J. H. DeLeach and R. R. Heusel shared a tent in Ragtown, one of the shanty towns established around the perimeter of the construction zone in 1931 as the project lured men seeking work from across the country.

12

Denizens of Ragtown during the first year of construction included worker families like this one awaiting the construction of homes in the more suitable environment of Boulder City.

13

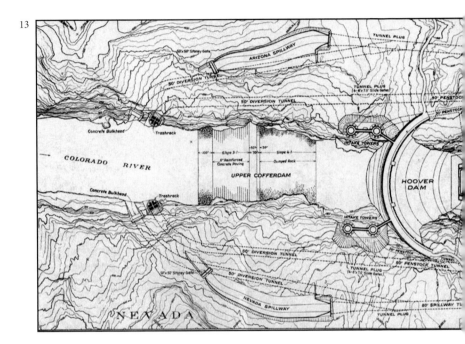

14

The Reclamation staff's overly busy exterior design, seen here, was transformed by California architect Gordon Kaufmann into an elegant machine-age aesthetic.

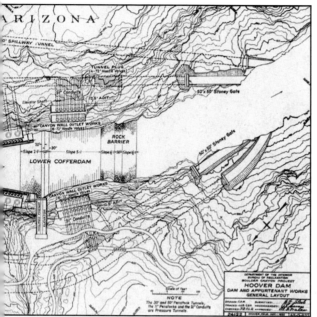

After numerous false starts, Reclamation design engineers finalized this arched configuration of Hoover Dam toward the end of 1930.

15

16

Frank Crowe, 1932.

Reclamation Bureau supervisor Walker R. Young (*left*) and the master dam builder of Six Companies, Frank Crowe (*right*), maintained a close professional relationship despite numerous disagreements over operations on the ground.

Six Cos. executives gather for a rare group portrait with government officials at the dam site in 1932. Left to right: Six Cos. publicity man Norman Gallison, Six Cos. executive Hank Lawler, Walker Young, Six Cos. directors Charles Shea and Edmund O. Wattis, Reclamation Commissioner Elwood W. Mead, Crowe, Reclamation Chief Engineer Raymond F. Walter, Six Cos. Chairman Warren "Dad" Bechtel.

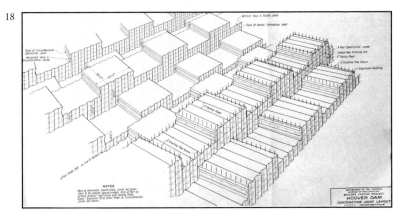

The system of interlocking concrete columns developed by Jack Savage's Reclamation design team. Poured five feet at a time, each column keyed into adjacent "lifts," as shown in this illustration from the official specifications. The spaces between the columns were later infused with grout to create a watertight seal.

19

The renowned high scalers, shown grooming the Arizona canyon wall seated on bosuns' chairs and suspended on ropes hundreds of feet above the river. Photo by the incomparable Ben Glaha.

20

Construction supervisors maintained an almost exclusively white workforce but appreciated Native Americans' talents aloft as high scalers. The subjects of this 1932 Glaha photo are described in official files as "one Yaqui, one Crow, one Navajo and six Apaches."

21

An arresting play of shadow and shape as the columns and forms on the downstream face rise from the riverbed in this Ben Glaha photo from October 1933.

22

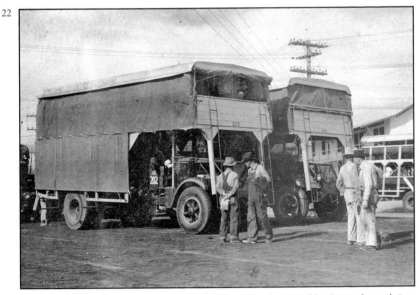

"Big Berthas" lined up to transport workers, 150 at a time, from Boulder City to the worksite eight miles away.

23

Once at the site, workers were transported by devices such as "monkey slides," platforms on rails set vertically on the dam faces and abutments. Photo by Ben Glaha.

24

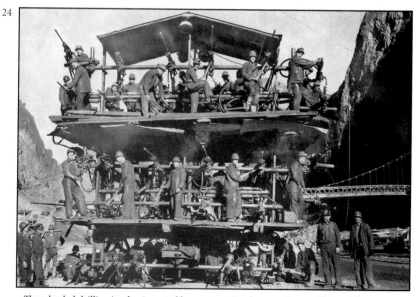

The wheeled drilling jumbo, invented by construction foreman Bernard "Woody" Williams, allowed as many as thirty drillers to attack the tunnel face simultaneously.

The jumbo principle was later applied to the lining of the tunnel walls with concrete. Here a sidewall jumbo, its chutes and buckets visible within the gantry, is ready to be wheeled to the next tunnel section to be concreted.

A crestfallen President Herbert Hoover visits the dam site on November 12, 1932, four days after his defeat by Franklin Roosevelt in an electoral landslide. Had he stayed until the next day, he would have witnessed a project milestone: the diversion of the mighty Colorado River.

27

Determined to maintain blue-nosed order in Boulder City, the government placed it under the jurisdiction of septuagenarian Sims Ely, shown here flanked by Reclamation officials Ralph Lowry and Walker Young.

28

Boulder City notables: (*left to right*) chief ranger Glenn R. "Bud" Bodell, "Whataman" Hudson and his evangelist bride "Ma" Kennedy, ranger Claude Williams.

29

Field management assembled in the gorge to mark the pouring of the millionth cubic yard of concrete, January 7, 1934—a sign of the breakneck pace established by Crowe. Left to right: Charlie Shea and Felix Kahn of Six Cos., Walker Young, Woody Williams, Reclamation office supervisor John C. Page, Frank Crowe.

30

Taking advantage of the opportunity for a bird's-eye view, the government's Boulder Dam Consulting Board rides a penstock section over the work site.

31

Wedged deep within a gallery inside the dam, a worker monitors the massive repair of the underground grout curtain after 1937. Under pressure from the filling Lake Mead, the dam's watertight seals failed, producing extensive seepage and dangerous instability of the entire structure. The repairs took nine years.

Among the country's most stalwart Republican newspapers, the *Los Angeles Times* signaled disapproval of Harold Ickes's removal of Hoover's name from the dam with this editorial cartoon on May 18, 1933. When Hoover went unmentioned during FDR's dedication, the paper reproduced the same cartoon with a telling alteration, October 1, 1935.

Hoover Dam (still officially "Boulder Dam") and Lake Mead, 1940. The young woman in the foreground is Gene Segerblom, twenty-two, whose husband Cliff was then the official Reclamation Bureau photographer.

# 16

# The Rising

**M**emories of Hoover's hurried visit faded quickly at the dam site in the frenzy of post-diversion construction. As soon as the smoke and dust cleared the high scalers were again aloft, preparing anchorages for the cofferdam replacing the temporary rock barricade.

Six high-capacity pumps had been churning night and day to drain water from the riverbed. This task was largely completed by November 21, only nine days after the diversion. What had been a half-mile of raging torrent was reduced to a few shallow pools and a thick layer of stranded, twitching fish, soon to be mucked out by bulldozers and transported to dumps up-river. Crews recovered the Marion dragline the Colorado had swallowed up on the eve of the diversion, hauling it out of the mud with the help of a sister machine anchored on shore. A month spent buried in the riverbed had taken its toll. Before it could be returned to service the enormous dredge would have to be disassembled down to its gears, every last piece cleansed of sand and silt, every inch of corroded wiring replaced.

The project's increasing prominence as a tourist attraction left the government ranger force hopelessly overmatched in its efforts to police the throngs of visitors. Fences and warning signs blocked public access to the most dangerous spots overlooking the canyon, but nothing could keep intrepid visitors from stepping beyond the boundary of safety. On November 16, six soldiers from Fort MacArthur, Los Angeles, made their way to Lookout Point and blithely strolled past a sign reading "Keep Out." Pfc. Theodore Wells ventured onto the steel awning of a floodlight, which promptly gave way, pitching him to his death in the riverbed a thousand feet below.

On a more uplifting note, the gorge was witness six days later to a heroic episode destined to grow in the telling. It started when a government inspector named Burl Rutledge leaned out over Lookout Point to examine equipment installed on an overhanging ledge. He lost his grip on his safety line, and in a flash was tumbling down the sheer cliff toward nearly certain death.

Oliver Cowan, a burly high scaler working from his bosun's chair twenty feet below the rim, glanced up just in time to see Rutledge fall. He pushed away from the wall and managed to intercept the falling man in the nick of time, clutching him by the trouser leg, the sturdy hemp line knotted to his chair squealing taut with the strain. The two men hung on to each other for dear life until a foreman swung over to lend a hand. All three were then hoisted to the rim.

Six Companies and the Reclamation Bureau played up the hair-raising rescue as an act of exceptional bravery. The next morning, newspapers coast to coast reported Cowan's quick-witted reaction, describing him as having "tim[ed] himself with the precision of a trapeze acrobat" in a "dramatic battle with death in mid-air." The distance Rutledge fell before being snatched from death's grasp was inflated from twenty feet to as much as four hundred, and Cowan's act magnified to his having grasped at the falling man's ankle as he flew past in midair. Cowan, with his ready smile and athletic six-foot frame, proved a ready subject for admiring reportage, if a bit bashful: "There wasn't much to it," he told reporters a few days later in Los Angeles. "I just held on until some of the other boys came to the rescue." His journey would take him to Washington, where he was said to be in line for a Carnegie Medal, an annual award for selfless, death-defying heroism. (It was not to be: when the 1932 awards were announced Cowan's name was missing from the list of seventy honorees.)

Cowan's act brought new renown to the high scalers, not that these daredevils were starved for attention. Already they were among the prime attractions drawing visitors to the canyon. Spectators gathered along the canyon rim to gawk at the teams of men drilling, jackhammering, or nonchalantly taking lunch while suspended hundreds of feet above ground on slender lines of braided hemp. It was not unusual for the men to stage impromptu acrobatic demonstrations for the onlookers, unnerving Walker Young, who tried to quell the scalers' midair bravado with threats of harsh punishment for unsafe behavior.

Young's concern was that the circus heroics would inadvertently draw public attention to the high human toll of the overhead work: at least a dozen men, most of them high scalers, would lose their lives in plunges from the canyon walls during construction. But Young was stymied by the desire of the bureau and the construction company for positive publicity. Neither could resist crafting heroic myths from the scalers' gymnastic routines. The exemplary high scaler was twenty-three-year-old Louis Fagan, a "human pendulum" (so dubbed by the *Las Vegas Age*) whose signature feat was to have transferred every member of a tunnel crew around an outcropping on the Arizona cliffside twice a day for three weeks in January 1932. His method involved locking his legs around each miner one at a time, kicking away from the wall, swinging out over the canyon and around the projection, and depositing the passenger on the far side. When not engaged in human transport, it was reported, Fagan transported crates of dynamite in similar fashion.

As the magnitude of Franklin Roosevelt's electoral victory sank in across the country, newly elected Democratic office holders moved swiftly to grasp the reins of government after twelve years of GOP control. Few prizes beckoned like the great project on the Colorado. On the Monday following election day, Nevada's newly elected Democratic congressman, James Scrugham, showed up in John Page's Boulder City office to declare a new era in the oversight of Hoover Dam. Scrugham, a former governor and the state's delegate to the compact commission, peppered the nonplussed Page with questions about the qualifications of the local Reclamation staff, evidently to quantify the potential for patronage jobs. (Page informed him that most of the staff had civil service protection.) Scrugham further grilled Page about the electioneering for Hoover that Sims Ely and other federal employees had conducted in the waning days of the campaign. This was illegal, he warned Page, adding that he meant to see that charges were brought against the lawbreakers.

Nothing came of Scrugham's threat. But the encounter signified that the project was in for a new style of supervision from Washington. The pampering of Six Companies by Wilbur and Mead, their tendency to see the interests of the contractor and the federal government as one and the same, were relics of the past. In the years to come government investigators would swarm over the canyon, training their gimlet eyes on every aspect of the work. The Six Companies books would be laid open to scrutiny by officials who by no means liked what they saw. Elwood Mead, who had been the final arbiter of all things in Boulder Canyon under Wilbur's indulgent leadership, would no longer have the last word. That authority would belong to the new interior secretary, Harold Ickes, a lapsed Republican from Chicago who would become known as the quintessential New Dealer.

The fifty-nine-year-old Ickes, a newspaperman turned lawyer and progressive political activist, had made his name crusading against the Chicago utility baron Samuel Insull, whom he fought, as *Time* magazine observed, "bravely but utterly without result for 25 years." (Insull's empire had finally collapsed in mid-1932, ruined by the Great Depression.) Ickes's record of Republican apostasy dated back to 1912, when he campaigned for the Bull Moose Progressive ticket of Theodore Roosevelt and Hiram Johnson. In the 1928 presidential election he bolted the party to support Democrat Al Smith, and in 1932, convinced that Hoover's renomination would spell disaster for the GOP, he launched a "dump Hoover" movement at the party convention. It failed for lack of a candidate willing to take up the colors.

Ickes's eventual appearance in Franklin Roosevelt's entourage seemed preordained. Yet the president-elect had never met him before naming him to the cabinet, and at first even mispronounced his name as "Ikes." (It is pronounced "Ickiss.") Distinctly more cantankerous than most of the cabinet members, he nonetheless harbored a vision of government that corresponded closely to the new president's. As he concisely distilled his philosophy for the press: "In times such as these the people should look to their government for assistance. . . . The days of the financial overlords are as dead as those of the feudal lords. We have a new social outlook upon things in general."

Determined to be a vigilant overseer of his department, Ickes spent the first two months of his tenure quietly taking the measure of the Boulder Canyon Project, the largest undertaking under his jurisdiction. Much of what he discovered, from the government's procurement process to Six Companies' labor practices, appalled him. Beginning in early May, he moved to institute change.

One of his first shots was purely symbolic: on May 8, he erased Wilbur's designation of the project as "Hoover Dam" by ordering Mead to call it "Boulder Dam . . . in correspondence and other references to the dam as you may have occasion to make in the future." News of the name change inspired a torrent of attacks largely from Republican editorial pages, not to mention "a number of insulting letters, some of them anonymous," Ickes complained to his private diary. The unexpected reaction forced him to elaborate publicly on his reasoning: He felt it was not "sound public policy" to name "a mountain, a dam, a park, a lake or anything of the sort after a living president . . . least of all . . . while that president is still in office," and that it was "distinctly in bad taste" for the naming to be done by a direct appointee of the honoree. In a further shot aimed directly at Hoover's *amour-propre*, he observed that many of the dam's original supporters considered Hoover's contribution to the project to have been "at best, very casual" and that the ex-president had been "at the very least, luke warm on the whole matter." Finally, he held that Wilbur had exceeded his authority by christening the dam without instructions from Congress, and that he had only restored its geographically appropriate name. This rationale was almost as disingenuous as Wilbur's had been in 1930, as the name "Boulder Dam" commemorated a canyon twenty miles from the project's actual location.

Hoover and Wilbur maintained a stoic public silence about the name change, but it plainly rankled. Hoover detected the hand of his old nemesis Hiram Johnson—a friend of Ickes's and the obvious source of the calumny that Hoover's contribution to the project had been "casual." Wilbur, searching for a simpler explanation, ascribed it to "pettiness," observing that Ickes changed the name less than a week after Hoover visited the construction site for the first time as a private citizen. (The unheralded visit in early May surprised many people in Boulder City, not least John Page's daughter Jean, who was in Walker Young's house helping to nurse the ailing superintendent when "a tall smiling gentleman" she recognized as the ex-president appeared on the doorstep asking after Young's health.) In the wake of the name change, Hoover would never pay another visit to Boulder City or Black Canyon.

The renaming of the dam may have been the most conspicuous volley in Ickes's campaign against the Hoover legacy, but there were others. On May 5 he rejected bids from ten manufacturers for 400,000 barrels of cement for the dam because they all had come in for exactly $1.29 a barrel, an obvious sign of collusion. Adding insult to injury, the price was nearly 20 percent higher than what they had quoted just two months earlier.

The cement cartel proved more steadfast than the administration, which desperately needed industry's support for its economic initiatives. Not long after Ickes's widely publicized rejection of the bids, Reclamation quietly reissued the cement order, compromising on a discount of about 10 percent. In return, the government suspended its attack on the industry's price-fixing behavior. The cement cartel would not be broken until 1938, when Reclamation accepted an outside manufacturer's bid for a dam project for the first time. The new bidder, who was hoping to become a major player in the cement trade, was Henry Kaiser.

Ickes aimed two other initiatives squarely at labor relations at the dam site, which had not significantly improved since the abortive strike of 1931. The first applied to Six Companies' policy of paying some wages in scrip, redeemable at face value only at its company store in Boulder City.

This arrangement cast a shadow over Boulder City's nascent commercial sector, which found itself competing with a huge and well-stocked department store with a captive clientele of wage earners paid in its owner's private currency. While the independent merchants were free to accept scrip in their own establishments, they could redeem it from Six Companies only at a discount and only for merchandise at the store, not cash. To protect themselves, they accepted scrip in their shops at a discount of up to 20 percent, subjecting themselves to a further competitive disadvantage. (Prostitutes in Las Vegas's notorious Block 16, it was said, also accepted discounted scrip, making regular pilgrimages to Boulder City to spend it at the Six Companies store.)

The company's stranglehold on the workers' custom seemed unbreakable. Their families typically lived paycheck to paycheck, dependent for survival on wage advances which the company would pay only in scrip. The Big Six's chief of employment in the canyon, the fearsome Earl McAdams, also applied unsubtle pressure on the workers to maintain a balance in their scrip accounts. "Everyone was supposed to patronize the company store," one worker recalled years later. "Anyone that did not had a stamp on the stub of their paycheck to see McAdams and explain why."

Scrip purchases consistently accounted for more than 10 percent of wages at the dam, amounting to $45,000 a month in guaranteed revenue for the company store. The desperate merchants fought back with ads in the local newspapers appealing to the employees' self-respect: "Do you Dare to be INDEPENDENT?" one read, featuring a drawing of that icon of sturdy self-reliance, Uncle Sam. "Do not draw scrip except as an emergency! GIVE INDEPENDENT MERCHANTS AN EVEN CHANCE!" But they could not overcome the economic fundamentals that placed laboring families at the mercy of the dominant employer in town.

The merchants appealed to Reclamation commissioner Mead, who brushed off their complaints, finding in September 1932 that the issuance of scrip was "standard business practice" and "the only practical system combining economy, simplicity, and service." Payment in scrip protected the contractor from an unnecessary drain on its scarce cash reserves, he observed, although he failed to mention that during the six weeks prior to his report in mid-1932, the Six Companies board had voted itself two dividends of $30 a share, or a total of $2.4 million, payable in cash from the money it collected from the government.

The only receptive ear the merchants found was that of Tasker L. Oddie, Nevada's Republican U.S. senator. Brooklyn-born, Oddie was a Nevada patriot, having served two terms as the state's governor and more than a decade as its senator. He found plenty to resent in Six Companies' flouting of state mining law and its refusal to pay local taxes, and regarded the scrip scheme as merely an extension of its policy of squeezing every drop of profit from the publicly funded dam project.

In August 1932, Oddie arranged for the Senate Irrigation Committee to hold hearings in Las Vegas and Boulder City to investigate Six Companies' behavior. This was a political triumph on paper that turned into a fiasco on the ground, as the committee chairman, John Thomas of Idaho, raced through the agenda, giving short shrift to four Boulder City merchants with prepared statements outlining the threat to their livelihoods from the Big Six's government-sanctioned quasi-monopoly. Thomas adjourned the hearing after an hour, led the committee to the Anderson mess hall for lunch, and then left town with a vague promise to give the complaints "every consideration." The *Review-Journal* could not conceal its disapproval of the whole affair, summing it up that evening with the headline, "Hearing Rushed and Witnesses Cut Short."

After two years of such torment, the merchants had begun to feel that deliverance would never come. But it would not take Ickes long to end a practice that struck him, predictably, as repugnant. Barely two months after taking office he summonined Bechtel to Washington and imposed a hard deadline of two weeks to end the use of scrip permanently. "I believe that a man is entitled to his salary in money," he explained to the press. Despite its claims over the years that scrip was the only system through which it could keep accurate records of employee advances, the board immediately capitulated and promptly instituted a charge system allowing workers to have purchases at the company store automatically deducted from their paychecks.

Ickes's second labor initiative did not go as smoothly. This involved discrimination against black workers.

In 1930, when the Boulder Canyon Project was launched, the black population of Las Vegas was minuscule—143 out of 5,165 residents, according to the U.S. Census—but they were the targets of bigotry nonetheless. Barred from joining the local AFL unions, they formed their own, the Colored Citizens Labor and Protective Association, which grew to 247 members by September 1931, when it started raising public objections to the systematic exclusion of Negroes from the dam project. The authorities responded largely with lip service. In May 1932, Wilbur issued a dutiful pledge to provide "all assistance possible" (in the *Review-Journal's* paraphrase) to place black laborers on the payroll. Bechtel followed with his own promise to hire blacks "when and if they had the necessary experience." Black workers in southern Nevada justifiably found these responses cynical and dispiriting. Bechtel's argument that blacks simply did not have the "experience" to compete for jobs was a transparent dodge. As one white dam worker recalled, most of the workforce had no construction background whatsoever: "I had never done this kind of work before. From what I could see nobody had. We just learned as we went along."

The Negro share of employment on the dam remained inconsequential. Only a few weeks after Wilbur and Bechtel delivered their ostentatious pledges, the roster of black dam workers reached thirty. That would prove to be the absolute high water mark of black employment at the dam, although it was described locally as a civil rights breakthrough that settled "this question of Negro labor on Hoover Dam . . . with justice and fairness" (as the *Age* wrote). Within a year, their number had dwindled to eleven, all but two of whom were minimum wage laborers employed on a segregated "colored" crew under a white foreman, Charlie "Dogface" Rose. The entire workforce by then exceeded four thousand. In July 1934, when employment peaked at 5,251 men, only fifteen black workers were on the job, all mired in the lowest pay grades, accounting for a bare $61 of the dam's total daily payroll of $21,674.

The indignities did not stop with their wages. The National Association for the Advancement of Colored People reported that black workers were barred with their families from residence in Boulder City, transported to and from the dam site in separate buses from the white workers, and further humiliated on the job "by such petty regulations as separate water buckets."

Within Boulder City, Sims Ely's hostility to Negroes was no secret. Everyone had heard of his confrontation with Clarence Newland, the Texas-born owner of the popular Green Hut restaurant, over Newland's black cook, McKinley Sales.

"Get rid of that colored cook," Ely had told Newland.

"Mr. Ely, how much money you got?" Newland replied.

"What bearing does that have on the subject?"

"Well, if you've got $80,000, you can have the Green Hut tomorrow and hire who you want. But as long as I own it, you're not telling me who to hire and fire."

From the moment of the project's launch, racial discrimination of the most casual variety was accepted as inevitable and rationalized as logistically necessary, based on the assumption that hiring black workers would require the construction of segregated dormitories and other facilities. In July 1931, while the workforce was ramping up by hundreds of men per month, Page declared in a memo to Mead that even though Six Companies believed, quaintly, that "negroes would probably be desirable on account of the extreme heat . . . no negroes [are] now employed on the construction work." The explanation: "[T]he matter of housing and segregation has so far rendered it impractical to plan on their employment."

Franklin Roosevelt's election seemed to herald a new era of opportunity for blacks at the dam. Especially encouraging was the appointment of Ickes, who boasted impeccable antidiscrimination credentials, including a stint in the 1920s as president of the NAACP's Chicago chapter. Upon taking office, Ickes had created the post of special advisor on Negro matters in the Interior Department, though to mollify Southern Democrats he gave the job to a white liberal from Georgia, Clark Foreman. The post of Foreman's top assistant, however, went to a Negro economist, Robert C. Weaver.

Alerted by the NAACP to the discrimination complaints against Six Companies, Ickes demanded a report from Mead. As usual, the Reclamation commissioner's sympathies lay entirely with the contractor. He assured Ickes that the builders had done their utmost to give "colored labor . . . a reasonable representation on the work," and repeated the argument that it would be "hardly feasible to provide separate dormitories and dining room facilities for the accommodation of a comparatively small number of colored employees. Experience elsewhere points to the conclusion that should this not be done unsatisfactory conditions are likely to develop."

To Mead it was self-evident that an integrated workforce would be wracked by dissension, even violence. He may also have picked up on concerns by Las Vegas civic leaders that providing opportunities for local black workers would only encourage an influx of blacks from all over the country. As the *Review-Journal* asserted, the small number of "colored job seekers" then in town were "merely the vanguard of thousands of Negro workers who would flock to the dam site on short notice" should the rolls be thrown open.

When Ickes challenged these explanations, Mead reminded him that Six Companies' labor policies lay outside the government's jurisdiction, except for the contractual specifications barring "Mongolian" labor and imposing the veterans' preference (the latter of which, in any event, the contractor regularly flouted). "I know of no way in which the Secretary [i.e., Ickes] or any other government official may legally dictate to the contractors the kind of labor that shall be employed," he counseled his new boss.

Ickes's ability to push further was constrained by politics. As long as Negro workers were poorly organized and economically weak, their gains would have to come at the expense of better organized groups that the administration did not wish to antagonize—in this case, white union members and white working-class voters.

Ickes's record on racial discrimination would persistently outpace the rest of the New Deal cabinet. In 1933, for instance, he inserted a unique nondiscrimination clause in all construction contracts let by the Public Works Administration, which under his jurisdiction would spend $3.3 billion on schools, housing, and other public projects. But the initiative did not apply at the dam, where he was hamstrung by the deal his predecessor had cut with Six Companies and the other contractors. The only blow he was able to strike for racial equality was embodied in Boulder City Order No. 12, promulgated by Ely in mid-1933 at Ickes's behest. The order opened residence in the city to all dam workers regardless of their "color or religious affiliation." But the paltry share of jobs awarded to black work-ers stripped the order of all significance; there is no record that any black employee exercised his new right to residency in Boulder City during the construction era.

Six Companies barely went through the motions of considering black workers for employment. One black applicant, O. B. Allbritton, reported in the *Age* that he had presented himself at the employment office, army discharge papers in hand, only to be brusquely turned away. "The answers were: We have no provisions." During that period turnover on the workforce averaged thirteen men a day. In the first two weeks of December 1931 alone, Six Companies hired 339 new men, none of them black. A few months later, the *Age* gave this "telling description" of the average dam worker: thirty-seven years old, "representing every state in the union," American-born, and white.

Not long after the river began flowing at full strength into the bypass tun-nels, a curious mark appeared on the Arizona canyon wall—a towering par-abolic dotted line reaching almost one hundred feet at its apogee. Painted by men on ladders equipped with buckets of whitewash, the line marked the contour of the immense cofferdam that would seal off the riverbed ahead of the spring floods.

The cofferdams designed to seal off Black Canyon at both ends were, like nearly every other component of the project, immense. The upper cof-ferdam required more than 650,000 cubic yards of sand, gravel, and rock, making it larger than most of the earth fill dams previously built in the United States. It was to be ninety-six feet tall at its crest and more than a seventh of a mile thick at its base—thicker than Hoover Dam itself by one hundred feet.

The original specifications dealt with the cofferdams' design in almost as much detail as the main dam. This reflected their critical role in the construction scheme—averting the dire consequences of flooding in the dry riverbed where two thousand men might be on the job at any given time. The specifications dictated the density of the cofferdams' silt, sand, and gravel fill and the characteristics of the compacting equipment ("having cast iron ball feet equally spaced over its cylindrical surface and its weight shall be not less than 1,000 pounds per linear foot of width of tread . . ."). The upper cofferdam, which would bear the brunt of at least three seasons of violent flood, received especially detailed treatment. Its earth fill core was to be lined with a three-foot layer of rock or boulders on the upstream side, "the maximum dimensions of which shall be not less than 4 inches nor more than 30 inches." This layer, in turn, was to be covered with six-inch-thick sheets of concrete reinforced with steel bars and laid down in longitudinal strips not wider than sixteen feet each. A wall of protective steel piles was to be driven at its foot across the full breadth of the canyon, and the entire structure was to be shrouded in a final layer of waterproof rubberized fabric. The goal was to keep the construction site dry even under the onslaught of a millennial flood, calculated at 200,000 cubic feet per second. (The greatest flood yet measured at the government gauge station at Lees Ferry, Arizona, had been 180,000 cubic feet per second.) While hydrologists calculated that this maximum projected flood would raise the river seventeen feet above the tops of the diversion inlets, the upper cofferdam provided a barrier thirteen feet higher yet. By Jack Savage's reckoning, nothing short of Noah's flood could inundate the work zone.

Still, the specifications were not proof against unexpected discoveries on the ground. Soon after Crowe's men began excavating the cofferdam foundations, the geology they unearthed provoked a bitter disagreement between him and Walker Young. The upper cofferdam site, it seemed, was littered with huge boulders, which made it impossible to simply drive steel pilings through the muck into stable bedrock. Instead, crews would have to dig a trench through the boulder field and line it with concrete to give the pilings a secure foundation. Clearly, this made the cofferdam far more expensive than Six Companies had anticipated. Crowe demanded compensation for the change in plans. Reasoning that the presence of unexpected conditions was a risk that the contract laid on the builders, not the government, Young turned him down. An infuriated Crowe vented his spleen to John Page a few days later "at considerable length," the office manager recorded—"threatens trouble if not remedied," Page observed.

The likely cause of Crowe's concern was his original unbalanced bid, through which Six Companies recorded most of its overall profit in the project's early stages. The crossover point was the completion of the diversion tunnels, by which time Six Companies had pocketed approximately $4.4 million, most of which was distributed to the partners via dividends. On subsequent stages of construction, however, the unit prices bid by Six Companies—so much per cubic yard of soil excavated or concrete poured—meant that on many tasks it would break even at best, or even lose money. For example, Crowe's bid quoted the removal of some 857,000 cubic yards of primordial muck and silt from the upper riverbed at $2.20 per cubic yard; compared to the $2.50 that Reclamation's design engineers thought that job would cost, the difference would produce a loss for the contractor of more than $250,000. Every additional cubic yard that had to be removed would add to the red ink.

Six Companies' economic incentives, therefore, changed dramatically once the tunnels were completed. Before then, any alteration in conditions or design approved by Reclamation officials and requiring more work—say, more extensive underground excavation—would increase the contractor's profit, as its unit rates for those tasks exceeded its costs. Afterward, however, the situation was reversed. It is hardly surprising that Crowe fought almost every subsequent change order to the hilt.

Several weeks after suffering Crowe's outburst, Page convened a summit meeting in Boulder City. Representing Six Companies were Crowe, Charlie Shea, and Augustine "Gus" Ayers, the contractor's chief of engineering. Across the table were Reclamation's Young, Page, and, dispatched from the Denver office, Jack Savage, the cofferdams' supervising designer. Sinclair O. Harper, the bureau's assistant chief engineer, took the chair. For nearly three full days, starting early in the morning of December 13, Shea and Crowe aired their grievances about costly change orders on the cofferdam and other parts of the project. Eventually, the solution was found in the project's very complexity. Reclamation agreed to combine all the mandated changes into a single order and net out their various costs and savings. The final tally would not be calculated until 1936. Perhaps unsurprisingly, it would come out in the Big Six's favor.

While the Big Six and the government bureaucrats squabbled over the work required in the riverbed, another crucial job was reaching completion on the canyon rim overhead. This was the stringing of five enormous cableways across the gorge, spanning the riverbed from the site of the intake towers all the way to the location of the powerhouses, nearly a mile downstream—the fundamental prerequisite for placing concrete in the dewatered gorge. Their construction had been launched on August 10, with four tons of dynamite stuffed into seven hundred holes obliterating part of the Nevada cliffside, including what was then known as Lookout Point, to create a foundation for two movable seventy-five-foot cable towers.

The cableways were the ultimate elaboration of the system Crowe had devised for Arrowrock Dam in 1911. There he had spent $73,000—an unprecedented sum for construction infrastructure at the time—to string three cables from a single tower on one side of the river to three separate anchorages 1,500 feet away. The cableways built to supply concrete to Hoover Dam would make those look like toys.

Crowe had mapped out the Black Canyon cableways even before his bid was final, representing them with lengths of white twine in the mockup of the dam project he had wheeled into Will Wattis's hospital room. Towering some eight hundred feet above the riverbed so they would clear the ultimate crest of the finished dam by fifty-seven feet, two lines would stretch 2,575 feet, making them the longest ever built. Four of the five would have movable towers at each end, standing on tracks running parallel to the canyon rim. The fifth, which would cover the powerhouse site at the downstream end of the canyon, would have a stationary head tower on the Nevada side and a mobile tower with six hundred feet of lateral travel on the Arizona cliffside. Because four smaller cableways had been in operation early in the project, the new lines were designated Nos. 5 through 9, counting from the upstream end of the canyon.

The cable towers were themselves striking additions to the landscape—pyramidal gantries nine stories tall, built as right triangles with the verticals situated on the side furthest from the river, so they resembled giant skeletons straining back against the sixty-ton steel lines suspended over the gorge. Each was counterbalanced by a solid concrete block weighing as much as fifty tons. Prodigious in scale, the cableways were also prodigious in cost, involving six separate subcontracts totaling more than $2 million ($31 million in modern terms), including the largest orders placed for supplies or equipment by the Big Six during the project. There was a $1 million order from Columbia Steel Co. of San Francisco for structural steel for the towers and braided steel cabling, and another $501,000 to Ingersoll-Rand Co. for compressors and air hoists. Westinghouse Electric Co. provided electric motors worth $293,000. All this was on the Six Companies tab, but if the board of directors saw any reason to kick at the enormous expense they kept it to themselves, for every dollar they spent on the cableways saved them much more in terms of the time and expense of pouring concrete.

By May 1933 they had been completed, five steel cables strung rim to rim over a dry gulch that had been the home of one of nature's wildest rivers and that would welcome her back, tamed, soon enough. Before that could happen, the river's imprisoning rampart would have to be poured. That moment had finally arrived.

# 17

# The Pour

**W**ednesday, June 6, 1933: A Midwestern heat wave had already claimed six lives and was expected to get much worse. In Washington the calendar was marking off the last of what President Roosevelt himself had dubbed the Hundred Days, that breakneck three-month rush of congressional action which brought into being fifteen new laws, including a farm relief program and new regulations for the banking and securities industries—"the starting of the wheels of the New Deal," as the president said in the third of his Fireside Chats.

In Black Canyon that day, another foundation was about to be set. At eleven in the morning Frank Crowe and Walker Young clambered onto a narrow ledge in the very depths of the riverbed, more than one hundred feet below the normal water level. From there they looked down on several square enclosures, fifty feet on the side, marked by walls of wooden slats faced with sheet metal and propped upright by timber bracing. At Crowe's signal, passed up the line by a system of electric bells, an engineer in the control shack of Cableway No. 6 lowered a steel bucket filled with sixteen tons of fresh concrete that had been hovering eight hundred feet overhead. It paused a few feet from the ground, directly above an enclosure designated as Block J-3. In the job site's system of alphanumeric coordinates, Block J-3 would be the foundation block adjacent to the dam's center line on the Arizona side and three sections in from its upstream face.

# COLOSSUS

Concreteman C. W. "Wince" Bingham strode across the enclosure and tripped the "dogs," the safety latches on the bucket's lower edge, with a swing of his long-handled shovel. The bottom sprung open, disgorging a truck-sized gob of wet concrete onto the exposed bedrock. Suddenly relieved of sixteen tons of cargo, the bucket recoiled twenty-five feet into the air as though rigged with springs, while the cableman in the control shack hastily rolled in the hoisting line to take up the slack. Meanwhile, Bingham and his seven-man crew had at the mound of concrete with spades and brooms, working it into every corner of Block J-3. When they had finished, it covered the 2,500 square feet of enclosed ground to a depth of slightly more than one inch.

The first bucket of concrete had been poured for Hoover Dam. Crowe and Young had wanted the event to take place with a minimum of ceremony. They got their wish. Few newspapers marked the pour with more than a few paragraphs on an inside page. Possibly inured to the headlong pace of work in the canyon, none bothered to mention that the pouring had commenced eighteen months ahead of schedule. Many more milestones would be passed in the next two years as the concrete monolith rose toward the sky. It was only one bucket, after all. Another half-million just like it would be needed to finish the job.

Excavating the river bottom down to bedrock had taken the men almost ten months. Six million cubic yards of muck, rock, and gravel was removed, some converted into fill for the cofferdams, the rest dumped in waste heaps a mile or so upriver. The process amounted to a major industrial deployment in itself—a fleet of more than seventy trucks moving loads out of the excavation zone at an average rate of five per minute, digging and jackhammering around the clock until bedrock was finally struck about 104 feet below the low waterline, or about six hundred feet above sea level.

The canyon sprang several surprises on the excavation crews. Early on they came upon a planed, sawed-off two-by-six-inch plank buried bizarrely forty feet deep in the river bottom. (Geologists concluded that it had come from Callville Wash, an upriver mining community flooded in 1922). In early June, just as the concrete pour was beginning, workers drilling a drainage well happened upon another artifact nestled in an old surveying bore fifteen feet deep in the bedrock: a drill bit studded with eight black diamonds that had been lost ten years before by Walker Young's original survey crew. The bit was encrusted with petrified silt and slightly dented, but as its 21.15 carats of diamonds were still serviceable (and worth about $3,700), it was shipped off to Denver for refurbishing.

The biggest surprise was the discovery of a deep trench running length-wise down the center of the riverbed, as if gouged out by a monstrous talon. No one knew how deep below it lay the bedrock, only that the trench, a primordial crevasse with hot springs discharging one-hundred-degree water and boulders twelve feet tall, was much deeper than anything hinted at by years of test borings. The discovery caused days of delay in the pour, as Crowe deemed the faulted and spalled ground exposed in the partially excavated trench to be an unsuitable foundation for his dam. More digging was needed, but most of the earthmoving machines had already been shifted out of the canyon. Crowe appealed to Young for approval to resume excavation, only to be stalled by the latter's habitual caution about unexpected expenses.

Inspecting the trench one day with Young, Crowe pressed him for an immediate ruling.

"I'll let you know what to do," Young replied testily.

"By tomorrow morning," Crowe shot back.

After a day of telegraphic discussions with his superiors in Denver and Washington, Young gave Crowe the green light. The machinery was back in the trench within hours. Bedrock was finally struck at 505 feet above sea level, or ninety-five feet below the main shelf. In this trench, dubbed the inner gorge, Block J-3 was staked out and poured.

The system Jack Savage's engineers developed for the pouring of 3,500,000 cubic yards of concrete in Black Canyon was the fruit of decades of research in the properties of bulk concrete—and of learned speculation, too, for no one had ever poured so much concrete in bulk. The one fact the bureau knew beyond question was that the concrete had to be systematically cooled by artificial means. The hardening of concrete is a chemical process in which the reaction of its cement with water generates heat, which makes the material expand. If this expansion is not controlled, it will produce internal cracking throughout a large block of concrete. In a monolithic block as massive as Hoover Dam, curing under normal conditions would take more than one hundred years and might very well leave the structure cross-hatched with cracks and as porous as a sieve.

The bureau had experimented with artificial cooling at the Owyhee Dam in Idaho, the largest mass of concrete ever poured before Hoover Dam. Owyhee was cooled by circulating water through internal coils for about a month, and only during the late stages of construction. This proved to be insufficiently thorough, for cracks appeared in the concrete shortly after its completion in 1932.

At Hoover Dam, which would be built from seven times as much concrete, more stringent measures were plainly needed. The bureau's basic plan was to build the dam not as a single monolithic mass, but in discrete concrete blocks—more than thirty thousand of them, measuring up to fifty feet square and five feet in height. These were to be poured one atop another in 230 separate columns. The sides of each column were corrugated to interlock with its adjacent columns, leaving interstices to be filled with the cement paste known as grout. The bureau's specifications stated that no more than five feet of concrete (a unit known as a "lift") were to be poured in any column in a seventy-two-hour period, and not more than thirty-five feet in any thirty days. No column could exceed the height of its immediate neighbors by more than thirty-five feet at any time.

On the surface of every lift would be laid rows of one-inch pipes, creating one of the true marvels of the project. This was the cooling system, which Jack Savage had refined following the Owyhee test. In its final configuration, the scheme required 662 miles of piping, its goal to reduce the temperature of the curing concrete to a target of forty-five degrees Fahrenheit at the upstream face and sixty-five degrees on the downstream side.

This was done in two stages. The "pre-cooling" stage circulated chilly river water through the piping to extract half the unwanted heat from the mass. In the second stage, the water was first passed through a refrigeration plant erected on the Nevada riverbank, which chilled it to about forty degrees before circulating it through the concrete. That was frigid enough to complete the cooling of a fifty-foot-tall block of concrete (i.e., ten lifts) in six to eight weeks.

The water pipes were connected to the cooling apparatus through lines in a vertical eight-foot-wide gap at the exact center point of the dam, known as the "slot." After sufficient cooling was achieved in each fifty-foot block, its waterlines were filled with pressurized grout and the slot concreted to the top of that level, like a zipper slowly being pulled closed. Once the cooling of a section was completed, the gaps between its columns were also filled with grout. This technique effectively created an intricate network of internal expansion joints, ensuring that cracking and shrinkage in the concrete occurred only where the designers dictated.

From Frank Crowe's standpoint, the raising of the dam was chiefly a problem of logistics. "We had 5,000 men jammed in a 4,000-foot canyon," he recalled years later in a *Fortune* interview. "The problem, which was a problem in materials flow, was to set up the right sequence of jobs so they wouldn't kill each other off."

Fortunately, solving this problem was second nature to Crowe, the master of what would much later become known as critical path management—the precise coordination of disparate but interconnected tasks so they will all interact with maximum efficiency. The pour in Black Canyon—involving the constant motion of men, equipment, and material twenty-four hours a day, seven days a week in and above a thousand-foot gorge in the desert—unfolded on a grander scale and comprised vastly more moving pieces than anything Crowe had ever attempted.

Every part of Crowe's great machine was monumental on its own terms. There were two full-scale concrete plants, each connected to the construction site by a railroad hung precariously on the Nevada canyon wall, 220 feet over the riverbed. (The tracks had originally been laid on dry land at the river's edge, but the draining of the canyon left them suspended partway up the cliff, anchored to the vertical rock wall by angled iron struts.) One hundred seventy-five carloads of cement and gravel aggregate entered the mixing plant each day. Nine trains were kept constantly in motion hauling filled buckets to the cableways and returning with empties. There were two tracks and nine switches, each equipped with signal lights and emergency whistles, which were often sounded to check the locomotive engineers' propensity for negotiating the maze at hair-raising speeds.

> Oh, I'll tell you, this was a mad confusion [recalled Richard "Curley" Francis, who served the project as both truck driver and locomotive engineer]. We had red lights and green lights to tell us when to go and how to go, and it was a real feat to run the switch car and keep all nine trains working. . . . All of a sudden you'd come around a turn and you'd hit a red light. Half the time you'd be looking down the track and see another train coming right for you, then all of a sudden they'd switch him around you.

It was not uncommon for a switchman to lose track of where all the trains in his charge were going, an alarming development that would send him lunging for his emergency whistle to let off a long blast. "Any time that man hung on to that whistle, everybody stopped dead because we all knew that he didn't know where everybody was at," Francis related. "It was an amazement to me that we didn't have more wrecks than we did."

The trains fed a never-ending supply of concrete to the five cableways, which had to haul it across the canyon in twenty-ton buckets and deposit it in the lifts with split-second timing. The professional demands on the men under Crowe's command had never been greater: from concrete mixers, locomotive engineers, and signalmen to the puddlers who spread the concrete in its wooden corrals hundreds of feet above the riverbed, every man had to know his job to the smallest detail and had to be ready to snap into action the moment his task was called.

One might best understand the complexity of the system by following the buckets—known as "Crowe buckets" in honor of their inventor, who was eventually awarded two patents for their design—on their round-trip journey between concrete plant and dam.

The buckets were cylindrical steel behemoths seven feet tall and nearly seven feet in girth. They began the cycle nestled in two of the four bays of a specially designed railcar, open at the top and at the side facing the dam to facilitate their removal and replacement. At the concrete plant, the locomotive engineer carefully positioned the railcar so each bucket was lined up directly under one of the plant's mixing spouts, which charged them with fresh concrete. This was a critical step, for each load was to be delivered to a different part of the dam, and therefore required a different grade of aggregate, ranging from pea gravel (the smallest grade) for the outer faces up to a mixture with nine-inch cobblestones, formulated to withstand the enormous compressive forces at the dam's core. Send the wrong grade to the wrong column, and it would have to be shoveled out before another bucket could be poured.

Once the buckets were filled, the railcar threaded its way along the tracks to the cableway terminus adjacent to the dam. Here the buckets had to be accurately spotted again, directly under the cable hoists that would carry them into position over their designated columns on the dam.

The next part of the operation was the trickiest. From his shack under the cableway tower an operator swung the filled bucket over the dam. It was up to him, assisted by signalmen, to know exactly where and when to brake the hoist so the bucket swung directly over the designated column. He then had to lower the bucket without endangering the waiting workers or slamming it into the forms; the process resembled a fisherman's laying his fly precisely over a trout's lair. The concreting crews whacked the safety latches free with their shovels and scrambled clear as the operator, still relying on the signals from his spotters, released the trapdoors and discharged the sixteen-ton load.

The concrete was immediately set upon by the placing crew—typically seven men shod in rubber hip boots—who worked it into every corner of the fifty-foot-square form using their shovels and feet, tromping up and down to deflate any air pockets. If the lift included a part of a gallery, stairway, or other interior structure, the men also settled the mass into its irregular corners and niches using pneumatic vibrators. Each pour added just over an inch to the concrete level on average, giving the lie to the popular mythology of bodies buried in the mass; not only was it impossible to cover a man's form with a single bucketload of concrete, but the presence of any soft spot within the hardening mass—say one left by an embedded human body—was a serious flaw that would so weaken the structure that it could not be casually overlooked.

The cableman closed the bucket doors with a tug on his cable sling and started the empty vessel back home, again timing its trajectory to glide it precisely into a vacant well in a waiting railcar. "Let it be said to the credit of the signalmen that there were but few times when the buckets were banged against the rock wall behind the loading point," Six Companies engineer Lawrence P. Sowles observed, "while there were thousands of instances where the buckets were landed neatly and smoothly on the cars." Once loaded with two empty buckets, the railcar returned to the concrete plant to begin the cycle anew.

This description only hints at the technical complexity of the pour. Atmospheric conditions wreaked havoc with the setting concrete. In the summer heat the concrete began hardening before the men could work it into the forms, a problem the concrete experts eventually solved by developing a special slow-setting grade for hot-weather pouring and by instructing the crews to pour on a bias, building up the lifts at the downstream edge with the first buckets and filling in the low sides with subsequent buckets. By reducing the area of wet concrete exposed to the air, this technique helped keep the surface "live," or workable. (Once cooler weather returned, the normal procedure of spreading each bucketful evenly across the form resumed.)

Many lifts contained more than concrete. Some eight hundred electrical thermometers and strain gauges encased in glass or metal tubes were installed in accordance with the engineers' blueprints, buried by hand deep in the wet concrete so they would not be crushed by subsequent pours, then coupled to the monitoring system that made Hoover the most heavily instrumented dam in history. There were also grout valves, water drains, and molds for the internal inspection galleries (there were to be fifteen of these on five levels, ten running from face to face perpendicular to the arch, and five traversing the dam from abutment to abutment), plus two elevator shafts and two spiral staircases leading from the crest of the dam down six hundred feet.

To prepare a dry lift to take new concrete, its surface had to be carefully primed. High-pressure jets of water and compressed air scoured the hardened concrete to rid it of dirt, rocks, and, especially, laitance. This was a syrupy residue of cement, sand, and water that leached to the surface from the setting concrete and, if not washed off, would prevent a tight bond from forming between lifts. After the cleaning, the wood and metal forms were winched five feet higher to shape the subsequent lift, and a team of Reclamation inspectors brought on the scene to certify their positioning. The first bucket poured on any new lift was always a slurry of pure grout to ensure a secure bond with the next pour.

Almost as innovative as the column-and-block configuration of the dam was the grout curtain, a feature designed by Jack Savage and his engineering staff to counteract the phenomenon of uplift, which occurs when water seeping under a dam exerts upward pressure on its mass. Uplift reduces a dam's effective weight, lowering its resistance to the tremendous force exerted by the water in its reservoir. In blunt terms, this can render a dam vulnerable to tipping over. The larger the dam, the greater the weight of its impounded reservoir and, therefore, the higher the pressure forcing water through unsealed faults in the foundation rock, creating seepage and uplift. As the world's largest dam impounding the world's largest reservoir, Hoover Dam would be subjected to uplift beyond anything dam builders had ever recorded.

Hoover Dam's grout curtain was designed as a line of four hundred holes drilled as deep as 150 feet into the bedrock and canyon walls and pressure-filled with grout. The expectation was that the grout would penetrate the subterranean fissures that might otherwise allow water from the reservoir to seep under or around the dam—in essence, creating an impermeable seal deep into the foundation and abutments.

Dam builders had not fully worked out how large a grout curtain was needed for any given dam—or, indeed, what the best grouting method might be for ensuring an adequate seal. In Black Canyon, these imponderables were compounded by less than complete knowledge of the underlying geology. The planners' assumption was that the bedrock was solid and stable—a 1933 government report praised its "unusually good foundation conditions" and recommended only minimal grouting, "primarily for sealing fine seams and joints." This would turn out to be a drastic miscalculation. Unbeknownst to the project geologists, the rock of Black Canyon was shot through with fractures, shears, and faults destined to come under tremendous pressure once the reservoir filled. Yet in this aspect of the design, the engineers relinquished their customary conservatism. Not only did they specify a minimal grout curtain—the single rank of relatively shallow bores—but they failed to monitor the grouting process to ensure that crews fulfilled their specifications.

The grouters, who were performing their work hastily to keep ahead of the concrete pour, kept running into problems that should have told the design engineers their picture of the underground geology was incomplete. At several points the crews struck hot springs, causing the grout to set prematurely and plug the drilled holes with hardened cement. Elsewhere they tapped into huge underground voids that consumed sack after sack of grout like insatiable monsters. In both cases, the workers simply abandoned the bores. In the end, they failed to fill completely fifty-eight of the 393 holes specified by the designers. What was supposed to be an unbroken underground bulkhead instead resembled a mouth with dozens of missing and broken teeth. The dismaying consequences would not be discovered for years, when they would place the dam's very integrity in question.

As the dam rose, it acquired a steel and wood exoskeleton composed of zigzagging catwalks, scaffolds, drainpipes, ramps, and the frame of an open-air platform elevator the men called the "monkey slide." Especially at night, when spotlights sliced through the pitch-black canyon, the site resembled the set of an impressionist film, all noise, smoke, steam, and the ceaseless motion of men at work on a towering edifice. The dam had become both the quintessential expression of industrial might and a living thing reaching from bedrock toward the sky—to which it got closer, inch by inch and foot by foot, every day.

Meanwhile a panoply of appurtenant structures took shape around the gorge. Upstream, overlooking the site of the reservoir, spires of concrete-encased steel reinforcing bars marked where four cylindrical intake towers were to rise in pairs, 390 feet tall, from shelves jackhammered into the cliffsides. The intakes fed thirty-seven-foot-diameter tunnels, which were to be lined with steel water pipes known as penstocks. Seventeen adits were being driven into the canyon walls to funnel water from the penstocks into the turbines of the powerhouse, a U-shaped structure under construction at the foot of the dam.

Two spillways were being bored out, one on either side of the canyon. These concrete channels would be fitted with movable gates to ensure that the reservoir could not overtop the dam even in the worst imaginable flood. Water finding its way into the spillway reservoirs would cascade into inclined, concrete-lined tunnels, which were joined to portions of the outer diversion tunnels underground. The inner tunnels were similarly incorporated into the penstock system.

The enormous penstocks, which were to carry water from the intakes erected in the reservoir to the power-generating turbines, were products of a vast foundry established on Nevada flatland a mile from the river, manned by eight hundred laborers employed by Babcock & Wilcox Co., an Ohio-based maker of steel pressure boilers. Recognizing its magnitude, Reclamation had carved the $11 million fabrication job out of the main contract, making it one of the few tasks in the canyon removed from Six Companies' direct control. What made the fabrication so challenging was the sheer size of the biggest outlet pipes. With a diameter of thirty feet, they were too large to be transported on any rail line or highway in the United States, mandating the construction of B&W's $600,000 foundry—an enclosure 670 feet long and five stories tall.

The foundry's location was christened Bechtel, Nevada, in honor of Dad Bechtel. The cofounder of Six Companies had died of a diabetic attack at sixty-one on August 28, 1933, in Moscow, where he had traveled at the invitation of the Soviet government to inspect its towering Dnieperstroy Dam outside Kiev, completed in 1932 and billed as the largest hydroelectric installation in Europe. (Though not in the world: at 167 feet in height it was shortly to be dwarfed by Hoover Dam.)

The penstocks were fabricated in sections, each comprising three twenty-three-ton steel flat plates twelve feet wide, thirty-seven and a half feet long and two and three-quarters inches thick. The sheet was run through a pair of vertical pressure rollers—the "largest diameter plate rolls and the most powerful ever built," Reclamation publicists dutifully reported—to achieve the required curvature. Then they were welded together into a thirty-foot ring. Two completed rings were in turn welded to each other to form a single section weighing (with fittings) 170 tons.

Transferring this gargantuan object from foundry to canyon presented another challenge. The existing rail line was too narrow to accommodate the sections, so government engineers instead regraded the construction highway and surfaced its winding curves with oiled gravel. A special trailer with its own steering and brake system was assembled by a Midwestern steelworks, and hooked to a tractor for towing to the canyon rim. (Luckily, the route was all downhill, although this meant that the trailer operator had to keep his foot on the brakes for the entire trip.)

At the rim, the sections were handed off to one last outsized feature of the construction landscape. This was a government-built cableway at the downstream end of the construction zone, the two-hundred-ton maximum capacity of which outstripped that of all five of Crowe's cableways combined. The penstock sections, braced by temporary internal frames of hub-and-spoke design dubbed "spiders," were strapped to the cableway hoist for the final leg of their journey, then deposited on another trailer at an outlet portal to be rolled into the tunnel and welded in place.

The pouring phase of construction introduced new dangers for the workforce. Although the toll of deaths and injuries on the pour never approached that of the tunnel excavations, the hazards were more various. There was more traffic of heavy vehicles in tighter quarters; more slippery surfaces for the men to move around on and higher heights from which they could plunge to their deaths; and twenty-ton objects careening through the air on cables that occasionally snapped apart in mid-journey, converting them into untethered projectiles.

Often, the only warning a frayed high-line cable gave before separating was a crack splitting the air like a pistol shot. On the night of January 3, 1935, the puddlers on Form B-1, at the upstream edge of the dam adjacent to the Arizona cliffside, heard this sinister alarum a split second before a full bucket came careening over the edge of the form. The bucket slammed into J. W. "Happy" Pitts, the boss pipefitter, and Ike Johnson, his signal-man, hurling Pitts off his perch atop the form walls and over the side of the dam before crashing into the canyon wall and discharging its load. Pitts was killed instantly, his mangled body retrieved from a catwalk 150 feet below. Search parties could find no trace of Johnson until someone spotted a light flickering in the gloom from midway up the dam face. There they discovered him on a scaffold, flat on his back and encrusted in already setting concrete nearly head to toe, his one free arm holding aloft a lighted match. He had been scooped into the wayward bucket, or possibly had clutched onto its rim for a hair-raising ride through the air, then dumped onto the scaffolding along with sixteen tons of wet concrete—battered, bruised, his eyes smarting from the lime in the wet cement, but otherwise unhurt.

Disaster could strike from any direction. Notwithstanding engineer Sowles's admiration for the cablemen's skills, even a minor operational mis-calculation could produce calamity. On the graveyard shift hours before dawn on October 1, 1933, a cable hoist went out of control and slammed its bucket into a waiting railcar, dislodging another bucket from its bay. The bucket fell sixty feet to the riverbed, where it crushed James A. Jackman to death. It was his third day on the job.

On the graveyard shift that November, W. A. Jameson and a second worker were carrying a timber strut down the catwalk that snaked along the front face. They had just reached the bottom when a form high overhead gave way, dumping a full lift of freshly poured concrete into the slot. The load, pregnant with eight-inch cobblestones, swept up forms, scaffolding, and refrigeration pipes on its way down before flattening Jameson, who was unfortunate enough to be standing directly underneath it. Rescue crews needed sixteen hours to dig his body out of the debris. His neighbors raffled off his 1927 Buick for the money to send his body home to his nearest relative, a sister in Winston-Salem, North Carolina.

Concreting the spillway inclines, or "glory holes," was another perilous job. The puddlers and finishers had to maintain their footing while handling balky equipment on forty-five-degree slopes slick with wet concrete and flowing water. Early on the morning of September 19, 1933, three carpenters and their foreman were trying to work loose a stuck wooden form when it gave way, plummeting down the incline with all four men aboard like a toboggan, gathering speed as it headed for a hundred-foot drop where the spillway intersected the diversion tunnel. One carpenter, thrown free, managed to hook his arm around a cable strung along the tunnel as a guard line and watched his fellows shoot past, shouting (or so it was reported), "We're comin' through!"

The form soared into the gap, pitching carpenter Jack McPhee into the current. He landed flat on his back, shattering his spine. The other two passengers, foreman Bill Partain and carpenter J. F. Armstrong, hung on to what was now their life raft. When they finally shot out of the downstream portal Woody Williams was waiting with a lifeline and a boat, with which he and his crew towed the men, injured and gasping for breath, to shore.

The victim of a later, similar accident was less fortunate. Seventeen-year-old Berthel Reaves, who had falsified his age as twenty-one so he could join his father on the job, was stripping concrete forms in the same incline on February 21, 1935, when he lost his grip on the slope. The bypass tunnel upstream of the spillway had been plugged and fitted with a valve so water could pass through to irrigate downstream farms. At the head end the water emerged from the valve at 7,200 feet per second, a blast that must have ripped through young Reaves's body like a mortar shell. He was swept away with barely the sound of a splash. Search parties, Reaves's father among them, scoured the riverbanks all night and through the next day before abandoning hope. Three weeks later his broken corpse finally washed up on a sandbar six miles downriver.

Some dangers were inherent in the new forms of transportation contrived to carry men across the dam and to the top of the concrete columns. Vertical transport was provided by four monkey slides (two on the upstream face of the dam, one on the canted downstream face, and the fourth descending from the rim on the Nevada cliffside). These were simple open platforms with waist-high railings that were locked into vertical tracks. Hoisting was provided by steel cables, the parting of which could send a cargo of fifty men in free fall toward the canyon floor.

Similar platforms, or skips, were hung from cableway carriages to transport crews across the canyon. Marion Allen experienced several hair-raising crossings this way, including one during which a full skip started spinning uncontrollably as it reached the canyon midpoint. The hoist cable soon became so tightly twisted it began to fray, emitting greasy smoke and a shower of sparks.

> There we were with two or three hundred feet of open space below us and nothing to stop us if the cable broke [Allen recounted]. Everyone was screaming to stop but the skip wound tighter and we screamed some more. . . . When the operator tried to move us the cable would scream, then we would scream until he quit.

The men spent three hours suspended in midair, baking under the open sun while foremen tried to find a solution for their increasingly desperate predicament. At one point an iron-nerved rigger crawled out on the main cable to attempt untangling the skip line manually, but was unable to loosen the tightly braided steel. The rescuers then hit upon the idea of sending an empty skip out on the adjacent Cableway No. 7 like a lifeboat, only to discover that even at its closest approach it remained tantalizingly just out of reach of the marooned crew. To overcome that last obstacle, they laid new rails to give Cableway No. 7 more lateral range—blasting several feet of cliffside flat to provide room for the new track. This allowed an empty skip to move within reach of the castaways. When they finally landed they were surprised to find a full complement of supervisors waiting for them, masking their concern with gruff banter. "Sorry I had to dock you guys most of the day," one said. "You better get over to the Nevada spillway and finish your shift."

The work hazards in the dewatered canyon presented an unusual financial issue for Six Companies, as the state of Arizona paid considerably better compensation than Nevada to families of men injured or killed on the job. The difference was reflected in the discrepancy in the rates Six Companies paid to the states' workmen's insurance funds: in 1931, the assessment was $25.04 per $100 of payroll in Arizona but a mere $5 in Nevada. Although the rates converged over time—in 1933 Arizona's charge had fallen to $9.86 while Nevada's had risen to $6.50—the difference was still so great that the Six Companies board considered buying its own injury insurance, only to drop the idea when it learned that a $60,000 premium would only save it the equivalent of a $1 increase in the public rates.

While it lasted, workers exploited the discrepancy between the two states' payouts. As soon as footbridges connected the tunnel sites on both sides of the river, men took to claiming, sometimes with the connivance of their fellows, that injuries incurred in Nevada had actually taken place on the other side. They were not alone in attempting to game the system: in the early months of construction, while the job was still split into two discrete locations separated by a raging river, Six Companies had instructed Crowe to employ only single men on the Arizona side "so far as practical," plainly to reduce the likelihood of a claim from families of injured or killed workers. Once the work coalesced into a single job site without a clear demarcation line, this stratagem lost its rationale. But crews on the ground still tried to finesse close calls onto Arizona's ledger. Tex Nunley, while serving as a Six Companies surveyor, was once given the responsibility of pinpointing the location of an accident that had claimed the life of a mucker near the riverbed's center line. Standing over the victim's mangled body in the mud, "an engineer gave me a three hundred-foot reel of tape," he recalled. "I took the tape and went to the Nevada side, read the tape, come back, went to the Arizona side, read the tape, come back. I could have called out anything, but he said, 'Tex, make it Arizona.'" The difference of a few feet meant compensation for the widow of hundreds, even thousands, of dollars more.

As a sign of his commitment to an accident-free job, Crowe called regular meetings of his foremen to press them for ever-greater vigilance against careless behavior. As these "Safety-First smokers" had been a regular feature of the job since its inception, it is fair to wonder if they still packed any punch by the third year of construction, or whether they were designed chiefly to impress visitors. "The keynote of the entire evening's discussion was the very human statement of Frank Crowe . . . that during his twenty-eight years of construction work the welfare and well-being of his workers had ever been closest to his heart," the *Review-Journal* attested after attending one meeting.

The company's concern with safety sometimes appeared to be little more than rhetorical. Early in the construction phase it had purchased goggles, safety belts, and some thirteen thousand safety helmets for distribution to all workers (the project acquired the reputation, inaccurately, as the first construction site to use hardhats) but the mandate to wear them was only spottily enforced. "Safety was something that was preached," recalled Marion Allen. "When you rode on the bus, the first thing you'd see was [a sign reading] 'Safety First.' . . . Working men, in a hurry lots of times, they forgot their hat, or they forgot their belt, but sometimes the foremen were a little lax and did not send them back. We had safety meetings. Nobody attended unless they were forced to, because they took up too much of what little leisure time you had."

Many rules were regularly flouted, such as the prohibition on men catching rides on heavy equipment being moved across the canyon by cable. The common rationale was, "It saved walking." One such daredevil stunt cost the life of Kenney Wilson, who hitched a ride on a ten-ton concrete pump on February 19, 1935. Jack Eagan, Wilson's foreman, heard the telltale pistol crack of a severed line. He looked up to see Wilson and the pump plummeting to earth from 350 feet in the air, even imagined his friend waving goodbye with a "cheerful smile" before he and the machine struck the lower cofferdam with enough force to become buried several feet deep in the soggy surface.

The most sustained rule breaking was perpetrated by Six Companies itself, as was made clear via a wave of lawsuits filed by workers who had served time on the tunnel excavations. The cookie-cutter lawsuits were the brainchild of Harry H. Austin, a Las Vegas lawyer who filed the first case on January 6, 1933. His clients' virtually identical complaints alleged that they had become permanently disabled by working long shifts underground enveloped in the dense blue haze of truck exhaust. They listed heart problems, chronic dizzy spells, headaches, and mental deterioration as their symptoms—all known effects of acute carbon monoxide poisoning—and sought judgments of $50,000 for their personal injuries, $25,000 for punitive damages, and hundreds or thousands more for lost work time. By the end of August, six Austin lawsuits were pending and dozens more were in the pipeline.

Six Companies plainly did not relish bringing these cases to trial. In fighting the Stinson lawsuit over Nevada's mining law jurisdiction it had narrowly managed to convince a federal judge that the tunnel work presented no danger to its employees. There were no assurances that it could rely on jurors to reach the same conclusion.

The company's potential liability was incalculable. More than two thousand men had worked in the diversion tunnels. Many had directly experienced bouts of headache, shortness of breath, dizziness, even loss of consciousness underground, or knew men who did. The workers had been routinely assured by their foremen and the company doctors that the air was clean, their symptoms transient, and their well-being among Frank Crowe's foremost concerns. Let a single plaintiff prevail on a claim that the work had brought him lasting disability, and these first raindrops of litigation would surely beget a downpour.

To forestall that possibility, Six Companies launched a fierce two-pronged defense. Its primary strategy was to question whether any exposure to carbon monoxide, even if severe, could cause lasting physiological damage. The company's position was that, although the gas was capable of killing, that could only happen under the most extreme, and rare, conditions. For the most part its effects would entirely disappear after no more than a few hours. In the stark formulation Six Companies' trial lawyer, Jerome White, put into the mouths of his expert witnesses, victims of carbon monoxide poisoning "either die or get well." By this standard, a plaintiff's appearance in the courtroom, standing on his own two feet and certainly not dead, was sufficient to prove the company's case.

But the "die or get well" standard was contradicted by more than a decade of research, tying chronic carbon monoxide exposure to memory loss, vertigo, spasticity, and impotence, among other syndromes. Nor was carbon monoxide poisoning an obscure subject of scientific scrutiny. The mountain of literature on the gas's effects dated back to Aristotle, who had described the symptoms of death from coal fumes in the fourth century B.C.

In short, the symptoms of carbon monoxide poisoning were not only well known to medical science but plainly rampant in Black Canyon. During the trial of Austin's first case in the autumn of 1933, a parade of witnesses testified that headaches and dizziness were commonplace in the tunnels. Foremen acknowledged that they routinely allowed men to take breaks in the open air to recover from spells of light-headedness, and that even the hardiest and brawniest laborers suffered headaches and nausea that could incapacitate them for a full shift or even days on end. Adding to its weight, much of this testimony was elicited by Austin's cross-examination of foremen called to the stand by the company's own lawyers, who expected them to parrot the official line that they had never seen any evidence of gas-related illness. Instead, almost every one confessed to having seen men overcome singly or en masse, twenty, thirty, even forty men at a time.

The picture that emerged from weeks of such testimony was of Six Companies' gross neglect of its workers' well-being. Especially reprehensible was the performance of its medical staff. Although men presented themselves at the Boulder City hospital with the unmistakable symptoms of carbon monoxide poisoning nearly every day, the staff never sounded the alarm. At best, the doctors showed indifference to their patients' health by counseling merely rest and a few hours of fresh air; at worst, they colluded with management by diagnosing gas poisonings as pneumonia, tuberculosis, or cardiac illness—all conditions for which the men were ineligible to claim injury compensation.

This was remarkable dereliction for a company that boasted of its commitment to its employees' well-being, citing as Exhibit A the $20,000 hospital for employees it opened in Boulder City in 1931. As it happened, this was where most of the specious diagnoses were delivered. Plainly, what had tipped the calculus against the tunnel workers was money—the $300,000 that Six Companies reckoned as the cost of assembling a special fleet of electric-powered vehicles and equipment to perform the underground excavations.

The second prong of the company's defense strategy was less esoteric than the attack on the scientific evidence. The goal was to shift the public's attention away from the company's deeds and onto each plaintiff's character. That job was assigned to Bud Bodell.

Bodell had left his job as chief ranger on the federal reservation in March 1933, shortly after a spectacular indiscretion put him on the wrong side of Sims Ely: he had staged a wild chase through Boulder City's residential neighborhoods in pursuit of a bootlegger, barely missing a woman and child and climaxing with a shootout in full view of terrified witnesses. After that escapade, his days on the federal payroll were numbered.

He resurfaced almost immediately as the Big Six's head of security, his first assignment being the preparation of dossiers on Harry Austin's six clients. It soon became evident that the weakest link in the group was Edward F. Kraus, a thirty-four-year-old truck driver. Kraus claimed that his five months of steady work in the tunnels from January through June 1932 had left him with chronic headaches, dizzy spells, heart palpitations, and a diminished sex drive. But the work history he cited did not conform to Six Companies records, which indicated that for most of his time on the job he had been working above ground.

More usefully, Kraus seemed to be a man of majestically poor judgment, given to fraternizing with a dubious crowd of ex–dam workers and loose women. The ultimate blow to his credibility was delivered on September 20, when he and two associates were arrested by Las Vegas sheriff's deputies for mugging an "aged prospector" named Jack McEachern and absconding with a $100 diamond ring.

As it happened, the arrest was based on a tip and evidence Bodell personally produced for the authorities. For the local press, he further inflated this purported midnight assault into a vast criminal enterprise, claiming that the arrests had busted "one of the most widespread gangs of racketeers ever uncovered in the state of Nevada," as the *Review-Journal* obligingly reported. He described Kraus, who was said to have a lengthy criminal record in his hometown, Salt Lake City, as the mastermind of a multifaceted plot to import $100,000 in counterfeit currency into Las Vegas, entice local businessmen into affairs with a mysterious femme fatale for blackmail, and extort insurance settlements from Six Companies by faking auto accidents on the job site. In the sensational atmosphere of the moment no one made much of the fact that one other gang member and the ostensible victim, the "aged prospector," were both Bodell acquaintances. Nor was it widely reported that Kraus's extensive rap sheet, closely inspected, boiled down to a single arrest for violating Prohibition laws by operating a Los Angeles beer garden.

Harry Austin arranged to defer Kraus's criminal trial until after the civil case, then steeled himself to lead his unsteady client into battle against Six Companies. The trial opened on October 17 in a jammed Las Vegas courtroom, Kraus on the stand. From the beginning, the local press barely concealed its indifference to the central issue of the case—whether Six Companies had knowingly exposed thousands of men to poisoning by carbon monoxide. ("Kraus Case Is Tiresome with Many Details" read the *Review-Journal* headline after a day of dense scientific testimony.)

The Big Six's defense team did its best to stave off the newspapers' ennui. Its lawyers presented evidence that Kraus had engaged in frequent trysts at roadside motels with "women not his wife," odd behavior for someone who claimed he had "lost his sex power." They described drunken late-night parties at which he was said to have "danced as though he were a well man." Their star witness was gang member John Moretti, a "dapper little Italian" (the *Review-Journal* again) soon exposed by Austin as a Bodell plant—a bootlegger and panderer whose assignment had been to entice Kraus and his friends into crime by plying them with liquor and girls.

It all left the jurors hopelessly confused. After nearly seven weeks of trial they spent two full days balancing the abstruse medical testimony against Kraus's unprepossessing character. Finally, on Wednesday, November 29— Thanksgiving Eve in the state of Nevada—they reported that they were deadlocked 5–7 with no prospect of agreement. The judge declared the case a mistrial. Under the circumstances, the outcome had to be counted a victory for Six Companies.

Four days later Kraus returned to the courthouse to answer the robbery charge with his alleged partners in crime, "Red" Belmain and Max Moore. Harry Austin again portrayed the star prosecution witness, Moretti, as an agent of a conspiracy stage-managed by Bodell. Belmain recanted the confession in which he had implicated Kraus, claiming that Bodell had promised him a light sentence if he cooperated.

In contrast to the interminable civil trial, this one was over in a flash—two days of testimony followed by a few hours of jury deliberations. Austin's attempt to tie Six Companies, Bodell, Moretti, and the local sheriff's deputies into one big conspiracy was rejected by the judge, who refused to believe the cast of characters capable of anything so Machiavellian. ("I've seen some dumb deputy sheriffs in my time," he observed, "but never any dumb enough to enter into a conspiracy of this kind.") But the jury scented enough foulness in the air to acquit Kraus, the alleged ringleader. Belmain and Moore, however, were convicted and sentenced to prison terms of six years each.

The verdict left the entire affair unsettled. Austin pronounced himself ready to retry the civil case as soon as a court date could be secured. But Kraus's claim would not see the inside of a courtroom again. Austin's next gas case would feature a more upstanding plaintiff, but it would not come to trial for more than a year, when an even more desperate Six Companies would show how low it could sink to avert a guilty judgment.

In the interim, the federal government would finally give a fair hearing to the workers' complaints about the company's workplace policies. Early in 1934 the first comprehensive investigation of labor conditions in Black Canyon was launched by the U.S. Department of Labor—now headed by FDR's confidante Frances Perkins, who took her regulatory responsibilities very seriously. On April 20, Page arrived at his Boulder City office to discover D. B. Burdick, a special agent for a new federal agency called the Department of Investigation, waiting at his door with orders to look into safety issues. (The following year the agency would be renamed the Federal Bureau of Investigation.) Burdick arrived just in time to witness a horrific accident, in which the snapping of the guide cable of a monkey slide halfway up the dam face dumped twelve men onto a pile of steel rods at the bottom, producing several ghastly impalements.

Burdick spent four days in Boulder City hounding Page and Six Companies for safety and wage records. He fed his data to Sidney Williams, a Labor Department investigator in Washington, who calculated that the death and injury rate on the job was twice the average of the concrete construction trade nationwide. Williams scoffed at Six Companies' defense that the size and difficulty of the job made an elevated accident rate inevitable. On the contrary, he found the "common hazards" at the dam to be wholly conventional: "falling from scaffolds or into floor openings, handling materials and tools, being struck by concrete buckets, other materials or objects falling." Williams believed the higher rate arose principally from the contractor's indifference to "modern methods of organized accident prevention including accident investigation and analysis." Six Companies had failed to place a full-time safety engineer or safety director on its payroll or assign enough signalmen on the cableways to ensure safety; Williams reported a complaint from Arizona government inspectors to the effect that they had to apply "considerable pressure" to force Six Companies to assign two signalmen to a cableway after they determined that one was insufficient. The contractors invited disaster by overworking crews with extended hours and double shifts; Williams pointed specifically to an accident on November 1, when a three-thousand-pound truck in the tunnel leading from an intake tower to the powerhouse ran out of control, killing three riggers. The crew that had failed to secure the truck had been on the job for more than thirteen hours straight. "Fatigue was probably a factor in this accident," he concluded dryly.

Yet for all its detail and its consistent findings of fault on the contractor's part, the Williams report produced no immediate consequences for Six Companies. This may have reflected the mildness of the report's recommendations: that the company "keep a detailed record of all disabling accidents . . . inform and stimulate the supervisory force, and . . . interest and educate the workmen in safe practices." But the Big Six would have been mistaken to assume that the lack of immediate action by the Labor Department put it in the clear. Governmental discontent with its treatment of labor still simmered, and would very shortly come to a boil.

Notwithstanding Crowe's ostentatious safety lectures, the main reason for the high injury rate was his relentless demand for progress. Indeed, the phenomenal pace of the job was a point of pride, with each remarkable milestone recorded for the news agencies by Ben Glaha's ubiquitous camera. When the millionth cubic yard of concrete was poured on January 7, 1934, seven months and a day after the first, Young, Crowe, Page, Woody Williams, Charlie Shea, and Felix Kahn gathered on the record-setting lift for a ceremonial photograph, balancing themselves on a timber slat laid across the wet concrete next to a hand-painted placard marking the event, with a crew of laborers in their winter garb of hardhats and overalls assembled as background scenery. The second millionth was marked in a similar fashion on June 2, 1934, or one year (minus four days) after the first bucket had been poured, and the third millionth on December 5. Just over three weeks after that, on December 28, the graveyard shift on Cableway No. 7 achieved a record pour of 240 buckets in eight hours—a prodigious 3,840 tons of concrete—and rewarded themselves with a ritual photograph. Their mark stood for less than forty-eight hours, bested on December 30 by the day crew, which poured 277 buckets. By then the ultimate milestone was lurking just beyond the horizon: the dam's final bucket of concrete would be poured at the crest on February 21, 1935.

Certainly nothing in the contract, the construction schedule, or the elements mandated such haste. Reclamation had budgeted for a pour lasting thirty-two months; Six Companies completed the work in 625 days, shaving a full year off the deadline. The contractor received no direct bonus from the government for this achievement, although by pocketing its completion fee two years ahead of schedule it earned several hundred thousand dollars in interest.

The exact number of workers killed or injured in the rush to pare another day, week, or month from the construction timeline can never be calculated. All that can be said is that many men paid for the Big Six's construction record with their lives.

# 18

# Reckonings

With every new step taken toward completion, the dam received more public attention. By late 1934 tourists were coming by the thousands to gather on the stone parapets constructed by the Reclamation Bureau on the Nevada cliffside (their sandstone masonry handcrafted by Dogface Charlie Rose's unsung Negro crew), and goggle at the intricately choreographed ballet of cableways, concrete buckets, and workmen.

The site had drawn the curious from the beginning, although in the early days of construction a visit required a mountaineer's agility. The lookout point then was accessible only by climbing a steep canyon trail to a concrete platform fringed with a chain link fence to keep visitors from pitching over the side. Despite its remoteness, the spot ranked highly as a local landmark, hosting the wedding ceremony of Ma Kennedy and Whataman Hudson in September 1931. It was renamed "Elks Point" the following year on Washington's Birthday, when members of that lodge erected a flagpole at the site and laid a copper plaque bearing a terse inscription by the country's pre-eminent Elk, Herbert Hoover: "Here man builds his vision into stone that generations to come may be blessed."

Hollywood ingenues were quick to divine the publicity value of posing against the dramatic backdrop of Black Canyon. A willowy Loretta Young showed up in February 1932 with a personal photographer and pilot, the latter of whom made news by flying below the canyon rims, a feat it was claimed had never been done before. Every year brought more glamorous stars—Clark Gable, Bette Davis, and Ronald Colman among them. Movie producers seeking exotic locations swarmed over the gorge, yielding process shots for the RKO drama *The Silver Streak* in 1934 and the scenario for a full-length feature, *Boulder Dam,* in 1936. An MGM crew brought to the site in 1932 by director Frank Capra (*It's a Wonderful Life*) must have gone home uninspired, however, for no picture resulted.

Movie people and other VIPs were spared the rigors of the hike up to Elks Point. They were customarily escorted to the riverbank by Reclamation or Six Companies functionaries, personally introduced to Frank Crowe, led in convoy around the thundering traffic of towering dump trucks and jumbos, and for a final thrill, driven through the three-quarter-mile Tunnel No. 2, not yet in operation. (This was the same treatment Hoover got on his post–Election Day visit.)

Privileged visitors sometimes overran the worksite at battalion strength. The 1932 American Legion convention in Las Vegas sent 177 cars of legionnaires; a few months later Tunnel No. 2 accommodated a caravan of four hundred autos carrying members of the Nevada Teachers Association. One afternoon 3,500 Shriners got the grand tour, and on another occasion the Mormon Tabernacle Choir, three hundred voices strong. Meanwhile there were more delegations of engineers and entourages of heads of state from all over the world, avid for a close-up view of a new Wonder of the World in the making.

Recognizing that the escorting of armies of visitors around the site "severely interfered with work at the government office," Walker Young closed the site to mass visits in 1933. As an alternative he issued a permit to Earl Brothers, the owner of the Boulder City movie theater, to establish a tourist bureau with a set tariff and program. Brothers was authorized to conduct visitors to a new Lookout Point on the Nevada abutment, then down to the lower cofferdam and back to Boulder City—a two-and-a-half-hour trip for which he was to charge no more than $1.50 a head.

At Crowe's insistence, Six Companies followed Young's example. Board members were instructed to cease giving letters of introduction to their cronies that might inconvenience the field management. Henceforth, any

board member granting VIP courtesies in the gorge would have to personally escort the guest—an imposition on the directors' time that effectively
choked off the flow of privileged traffic. Crowe, additionally, extracted an
understanding from the board that he had the right to refuse admission to
the site to any visitor, no matter how grand.

The dam reigned as the principal tourist draw for Las Vegas, despite
the city's burgeoning reputation as a legal haven for gambling, drinking,
and whoring. For promotional purposes the municipality dubbed itself the
Gateway City—the gateway, that is, to Black Canyon. In mid-April 1933,
at the time of year when southern Nevada's climate is at its least intolerable, the chamber of commerce counted 1,500 tourists registered at hotels
and auto camps within the city limits, a record up to that time. That most
were passing through on their way to see the dam rather than partake of
sin could be gleaned from the fact that they included a delegation from the
Los Angeles Bureau of Power and Light, a study group from the American Institute of Mining and Metallurgical Engineers, and two troops of Boy
Scouts. In mid-1935, *Harper's Magazine* writer Theo White took pains to
explain to his readers that the "small town called Las Vegas" serving as the
jumping-off point for dam visitors was "not to be confused with the New
Mexican town of the same name," which was well known to travelers in the
West as an important depot of the Atchison, Topeka and Santa Fe Railroad.
Las Vegas, N.M., would soon slip into the shadow of its Nevada namesake
forever.

Some 92,000 visitors came to the canyon in 1932, more than 130,000
the following year, and 265,000 the year after that. Certainly one explanation for the growth was the canyon's greater accessibility to motor traffic
after Nevada completed paving the Las Vegas–Boulder City highway. But
opinion makers did their part to stoke the tourist trade. Will Rogers, whose
homespun persona straddled the worlds of Hollywood and letters, reported
on a visit to the canyon in one of his daily "telegrams" syndicated in newspapers coast to coast. "Don't miss seeing the building of Boulder Dam," he
urged his vast audience. "It's the biggest thing that's ever been done with
water since Noah made the flood look foolish."

The *Los Angeles Times,* intent on obliterating all memory of its early opposition to the Boulder Canyon Project, urged readers to make the 297-mile, seven-hour journey from Southern California—"over splendidly paved roads"—to see "the Greatest Drama of the West" play out. Its issue of Sunday, June 18, 1933, offered no fewer than four features on the project, which, as befit a rock-ribbed Republican newspaper, it continued to call "Hoover Dam." As an essential component of its mythmaking, it carried forward the lionization of Frank Crowe as the nation's master dam builder. "He has the physique of an Olympic gladiator, temperament of an artist, hand of a musician, judgement of a Solomon, patience of a Job, poise of a Chief Justice, and the sociability of an Elk," *Times* correspondent Chapin Hall wrote without a trace of self-consciousness. Crowe had become such a household name that Buick enlisted his endorsement for its automobiles. "He demands that which will do the job best," read its newspaper advertisement, under a photograph of Crowe leaning on one its sedans at the job site. "That is why Buick is his steadfast motor car choice."

Interest really exploded in 1935, when excitement over the dam's impending completion conjoined with the promotion of new vacation amenities on the shore of the filling reservoir "in the hitherto worthless mountainous desert section of the Rockies" (*The New York Times*). Nearly a half-million visitors would make the trip that year, many of them attracted by what promised to be a historic event—the formal dedication of the dam by President Franklin D. Roosevelt.

The tourism surge prompted Young and Ely to redouble their efforts at cleaning up the reservation and its environs. Their chief target was the miasma of vice lurking just beyond their formal jurisdiction. From time to time Bud Bodell and his rangers had ventured across the federal boundary line to demolish bootleggers' shacks along the Las Vegas–Boulder City highway, as in their heroic raid just before Christmas 1932, during which they shut down twenty-three speakeasies and saloons on eighteen miles of road. But such efforts were never more than a temporary expedient, as the "resorts" invariably sprouted again like weeds.

The most resilient among them was a cluster of bars, gambling dens, and whorehouses at Railroad Pass, seven miles from the Boulder City gates. This community's foremost entrepreneur was Peter Pansey, a Las Vegas club owner whose outpost comprised a casino, a gin mill, and a string of detached one-room "cribs" for prostitutes. Ever audacious, Pansey offered a free lottery ticket with every drink at his Boulder Inn; first prize was $25, second prize a case of bottles of effervescent fluid purporting to be champagne. He arranged with Frank Gottwals, the holder of Boulder City's lone taxicab permit, to pay the fare for any customer Gottwals ferried to the cribs, which were then situated a mile and a half from the highway, demurely out of sight of passing traffic.

Ely quickly ended this arrangement by revoking Gottwals's business permit. His solution backfired, however. Pansey, deprived of the easy flow of trade, relocated the cribs to the highway shoulder and draped them, unsubtly, with garlands of red lights. Then he advertised the location in the Boulder City and Las Vegas newspapers as "The New Boulder Inn—Now Right on the Highway."

Ely and Young took this setback hard. Appealing to federal prosecutors to clean up Railroad Pass, Young ticked off the location's "pernicious" attributes.

> The bootleg liquors dispensed have been of such vile quality that many workers were made "crazy drunk," and on returning to this camp became so disorderly that we felt compelled to expel them for short or long periods. Numerous wives have told us pathetic stories of the total loss of their husbands' paychecks at these gambling resorts. Cases of venereal disease in great number incurred at these resorts have come to the attention of the health office.

To their frustration, however, Pansey held a strong hand. His standing as a Las Vegas club owner of long vintage had earned him political clout he was not too shy to deploy. Interior officials heard from U.S. senator Pat McCarran, who asked that a "more thorough investigation" be made of the Railroad Pass matter based on Pansey's record as "a heavy taxpayer in Clark

County, Nevada [who] has, according to the authorities in Clark County, conducted his business at all times in an orderly manner."

Moreover, only a small portion of Pansey's resort (three cribs, to be exact) actually occupied federal property—"withdrawn" land from which the government had legal authority to evict squatters. The authorities were quietly allowing others to occupy similar parcels—chiefly dam worker families whom Young judged "quiet, good people" and whose occupancy "we have informally suffered . . . in order not to be oppressive, unreasonable, or captious in our treatment of good citizens." If Young evicted the noxious Pansey he might also have to dispossess the more upstanding squatters, a step Pansey must have known he would be reluctant to take.

For four years, Pansey fought Ely and Young to a draw. Sometimes he demanded huge sums to relocate, and sometimes he tried to dicker—once asking Ely if he could keep the casino and bar if he would "get rid of the girls." Ely rejected the overture, replying that "the whole business is objectionable." But the resort's unsavory character finally caught up with it on Saturday night, April 6, 1935, when a gunfight broke out on the premises. ("Bullets flew in considerable profusion," reported the *Boulder City Journal*.) Within a week, the Clark County liquor board revoked Pansey's license. He managed to hold off Young and Ely with one hand and the Clark County commissioners with the other for one more year. Finally, in May 1936, having pocketed handsome profits from liquor, gambling, and prostitution for five fat years, he accepted a token payment of $50 from the federal government and abandoned his leasehold in the pass.

By then Railroad Pass was on the wane. As the dam had neared completion, Crowe had cut the workforce to a single shift and laid off more than a third of his men. Every month Reclamation was transferring more of its field engineers to new projects. Overall employment, including Reclamation personnel and workers for Six Companies and its subcontractors, peaked at 5,251 men in July 1934, dwindled to 3,200 by April 1935, and continued its downward slope thereafter. Whether Boulder City itself would remain occupied after the completion of Boulder Dam was an unresolved question.

Young's crusade to burnish the image of the reservation and project was not limited to Railroad Pass. In late 1934 he undertook the chore of vetting the film script of "Backfire," which Warner Bros. proposed to shoot on location in the canyon. Showcasing some of the studio's most promising young stars, "Backfire" was to expose its characters to all sorts of colorful job-related perils in a decidedly shady environment more closely resembling the mining camps of Zane Grey stories than real-life, sober Boulder City. Young found most of this highly objectionable. He communicated his umbrage via a Warner Bros. underling to the producer, Hal Wallis, in three crisp pages of notes, single-spaced.

> On pages 34 and 35 there are scenes of bums loitering and sleeping in the public park. You must know that there is no possibility of this happening in Boulder City. . . . We do not appreciate the inference that we have bums in Boulder City, nor that they exist on garbage. . . . Beginning on page 41 there are numerous scenes laid in the "HI-DE-HO CLUB." While it is true that honky-tonks, pawn-shops, gambling halls, saloons and night clubs do exist in this vicinity, they will not be found in Boulder City. . . . The scenes beginning on page 110 depicting Novak's death as a result of a cave-in in one of the tunnels, while probably not overdrawn, are not good publicity for the job. . . . The accident scenes described on pages 124 to 133 are rather overdrawn and absurd, especially in that the cableway fails under the weight of a single man. These scenes may be interesting in a movie but are most certainly poor publicity for the Government and the contractor.

Wallis sent back a revised script incorporating "practically every change" except the two fatal accidents, which he deemed "very essential to the dramatic value of the story." Retitled *Boulder Dam*, the movie premiered in March 1936 to tepid reviews and was quickly forgotten.

Only once did Young allow enthusiasm to overcome his dignified judgment. In July 1935, Bunny Dryden, a high-wire walker who had made a sensation at the 1933 Chicago World's Fair, proposed to stroll across the canyon atop a cableway during the dedication festivities. Young's instincts told him such a publicity stunt would be borderline inappropriate, but he was plainly intrigued, describing Dryden to Mead as "an unusually enthusiastic young man, 23 years of age, 6'-1" in height, and 185 pounds of wonderfully fine physique. . . . He walks blindfolded, handcuffed, and carries others on his shoulders, balances on a chair, and turns flip-flops in the air."

Mead's instincts ran truer to form. "It's thumbs down on Bunny Dryden's proposal," he replied crisply. "It would cheapen the occasion. Personally I don't enjoy stunts of that kind but even if I liked them would regard it as a mistake for a dedication of this great work."

But other developments were threatening to ruin the dedication party. These involved Six Companies, which in early 1935 faced reckonings on three fronts for its more than four years of abusing its workforce.

The first front opened on Tuesday, February 26, when U.S. Attorney Edward Carville, two Public Works Administration inspectors, and a U.S. marshal burst into the contractor's office in Boulder City and proceeded to rifle its files. Alerted by a frantic Crowe, Page hastened over, only to be informed by Carville that he carried orders from Attorney General Homer Cummings to investigate an allegation that the Big Six had been paying illegal overtime for years.

The charge originated with John F. Wagner, a former Six Companies payroll clerk. In 1934, Wagner had taken a job with the Reclamation Bureau in Washington, a perch from which he broadcast the accusation that the Big Six kept two sets of books, one documenting the regular eight-hour payroll and another covering "emergency" overtime. This maneuver, he contended, allowed the contractor to conceal from Reclamation auditors that it had made sixty thousand illicit payments. Calculated at the statutory fine of $5 per violation, the contractor was potentially liable for a penalty of $300,000. For a year Wagner was largely ignored. Then his story came to the attention of Louis R. Glavis.

Glavis occupied a unique sinecure in the Interior Department as Harold Ickes's personal anticorruption sleuth. It was not a role that endeared him to official Washington, especially given that Ickes often sicced him on his enemies—real and imagined—within the administration. Glavis's personality did not help; he was a gimlet-eyed investigator who assumed all people guilty until proven innocent. Ickes privately described him as "somewhat of a man-eater." On one occasion Glavis's investigation of a construction contract let by Treasury Secretary Henry Morgenthau, Jr., so poisoned the cabinet room that President Roosevelt had Ickes instruct him to "stay in his own back yard" (i.e., stick to investigating Interior Department programs). On the plus side of the ledger, by Ickes's estimate Glavis's snooping had saved the government more than $64 million in federal public works funds. It was in this spirit of ferreting out fraud that Glavis lent an eager ear to Wagner's story.

The charge was serious. If proved, it exposed Six Companies not only to fines, but to criminal prosecution for defrauding the government. The furor also threatened to reflect badly on Young and Page, who had let their responsibilities for overseeing Six Companies' payroll practices slide under the indulgent leadership of Secretary Wilbur and Commissioner Mead. Now they were on the spot. The limitation of an eight-hour workday on government contracts had existed in federal law since 1912 and was specifically written into the Six Companies contract in 1931, when the need to spread government paychecks widely was deemed especially acute. Exceptions were permitted only for genuine emergencies.

Now that the horse was out of the barn Young moved to shut the barn door, issuing a memo to Reclamation staff on March 15 observing that "there is evidence that many violations of the eight-hour law . . . have escaped detection" and ordering all government employees "to make a special effort to detect any violation by employees of Six Companies Inc., the Babcock & Wilcox Co., or any of the subcontractors."

That did nothing to halt the investigation. Glavis's men kept Boulder City in an uproar for most of that cold and rainy March. They established living quarters in a vacant Six Companies dormitory and commandeered two offices in Reclamation's hilltop administration building along with a basement vault, to which they ordered the contractor to deliver truckloads of payroll records. They tied up company clerks for hours on end reconciling every overtime chit with a specific "emergency." The only break in their routine came on March 9, a day they spent briefing Louis Glavis, who had personally come west to underscore the gravity of the matter.

The investigation could not have come at a worse time for the local Reclamation staff, who were already overburdened with formalities connected with the dam's completion. The last open diversion, Tunnel No. 4 on the far Arizona side, had been sealed on February 1, its 1,200-ton steel gate descending majestically to choke off the river's flow underground, a procedure that took ninety minutes. A concrete plug four hundred feet thick was to be poured behind the gate, which would be left to rust away six hundred feet below the surface of the new reservoir. The reservoir, then known as Boulder Dam Lake and eventually christened Lake Mead, had already begun to fill. Three weeks later, on February 21, the last bucket of concrete was placed on the crest of the dam.

A flurry of final arrangements still demanded attention before Six Companies could formalize the turnover of the project to the U.S. government, the necessary precedent for collecting its final check. Crowe hectored Page incessantly to complete the required paperwork. Yet Glavis's men displayed little solicitude for their harried fellow public servants. On the evening of March 13, they hauled Page into their office for several hours of harsh questioning about his failure to assess a single overtime penalty against the builders. (Ostentatiously they kept a stenographic record, just as Crowe had done to intimidate the leaders of the 1931 strike.) Young's turn came the following morning. Both answered that Six Companies had justified every overtime claim on emergency grounds. This was to be the core of the company's defense, too.

Two more Public Works Administration investigators showed up on March 16, with a new directive ordering Page to produce statistics on accidents at the job site, a follow-up to the visit of Labor Department investigator Burdick the year before. Page's diary entry for March 31 included a weather report that might just as well have summed up that entire trying month: "Windy and raw."

Nor was Six Companies having an easier time of it. While criminal charges hovered over the heads of its board members and field executives, on March 27 the carbon monoxide issue, quiescent since the Kraus verdict in 1933, blew up again. As before, Bud Bodell was at the center of the controversy.

Harry Austin's second carbon monoxide trial had opened on February 18, in the same courtroom and before the same judge, William Orr, as the first case. But his second client displayed nothing like the indiscretion or witlessness of Ed Kraus. He was Jack Norman, a forty-eight-year-old family man who claimed to have been reduced to a "physical derelict" by gas he had inhaled in the bypass tunnels.

With Six Companies deprived of grounds for sullying the colorless Norman's character, the trial moved smartly along, reaching the jury on March 16 after a mere four weeks of technical testimony. Austin felt so confident of a victory that would lay the foundation for a sustained assault on Six Companies that he had already prepared dozens more complaints. Eventually he would file forty-eight, seeking a total of $4.8 million in damages.

But Bodell had not been idle. Austin's law partner Clifton Hildebrand caught wind of what he had been up to on the day the jury retired for deliberations. The discovery occurred at the bar of the Apache Hotel, a stylish Las Vegas watering hole. There Hildebrand ran into a soused James Begley, whom he knew as a henchman for the Six Companies defense team. Begley took advantage of the encounter to gripe about Frank Crowe, who, he complained, had barred him from the job site despite all that he and Bodell had done for the defense.

Hildebrand's ears pricked up. "What did you do?" he asked.

"We're the ones who know how to fix juries," Begley said.

How many jurors were fixed? Hildebrand asked.

At least five, Begley replied. Perhaps detecting a hint of censure in Hildebrand's expression, he added: "What the hell, you'd do the same thing if you could."

At that moment Jerome White, the Big Six's trial lawyer, entered the barroom. Discovering one of his employees deep in conversation with plaintiff's counsel, he intervened on the spot. "Shut up," he ordered Begley. "You talk too much when you get drunk."

Hildebrand related the conversation to Austin, who had earlier had a disquieting encounter at the Apache with Woody Williams, also apparently drunk. "We have at least three men on that jury that we are sure of and perhaps four or five," Williams told him. "You fellows may think you are going to get a verdict but you haven't a chance in the world," he added—or "words to that effect," as Austin reported in an affidavit.

Any inclination Austin might have had to dismiss Begley and Williams merely as mouthy drunks evaporated at 8 P.M. the next day, when the jury returned a 9–3 verdict in Six Companies' favor. Over the next week he and Hildebrand interviewed jurors, their friends and wives, and assorted other courtroom hangers-on, gathering evidence of a conspiracy by Six Companies, its lawyers, and Bud Bodell to fix Norman's trial. Their sources told them that J. H. Hazard, the foreman of the Norman jury, got $5,000 to secure a verdict in the Big Six's favor. Two other jurors who fell into line received $500 each to cast their votes in the company's favor, another juror said.

"What makes you think they got money?" Austin asked him.

"Because I myself was offered $1,000," the juror replied.

On March 27, Austin presented a sheaf of notarized declarations to Judge Orr, causing an immediate sensation in the courthouse. The excitement was short-lived, however, as Orr summarily rejected Austin's application for a new trial, invalidating every one of the damning statements as hearsay.

Orr's action drove the carbon monoxide issue off the front pages, at least for the moment. The denouement would not occur for another ten months, when on the eve of the trial of a third carbon monoxide lawsuit Six Companies quietly settled Norman's case along with forty-seven others that Austin had filed. The terms of the settlements were never disclosed.

Suppressing the overtime allegation would prove more difficult, if only because the Big Six's adversary in the case was not a provincial plaintiff's lawyer but the redoubtable Harold Ickes. Henry Kaiser, who placed himself in charge of the defense, initially mapped out a counterstrike on political rather than legal territory, inundating leading decision makers in Washington with telegrams asserting that every hour of overtime had been justified under the emergencies exemption.

For once, Kaiser's instincts failed him. The telegrams only succeeded in infuriating Ickes, who resented having to field inquiries on the subject from members of Congress and White House functionaries. "Mr. Kaiser's telegraphic bombardment has not made a favorable impression upon me," he complained to Key Pittman, Nevada's senior Democratic senator. "Mr. Kaiser has telegraphed to me, he has telegraphed to the President, he has telegraphed to you, and he has telegraphed to others who have telegraphed to me. . . . Frankly, he is doing himself and his company no good by his lack of composure."

Kaiser moved hastily to make amends. "Your personal assistant, Mr. Slattery, suggested that I be patient," he wrote the secretary, promising to follow this "constructive suggestion."

But by nature Kaiser was not a patient man. He had already prepared a second line of defense. The fruit of this effort appeared late in 1935: a slender 116-page volume produced by a writer from Berkeley named George Albert Pettitt, elegantly bound in soft leather and delivered to a few thousand congressmen, senators, journalists, and other opinion makers nationwide. It was entitled *So Boulder Dam Was Built.*

*So Boulder Dam* portrayed the Boulder Canyon Project not as a solid triumph over nature and circumstance by muscular American industry, as one might expect from a corporate public relations effort, but instead as an unrelenting sequence of near-disasters, each averted by work crews summoned to the scene and paid, naturally, on overtime. The root of these emergencies, Pettitt specified, was the federal government's own eagerness to get the project underway so it might succor the "hundreds of men sitting around hungry and children ravenously sifting through the garbage cans outside of the workers' mess."

The book did not shy from providing details of windstorms and flash floods, the murderous heat of the canyon, and accidents large and small. "On the average of once every fortnight during the major part of the construction period Death struck down someone on the Black Canyon project," Pettitt wrote, perhaps the only time Six Companies was willing to put its name to such an admission. Under the circumstances, the contractor could scarcely be expected to keep track of overtime hours or to prove "that every hour of overtime authorized during four years of construction on a schedule of seven days a week and twenty-four hours a day, had been justi-fied. . . . They were as difficult to trace as needles in a haystack."

*So Boulder Dam Was Built* was a legal brief disguised as narrative. Yet as a chronicle of the construction period it was so well dramatized that Walker Young recommended Pettitt to Mead as a publicity writer. The book may have been "propaganda," Young reported, but "Mr. Pettitt got the atmo-sphere of the job as no other writer has, to my way of thinking. . . . While I was reading it I lived the job all over again." How much Kaiser paid Pettitt for his invaluable effort is not recorded, although it is known that Six Com-panies showed its gratitude by allowing Pettitt to spend his honeymoon in the Boulder City guest lodge, gratis.

Policymakers in Washington could not help but take note of the book and associated publicity campaign—not to mention the growing public standing of Henry Kaiser, who granted interviews for publication and took to the radio airwaves nonstop in defense of a project he represented as a symbol of national resolve. The effort helped Kaiser transform himself into a popular icon of American industry. In the coming years of war, economic reconstruction, and prosperity, he would build his wealth on that founda-tion, drawing on the assistance of such admirers as magazine baron Henry Luce, whose *Time, Life,* and *Fortune,* intent on documenting America's eco-nomic preeminence in the twentieth century, would glorify Kaiser in article after article as an exemplary American business genius.

Further leverage in Six Companies' favor came from Kaiser's improv-ing relationship with Ickes, who sought his advice on industrial policy with increasing frequency and would later accept his help to break the cement cartel. On February 17, 1936, Ickes closed the overtime case with an assess-ment of $100,000, one-third of the original penalty. Buried in the secretary's announcement was the disclosure that the government had simultaneously accepted the Big Six's claim for $175,000 for extra excavation and other change orders at the dam. In other words, instead of paying the statutory $300,000 penalty for violating the overtime law, the company walked away from the affair with a net profit of $75,000.

\* \* \*

The last and potentially most disruptive challenge to Six Companies' work-force policies arose in July 1935, the final summer of construction, with the project's most serious outbreak of labor unrest.

After the Wobblies' strike of 1931, labor relations on the job had stayed largely untroubled. There was one more episode of IWW agitation in August 1933, provoked by a new effort by Six Companies to eject all known Wobblies from the payroll. On that occasion the strike committee, again led by Frank Anderson, failed utterly to rouse a workforce that had become exquisitely sensitive to the chill of unemployment. After haranguing the morning shift at the Anderson mess hall, the crestfallen Wobbly organizers were left behind when the men strolled off to board the Big Berthas. IWW historians would lament the episode as the only time the union had called men off a job and failed, but that invests it with a stature it does not deserve. In reality it was the reflexive twitch of a corpse all but declared dead after the abortive strike of 1931.

The 1935 strike was a different matter. After Roosevelt's election, a seis-mic shift had occurred in the federal government's relationship with orga-nized labor. Support from the American Federation of Labor had been an important factor in the Democratic victory, and although the president did not always disport himself in office as labor's steadfast friend, in the Demo-cratic Congress sentiment favoring union rights took root. The change was manifested in the celebrated section 7(a) of the National Industrial Recov-ery Act of 1933, which guaranteed workers the right to bargain collectively. After the Supreme Court overturned the NIRA in 1935, the pro-labor spirit resurfaced with passage that same year of the Wagner Act (formally known as the National Labor Relations Act), which reinstated the collective bar-gaining provision and forbid employer reprisals against union organizers.

In Boulder City, organized labor began gingerly to emerge from the shadows. Ragnald Fyhen, a union machinist whose thick accent proclaimed his Norwegian origin, was assigned by his international in 1934 to establish a local at the project site. At first he kept his activities secret, convening or-ganizational meetings late at night in a darkened back room of the Boulder City barbershop. But by the end of that year he was sufficiently emboldened to organize the Central Labor Council in partnership with the carpenters and electrical workers unions. In those pre–Wagner Act days, Fyhen understood that there was little to prevent Six Companies from firing him on any pretext to discourage his labor activity. The blow duly fell, and the very day after his sacking one of Bodell's men dragged him before Sims Ely with a request that he be given a "floater"—that is, an order to vacate the city for lack of employment.

"What has he done?" Ely asked.

"Organized a union."

"What union was it? The I.W.W.'s or the A.F. of L.?"

Informed it was the latter, Ely responded, "Why, that's permissible." Consulting his records, he saw that Fyhen held down a second job as a sales representative for the Mutual of Omaha insurance company. That preserved his eligibility for residence in Boulder City, he ruled, sending Bodell's man packing. "The language used upon [his] leaving was not the most pleasant," Fyhen recalled.

The Central Labor Council acquired enough political weight to attract a full roster of community leaders on May 30, 1935, to the unveiling of a tablet honoring workers killed on the job. The program featured speeches by Walker Young and Senator Pat McCarran, the latter seizing the opportunity to inveigh against communism, a theme that would come to define his political career. No one from Six Companies attended. (The original plaque has since been relocated to the monument plaza on the Nevada side of the canyon, where it stands adjacent to a more elaborate memorial to the dead designed by the Norwegian-born sculptor Oskar Hansen.)

Boulder City's newfound respect for union action was put to the test scarcely six weeks later, when a ham-handed move by a Six Companies middle manager set off the longest work stoppage of the construction period.

The culprit was Sheldon Modglin, whom Six Companies had installed as construction superintendent of the powerhouse taking shape at the foot of the dam. Modglin's officious personality may have sprung from his standing as a relative of Frank Modglin, Felix Kahn's right-hand man at MacDonald & Kahn (and Alan MacDonald's eventual successor as Kahn's partner). On July 11, while Crowe was absent from the canyon, Modglin unilaterally rescinded a long-standing policy of paying the men for a half-hour lunch. Effective immediately, he declared, the day shift would start at 7 A.M. rather than 7:30, so that lunch could be taken on the men's time without cutting into the hours they owed the company.

This order had the effect of jabbing a hot poker at a workforce that had not received a raise in five years—in fact, had been subjected to incessant penny-pinching by employers pocketing millions of dollars in dividends. The first men to down tools were 335 carpenters and steelworkers. Fyhen's Central Labor Council promptly released a statement blaming the Big Six for "touching off the spark of unrest that has been smouldering in the minds of the workmen for over a year."

The strike unfolded in a decidedly *fin de régime* atmosphere. The final bucket of concrete had been poured more than four months earlier. Six Companies' payroll had dwindled to 1,700, or less than a third of its peak size, with most of the men assigned to pouring concrete and installing steel girders on the powerhouse. The Six Companies partners were already pre-occupied with new projects. Kaiser and Pacific Bridge were helping to build the Golden Gate Bridge. Shea, Kaiser, and Pacific Bridge had the contract for Reclamation's Bonneville Dam on the Columbia River. Crowe's attention was increasingly diverted by the start of construction for Parker Dam, 150 miles downstream from Black Canyon, a Reclamation project for which he had drafted Six Companies' winning bid. Demand for the individual firms' expertise on highways, railroads, and tunnels was expanding as the Roosevelt administration primed the economic pump with unprecedented spending on public works.

Still, a standard script guided the official response. Reservation rangers stepped up inspections of incoming vehicles at the Boulder Highway gate, and sales of 3.2 beer—the only alcohol permitted in Boulder City following the repeal of Prohibition in 1933—were summarily halted. A rumor spread that the strikers had dynamited the road from Boulder City to the job site; the truth was that Bodell's crews had blown up an old smuggler's trail through "Bootleg Canyon," a ravine abutting the federal reservation, to prevent thieves from using it to ransack storehouses in the gorge. The strikers, for their part, acted with due solicitude for a project that still commanded their pride of workmanship, granting dispensation for crews to water the curing concrete and keep the penstock tunnels pumped dry.

Crowe hastened back to Boulder City to find all other work halted. He reversed the lunch hour decree but the strikers, heartened by the support of the Central Labor Council, had expanded their demands to include a pay raise of as much as 25 percent, to $1.25 an hour for foremen, $1.00 for skilled laborers, and 75 cents for unskilled laborers. On July 15, the start of a new workweek, more than six hundred workers were on strike, enough to effectively shut down the job. Although nearly 1,100 men were still reporting to their shifts, Six Companies acknowledged that they were doing "little or no work."

The strike presented administration officials with a quandary: the White House, eager to place the New Deal's stamp on the project, was planning a gala dedication ceremony at the canyon with FDR in personal attendance. The plans were as yet a closely held secret. ("The prospects are good for a visit from the President in September," Mead had written Young on July 16. "Keep this confidential.") Any significant delay in the work, much less an ongoing labor confrontation, would surely require cancellation of the event.

Accordingly, Reclamation wasted no time in summoning a government "conciliator," Edward H. Fitzgerald, from Los Angeles. But while Fitzgerald worked to assemble an arbitration panel to review the demand for a wage hike, the Big Six's position hardened. On July 22, with the walkout entering its second week, its board flatly rejected any wage increase and withdrew permission for Crowe, who had already been named to the arbitration panel, to participate in its deliberations. The company directors plainly calculated that the strikers were approaching the limits of their resources. They were correct. That very day the Federal Emergency Relief Administration announced that it would absorb up to a thousand dam workers facing destitution into its make-work projects in Las Vegas. This was cold comfort: the maximum FERA paycheck was $79 a month, just over half the lowest wage at the dam—and that was for a family of ten. Boulder City's American Legion post had already taken up a collection to help clothe the strikers' increasingly impoverished families, and the Anderson Brothers were donating fresh milk.

Finally, after three days of hectic consultations with Washington, Fitzgerald contrived a settlement that provided a face-saving retreat for the workers, if little else. The wage issue was to be dumped in the lap of Harold Ickes, who would endeavor to find money to raise Boulder Dam wages to the minimum Public Works Administration standard of $1 an hour.

Whether Ickes took this promise seriously is hard to gauge. It is possible that he gave his assent to the solution in a moment of distraction, as his attention was wholly consumed during this period by a controversy over the U.S. Virgin Islands, where his attempt to remove a flagrantly corrupt and incompetent administrator had provoked a congressional donnybrook. In any case, the promise was an empty one. Although Reclamation projects henceforth would be held to the PWA standard, wage rates at Boulder Dam would not change for the duration of construction.

Six Companies had won the final skirmish with its workforce. More important, it had cleared the way for the dam's dedication on September 30, and soon after that for its ultimate handover to the United States government.

# 19

## The Crest

The president had left Washington on Thursday, September 26, accompanied by the first lady, a few members of his cabinet and the informal advisory team known as the Brain Trust, and seventy staff aides. The traveling party's ten-car train was said to be the longest special to have departed the capital's Union Station in years; the president's car, nicknamed the *Robert Peary* after the Arctic explorer, was the Union Pacific's most luxurious—"five bedrooms, dining room and observation platform, air-conditioned, finished in mahogany and equipped with radio," according to a newspaper's painstaking inventory.

Initially the trip had been billed as an official fact-finding tour, but the cover story could not be sustained. Roosevelt had not visited the western United States since his election in 1932, and the 1936 election already bulked large on the horizon. The most influential newspapers on the two opposite coasts came to identical conclusions, the *Los Angeles Times* declaring that the trip was taking place with "all non-political pretense abandoned" and the *New York Times* labeling it "the first forced march of [Roosevelt's] campaign for re-election." The issues on which the next election would be fought, such as farm support, work relief, and electrical power policy, would get a thorough airing on the week-long journey, which was to be capped by two political rallies in California, a fishing trip along the West Coast, and a return home by sea via the Panama Canal.

# The Crest

The dedication of the great dam on the Colorado River was to be the journey's high point. One of FDR's purposes in making the speech was to resolve the contradictions of his myriad policy statements on public works and power policy over the years. During the 1932 campaign he had sniped relentlessly at Hoover's grandiose construction program, but had also pledged his support for four great dams proposed or already under construction (including the project at Black Canyon). In his first year in office, he launched a $3.3 billion public works program of his own. When it came to the debate over public versus private power generation he had also talked out of both sides of his mouth: in a single campaign speech he had both urged the generation of power by public entities to create a "yardstick" to measure the cost of electricity, and stated "categorically" that the development of power was the job of private initiative and capital. But Franklin Roosevelt was a master at making paradox look like consistency. In this case he would make people overlook his contradictions by focusing their attention on the landmark of human achievement he had come to celebrate.

He also came to appropriate. The dedication was his way of placing his indelible stamp on a project that had been brought to fruition by three predecessors: the dam had been conceived by his cousin Theodore Roosevelt; its congressional authorization had been signed into law by Calvin Coolidge; and its construction had been launched by Herbert Hoover. Now that the dam was hailed as a wonder of the modern world and treasured as a source of employment for thousands of desperate men and relief for their families, Roosevelt hoped that his appearance at the edge of the Colorado River gorge would eradicate from public memory the project's decades-long gestation under three Republican presidents and transform it into a visible symbol of the New Deal.

As his train clattered westward, the president spent each day in his customary bustle. There were audiences with local politicians in St. Louis and Kansas City, and crowds to be acknowledged from the back platform at innumerable whistle-stops across the Midwest. A constant irritant was the tug-of-war between emergency relief czar Harry Hopkins and Interior Secretary Ickes over a new $4.8 billion works relief program, which fell within their joint jurisdiction; FDR hoped they would settle their quarrel in the tranquillity of the journey-ending cruise. (They would not.) A compensating triumph occurred on Friday evening, September 27, when his major speech on agricultural policy in the corn belt town of Fremont, Nebraska, was received enthusiastically by an audience of 25,000.

Approaching Salt Lake City, the train turned south on the Union Pacific tracks. The dam, still a day's travel away, loomed ever larger in the president's thoughts. He retreated for long stretches into his private car, polishing his speech into a manifesto of New Deal policies on public power, natural resources, industrial development, and government work relief. The risk of a misstep was great, for the address would be heard coast to coast by a radio audience in the millions, its every word ruthlessly parsed by politicians of both parties for its possible impact on the coming campaign. Perhaps for these reasons the president submitted his oration to the sharp critiques of Ickes, Marriner Eccles, and Steve Early, a White House aide who served as press secretary.

Well after 2 A.M. on Monday morning the train chugged through Las Vegas without stopping. This was not an oversight but a deferred compliment, for although the train skirted the municipality on its way to the dam, as a sign of the city's new stature the president would stop in town for a formal visit after the ceremony—making FDR the first American president to visit Las Vegas, but assuredly not the last.

By 4 A.M. the special had pulled up at a siding on the outskirts of Boulder City, where 120 infantrymen from Fort Douglas, Utah, were encamped to safeguard the sleeping president and his guests. But the troops were powerless to protect the president from a rude jolt at 5:40 A.M., when the air was shattered by the Boulder City mess hall whistle summoning the day shift to breakfast.

A few hours later came a bigger shock. Radio was still a novelty as a public medium and the logistics of cross-country broadcasting yet in their infancy. From Washington, Ickes had set a schedule for the dedication day built around a presidential speech at 2 P.M., and so instructed the organizers in Boulder City. But no one had thought to translate his orders from Eastern time to Pacific, possibly because the arrangements had been made in an atmosphere of the utmost haste. ("We had only about one week to complete preparations," one of the local planners said later.) No one realized that Ickes meant 2 P.M. East Coast time—11 A.M. at the canyon—until the early morning, when Walker Young reported to Ickes's rail car for a last-minute briefing. A nonplussed Young informed Ickes that if he kept to his schedule, twenty thousand local residents would still be making their way to the dam site while the ceremony was taking place. Most would miss the event.

"We don't care about twenty thousand people," Ickes barked in reply. "We're talking about the twenty million who are going to listen to us on radio."

Young descended from the train car to find himself enmeshed in a political scrum. The dignitaries who had ridden with the president were jostling with a throng of local worthies to grab the lone spare seat in the president's open car for the ride to the dam site. "There was the governor, there were senators from other states," Young recalled, "all of them claiming to have a great deal to do with the appropriation of money for the construction of the dam." Steve Early was pondering how to anoint one individual to ride with the president without offending the others, most of them Washington politicians with limitless memories for slights. Young, a neutral player, might have been delivered by providence. His ulcers could not have been soothed when Early suddenly installed him between the president and Mrs. Roosevelt in the back seat, behind the chauffeur and a man from the Secret Service. His most vivid recollection of the event would be the experience of dodging the lit end of the president's cigarette, all the way down to the gorge.

Without further ado, precisely at 9:30 A.M. as dictated by Ickes's agenda, the car pulled away from the depot, followed by a caravan of nineteen limousines. "I could at least get them down to the dam on time," Young later observed wryly. "I knew where it was, you know."


If Franklin Roosevelt had one personal characteristic on which all witnesses agreed, it was his compulsive loquacity, a prodigious flow of observation and inquiry that often left his companions feeling overwhelmed by a "Niagara of verbiage." Nothing unleashed this garrulous torrent like a new, unfamiliar environment: He "could see more in an hour's drive than anyone I had ever known," the Brain Truster Rexford G. Tugwell reported. "To ride with him was to be deluged with talk." The eight-mile journey to the dam must have provided plenty of raw material for the president's unremitting conversation.

First there was Boulder City itself, which despite its four years of development could still strike newcomers as "a community stranded on a desert island," in the words of a contemporary observer. Yet the town was populous enough to muster two thousand "gaily bedecked" schoolchildren on the broad lawn in front of the Reclamation building to greet the president in his car.

Then the motorcade hastened to the river on a paved road built under the first contract let on the dam project in 1931. Roosevelt would not have overlooked the considerable engineering achievement of its construction. It descended two thousand feet to the river via eight miles of switchbacks and hairpin turns, sandwiched for much of its distance between a sheer cliffside and a narrow, deep ravine. Crags in shades of red and pink, indicating the heavy concentration of iron in the geology, formed a serrated horizon. A few miles out of town, at a broad plain affording an unbroken vista of the terrain looking east, the motorcade pulled off the road to peer at a distant ribbon of water. This was the doomed Moapa Valley. Within a few short years it would lie entirely submerged beneath Lake Mead. The reservoir had begun filling the previous February and had already reached a level sufficient to support a flotilla of tourist boats offering round-trips to the dam's upstream face for 80 cents per passenger. But what the visitors saw that day scarcely hinted at the mighty 115-mile-long lake that would one day hold enough water to irrigate a quarter of a million acres of farmland and slake the thirst of tens of millions of Americans.

Underway again, the caravan descended down a steep escarpment. The road curved to the left around one last salmon-tinted outcropping, and suddenly there was the gorge, excavated down to the bedrock and spanned by a vast arched keystone of alabaster concrete.

# The Crest

The cars rolled past the temporary platform erected on the canyon rim for the president's address and continued over the dam's crest on a ribbon of fresh tarmac, forcing a milling crowd to the concrete sidewalks. Just beyond the abutment on the Arizona side of the river, the motorcade halted again.

Ever sensitive about voters' perception of his health, Roosevelt strived at every public appearance to simulate vigorous activity while concealing the tremendous physical effort this cost him. The visit to the dam, in blinding sunlight and stifling heat, would tax his ability to carry out this subterfuge, but he played his role with customary determination and evident good humor. As soon as his car parked, he pulled himself upright, using an iron bar built into the seat in front of him for leverage. His leg braces were snapped into place and a pair of aides gently deposited him on solid ground. Then, a jaunty straw-yellow Panama hat on his head, his right arm leaning on a walking stick and his left clutched tightly around the elbow of a military aide, he headed for a stone parapet overlooking the canyon, employing a rocking motion that, to distant observers unaware of the crucial support provided by the man at his side, looked very much like walking. At the wall he obligingly posed for news photographers, making a show of scrutinizing the government's handiwork and using his stick to draw the first lady's attention to the slowly filling reservoir. Asked for his impression by a reporter, he gave an uncharacteristic response. "I'm speechless," he said.

Mrs. Roosevelt went off to gather her own impressions. Joined by Hopkins, she descended in a cable skip to the downstream floor of the gorge, where the hydroelectric plant was still under construction. The experience of staring up at a 727-foot monolithic wall of concrete from the bottom of a dry riverbed, enveloped in the commotion of a worksite that two years earlier had been under 140 feet of turbulent water, would stay with Eleanor Roosevelt to the end of her life. She would tell friends that the visit had brought home to her the sweeping achievement of the New Deal as though for the very first time. For all that it had been conceived and launched under Republicans, the dam in its finished form seemed to give tangible expression to her husband's policies. It represented gainful employment, cheap hydroelectric power, reliable irrigation, and protection from the obstinate elements, all wrought from the forbidding land by a visionary federal government embarking on a new role in national life.

The first lady returned to the crest and joined the president on the grandstand. The crowd closed back over the roadway, where people stood shoulder to shoulder almost all the way to the Arizona side. A few agile souls scampered onto the parapets or scaled the flagpoles ringing the reviewing plaza for a better view, only to be ordered back to earth by vigilant police officers. Despite the timing miscue that left countless pilgrims still on the road as the ceremonies started, despite the 102 degree heat under the pitiless sun, an estimated ten thousand onlookers were on hand.

As the first speaker, Ickes filled the stagnant air with pedestrian bromides about the eternal conflict between man and nature. ("Just as nature, untamed and invincible, in her sullen immobility, has destroyed not only the works of man but man himself, so has man in his turn wreaked his vengeance upon nature . . .")

Sensitive ears might have detected the insult to Hoover implied in Ickes's fulsome praise for Hiram Johnson, whom he identified as "more intimately associated with Boulder Dam than . . . any other man." He added: "It has been well said that if this dam should bear the name of any living person, then it should be christened Johnson Dam." The thought of Hoover reading these words in a newspaper account of the celebration must have given a frisson of malicious glee to Ickes, who had made no secret of his intention to use the dedication "to try to nail down for good and all the name Boulder Dam." To that end he had also arranged for a commemorative U.S. postage stamp to be placed on sale in Boulder City that day, denominated at the standard first-class letter rate of 3 cents and bearing the inscription "Boulder Dam—1935."

After Ickes's speech and an introduction by Senator Key Pittman of Nevada, FDR came to the podium. Wedged into a support frame of tubular steel, his braces once again locked in place, the president placed his weight on the lectern and opened with an extemporaneous flourish: "This morning I came, I saw, and I was conquered, as everyone will be who sees for the first time this great achievement." There was a moment's interruption when Ickes, seated a few feet behind the podium and jingling the change in his pocket, dropped it with a clatter on the wooden platform. ("Oh, I wanted to choke that man," a member of the audience recalled nearly forty years later.) FDR pressed on. His theme was much the same as that of his interior secretary—the taming of nature for the benefit of all mankind—but when invested with his distinctive cadence his oratory commanded attention. "Ten years ago the place where we are gathered was an unpeopled, forbidding desert," he observed. "The transformation wrought here is a twentieth century marvel."

He acknowledged "the energy, resourcefulness, and zeal of the builders, who under the greatest physical obstacles, have pushed this work forward to completion, two years in advance of the contract requirements. . . . Especially we express our gratitude to the thousands of workers who gave brain and brawn to the work of construction." He reminded his listeners of the effort to work out an "equitable division" of the Colorado's waters among the seven states of its basin without naming the steward of that effort, Herbert Hoover. He noted that the contracts governing the sale of its hydroelectricity would cover the dam's construction cost within fifty years while providing light to consumers at low public rates, without mentioning that the pacts had been reached during his predecessor's administration. In a seeming burst of false modesty, he acknowledged that "throughout our national history we have had a great program of public improvements, and in these past two years all that we have done has been to accelerate that program." He added, lest anyone forget the crisis that had returned the White House to Democratic control after twelve years of Republican rule: "The reason for this speeding up was the need of giving relief to several million men and women whose earning capacity had been destroyed by the complexities and lack of thought of the economic system of the past generation."

The absent Hoover cast his shadow over the entire ceremony like an unacknowledged wraith, his name uttered from the grandstand not once during the long day. Yet Roosevelt's attempt to write Hoover out of the story was unavailing in the West—especially in California, which claimed the Stanford-educated Hoover as a favorite son. "It was Hoover, the far-visioned engineer, who was among the first to conceive the project's vast possibilities," editorialized the loyal Republican *Los Angeles Times*; "Hoover's hand that was at the helm and Hoover's energy, ability and determination that made possible the successful outcome." Ascribing the dam's rechristening to Ickes's "almost inconceivably petty political pique," the newspaper underscored the point by republishing a cartoon it had run at the time of the original renaming, depicting the secretary as a minuscule figure trying to remove the enormous words "Hoover Dam" from the edifice with a chisel. Then the caption read: "It Can't Be Done, Mr. Ickes." The new version showed a tiny FDR joining Ickes on the dam face with his own chisel. The caption now read: "And Still It Can't Be Done."

Yet in a larger sense FDR was justified in claiming the great dam as a signature work of the New Deal. In its time Hoover's public works program may have been unprecedented in scale, but he conceived it as an emergency measure in a period of economic crisis, made necessary only because private enterprise had refused to accept a leadership role in the crisis. By 1935, Roosevelt had come to see public works as a central function of the federal government—indeed, an essential function, and one likely to carry his presidential legacy tangibly into history. Early in his administration he had handed responsibility for the government's outsized $3.3 billion public works budget to Harold Ickes not only because he expected the cautious and thrifty interior secretary to make every dollar tell, but because he knew that Ickes would demand that every bridge, tunnel, highway, or dam built with the taxpayers' money endow posterity with positive, ineradicable benefits.

Herbert Hoover was heir to the concept of a small, circumspect federal government, empowered to wage limited war and secure the nation's borders but not much else; even his halting efforts to ameliorate the economic crisis between 1930 and 1932 had stretched the limits of what was then regarded as permissible federal action. FDR, by contrast, would bequeath his successors an assertive federal bureaucracy capable of projecting its power to all the forty-eight states and beyond to the rest of the world. His was an expansive view of executive authority that harked back to Alexander Hamilton and the Federalists and looked ahead to presidencies that would be more imperial than his own. Hoover saw the dam mostly as a regional boon for seven Western states; Roosevelt as a gift to the whole country. "The mighty waters of the Colorado were running unused to the sea," he told his audience on September 30, 1935. "Today we translate them into a great national possession."

By almost any standard, Franklin Roosevelt's dedication speech had to be judged a political triumph. The occasion received front-page attention from newspapers across the country; a 2,700-word report led the *New York Times,* which also published the verbatim text. Many articles complimented the president for gracefully abstaining from partisan politics on this, his first trip to the West since his inauguration. That is not to say that everyone in the audience was equally pleased. "Sizzling hot today," recorded Harry Morrison's wife, Ann, fuming to her diary about the poor accommodations provided at the dedication for all but the few VIPs shown to a sheltered platform with comfortable seats. "An uncovered platform for the overflow. That's where the wives wound up. We nearly melted—all got sunburned and blistered and could hear only parts of the speeches."

Perhaps unavoidably, there were a few hitches in the festivities. One spectator suffering from heat prostration was taken away by ambulance. Later that afternoon, the president's party took a detour on their way out of the gorge to visit a Civilian Conservation Corps camp in the Charleston Mountains. The twenty-vehicle motorcade, with the president and first lady in the lead car, negotiated several hair-raising curves on a rutted dirt road, took a wrong turn in the mountainous wilds, and heedlessly drove past a sign warning "No Vehicles Allowed." One mile later the road ended at a sheer mountain wall.

The drivers helped the president bodily from his car and perched him on a boulder while they hustled to get the procession turned around. In the next hour the sun dipped behind the mountain range, the temperature—of Mrs. Roosevelt's disposition as well as the ambient air—plummeted, and aides waiting at the Las Vegas train depot began to lose their composure over the disappearance of President Roosevelt's vehicle and nineteen other carloads of dignitaries. At last the motorcade arrived back at civilization, safe but nearly two hours behind schedule.

Amid the celebratory pomp it was easy to forget that Boulder Dam was not quite finished. Upstream, the reservoir was already filling, transforming the lowest hillocks of the Moapa Valley into islands, some of which harbored small herds of stranded sheep. The dedication spectators were struck by the lake's serene beauty, its water left a sapphire blue by the settling out of the Colorado's red silt.

But on the downstream side, the gorge remained very much a construction zone. The U-shaped powerhouse nestling against the dam's downstream face was an unroofed shell, with huge circular spaces in its poured concrete floor indicating where the dam's enormous turbines were to be installed. Still on the drawing board was a whole array of memorial adornments to the canyon rim. Gordon Kaufmann's stripped-down art deco design reinforced the dam's implicit power, but any great project financed from the public purse required that a host of edifying, not to say self-congratulatory, narratives be provided for visitors by plaque and memorial display.

Some of these were straightforward enough: in late 1936 four five-foot bronze placards were installed flanking the elevator doors on the crest to list the project's chronology, specifications, and political patrons. The honorees included presidents Harding, Coolidge, Hoover, and Roosevelt; legislators Swing and Johnson; interior secretaries Wilbur and Ickes; the Reclamation Bureau staff (commissioners Mead and Arthur Powell Davis at the top); and the contractors. This last plaque had to be recast, according to Walker Young's recollection, when it was discovered that it identified the project's general superintendent as "Patrick J. Crowe." Each of the Six Companies founding partners was named, as if to fulfill Henry Kaiser's long-ago promise to Dad Bechtel that his name one day would be embossed upon the greatest public work of its time. Only the fact that Dad, like Will and Ed Wattis, did not live to see that day arrive might have tempered the pride felt by Kaiser and the other surviving partners. A few months after Mead's death on January 26, 1936, a separate plaque in his honor was installed overlooking the reservoir, which had been duly re-named Lake Mead.

Certainly the monument telling the most unusual story was the one dedicated to a dog. A part-Labrador stray with a jet black coat and a white blaze on his chest, the dog had been born in the crawlspace beneath a con-struction barracks in 1932. He was brought down to the riverbed by a la-borer while still a puppy, frequented the worksite as a cherished companion to the workers for nearly a decade, and acquired a name whose spectacular impropriety would not register in the public ear for another half-century. The men called him "Nig."

Making his sure-footed way around the canyon on its crosswalks and catwalks, Nig was the site's unofficial mascot. "He'd climb ladders, he was in the tunnels, he was everywhere," one worker recalled. When the whistle blew to end the day shift he appeared at the foot of the elevators, ready to hop the first lift up to the Boulder City transports. Legend had it that he would shun proffered treats from anyone but a dam worker. The workmen treated the dog with the utmost solicitude, sometimes to his disadvantage. When his health was affected by his irregular diet of candy and ice cream, notices were placed in the Las Vegas and Boulder City newspapers warning:

> *I Love Candy but it makes me sick*
> *It is also bad for my coat*
> *Please don't feed me any more.*
> Your friend, Nig.

Henceforth the Anderson mess hall would provide him with a daily lunch bag, which he would carry in his mouth down to the site, waiting for the lunch whistle to blow before wolfing down its contents.

After the Six Companies workforce dispersed, the dog kept company with crews manning the hydroelectric turbines for the Los Angeles munici-pal utility, the Department of Water and Power. His tenure lasted until February 21, 1941, an unseasonably hot day on which he decided to seek refuge from the sun under an idling truck. When the unwitting driver returned and drove off, the dog was crushed beneath its wheels.

"Rough, tough rock-hard men wept openly and unashamed," a newspaper article later recounted of the effect the dog's passing had on the human beings of Boulder City. He was buried in a concrete crypt near the Nevada abutment and memorialized with a plaque identifying him as "Nig, The Dog That Adopted a Dam."

This plaque stayed up until 1979, when it drew the offended attention of a Wisconsin tourist. Clarence Kailin was a veteran of the Abraham Lincoln Brigade, the unit of American volunteers that had fought on the anti-fascist side in the Spanish Civil War from 1936 to 1939 under the command of a black officer. He was dismayed to find a racial epithet posted on public property even in abbreviated form, and brought his complaint to a Reclamation Bureau supervisor, only to be cavalierly dismissed. "I told him that it was a racist name and the plaque should be taken down," he related. "He said, 'No way.'"

But the plaque could hardly survive in an era in which standards of racial identity had evolved so far from those of the construction period. Once Kailin returned home to Madison and complained to his congressional representatives its days were numbered. It was removed on March 21, 1979 (over the objections of numerous older Boulder City residents), and replaced with a marker set in the sandstone wall of the canyon, describing the dog simply as "the Hoover Dam construction crew's mascot" and a "devoted animal." To this day that marker consistently attracts a charmed and appreciative crowd.

The dam's final decorative touches were the work of two artists selected personally by Gordon Kaufmann. To beautify the interior spaces—the elevator lobbies, subterranean tunnels, and galleries that crisscrossed inside the dam and serviced the powerhouse—he appointed Allen Tupper True, a Denver muralist who drew his inspiration from the crafts of the Southwest Indians and whose work could be found in public buildings across the West. (His silhouette of a cowboy astride a bucking bronco has adorned Wyoming's license plates since 1934.)

True chose motifs from Pima baskets, pre-Columbian bowls, and Pueblo wall paintings to relieve the "oppressive monotony" of the workspaces. To leaven the dreariness of the public tunnels leading from the elevator lobbies to the powerhouse—"mole holes a city block long" through which a thousand visitors a day would pass—he created geometric patterns in green, red, and black, at once aboriginal and compellingly modern. In his hands the utilitarian interior spaces acquired a lively continuity. No longer expanses of gray concrete, they henceforth evoked "stepped mesas, rain, lightning, and clouds, [and] lizards, plumed serpents, and birds," all in the inventive imagery of the region's oldest human inhabitants.

As of this writing, almost none of True's arresting designs remain accessible to public view, the barring of visitors from most of the structure's interior being one of the more dismal consequences of the federal government's preoccupation with security.

To design a grand exterior plaza celebrating the project as a unique public achievement, Kaufmann engaged the cranky forty-three-year-old Norwegian sculptor Oskar Hansen, who specialized in the casting of monumental bronzes in impeccable art deco style. For the plaza's centerpiece Hansen ordered an enormous block of igneous black diorite, which would serve as the base of a 142-foot flagpole and the pedestal for two towering winged figures, ancient Egyptian in appearance, their sinewy arms thrusting skyward. The diorite block was so fragile that to keep it from chipping or cracking during installation it had to be set upon several blocks of ice and nudged gently into its foundation as the ice melted away.

The plaza's most distinctive feature is a terrazzo star map laid out in a great circle around the diorite pedestal. A product of Hansen's amateur fascination with astronomy, the map marked the positions of the northern sky's celestial bodies at the exact moment of FDR's dedication—in Hansen's calculation, September 30, 1935, at 8:35 and 2.25 seconds P.M. by "astronomical time," or 11:35 A.M. local Nevada time. Hansen spent three years executing this commission. Every day he could be spotted on the

Nevada abutment, a kneeling, pith-helmeted figure surrounded by "Keep Out" signs, plotting the map with the aid of an intricate framework of compasses, calipers, and protractors, shunning conversation with inquisitive onlookers.

But once the work was completed he emerged from his shell, explicating his conception in florid prose by the ream. He strived to invest the bronze figures—the "Winged Figures of the Republic," he called them—with a mythological yet fundamentally American significance, explaining that he had given them "the look of eagles . . . the vital upward thrust of an aspirational gesture; to symbolize the readiness for defense of our institutions and the keeping of our spiritual eagles ever ready to be on the wing." They were nude, he explained, but modeled "not to seem naked . . . [so] that my spectators should find them mighty of body and clean of soul; armed only in the winged imagination of their own thoughts."

As for the star map, "a legend has arisen to the effect that only five people understand the information given," Hansen wrote, rather pridefully. "While the number is not so limited . . . it is not necessary that the average visitor should be able to solve, along with top-flight astronomers, their most difficult problems." Rather, it is enough that the visitor understand that "time, the intangible governor of all our acts, is measured to us by the external relations of our Earth to other worlds in space."

Hansen's grandiloquence, so out of tune with his sculptures' art deco simplicity, suggests that he might have been well advised to let his artwork speak for itself. It does so with an elegance that invests the heroic aspirations implicit in the dam's pure bulk with a wholly human self-consciousness. Hansen's artistic style situated Hoover Dam in its time more precisely than the abstruse configurations of his star map ever could. Hoover Dam was born in the Jazz Age, built in the Machine Age, and in every respect represented the Modern Age. It stands today as the perfect melding of form and function, a landmark of engineering, architecture, and muscular industry. Hansen celebrated these qualities with soaring, silent art deco bronzes that rendered his verbiage entirely superfluous.

\* \* \*

One final adornment, this one figurative rather than physical, was made in 1947: the restoration of Herbert Hoover's name.

In that year the 80th Congress—the first since 1933 to have a Republican majority—resurrected the irksome issue of the dam's christening. The truth was that Harold Ickes's 1933 "Boulder Dam" decree had never fully taken root. Mapmakers remained divided about the nomenclature and many Americans used both of the dam's names interchangeably. A few stalwart Republican newspapers, such as the *Los Angeles Times*, had steadfastly refused to go along with the change at all.

For all that Hoover's name had been widely cursed during the depth of the Depression in 1933, that was no longer the case in 1947. The ex-president had restored his reputation by such humanitarian good works as founding the Polish Relief Commission after the German invasion of 1939 and leading a postwar European famine commission (at President Truman's invitation) in 1945.

On Capitol Hill the restoration was resisted by a few Democrats led by Senator Pat McCarran of Nevada, who argued lamely that the cost of new signs and stationery would inconvenience businesses in Boulder City. Harold Ickes, retired from the cabinet, waged a rearguard battle against the initiative as a private citizen. ("I didn't know Hoover was that small a man to take credit for something he had nothing to do with," he grumbled to reporters.)

Most politicians chose to get out of the way of a juggernaut. Even Phil Swing, who had become the last surviving standard-bearer of the Boulder Canyon Project Act with Hiram Johnson's death in 1945, signaled his support, more with resignation than enthusiasm. "Mr. Hoover as the only living ex-president demands the respect of most Americans," he wrote a friend. "If something worthwhile should be named after him in order to perpetuate his memory, other than his actions or failures in office as president, then, of course, I suppose our project was as good as any to pick on."

The bill restoring Hoover's name passed unanimously in both houses. Truman signed the act on April 30. "Vindication!" crowed the *Los Angeles Times*, referring less to Hoover's victory than to its own in its "fight for maintenance of the Hoover name."

By then all of the dam's "appurtenances," as they were labeled in the original specifications, were fully functional. The 1,180-foot paved roadway over the crest was opened to traffic the week before Christmas 1935, although for a time cars were permitted to cross only in convoys escorted by federal rangers. Milestones crowded upon each other over the succeeding months, though not all were welcome signs of progress. On December 20, 1935, Reclamation electrician Patrick Tierney, twenty-five years old, lost his footing on one of the Arizona intake towers and plunged 320 feet to its base. His was the last death to be officially recorded during the dam's construction, and followed that of his father, J. Gregory Tierney, one of Walker Young's original canyon surveyors, by fourteen years to the day—father and son the first and last men to die on the project, an eerie closing of a woeful circle in the history of the Tierney family and of Black Canyon.

On March 1, 1936, with a minimum of ceremony, the United States government had accepted Hoover Dam from Six Companies as a completed project. That it was truly finished was an arguable point, for there was a year's worth of detail work and cleanup yet to be performed, jobs that normally would fall within the contractor's responsibility. The early handover was widely regarded as another victory for Henry Kaiser, who had persuaded the Reclamation Bureau that it was in the government's interest to assume full jurisdiction as soon as possible, without making too much of the fact that the transfer also meant money in the bank for his own partnership. ("It's one thing to build a great public works, it's something else to get a government bureau to admit it's finished," Felix Kahn later observed to *Fortune*. "Unless you can saw the main job off . . . they'll have you adding power equipment, transmission lines, roads, and other extras for the rest of your life.") Six Companies filed an immediate claim for the portion of its contract fee ($2.5 million) withheld by the government as a completion guarantee. Added to the sums already paid out, that produced a final profit for the Six Companies partners of $10.4 million, after taxes. The sum is the equivalent of more than $160 million in 2010 dollars.

The dam is often said to have been finished ahead of schedule and under budget. The first of these assertions certainly is true. The government contract required the project to be completed within 2,565 days of the signing. Taking the start date as April 20, 1931, when Interior Secretary Wilbur inscribed his signature to the document and issued the formal order to Six Companies to begin work, the deadline was April 28, 1938. Frank Crowe beat that mark by two years and fifty-eight days. But the dam came in over budget, not below. Change orders issued by the bureau during construction raised the contract payments to $54.7 million, or about $5.8 million more than Six Companies had bid in March 1931.

Other than the partners and their investors, the only profit participant was Frank Crowe, whose original contract had called for a salary of $18,000 a year plus 2.5 percent of the gross profit—much of the latter attributable, after all, to Crowe's skill at completing a job of unparalleled size and complexity with time to spare. At the final accounting, his bonus came to more than $300,000, of which $250,000 already had been advanced to him during construction.

The night before the formal transfer, Crowe had quietly handed over his command to a new general superintendent. This was Ralph Lowry, a Reclamation engineer who had ably served as John Page's assistant for five years.

"Take it, Ralph, it's yours now," Crowe told Lowry, perhaps unconsciously echoing the timeless words ("There it is. Take it.") William Mulholland had uttered when he endowed his city with the waters of the Los Angeles Aqueduct in 1913.

"It's a great dam, Ralph," Crowe added.

"Well, Frank," Lowry replied, "you oughta know."

At precisely 7:36 P.M. on October 9, 1936, Miss Elizabeth Scattergood, the daughter of the general manager of the Los Angeles Bureau of Power and Light, stepped onto the broad front lawn of the downtown county courthouse. Before a dignified crowd she pressed a button transmitting a signal 226 miles to the Boulder Dam powerhouse, where the dam's newly installed generators cranked obediently into action. A noticeable crackling sound came from high over the heads of the Los Angeles crowd, and sixteen enormous arc lamps installed on the twenty-seventh floor of City Hall blazed into life. The first hydroelectric power had been delivered to Los Angeles from the Colorado River.

The metropolis, born 155 years before as a tiny pueblo on the edge of the desert, responded as if it had been released from epochs of darkness. "The dim-lit city, starting up like an aroused sleeper . . . was in an instant clothed with such flaming radiance as man has never made before," reported the *Los Angeles Times,* with a perhaps pardonable excess of enthusiasm. Along Broadway, one hundred searchlights swept the night sky. Marching bands, mounted corps, and floats began snaking through downtown, where an estimated one million residents had gathered for the greatest civic celebration since the Armistice.

Among the honored guests at the luminous inauguration was Phil Swing, three years retired from the House of Representatives, his place in the history of the great enterprise recognized at last. Addressing several hundred listeners seated on folding chairs, he summoned up the "many weary days of seemingly hopeless contest . . . fifteen years of effort, eight years of legislative struggle" that had passed between the conception and completion of the Boulder Canyon Project.

Swing did not dwell on the political strife that had begotten the Colossus of Black Canyon. Now, as always, his eye remained focused firmly on the goal that he had carried from the dusty Imperial Valley to Washington. There were many times during the journey when he had despaired of ever getting to the end. But those moments had withered to insignificance with the achievement they were honoring on that day-lit night.

"The dream has come true," he told the crowd. "We celebrate not only the greatest power plant on earth but also the conquest of the Colorado.

"It is no longer the master. It is now the servant of man."

# 20

# Legacies

The dam was capped off, Lake Mead was rising, and the generators were illuminating a great city more than three hundred miles away. But the process of measuring the implications of the great project in Black Canyon was just beginning.

At first it was driven more by conjecture than fact. In the summer of 1936, when the reservoir reached a depth of four hundred feet and extended more than one hundred miles upstream—already the world's largest man-made body of water—government officials addressed speculation by local residents that the lake had altered their climate and weather. Reclamation engineers anchored a timber raft on the surface with an evaporation pan, a flat tin saucer equipped with instruments that could measure changes in the surface to a thousandth of a foot, hoping to calculate how much water the giant reservoir might be evanescing into the atmosphere. The results told them that the lake's level was falling by six-tenths of an inch per day, meaning that about 25,000 gallons were evaporating every second. (At the time the lake surface was about two thousand feet, or 25 percent, below its maximum height, although as measured by volume of water it was less than half-full.)

In absolute terms this sounded like a lot of water to squander, amounting to 7 percent of the reservoir's capacity over a year.* It was enough, according

---

* Later studies have confirmed this estimate, placing the average annual evaporation rate from Lake Mead at 6 to 8 percent by volume.

to statisticians queried by the press, to fill a canal twenty-seven feet deep reaching from coast to coast. But it was judged to be insufficient to alter the weather in any detectable way. "The water in a pitcher on a speaker's stand is about as effective in air conditioning an auditorium as Lake Mead is in modifying the climate," reported J. Cecil Alter, the government's chief meteorologist in Salt Lake City.

Other indications of the lake's impact on the environment could not be so easily dismissed. The weight of 41.5 billion tons of water deformed the earth's surface along the entire reservoir valley. There was no reason for concern about the integrity of the dam, Reclamation officials assured the public—after all, it had been structurally engineered to resist even larger forces. What they could not predict, however, was the effect this unprecedented man-made load might have on the earth's malleable crust. One could only hope that the consequences would not be catastrophic.

The bureau's complacency ended abruptly at 12:44 P.M. on Thursday, May 4, 1939, when a powerful earthquake rumbled across the desert floor between Boulder City and Las Vegas, tumbling chimneys, buckling roads, and raising eerie clouds of dust on the open range. Measuring 5.0 on the Richter scale, the quake could be felt from Los Angeles to Phoenix and south to the Mexican border. It was followed over the next four days by aftershocks registering as high as magnitude 4.0. On June 11 a second 5.0 quake struck the same area.

There was no doubt the seismic activity was connected to Lake Mead, which by then had risen to within fifty feet of its maximum height. The region was not traditionally considered an active quake zone. The U.S. Coast and Geodetic Survey had installed its first seismograph near the dam only after the lake began filling in 1935, but in scouring the public record as far back as 1915 it had not turned up a single anecdotal report of an earthquake in the area. Over the following ten years, its instruments recorded six hundred quakes within a few miles of the reservoir, many of them strung along previously undetected faults crossing the lake bed.

It would later be determined that the most intense earthquake activity was associated not with peak water levels so much as with rapid changes in the lake, as during its seasonal filling and draining. Hoover Dam would remain a prodigious earthquake producer well into the 1960s, when the construction of Glen Canyon Dam and the impoundment of Lake Powell three hundred miles upstream allowed the Reclamation Bureau to better moderate flows into and out of Lake Mead.

The rising reservoir had a pronounced effect on the dam itself. Notwithstanding the bureau's reassurances about the structure's absolute safety, the water sought out and exploited imperfections in the underlying geology that government engineers had not even guessed at. Beginning in 1937, under the intense pressure exerted by the filling reservoir, the dam began to show the strain.

The weak link was the grout curtain, that single row of 150-foot boreholes pressure-filled with cement paste just ahead of the concrete pour. This program to block seepage in the foundations had been an innovative feature of the dam's design, but it was also highly experimental. Indeed, as an expert later observed, it was based largely on "guesswork"—about the geology of the site, the pressure of impounded water, and the formulation of the grout mixture itself.

Given these circumstances, the need to reexamine the grout curtain after the reservoir filled was "not altogether unexpected," a Reclamation technical team reported later. But no one anticipated the extent of the grout curtain's failure. Seepage and leaks, some of them sizable, had been seen in the galleries since the reservoir had begun to fill but had been treated as inevitable; the galleries had been equipped with drains in recognition of this very phenomenon. But in June 1937, as the reservoir reached a depth of five hundred feet, the situation became alarming.

Water began pouring into the dam's interior galleries at a rate of two hundred gallons per minute and cascading from faults in the downstream canyon walls. The inflow overwhelmed the drains serving the galleries, some of which had to be bailed out manually by bucket brigades. By January 1938, crews were carrying out hundreds of buckets a week. In the powerhouse, where water pooling near the generating turbines posed an obvious electrocution risk, trenches were cut in the concrete floor to sluice it back to the river. A conspicuous spring in the Nevada canyon wall rained down on the powerhouse roof as an unnerving sign to visitors that Boulder Dam was not nearly as watertight as advertised.

The seepage displayed the ability of flowing water to seek out the dam's weakest spots. These included the concrete lining of the diversion tunnels, now performing extended duty as penstock conduits. The arch concrete, which had been pumped into the overhead voids by pneumatic guns, was riddled with gaps and cracks through which warm alkaline water from underground springs drizzled onto the steel penstock pipes. Inspections soon revealed that the pipes were riddled with corrosion and in several spots completely eaten through.

The gravest concern was caused by the dreaded phenomenon of uplift, produced by seepage under the foundation pushing up against the dam's mass. Abnormal uplift first appeared in the pressure gauges along the Nevada abutment and beneath the central section of the powerhouse around the same time that leaks appeared in the abutment walls and water began pouring into the galleries. The readings told Reclamation's engineers that the balance of power within the reservoir valley had shifted dangerously in the water's favor.

In September 1938, Reclamation retrieved core samples from the rock foundation deep under the dam. The results were shocking: the bedrock was riddled with faults, shears, and veins of soft manganese through which water flowed freely. It was now evident that the geological mapping of the canyon in the 1920s and 1930s, viewed at the time as exceptionally thorough, in fact had been woefully superficial. As a consequence, the original grout curtain was too shallow. Even more troubling was its slapdash construction. The abandonment of fifty-eight grout holes by the drillers compromised the entire arrangement. Instead of sealing the bedrock against seepage, the grout curtain was letting water through and even, in spots, concentrating the forces of uplift.

All those errors were in the past. The urgent question was how to stem the increasing seepage. Reclamation's answer was to massively augment the grout curtain with two more ranks of boreholes, some of them twice the depth of the originals or as much as three hundred feet into the rock. The deepest hole, D-23 on the Nevada side of the foundation, would reach nearly 480 feet into solid rock, or fully 60 percent of the height of the dam towering above it. This time, no hole was to be left unfilled no matter how much cement it consumed; hole A-124 in the Arizona abutment, which crossed a gaping void in the rock, would swallow 8,258 sacks of cement (more than four hundred tons of grout) before it was sated.

The repair project was launched in late 1938 with a budget of nearly $2 million. It would take nine years to complete, or more than twice as long as Frank Crowe's men had needed to pour the dam itself, and require nearly twelve thousand tons of cement.

The effort presented its own set of novel technical challenges. Reclamation engineers found that existing formulations of grout cement, mostly developed for the oil drilling industry, were unsuited to the pressures and temperatures of Black Canyon, and in an echo of the original concrete studies, embarked on a new research program to develop new materials.

The effort also taught the engineers why it was critically important to complete the grout curtain before the completion of a high dam, not afterward. The holes had to be drilled from inside the dam, using a drainage gallery running horizontally along the structure's upstream foot—a cramped space barely wide enough to accommodate a man wedged in with his drills and pumps. Drill holes sometimes penetrated subterranean streams that sent torrents of hot water cascading into the gallery, forcing the drillers to scurry for safety. On one occasion, the slip of a wrench caused four hundred feet of drill rods to rebound from a hole "as if they had been shot out of a cannon." Fortunately, the supervising engineer reported, "the only casualty was a mangled mass of drill rods." After that, only the most experienced and seasoned drillers were allowed on the project.

Construction of the supplemental grout curtain was conducted entirely outside public view and known only to a small fraternity of engineering geologists. To this day it is left out of the presentation to the tourists thronging the canyon with their guides, ogling a project supposedly engineered to perfection. But it saved the dam from what might have been catastrophic damage. After its completion in 1947, uplift fell below the level that had been forecast in the dam's original engineering studies.

When the dam was built no model existed for preparing the foundation and abutments for concrete dams of its size. Without precedent or experience to go by, the grout curtain's designers relied on guesswork, and for the most part guessed wrong. But five years later, the construction of the supplemental grout curtain established firm principles for investigating the geology underlying massive dams and sealing the bedrock and abutments—one more contribution by Hoover Dam to the disciplines of dam building and engineering geology.

The unexpected seepage and leaks raised questions about other features of the project that had been difficult to model during the design stage. Concern focused on the two spillways, which were the largest in the world, each theoretically capable of accommodating twice the volume of Niagara Falls. Their role was to guarantee that the reservoir never overtopped the dam even in an emergency, for spillover would severely weaken the concrete. Although the spillways were expected to carry water only rarely, any flaws in their operation would have dire implications. Consequently, the government decided in the summer of 1941 to raise Lake Mead to its maximum level of 1,220 feet above sea level and give the spillways a full-scale test—a belated shakedown run five years after their completion.

The bureau extracted the maximum publicity value from this exercise, promoting the spillway test as an unsurpassed tourist spectacle. On August 6, before thousands of onlookers, the dam operators lowered the steel bulkheads of the Arizona spillway by twelve inches. A thundering cascade of emerald water flecked with foam poured over the gates and disappeared into the 2,200-foot incline, bursting moments later from the downstream outlet with a deafening roar.

The entertainment awed tourists for two more months. Then, on October 28, one control gate failed, springing fully open and tripling the rate of the test flow to nearly 300,000 gallons per second. When the gates were finally closed and the torrent choked off, inspectors discovered to their dismay that the turbulent water had chewed the spillway tunnel's concrete into rubble. The worst damage, at the spot where the spillway incline was joined to the original diversion tunnel, left a gaping hole 115 feet long and forty-five feet deep.

Engineers suspected that the cause was an infinitesimal misalignment of the concrete bore at the foot of the incline. The hole was repaired with specially formulated heavy-duty concrete, and the bore polished mirror-smooth. Whether the patching served its purpose would not be known for forty-two years, or until the next time the spillways were opened.

The bureau promoted the 1983 event as another tourist spectacle, scheduling the gate openings for a Fourth of July holiday weekend certain to attract huge crowds from Southern California. Yet this was no test, but the real thing: the Colorado was on a rampage, triggering emergency reservoir discharges along the river from the Grand Canyon to the Mexican border and making the spillway activation mandatory.

Lake Mead reached its all-time record elevation of 1,225.44 feet on July 24. Water continued to cascade into both spillways until early September, when the gates were again shut. Then the dam engineers discovered that the 1941 repairs had failed to achieve a permanent fix. The spillway concrete once again had been chewed to pieces.

This time the cause was identified as the poorly understood phenomenon of cavitation, which occurs when vapor pockets develop in currents flowing swiftly over irregular surfaces, even carefully finished concrete. The collapse of these pockets under the surface can pack the wallop of an explosive charge—especially in places where water cascades over an edge, as at the elbow of a spillway incline.

The theory that cavitation was the culprit gained credence from examination of the spillways at Glen Canyon Dam, which had also run at maximum capacity during the summer flood. There engineers found even worse damage, including seventy-foot holes in the underground conduits that undermined the dam's very foundation.

A second major repair program was hastily organized to equip the spillway inclines with aeration slots, or ridges to break up the water current as it cascades down. Tests at Glen Canyon Dam the following year showed that the new design worked, in principle. Whether it would eliminate cavitation damage at Hoover Dam has never been established, as the spillways have never been used again.

The Colorado's 1983 deluge damaged more than the Hoover Dam spillways. It undermined the dam's reputation, born of nearly a half-century of flawless operation, as a steadfast bulwark against the ravages of flood. Hundreds of houses, farms, and tourist resorts were destroyed or swept away by the raging river, causing hundreds of millions of dollars in damage. Considering that the Boulder Canyon Project had been represented from its inception as above all else a shield from flood, this was a serious blow.

The disaster showed that the dam had been oversold as a barrier against the river. Adequate flood control, it became evident, depended on the interaction of the dam with control operations up and down the river as well as the cooperation of Mother Nature. None of these factors had performed as expected.

The unpredictability of the elements was the key factor in the flood. After an unusually wet winter, the Rocky Mountain snowpack had reached three times its customary depth. That would not necessarily have been a major problem except that a surprise thaw in late May caught the Reclamation Bureau unprepared to deal with the surging runoff. In late June, when the bureau recognized the magnitude of its mistake, it was already too late to lower the levels of lakes Powell and Mead to absorb the coming wave. The bureau's sole option was to pass the overflow through the spillways, which only transferred the problem downstream. The result was the inundation of the floodplains of the lower Colorado, which had filled with homes and resorts during decades of complacent overbuilding.

The grief and anger the flooded-out landowners directed at the government were not assuaged by Ronald Reagan's overbearing interior secretary, James G. Watt, who ostentatiously praised the Reclamation Bureau's flood control efforts even as they were bringing the landowners bankruptcy and ruin. Watt added insult to injury by blaming the landowners for their own folly in building in the flood zone. This was revisionist history, for the most enthusiastic promoter of development in the floodplain had been Watt's department. For years, Interior's Bureau of Land Management had enticed resort developers into the floodplains by relaxing its building codes. Interior bureaucrats extended lease terms on shoreline parcels to encourage ever more ambitious proposals, hoping to generate a robust stream of revenue for the government from "camping space, food services, general stores, marine supplies, laundry facilities, playgrounds and water-oriented facilities." The Reclamation Bureau, to its credit, tried to sound the alarm about this crescendo of vulnerable construction, but the Bureau of Land Management, its sister Interior agency, steamrollered over its objections and concealed them from the leaseholders.

There could be no winners in this new battle between landowners and the government—except, as always, the river, which again reminded its would-be masters that, like any wild creature, it could be tamed only up to a point. The disaster made clear that the Boulder Canyon Project could never have fulfilled all of its creators' expectations. The dam could not guarantee an end to flooding or drought, any more than the river could provide the limitless supply of water assumed by the drafters of the compact of 1922.

Nor could it end interstate quarreling over water, as the fathers of the compact and the Boulder Canyon Project Act had hoped. If anything, the building of the dam sharpened the conflicts over the river's bounty. This was demonstrated by the long battle waged by Arizona against California and numerous other adversaries in the Colorado watershed starting as early as 1923. The fight encompassed a 1934 attempt by Arizona governor Benjamin Baker Moeur to block construction of Parker Dam, which was designed to divert California's claimed share of the river into the new Los Angeles Aqueduct, by calling out the Arizona National Guard. The guardsmen commandeered a ferry boat to reconnoiter the construction site and, in a moment out of Gilbert & Sullivan, promptly ran aground on a sandbar. Congress ended the skirmish by voting to turn Parker Dam into a federally sanctioned project.

In 1952, Arizona filed a new lawsuit, this time challenging what the state viewed as another water grab by California. The case, the third to bear the title *Arizona v. California,* would go down in history as one of the longest, costliest, and most complicated in Supreme Court history.

By then much more was at stake in the division of the Colorado than ever before. During the first postwar decade demand for water across the lower basin had exploded. As always, the Golden State had the largest appetite. From 1920 to 1950 the population of Los Angeles had nearly quadrupled to two million—growth fed in part by the water supply from the river. Southern California consumed every drop of the 4.4 million acre-feet it was allotted annually by the Boulder Canyon Project Act, and more. Indeed, the region had become addicted to its temporary entitlement to water unclaimed by Nevada and Arizona—another 900,000 acre-feet a year, bringing Southern California's total annual consumption to 5.3 million acre-feet.

But Arizona was also booming, Phoenix having evolved since 1920 into a metropolis of nearly 450,000 souls. Other new claimants unanticipated, or at least ignored, by the compact delegates in 1922 included five Indian reservations adjacent to the river, of which the Navajo reservation alone was deemed to be entitled by law to 600,000 acre-feet. Then there was the claim of Mexico, which had been awarded 1.5 million acre-feet a year by the U.S.-Mexico treaty of 1944.

The darkest shadow over the river apportionments was cast by the belated realization that Arthur Powell Davis, in promising that the river would always provide enough water to satisfy all demands, had perpetrated a fraud. Powell must have known, or at least strongly suspected, that the streamflow estimates he placed before the compact delegates were vastly overstated. But given the certainty that the negotiations would collapse if the truth became known, he had swept that fact under the rug, possibly with Hoover's connivance.

The compact rested upon the assumption that the river would deliver as much as 17.5 million acre-feet every year, allowing at least 7.5 million acre-feet to be allocated annually to the three lower basin states. But that figure had been extrapolated from a mere two decades of gauging, 1899–1921, which Davis surely knew to be an incautiously brief period of measurement. Indeed, as was shown by later studies based on tree ring data, in the Colorado watershed those years had been among the wettest in centuries. In known history the Colorado had never run with the abundance required by the compact terms. Rather than producing a reliable bounty of 17.5 million acre-feet a year, the river's flow averaged between 13 and 14 million in the post-compact years, creating an unremitting shortfall. In the twenty years prior to Arizona's lawsuit, the annual water flow at Lees Ferry exceeded 17.5 million acre-feet only four times. Unless the Supreme Court stepped in, Arizona feared, it might never recover its right to the water being consumed by California.

In light of the complexity of the underlying issues and the history of rancor between the states, it was hardly surprising that Arizona's lawsuit would drag on. But no one anticipated that it would do so for eleven years, entangling in a web of litigation not only the two named states but Nevada, New Mexico, Utah, the cities of Los Angeles and San Diego, four California irrigation districts, and the federal government. By the time the lawsuit limped to its conclusion in 1963, some 340 witnesses had testified, producing 26,242 pages of transcript to go with four thousand exhibits.

The justices' 5–3 decision appeared at first to reward Arizona with a knockout victory after its long years of obstinacy. They ruled that Congress had intended through the Boulder Canyon Project Act to limit California strictly to the 4.4 million acre-feet written into the measure and to award Arizona an irreducible 2.8 million acre-feet a year from the Colorado.

Some 900,000 acre-feet of Colorado water that had been nourishing Southern California's boisterous growth—nearly 20 percent of its consumption—was suddenly snatched from its control. Worse, the Court ruled that the sole authority to apportion surpluses and shortages from Hoover Dam belonged to the secretary of the interior. This was an astonishing expansion of federal power, granting Washington the ability not only to impose its will in interstate quarrels, but to make decisions that until then had belonged to state governments alone. Statewide farm regulations, urban growth policy, industrial development—on these and a myriad other issues, any state dependent on water from the Colorado henceforth would have to defer to the U.S. Interior Department.

This aspect of the ruling was by far its most controversial. Among its fiercest critics was Justice William O. Douglas, whose dissent blistered the majority for giving the government "a power and command over water rights in the 17 Western states that it never has had, that it always wanted, that it could never persuade Congress to grant, and that this Court up to now has consistently refused to recognize . . . the life-and-death power of dispensation of water rights long administered according to state law." The decision, he wrote, was destined to be "marked as the baldest attempt by judges in modern times to spin their own philosophy into the fabric of the law."

Hoover Dam, born in an effort by Southern California farmers and ranchers to rule their own destinies, had become the instrument by which they lost control over their destinies forever. A new set of internecine conflicts over water—between cities and farms, big cities and small towns, wet regions and arid zones—would be adjudicated not in state capitols and city halls, but in Washington, D.C. For the citizens of the seven states of the Colorado watershed—and especially the three states of the lower basin—the most important cabinet appointee in any new administration would no longer be the secretary of defense or state, but the secretary of the interior.

Arizona moved quickly to capitalize on its victory by resurrecting an old dream—the Highline Canal conceived by George Maxwell in 1922 as an alternative to the Boulder Canyon Project. In 1968, reconstituted as the Central Arizona Project, the plan was approved by Congress in the form of a $1 billion, 241-mile aqueduct to siphon Colorado River water to burgeoning metropolitan Phoenix.

Congress did not stop there. The *Arizona v. California* decision inspired the federal government to an even larger undertaking, the vast Colorado River Storage Project, a system of dams and reservoirs designed to serve the upper basin states, which, like Arizona, had never lost their fear of California's voracity for water. The project would ultimately encompass nine dams on the main stem of the river and its upstream tributaries, with the Glen Canyon Dam just upstream of the Grand Canyon as its centerpiece, all positioned to sequester the Colorado's streamflow before California or Arizona could grab it. Nor was that all: by the 1970s, seven new dams were raised downstream of Lake Mead, most of them storing water for diversion to California aqueducts and the All-American Canal.

This epidemic of dam building turned the Colorado into the most heavily exploited river in the Western Hemisphere, with virtually every possible dam site occupied by a man-made rampart and reservoir. All came on line during what hydrologists call the age of abundance, a twenty-year wet period beginning in the mid-1960s that fed unprecedented population growth across the Southwest, swelling the Colorado watershed's population to more than 33 million.

At first glance, it made sense to husband the Colorado's water to serve this thirsty migration. But Reclamation's dams and reservoirs created only the illusion of abundance, not the reality: more than 62 million acre-feet of storage capacity now existed on a river that produced an average of less than 14 million acre-feet a year. No amount of storage could erase the fundamental truth that there would not be enough water to fill it. Indeed, the profligate construction of reservoirs only contributed to waste, for 20 percent of the river's production was lost each year to evaporation. In the desert reservoirs of Lake Mead and Lake Powell, enough water disappeared into the arid skies on a single weekend to serve the domestic needs of seventeen thousand households for a year.

People kept coming. The seven basin states doubled in population to more than sixty million in the last three decades of the twentieth century. During the 1990s Las Vegas reigned as the nation's fastest-growing metropolitan area, its growth rate supported by water and electricity provided by a single source, Hoover Dam. But what the dam bestowed, nature could take away. A protracted drought began in 1999. In 2002 the river's flow dropped to six million acre-feet, the lowest mark since 1906. In the Western United States of the 1980s and 1990s, the National Academy of Sciences observed, "unlimited population growth [was] taken as an article of faith." But by the beginning of the new century, it was indisputable that the Colorado had no more surplus to be tapped. Lake Mead, already shriveled to 60 percent of maximum capacity (in 2004 it fell to its lowest level in four decades), was doomed to shrink further: An average 9.0 million acre-feet a year came in, but demand in the lower basin and apportionments to Mexico subtracted

9.5 million, and another 800,000 acre-feet were lost to evaporation. The distinctive "bathtub ring," a stratum of bleached rock encircling Lake Mead that showed graphically how far below the high water mark its level had fallen, would only grow wider.

The forecasts turned more pessimistic. Research on the effects of climate change on the watershed pointed to "reductions in snowpack, an earlier peak in spring snowmelt, higher rates of evapotranspiration, reduced late spring and summer flows, and reductions in annual runoff and streamflow," the National Research Council reported in 2007. After a momentary respite from drought in 2005, dry conditions returned in 2006, exacerbated by a warming trend: July 2006 was the second hottest July on record in the continental United States, the year as a whole the warmest ever recorded.

For a population dependent on allocations that already exceeded the river's capacity, the era of limits had arrived.

The persistent shortages underscored the changes not only in the population of the Colorado basin since 1922, but in its economics. The principal concern of the Bishop's Lodge delegates had been water for irrigation. During the intervening eighty years agriculture had taken a back seat to the exploding urban population, which demanded water for drinking and industrialization.

The urgent need to redistribute the dwindling water supply brought delegates of the seven states together in 2003 with seven water districts, five Indian tribes, and the federal government. The result was a complex of twenty-four agreements transferring 200,000 acre-feet of Colorado River water annually from Imperial Valley farmers to urban users. As compensation, the government agreed to line the All-American Canal with concrete to reduce losses from seepage. California, as always the linchpin of any distribution agreement involving the Colorado, pledged to reduce its annual consumption to its statutory maximum of 4.4 million acre-feet—albeit gradually, over a period of years, in the hope of achieving what the state's water officials called a "soft landing."

On the surface, this appeared to meet the new pattern of demand in the watershed. At a signing ceremony on October 16, held on the crest of Hoover Dam, Interior Secretary Gale Norton allowed herself to get carried away with enthusiasm. "With this agreement, conflict on the river is stilled," she declared.

As an expression of blind optimism this approached Neville Chamberlain's vision of peace at Munich. For the inexorable reality of the river could not be wished away. The tug-of-war between the farmers and the cities would only grow worse, as urban and suburban populations continued to climb.

John Wesley Powell, the great sage of Colorado exploration, had foreseen the river basin's destiny. Attending an irrigation congress in Los Angeles in 1893, he had listened with rising indignation as William Ellsworth Smythe and George Maxwell proclaimed the coming irrigation paradise. At length he got to his feet, a grizzled and one-armed icon and a prophet unheeded by his own erstwhile followers. There was not enough water in the region to achieve even a fraction of what they were proposing, he warned. "I tell you, gentlemen," he said, "you are piling up a heritage of conflict and litigation over water rights, for there is not sufficient water to supply the land."

Then he left, driven from the hall by a chorus of catcalls and boos.


Hoover Dam simultaneously built the West and confined it in a straitjacket. Development of the Arid Lands, as nineteenth-century Congresses so quaintly called the desert zone of the West, had always been subject to the unforgiving limitations of climate and resources. The dam relaxed these limitations, but it could not eradicate them. The dam allowed the West to join in, even help drive, America's transformation into the richest and most powerful nation on earth. But notwithstanding the expectations of its builders, its capacity to do so was finite.

The task facing the people of the Colorado basin today is to learn how to live in harmony with the river, as did the Indians of the plains and desert in millennia past. But it will be a difficult adjustment. Those tribes' very cultures arose out of the river's rhythms and moods; ours, by contrast, are based on the assumption that we can bend the river to our will, just as we assert our dominance over all of nature's manifestations.

Striking the necessary balance will demand all of modern man's resource-fulness and invention. The river is bountiful, but as the National Academy of Sciences reported in 2007, the traditional instrument of its control, the construction of surface reservoirs, has reached its "physical, economic, and political limits." The key to exploiting the river as a permanent resource is to shift away from the construction of public works and toward such sustainable strategies as conservation, water-efficient agriculture, and recycling. The three contentious constituencies of modern water policy—farmers, city dwellers, and environmentalists—also will have to better understand each other's needs and interests and reach mutual accommodation. Hoover Dam did its part in the harnessing of the Colorado by proving its potential to irrigate and water an explosively growing West; it is up to us to extend that potential into the future.

Given its importance, it is proper to ask if Hoover Dam could be built today. The obstacles to its construction in the 1920s were regional politics and the power trust. Political and economic opposition would certainly exist today, but to them would be added an entirely new roster of public concerns.

Foremost among these is the environment. The environmental impact statements mandated today for large-scale public and private developments by the National Environmental Policy Act of 1969 and subsequent legislation certainly would have consumed years, if not decades, of study and debate, and surely would not have become final without several rounds of litigation. Under the Endangered Species Act of 1973, a further assessment of the dam's impact on wildlife habitats in the reservoir zone and downstream would be required prior to construction. America's unconcern with those issues in the 1920s and 1930s facilitated the construction of the dam, but also led, doubtlessly, to the eradication of undiscovered, unrecorded, and unrecoverable habitats and the extermination of untold species of flora and fauna.

Legal rights ignored or casually dismissed in the 1920s, including those of Southwestern Indians and the Mexican people, could not be easily dismissed today. In light of what is known about the Colorado River's stream-flow, the water rights of those communities and others might conceivably shift the economic calculus against building the dam at all.

Seismic issues, almost entirely neglected during the original planning and design, would today be taken more seriously. Geologists have mapped twenty-six faults intersecting the abutments of Hoover Dam, most of which were unknown or underappreciated at the time of construction. Studies conducted in the late 1990s concluded that the dam would withstand what engineers call the "maximum credible earthquake" in the vicinity—a quake measuring 6.75 on the Richter scale on a fault running as close as 1.8 miles from the structure—with some cracking as far as 150 feet below the crest, but not enough to provoke failure. Yet questions about the seismic landscape around the dam site would certainly attract attention, and might conceivably rule out Black Canyon as the site for a major structure.

In the United States today, the building of great dams has fallen out of fashion. Their effect on the environment, their cost, their fallibility, and their lifespan limitations due to aging and the silting of their reservoirs—a phenomenon reduced in Lake Mead, but not eliminated, by the creation of reservoirs upstream—have all guided society to seek out other ways to harvest and conserve that most precious natural resource, water.

Still, the question of whether Hoover Dam could be built today is fundamentally unanswerable. The movement to preserve America's wild rivers is powerful, but it never had to confront a river with as much exploitable potential as the Colorado. Dams are products of their eras as well as makers of new eras. Many of the obstacles and objections that would be raised against a Hoover Dam today were to a large extent inspired by Hoover Dam's construction. In the end, speculation on what might have been is just that—speculation.

For some of its builders, Hoover Dam was the high point of a career; for others the foundation of industrial empires yet to come. Three of the fathers of Six Companies did not live to see Hoover Dam built. Will Wattis died in

1931 without ever setting foot in Black Canyon; his younger brother, Ed, who had seen the colossus begin construction, died before its completion, in 1934. By then Dad Bechtel, who had suffered his fatal mishap in Moscow, was already two years in the grave.

Charlie Shea died in 1942, age fifty-eight; the pallbearers at his San Francisco funeral included Crowe, Kaiser, Kahn, and Morrison, on what was very likely the last occasion they were ever seen together. Shea's company, J. F. Shea, had been liquidated a few years earlier for tax purposes. Felix Kahn died in 1958. Buried with him were the last vestiges of MacDonald & Kahn, which had been supplanted by a partnership he had started with Frank Modglin, his top lieutenant, and later dissolved.

At Utah Construction, Marriner Eccles succeeded the Wattis brothers as president and chairman. He remained in the latter post until 1948. That year he passed the title to Lester Corey, a Wattis cousin, the better to focus his own energies on reforming the Federal Reserve System, which he served as chairman and governor. (In recognition of his vital role in the Fed's reformation in the New Deal, the central bank's headquarters building in Washington today bears his name.)

The Japanese attack on Pearl Harbor found Utah Construction at work on a complex of secret fuel depositories under the volcanic mountains of Oahu, the first of many war contracts that would earn it $750 million. Corey transformed Utah into a leading international mining contractor, but after his death in 1964 the company hit a financial wall: it was too small and undiversified to outlast the mining downturn of that period, and too narrowly held (mostly by members of the Wattis and Eccles families) to raise new capital in the public markets. In 1976 it merged with the General Electric Company and disappeared from the roll of independent corporations. At the time of the GE deal, Utah, which had been founded in 1900 with $4,000 in capital, was worth $88 million.

Morrison-Knudsen followed a similar arc. By the 1950s the company, still under Harry Morrison's direct control, ranked as one of the biggest construction firms in the world, with nearly two hundred projects underway in the United States and another thirty-five overseas. In 1954, Morrison received that quintessential honor of American celebrity, a cover story in

*Time,* where he was labeled (immoderately) as "the driving force behind Hoover Dam" and (still more immoderately) as "the man who has done more than anyone else to change the face of the earth."

After his death in 1971, the firm continued to grow—for a time. In the 1980s a new chairman, William Agee, plunged into the rapid transit construction business, winning contracts for subways and rail lines in San Francisco, Chicago, and Washington, D.C., often with lowball bids that, it transpired, could not be fulfilled at a profit. When the government's enthusiasm for rapid transit evaporated in the 1990s, its decline into bankruptcy was hastened. The Seattle tycoon Dennis Washington bought Morrison-Knudsen out of bankruptcy in 1996 for $250 million, a mere 15 percent of its revenues the previous year, and the once great name of this most entrepreneurial partner of Six Companies disappeared, like those of Shea, MacDonald & Kahn, and Utah, into history.

Of all the partners, the names that burned brightest after the triumph of Black Canyon were Kaiser and Bechtel.

For Henry Kaiser, Hoover Dam proved to be the ideal launching pad for an impressively diverse career. Contracts for Bonneville and Grand Coulee dams were only the start. Six Companies had been underbid for the $36 million Shasta Dam in the mountains of Northern California, but Kaiser secured the $11 million contract to provide its construction cement, breaking the cement cartel that had bedeviled Harold Ickes in 1933. As war loomed in Europe, Kaiser moved into shipbuilding, ultimately delivering 1,409 "Liberty Ships" from four West Coast yards, the basis of his claim to be the most prolific shipbuilder in history. He was also among the most efficient: construction of the first Liberty Ship, built for the British government, took 196 days; by the end of 1943 that figure had been reduced to twenty-five days and the yards were launching new ships every ten hours. To meet the shipyards' demand for steel, Kaiser built the first integrated steel plant on the West Coast, locating it far from the ocean in the smoggy California hamlet of Fontana to keep it safe (so he said) from marauding Japanese bombers.

War's end brought successful new ventures in the mining and production of magnesium and aluminum and in home building—and a rare failure, the Kaiser-Frazer auto manufacturing company. Kaiser-Frazer built big sedans and a compact runabout called the Henry J, which was cheap, plain, and marketed through Sears. But the company could not compete with better-established automakers like General Motors and Ford. It went out of business in 1955, having accumulated losses totaling $111 million.

After Kaiser's death in 1967 his empire went into a tailspin. The generation of executives he had personally trained died off or retired, leaving his companies in the control of finance managers rather than engineers or entrepreneurs. In the 1980s Kaiser Steel became the prize in a takeover battle waged by, among others, the infamous insider trader Ivan Boesky and the Minneapolis corporate raider Irwin Jacobs, whose sinister nickname was "Irv the Liquidator." Eventually it was taken private in a debt-ridden buyout. Crushed by interest payments and competition from foreign steelmakers, the firm went bankrupt in 1987.

Dad Bechtel's sons Steve and Warren managed the family company after their father's death. They continued his close relationship with Henry Kaiser through the war years, joining him in shipbuilding, cement, and steel. But by 1946 they had tired of their irrepressible and publicity-hungry partner. "When you're in trouble, there's no better partner than Henry Kaiser," Steve was fond of saying; "but when you're not, he's just unlivable."

The brothers veered off into engineering and construction management, fields at which their father had excelled. Dad's little road building company evolved into the largest international contractor in the world, synonymous with monumental projects: nuclear plants, subways, industrial parks the size of cities. Bechtel Group built pipelines across the Arabian Desert and the Canadian Rockies, oil platforms in the North Sea, and the Channel Tunnel. It supervised the cleanup of Three Mile Island and the quenching of the Kuwait oilfield fires after the first Gulf War. Even its failures were gargantuan: when a Bechtel consortium was accused of slipshod supervision on Boston's massive Big Dig highway tunnel, the firm settled the accusations for $407 million—three times the consortium's profits on the project over its twenty years of construction, but a small price to pay to avert criminal charges that were speculated to be in the offing.

Despite such setbacks, Bechtel Group held an unassailable position atop the contracting world, renowned for its institutional secretiveness and gilt-edged political connections. These dated back to John McCone, an early partner of Stephen Bechtel's who became chairman of the Atomic Energy Commission (at about the time, fortuitously, that Bechtel Group began building nuclear power plants), and subsequently director of the Central Intelligence Agency. The revolving door between Bechtel's San Francisco headquarters and the corridors of power in Washington was a byword. Among the firm's executives, general counsel Caspar Weinberger later became secretary of defense and George Shultz sandwiched a stint as Bechtel president between appointments as secretary of labor and secretary of state in successive Republican administrations.

The Bechtel family's social and business connections defined the old boys' network. At the annual encampment of Bohemian Grove, the Bay Area men's club of which Herbert Hoover had been a prominent member, the Bechtel lodge hosted Henry Kissinger and Gerald Ford, along with prime ministers of countries around the globe and CEOs of major corporations—many of them current, former, or potentially future clients. As the twentieth century yielded to the twenty-first, Bechtel Group stood as the lone survivor of Six Companies, the last of its breed. Dad had started the business with a single steam shovel; his grandson and great-grandson, Steven D. Bechtel, Jr., and Riley Bechtel, were billionaires. The fulcrum on which the transformation of the family fortune had turned was Hoover Dam.

After Hoover Dam, Walker Young was named engineer in charge of Reclamation's Central Valley Project, which encompassed Shasta Dam and a system of related canals. This was a consolation prize, for he had been passed over for the job of Reclamation commissioner after Elwood Mead's death in favor of his onetime underling, John Page. Young retired from the bureau in 1948 and spent much of his remaining years assiduously monitoring articles and books published about the great project on the Colorado; friends who mailed him publications for his enjoyment often received them back with blue-penciled corrections to the text and vexed comments in the margins. He griped about writers who relied on "sensationalism" and "misinformation" in their work, for example by depicting Crowe and his foremen as "rough and tumble, tough and crude," a characterization he rejected vigorously. He died on April 23, 1982, in a nursing home in San Rafael, California, at the age of ninety-six.

Sims Ely outlasted his reputation as Boulder City's "first Hitler," as John Page had described him so indecorously. His long years of service had made him an institution in the town, seemingly as permanent and indispensable as the water tower on the hill. Although a 1932 federal law mandated his retirement as city manager in April 1939 (at the age of seventy-seven), he applied for and received a one-year deferment, and then a second. Implausibly, he seemed to have wormed his way into the good graces of Harold Ickes, who was moved to learn that Ely had once been a confidant of his own political hero, Theodore Roosevelt. In an uncharacteristic moment of sentimentality, Ickes informed Ely's son Northcutt, the former assistant to Ray Lyman Wilbur, that his father had done "a fine job out there; it was a tough one, and he has made that town something to be proud of." Ely retired to the East Coast, where his son and daughter had made their homes, and died in a Rockville, Maryland, rest home on November 11, 1954. He was ninety-two.

After the dam's completion, the city Ely had helped nurture into being struggled through a long period of existential doubt, like a roadside hamlet bypassed by a new superhighway. Some members of its business community fought to maintain its status as a federal reservation, counting on the government's restrictions on growth and its blue-nosed legal regime to preserve their diminished but still profitable franchises. They were supported by the town clergy, who cherished Boulder City as a tiny refuge from the vice-ridden territory outside the city limits. But they were opposed by the federal government, which had wearied of supporting a municipality whose raison d'être as a government protectorate had long since passed, and by an incipient pro-growth constituency, which saw great opportunities for real estate development and commercial expansion if it were turned into a conventional municipality.

The latter forces won the battle. Boulder City was incorporated as a Nevada municipality on January 4, 1960. The Prohibition-era moral code established by Sims Ely persisted for a few years more: the first bottle of liquor to be legally sold within the city limits was purchased by one Stella Kilday on September 8, 1969. Today the city continues to thrive as one of the more salubrious suburbs of Las Vegas.

Frank Crowe remained his taciturn self to the end of his life. He built three dams after Hoover, but granted precious few interviews—typically monosyllabic and self-effacing—and left behind no recorded oral histories or substantial written memoirs. It was as though he preferred to be remembered in the same vein as the great English architect Christopher Wren, whose epitaph reads, "If you seek his monument, look around you." Crowe evidently wished his works to speak for him.

His last dam, the nineteenth of his career, was Shasta, in the foothills of California's Sierra Nevada range. In 1941 he prepared the bid for Six Companies, which had been goaded into pursuing the job by Henry Kaiser, only to lose it to a competing consortium by a bare $263,000. The partners were stunned to realize that they would be on the outside looking in on what very likely would be the last great dam built in the West. Another shock promptly followed: Crowe accepted the victor's offer to become the project's boss.

In bulk, Shasta would be half-again as large as Hoover Dam, 6.2 million cubic feet of concrete. For Crowe it was the last opportunity to deploy the men and techniques that had defined his career, and their last chance to respond to his beckoning call. One day Crowe strolled down the main drag of Redding, California, the staging point for the dam site, with its mayor, greeting the old worthies who had already assembled to build the project. After they had walked a few blocks, his companion exclaimed, "My goodness, man, you know more people in this town than I do."

Shasta was finished in 1945, characteristically several months ahead of schedule. With war's end, Crowe received an offer from the War Department to become engineer-in-charge of the reconstruction of Germany in the American occupation zone. But for the first time in his life, he was confronted with a job he did not think he could handle. He was sixty-two and, unbeknownst to anyone but his family and a few close friends, had already suffered one heart attack. He preferred to remain at home in Redding, taking on the occasional consulting assignment from Morrison-Knudsen and living the life of a gentleman rancher. "My cow business is very good," he wrote to his sister Catherine on Christmas Day 1945. "I sold 10 little 2 year old steers yesterday for $178.80 each. I think I can raise them for $100.00 each." Nine weeks later, on February 26, just after a trip to the Shasta Dam site, he was stricken by another heart attack, this one fatal.

The encomiums poured in, invariably describing him as the greatest dam builder of the age, perhaps any age. This was a title he might well have accepted with mixed feelings, or at least recast as a shared achievement. As he told a reporter from *Time* in one of the last interviews he ever gave, on the occasion of the pending completion of Shasta: "If you want to see the fellow who really built this dam, go over to the mess hall. He wears a tin hat, his average age is thirty-one and he can do things."

For thousands of men who labored in Black Canyon with Frank Crowe—the real builders, as he acknowledged—their work on the project during the darkest days of the Great Depression would be the defining achievement of their lives, one they were proud to relive for the interviewers who began showing up on their doorsteps in the mid-1970s, hoping to capture their recollections before Time, the great destroyer, forever erased their memories. They testified to the heat, loneliness, toil, injury, and death the workforce bore for a few dollars a day, but also to the pride of vanquishing nature by creating something bigger than any of them, and more enduring.

Robert Parker, who had started working in Black Canyon at the age of seventeen scrubbing floors and hauling garbage at the Anderson mess hall and had worked up to shift supervisor at the Himix concrete plant, gave his witness to an interviewer from the University of Nevada in June 1986. Did he think the dam would turn out to be as important as it was? he was asked.

He replied: "I had an idea that it would make history."

# NOTES

## ABBREVIATIONS USED IN NOTES

BCMHA    Boulder City Museum and Historical Association

JCP    John Chatfield Page diary

*LAT*    *Los Angeles Times*

*LVA*    *Las Vegas Age*

*LVRJ*    *Las Vegas Review-Journal*

NARA    National Archives and Records Administration

*NRE*    *New Reclamation Era**

*NYT*    *New York Times*

OH    Oral History

OPM    Office of Personnel Management

*RE*    *The Reclamation Era*

UNLV    University of Nevada, Las Vegas

UNR    University of Nevada, Reno

USBR    United States Bureau of Reclamation

## INTRODUCTION

x    *"All thought"*: Ickes, *The Secret Diary of Harold Ickes*, Vol. 1, p. 445.

x    *"For a generation"*: *RE*, Oct. 1935, p. 194.

---

* The name of USBR's house organ changed from *New Reclamation Era (NRE)* to *Reclamation Era (RE)* with the January 1932 issue.

xi   *Within a year of Roosevelt's address:* Ward, *Water Wars,* p. 61.

xi   *"How about it?":* Ibid.

xi   *brackish stream:* Fradkin, *A River No More,* p. 321.

xii  *"the greatest dam":* RE, Oct. 1935, p. 193.

xii  *"This is what":* J. B. Priestley, "Arizona Desert," *Harper's Monthly,* March 1937, p. 365.

## CHAPTER 1: The Journey of Death

3    *By any customary measure:* See U.S. Geological Survey, "Largest Rivers in the United States," at http://pubs.water.usgs.gov/ofr87242 [accessed July 23, 2009].

4    *"an American Nile":* J. B. Lippincott, "The Colorado River," 1915, J. B. Lippincott papers, Water Resources Center Archives, University of California, Berkeley.

4    *"Every tree":* Commencement address, Brown University, June 1916; cited in Pisani, *Water and American Government,* p. 115.

4    *"The Colorado River flows":* William Ellsworth Smythe, "An International Wedding," *Sunset,* Oct. 1900, pp. 293–94.

5    *"the women wore":* Flint and Flint, eds., *The Coronado Expedition from the Distance of 460 Years,* p. 34.

6    *"the largest single western movement":* Bieber, ed., *Southern Trails to California in 1849,* p. 17.

6    *"the explorations already made":* James K. Polk, State of the Union address, Dec. 5, 1848, at http://www.gutenberg.org/dirs/etext04/supol11.txt [accessed June 20, 2009].

6    *Some 300,000 Argonauts:* deBuys and Myers, *Salt Dreams,* p. 34.

7    *"tall, strong and alert":* Maria R. Audubon, in John Woodhouse Audubon, *Audubon's Western Journal,* pp. 34, 37.

7    *"muddy stream":* Ibid., p. 166.

7    *"There was not a tree":* Ibid.

7    *"Truly here was a scene":* Ibid., p. 167.

7    *"a tincture of bluelick":* John E. Durivage, in Bieber, ed., *Southern Trails to California in 1849,* p. 234.

8    *As a U.S. senator:* Davis, *Jefferson Davis,* p. 233.

8    *"a discoloration":* William Phipps Blake, "Geological Report" in *Explora-*

*tions and Surveys for a Railroad Route from the Mississippi River to the Pacific Ocean*, p. 97.

8 *"could be traced"*: Ibid.

9 *"a tradition"*: Ibid., p. 98.

9 *"The alluvial soil"*: Ibid., p. 249.

9 *The desert was in fact a deposit*: Worster, *Rivers of Empire*, p. 195.

10 *Between 1824 and 1905*: See Salton Sea Authority, "Historical Chronology," at http://www.saltonsea.ca.gov/histchron.htm [accessed July 23, 2009].

10 *"It is, indeed"*: Blake, *Explorations and Surveys*, p. 250.

11 *"The heat was so intense"*: See Howe and Hall, *The Story of the First Decade in Imperial Valley, California*, p. 25.

11 *"It was then"*: Tout, *The First Thirty Years*, p. 25.

11 *The tract he sought*: Taze and Jessie Lamb, "Dream of a Desert Paradise," *Desert*, June 1939, p. 23.

12 *"rather mythical"*: Ives, *Report Upon the Colorado River of the West*, p. 25.

13 *"the accounts of one"*: Ibid., p. 21.

13 *"practical head of navigation"*: Ibid., p. 5.

13 *"Ours has been the first"*: Ibid., p. 110.

14 *"About nine o'clock"*: Ibid., p. 28.

14 *"pigmy"*: Ibid., p. 32.

15 *"The women generally"*: Ibid., p. 39.

15 *"Every point of the view"*: Ibid., p. 79.

15 *"like a teetotum"*: Ibid., p. 81.

15 *"For a second"*: Ibid., p. 82.

16 *"The river was narrow"*: Ibid., p. 85.

17 *"not in a condition"*: *Congressional Globe*, U.S. House, 37th Congress, 2nd Session, May 27, 1862, p. 2379.

17 *Members demanded to know*: Barbara Ann Metcalf, "Oliver M. Wozencraft in California" (master's thesis, University of Southern California, 1963), p. 94; *Congressional Globe*, May 27, 1862, p. 2381.

17 *"a heritage"*: Stegner, *Beyond the Hundredth Meridian*, p. 343.

18 *He was seventy-three*: Metcalf, "Oliver M. Wozencraft in California," p. 95.

18 *his landlord summoned*: Lamb, "Dream of a Desert Paradise," p. 27.

18 *"My dear father"*: Metcalf, "Oliver M. Wozencraft in California," p. 98.

## CHAPTER 2: Born of the Desert

19    *"To no other man"*: Otis B. Tout, cited in Margaret Darsie Morrison, "Charles Robinson Rockwood: Developer of the Imperial Valley," *Southern California Quarterly*, Dec. 1962, p. 307.

19    *President Theodore Roosevelt*: "Message from the President of the United States," Jan. 12, 1907, Senate Doc. No. 212, 59th Congress, 2nd Session.

20    *"They call him the Seer"*: Wright, *The Winning of Barbara Worth*, p. 24.

20    *Robinson chose to stay behind*: Philbrick, *Mayflower*, p. 21.

20    *Before Charles Rockwood's birth*: Morrison, "Charles Robinson Rockwood," pp. 308–9.

20    *"great hands"*: Woodbury, *The Colorado Conquest*, p. 45.

22    *"cabinet ministers"*: Alexander, *The Life of George Chaffey*, p. 280.

22    *"He took all men"*: Woodbury, *The Colorado Conquest*, p. 45.

22    *"show cases and tables"*: Rockwood, *Born of the Desert*, p. 5.

22    *"After getting his supper"*: Ibid., p. 3.

23    *"sort of a central"*: Heffernan, *Personal Recollections*, p. 2.

23    *"a glad hand artist"*: Ibid.

23    *"Of all the men"*: Ibid., p. 7.

24    *"I have been trying"*: Rockwood, *Born of the Desert*, p. 12.

24    *"believing without doubt"*: Ibid., p. 13.

25    *"I advised him"*: Heffernan, *Personal Recollections*, p. 9.

25    *"I believe I shall"*: Alexander, *The Life of George Chaffey*, pp. 283–84.

25    *"struggled through adversity"*: Hearing, U.S. House of Representatives, Committee on Irrigation of Arid Lands, March 21, 1904, p. 87.

26    *Chaffey's roots*: Frederick D. Kershner, "George Chaffey and the Irrigation Frontier," *Agricultural History*, Oct. 1953, p. 115.

26    *"the best cash crop"*: Elwood W. Mead, in Alexander, *The Life of George Chaffey*, p. xiii.

27    *The firm of Chaffey Brothers*: Alexander, *The Life of George Chaffey*, p. 36.

27    *Intrigued, Chaffey disappeared*: Ibid., p. 284.

28    *"Let me do"*: Ibid.

28    *"vital misrepresentations"*: Ibid., p. 285.

28    *"the sine qua non"*: Ibid., p. 287.

28    *deeply in the red*: Robert G. Schonfeld, "The Early Development of California's Imperial Valley," Part I, *Southern California Quarterly*, Sept. 1968, p. 288; Alexander, *The Life of George Chaffey*, p. 282.

28    *"had taken not one"*: Alexander, *The Life of George Chaffey*, p. 347.

28    *Chaffey's contract*: Letter, Chaffey to Charles D. Walcott, Feb. 16, 1907, cited in Ibid., pp. 347–48.

28    *"payable when the company"*: Alexander, *The Life of George Chaffey*, p. 348.

28    *In practical terms*: Tout, *The First Thirty Years*, p. 47; see also *LAT*, Dec. 20, 1905.

29    *"without so much"*: Tout, *The First Thirty Years*, p. 48.

29    *"the project, by creating"*: Ibid., p. 292.

29    *the valley quickly attracted settlers*: Kennan, *The Salton Sea*, p. 25.

29    *The very first arrived*: Cory, *The Imperial Valley and the Salton Sink*, p. 1268; Tout, *The First Thirty Years*, p. 58.

29    *"the land is free"*: Schonfeld, "The Early Development of California's Imperial Valley," p. 289.

30    *Hitching up their Fresnos*: deStanley, *The Salton Sea*, p. 23.

30    *Buzzards Roost*: Tout, *The First Thirty Years*, p. 25.

30    *"Water turned through gate"*: Alexander, *The Life of George Chaffey*, p. 292.

31    *The most prominent vegetation*: Helen Hosmer, "Triumph and Failure in the Imperial Valley" in Watkins, *The Grand Colorado*, p. 209.

31    *"only a trickle"*: Waters, ed., *The Colorado*, p. 299.

31    *"of questionable pedigree"*: Heffernan, *Personal Recollections*, p. 10.

31    *"a 500,000-acre bowl"*: Imperial Irrigation District, "The Colorado River and Imperial Valley Soils," p. 6.

32    *"My brother, Harold"*: Evalyn B. Westerfield in Tout, *The First Thirty Years*, p. 72.

32    *"in the back room"*: Howe and Hall, *The Story of the First Decade in Imperial Valley, California*, p. 147.

33    *"Quitters helped"*: Tout, *The First Thirty Years*, p. 63.

33    *"an accursed region"*: Alexander, *The Life of George Chaffey*, p. 272.

33    *two thousand settlers*: Hundley, *Water and the West*, p. 21.

33    *One year later*: Cory, *The Imperial Valley and the Salton Sink*, p. 1269.

33   *1905 statistics:* Ibid.

34   *"swamped by prosperity":* Sykes, *The Colorado Delta,* p. 112.

34   *Los Angeles banks refused:* Cory, *The Imperial Valley and the Salton Sink,* p. 1259.

34   *"with no money":* Rockwood, *Born of the Desert,* pp. 20–21.

34   *"a craft loaded":* Alexander, *The Life of George Chaffey,* p. 298.

### CHAPTER 3: Rockwood's Gamble

35   *Rockwood obtained the funds:* Heffernan, *Personal Recollections,* p. 18.

35   *"I fell heir":* Ibid., p. 19.

35   *"birds of evil omen":* Tout, *The First Thirty Years,* p. 96.

36   *On average, the river carried:* Waters, *The Colorado,* p. 300.

36   *the greater the volume of water flowing:* Kennan, *The Salton Sea,* p. 32.

36   *requiring thirty dredges:* Hearings, Southern Pacific Imperial Valley Claim, House Committee on Claims, Feb. 24, 1908, p. 5.

37   *damage claims:* Cory, *The Imperial Valley and the Salton Sink,* p. 1277.

37   *one foot higher:* Ibid., p. 1278.

38   *"not merely a matter":* Smythe, *The Conquest of Arid America,* p. 266.

38   *"Government ownership":* Alexander, *The Life of George Chaffey,* p. 331.

39   *"a blunder":* Cory, *The Imperial Valley and the Salton Sink,* p. 1290.

39   *"I doubt as to whether":* Rockwood, *Born of the Desert,* p. 34.

40   *The first warning:* Howe and Hall, *The Story of the First Decade in Imperial Valley, California,* p. 101.

40   *"We were not alarmed":* Rockwood, *Born of the Desert,* p. 35.

40   *His solution was to blockade:* Howe and Hall, *The Story of the First Decade in Imperial Valley, California,* p. 102.

40   *"a warning cry":* Ibid., p. 103.

41   *stringent terms:* Hearings, Southern Pacific Imperial Valley Claim, House Committee on Claims, April 1, 1908, pp. 172–74; *LAT,* May 27, 1905.

42   *Epes Randolph arrived:* Klein, *The Life and Legend of E. H. Harriman,* p. 379.

42   *"considering everything":* Hearings, Southern Pacific Imperial Valley Claim, Feb. 24, 1908, p. 6.

42   *"playing with fire":* Ibid., p. 7.

42    *"Are you certain"*: Klein, *The Life and Legend of E. H. Harriman*, p. 380.

43    *At least once the cable snapped*: Tout, *The First Thirty Years*, p. 101.

43    *"The water was higher"*: Ibid.

44    *At 5:12 A.M.*: Fradkin, *The Great Earthquake and Firestorms of 1906*, p. 52.

44    *San Francisco was the western hub*: Ibid., p. 186.

44    *"the bustle"*: Cory, *The Imperial Valley and the Salton Sink*, p. 1315.

44    *Cory was an accomplished engineer*: See Tout, *The First Thirty Years*, p. 103.

45    *"The water"*: Hearings, Southern Pacific Imperial Valley Claim, Feb. 24, 1908, p. 8.

45    *The drop in elevation*: Cory, *The Imperial Valley and the Salton Sink*, pp. 1292–93.

45    *"This would mean"*: Hearings, Southern Pacific Imperial Valley Claim, Feb. 24, 1908, p. 10.

46    *the main business district collapsed*: LAT, July 1, 1906.

46    *Mexican tax inspectors*: Hearings, Southern Pacific Imperial Valley Claim, Feb. 24, 1908, p. 11.

47    *"most capable and efficient"*: Heffernan, *Personal Recollections*, p. 21.

47    *The gate buckled*: Hearings, Southern Pacific Imperial Valley Claim, Feb. 24, 1908, p. 12; Cory, *The Imperial Valley and the Salton Sink*, p. 1320.

47    *"by exhausting the capacities"*: C. W. Runge, "Fruitful Imperial—A Dream Come True," in *Southern Pacific Bulletin*, May 1921, p. 11.

47    *"into that hole"*: Hearings, Southern Pacific Imperial Valley Claim, Feb. 24, 1908, p. 8.

48    *a mere $20,000 in profit*: Ibid., p. 32.

48    *"I would not recommend"*: Ibid., p. 9.

48    *Harriman-Roosevelt relationship*: Klein, *The Life and Legend of E. H. Harriman*, pp. 360–71.

48    *"malefactors of great wealth"*: Kennan, *The Salton Sea*, p. 79.

48    *"It does not seem fair"*: Senate Doc. No. 212, 59th Congress, 2nd Session, p. 161.

48    *"I assume"*: Ibid., p. 162.

49    *"Can you bring"*: Ibid.

49  *"Close that break"*: Tout, *The First Thirty Years,* p. 107.

50  *"purely a gratuity"*: Hearings, Southern Pacific Imperial Valley Claim, House Committee on Claims, Jan. 23, 1917, p. 23.

50  *"That was the best"*: Kahn, *Our Economic and Other Problems,* p. 49.

50  *"This valley was worth saving"*: Kennan, *The Salton Sea,* p. 105.

51  *"diversion dams and distribution systems"*: The text of Roosevelt's Jan. 12, 1907, address to Congress, much of which was devoted to a fruitless plea for the lawmakers to make good his pledge of reimbursement to E. H. Harriman, is in Roosevelt, *Presidential Addresses and State Papers,* vol. 5, pp. 1082–1095.

## CHAPTER 4: The Lord's Dam Site

52  *"We had in the back"*: Edna Jackson Ferguson OH, April 15, 1975, Boulder City Public Library.

53  *Four barges:* Wesley R. Nelson, "Construction of the Boulder Dam: Government Engineers and Surveyors Have Made a Notable Record on Exacting, Perilous Work," in *The Story of the Hoover Dam,* p. 134.

54  *the first white woman:* Ferguson OH.

54  *U.S. Geological Survey:* The report of the Grand Canyon expedition appeared in *National Geographic,* May 1924, p. 472ff.

55  *"We would walk"*: Ferguson OH.

55  *Edison Electric Company:* See Myers, *River of Controversy* [unpag.].

56  *Its engineers cooked up:* Details of the plan are in Arthur Powell Davis, *Report on Problems of Imperial Valley and Vicinity.*

56  *"the unprecedented character"*: Ibid.

57  *"A rock-fill structure"*: Ibid.

57  *Imperial Valley population and valuation:* Robert G. Schonfeld, "The Early Development of California's Imperial Valley," Part II, *Southern California Quarterly,* Sept. 1968, p. 418.

57  *the president's half-brother:* See Hearings, House Committee on Irrigation of Arid Lands, H.R. 6044, July 9, 1919, p. 41.

58  *"They have as many"*: Hearings, House Committee on Irrigation of Arid Lands, H.R. 11449, June 15, 1922, p. 8.

58  *"we took out"*: Ibid., p. 270.

58     *The Ohio-born Harrison Gray Otis:* Gottlieb and Wolt, *Thinking Big,* pp. 17–21.

59     *The unions acknowledged:* Ibid., p. 84ff.

59     *Harry Chandler:* Ibid., pp. 121–23.

59     *"we have no rights":* Hearings, House Committee on Irrigation of Arid Lands, H.R. 6044, July 9, 1919, p. 34.

59     *unpaid bills:* Ibid., p. 119.

59     *"Not one cent":* Ibid.

59     *"To save themselves":* Hearings, House Committee on Irrigation of Arid Lands, H.R. 11449, Feb. 23, 1924, p. 248.

59     *soared in value:* Hearings, House Committee on Irrigation and Reclamation, H.R. 2903, Feb. 29, 1924, p. 1586.

60     *"There is an unfortunate":* Gottlieb and Wolt, *Thinking Big,* p. 169.

60     *"imminent danger":* Hearings, House Committee on Irrigation of Arid Lands, H.R. 11449, Feb. 23, 1924, p. 8.

61     *The road was soon carrying:* Hearings, Senate Committee on Irrigation and Reclamation, S. 727, Dec. 17, 1924, p. 178.

63     *"How soon":* Walker Rollo Young OH, June 23, 1975, Boulder City Public Library.

63     *"The Colorado":* Ibid.

63     *Mishaps on the water:* Wesley R. Nelson, "Government Engineers and Surveyors Have Made a Notable Record," p. 134.

64     *Passing storms:* Ibid., p. 133.

64     *a violent squall:* Ibid.

64     *It was possible to reach:* Wesley R. Nelson, "Surveying in Black Canyon," *RE,* Oct. 1932, p. 173.

65     *"In the sun":* Ibid.

65     *cheerful, redheaded youth:* Young OH.

65     *"a miserable government camp":* Murl Emery OH, undat., UNLV.

67     *Fall-Davis Report:* The report is formally designated Senate Doc. No. 142, 67th Congress, 2nd Session.

68     *Young and Black Canyon:* Young OH.

69     *Nature struck back:* Nelson, "Government Engineers and Surveyors," p. 134.

69   *Because the new site sat:* Young OH; Donald C. Jackson, "Boulder Dam: Origins of Siting and Design," Symposium on the History of the Bureau of Reclamation, June 2002, at www.usbr.gov/history, p. 6.

69   *"As I've said many times":* Young OH.

## CHAPTER 5: Hoover Steps In

73   *"endless litigation":* Colorado River Commission, *Minutes of the First Meeting,* Jan. 26, 1922, p. 2.

73   *"to secure development":* Ibid., p. 3.

74   *The U.S. Constitution allows states:* See Article I, Section 10.

75   *Rainfall and snow:* Olson, *The Colorado River Compact,* Appendix II, Exhibit JJJ.

75   *Arizona had the largest share:* Ibid.

76   *The riparian doctrine:* For cogent discussions of the riparian and appropriation doctrines, see Worster, *Rivers of Empire,* p. 88, and Hundley, *Dividing the Waters,* pp. 68–73.

77   *Kansas v. Colorado:* See 206 U.S. 46, 95.

77   *"probably 100":* Hearings, House Committee on Irrigation and Reclamation, H.R. 2903, Feb. 9, 1924, p. 45.

77   *He believed:* Olson, *The Colorado River Compact,* p. 60.

78   *"the energetic":* LAT, April 2, 1920.

78   *"barren desert":* LAT, April 12, 1920.

78   *Delph Carpenter was convinced:* Tyler, *Silver Fox of the Rockies,* p. 119.

78   *Carpenter and* Wyoming v. Colorado: Ibid., p. 134.

79   *The delegates found this logic:* Hundley, *Dividing the Waters,* p. 108.

79   *Arthur Powell Davis's estimates:* See Davis, "Report on Problems of Imperial Valley and Vicinity," (Fall-Davis Report) Table No. 4, p. 33.

79   *A dismayed Davis:* Colorado River Commission, *Minutes of the Sixth Meeting,* Jan. 30, 1922, p. 77; see also Davis to Hoover, Feb. 3, 1922, cited in Hundley, *Dividing the Waters,* p. 146.

80   *In the heat of debate:* For the angry contretemps, see Colorado River Commission, *Minutes of the Seventh Meeting,* Jan. 30, 1922, p. 95.

80   *"I have to look":* Ibid., p. 100.

80   *Hammered by its worst blizzard: Washington Post,* Jan. 29, 1922.

81     *"Is it worth while"*: Colorado River Commission, *Minutes of the Seventh Meeting,* Jan. 30, 1922, p. 141.

81     *Wyoming had filed:* Hundley, *Dividing the Waters,* p. 76.

82     *"Each state":* Wyoming v. Colorado, 259 U.S. 419.

82     *"We simply must use":* Carpenter to Emerson, Sept. 7, 1922, cited in Hundley, *Dividing the Waters,* p. 181.

83     *"In order to get":* Arnold Kruckman, "Inside Story of River Conference," *Saturday Night,* Nov. 18, 1922, p. 5.

84     *Carpenter proposed simply:* Colorado River Commission, *Minutes of the Eleventh Meeting,* Nov. 11, 1922, p. 20.

84     *"I scribbled it":* Hoover, *Memoirs,* Vol. 2, p. 116.

84     *Carpenter's proposal had been circulating:* Moeller, *Phil Swing and Boulder Dam,* p. viii.

84     *annual flows to be highly variable:* See Fall-Davis Report, p. 5.

85     *Later research:* See National Academy of Sciences, *Colorado River Basin Water Management: Evaluating and Adjusting to Hydroclimatic Variability* (2007), p. 81.

85     *"Don't we predicate":* Ibid., p. 91.

85     *"again open a matter":* Colorado River Commission, *Minutes of the 21st Meeting,* Nov. 20, 1922, p. 108.

86     *"Mr. Carpenter":* National Academy of Sciences, *Colorado River Basin Water Management,* p. 111.

86     *"California should let it":* William J. Carr OH, 1959, UCLA Special Collections, pp. 142–43.

86     *Californians and Hoover:* Ibid., pp. 143–44.

87     *"the early construction":* Colorado River Commission, *Minutes of the 27th Meeting,* Nov. 24, 1922, p. 303.

88     *Ben Hur Room: LAT,* Nov. 25, 1922.

## CHAPTER 6: Battlegrounds

89     *Swing on the cliff:* Swing, "The Struggle for Boulder Dam," pp. 58–59, Swing Papers, UCLA.

91     *only incorporated city:* Moeller, *Phil Swing and Boulder Dam,* p. 9.

91     *"Every member in there":* Swing, "The Struggle for Boulder Dam," p. 49.

91    *"I soon found out"*: Ibid., p. 63.

92    *"Michigan members"*: Mullendore to Stetson, undated [1923], in Olson, *The Colorado River Compact,* Appendix II, Exhibit DD.

92    *George Hebard Maxwell*: Nelson, *The Lobbyist,* pp. 22–27.

93    *"We believe"*: Maxwell's *Talisman* 6 (March 1906), cited in Pisani, *Water and American Government,* p. 18.

93    *"The establishment"*: Hearings, Development of Lower Colorado River Basin, Federal Power Commission, Sept. 23, 1923, p. 97.

94    *"My recommendation is"*: Hoover to George Christian, Jr., Dec. 12, 1922, Hoover Papers, Hoover Presidential Library, West Branch IA, cited in Hundley, *Dividing the Waters,* p. 234, n44.

95    *"The pages of space"*: George W. P. Hunt, "Why I Oppose the Approval of the Colorado River Compact," pp. 2–3, Central Arizona Project Collection, Arizona State University.

95    *Los Angeles seized*: Myers, *River of Controversy* [unpag.]

96    *"Shall California Be Sovietized?"*: Thompson, *Confessions of the Power Trust,* p. 514.

97    *"No great project"*: Burdett Moody, "The Colorado River–Boulder Canyon Project and the All-American Canal" [1925], Special Collections, Young Research Library, UCLA.

97    *nine boat trips*: Water Supply Paper 556, U.S. Geological Survey, 1925.

97    *"the most gigantic"*: Boyer and Webb, *Damming Grand Canyon,* p. 268.

97    *His counterproposal*: Ibid., pp. 264–65.

98    *he proved so surly*: Ibid., p. 266.

98    *sagging farm economy*: Robinson, *Water for the West,* p. 43.

99    *farmers had repaid*: Rocca, *America's Master Dam Builder,* p. 138.

99    *"They have erected"*: Quoted in Pisani, *Water and American Government,* p. 138.

99    *"the resignation of one"*: Work to Benjamin Fly, June 26, 1923, Box 136, Swing Papers, UCLA.

100   *"selfish, calculating"*: Johnson to his sons, Dec. 7, 1920, *Diary Letters.*

101   *"particularly . . . the hold"*: Johnson to Swing, Aug. 25, 1924, Swing Papers, UCLA.

101   *"I am here"*: Hearings, House Committee on Irrigation and Reclamation, H.R. 2903, Feb. 15, 1924, p. 97.

102  *"This committee has got"*: Ibid., p. 99.

103  *"The coming of the city"*: Hearings, House Committee on Irrigation and reclamation, H.R. 2903, Feb. 15, 1924, p. 100.

103  *"All the opposition"*: Ibid., p. 123.

103  *"I have given it"*: Ibid., p. 121.

104  *"The allied forces"*: Swing to Earl C. Pound, April 11, 1924, Swing Papers, UCLA.

104  *eleventh-richest person*: Gottlieb and Wolt, *Thinking Big*, p. 125.

105  *"economic absurdity"*: Hearings, House Committee on Irrigation and Reclamation, H.R. 2903, April 18, 1924, p. 1596.

105  *"Well, I do not know"*: Ibid., p. 1613.

105  *"just another one"*: Childers to Swing, April 16, 1924, Swing Papers, UCLA.

105  *three-to-one margin*: Moeller, *Phil Swing and Boulder Dam*, pp. 65–66.

106  *Carpenter hoped that Arizona*: Hundley, *Dividing the Waters*, pp. 253–54.

107  *"taking the project"*: Hoover to Tax Payers Association of Imperial County, Dec. 30, 1922, cited in ibid., p. 229.

107  *"Whenever we uncover"*: Johnson to "My dear Boys," May 8, 1928, *Diary Letters*.

107  *"Dr. Work . . . and I"*: Hoover, *Memoirs*, Vol. 2, p. 117.

107  *"assail, belittle"*: Swing, "The Struggle for Boulder Dam," p. 86.

108  *"the most disagreeable thing"*: Johnson to Boys, March 2, 1928, *Diary Letters*.

108  *"the stupendous importance"*: Johnson to Archibald M. Johnson, Dec. 12, 1925, *Diary Letters*.

108  *"It is the old method"*: Johnson to McClatchy, Dec. 9, 1925, *Diary Letters*.

108  *"I believe"*: Mellon to Smith, March 18, 1926, copy in Squires Papers, Special Collections, UNLV.

109  *Midwest flood of 1927*: McPhee, *The Control of Nature*, p. 42.

109  *"completely under water"*: Swing, "The Struggle for Boulder Dam," p. 72.

109  *he found the farmers*: See Moeller, *Phil Swing and Boulder Dam*, pp. 98–99.

110  *"A train load"*: Swing, "The Struggle for Boulder Dam," p. 73.

110  *"publicity bureau"*: Schlesinger, *The Crisis of the Old Order*, p. 65.

110  *"chloroforming"*: Lower, *A Bloc of One*, p. 235.

110  *College professors*: See *NYT*, May 30, 1928; June 2, 1928; June 21, 1928.

110  *"The article"*: *Washington Herald*, undated, in Swing Papers, Box 138, UCLA.

111    *Some of this money was handed:* See *NYT,* April 25, 1928; *LAT,* April 30, 1928; Hundley, *Dividing the Waters,* p. 273.

111    *Material from the FTC's investigation:* Thompson, *Confessions of the Power Trust,* p. vii.

111    *"defy the power lobby":* Moeller, *Phil Swing and Boulder Dam,* p. 112.

111    *He had been summoned:* See J. David Rogers, "Failure of the St. Francis Dam," at http://web.mst.edu/~rogersda/st_francis_dam/ [accessed July 3, 2009].

112    *"Of all the dams":* Los Angeles Coroner's Inquest, 1928, p. 13, quoted in Outland, *Man-Made Disaster,* p. 46.

112    *Pronouncing the structure safe:* Outland, *Man-Made Disaster,* p. 68.

112    *At an Edison construction camp:* Catherine Mulholland, *William Mulholland and the Rise of Los Angeles,* p. 321.

113    *It still reigns as the worst failure:* Rogers, "Failure of the St. Francis Dam."

113    *"envied those":* Ibid.

113    *Mulholland nursed suspicions:* Mulholland, *William Mulholland and the Rise of Los Angeles,* p. 327.

113    *A dozen inquests:* Rogers, "Failure of the St. Francis Dam."

114    *"an indictment":* Wall Street Journal, March 16, 1928.

114    *"men of the same":* Guy L. Jones, "San Francisquito Canyon Dam Disaster Report," 1928, quoted in Outland, *Man-Made Disaster,* p. 194.

115    *In the waning afternoon daylight:* Moeller, *Phil Swing and Boulder Dam,* p. 115; *NYT,* May 26, 1928.

115    *an uproar ensued:* NYT, May 30, 1928.

116    *"I am a good deal disturbed":* Quint and Ferrell, eds., *The Talkative President,* p. 111.

117    *"As private enterprise":* Calvin Coolidge, Sixth Annual Message, Dec. 4, 1928, at www.presidency.ucsb.edu/ws/?pid=29569 [accessed July 3, 2009].

117    *"the danger":* NYT, Dec. 13, 1928.

117    *The panel endorsed:* "Report of the Colorado River Board on the Boulder Canyon Project," Nov. 24, 1928, p. 3.

117    *"competent to carry safely":* Ibid., p. 4.

118    *"death knell":* LAT, Dec. 4, 1928.

118    *"it now is":* Ibid.

118    *"unduly pessimistic":* *LAT,* Dec. 5, 1928.

119    *Among the other guests:* Donald C. Jackson and Norris Hundley, "Privilege and Responsibility: William Mulholland and the St. Francis Dam Disaster," *California History,* Fall 2004, p. 47.

120    *"a challenge":* Elwood W. Mead, "The Boulder Canyon Project: A Colossal Enterprise," *Civil Engineering,* Oct. 1930, p. 3.

120    *Of that sum:* Ibid.

120    *"I really think":* Johnson to Boys, Dec. 18, 1928, *Diary Letters.*

121    *Squires's arrival in Las Vegas:* Charles P. Squires, "Las Vegas, Nevada, Its Romance and History" [unpub.], pp. 267–68, Squires Papers, Special Collections, UNLV.

121    *He became intimately involved:* "A Pen Picture of the Colorado River Commission and Its Work," *Nevada State Journal* (Reno), Nov. 25, 1922.

122    *"There was people":* Leon Rockwell OH, 1969, UNR.

122    *"People started":* Dean Pulsipher OH, Aug. 9, 1986, Boulder City Public Library.

## CHAPTER 7: Hurry-Up Crowe

123    *"he was all over":* Robert Parker OH, June 2, 1986, Boulder City Public Library.

123    *"Down by number nine":* Bud Keating OH, Sept. 7, 1997, Boulder City Public Library.

124    *"A lanky young man":* Paul, *Desperate Scenery,* p. 51.

124    *"Bums and Bohunks":* Ibid., p. 76.

124    *"5,000 men":* "The Earth Movers—I," *Fortune,* Aug. 1943, p. 212.

124    *"Frank Crowe was":* Richard "Curley" Francis OH, March 4, 1975, Boulder City Public Library.

124    *"I only knew him":* Marion Allen OH, April 14, 1986, Boulder City Public Library.

124    *"I will go":* Frank Crowe to Emma Crowe ("Mamma"), Aug. 25, 1909. The author is indebted to John Hollstein for providing a copy of this letter.

125    *Marie Crowe was dead:* Rocca, *America's Master Dam Builder,* p. 35.

125    *He knew every man:* Robert Parker OH, June 2, 1986, Boulder City Public Library.

125    *his daughters could not recall:* Allen OH.

# NOTES

125  *It became Crowe family lore:* Interview, John Hollstein.

125  *Crowe and lieutenants:* See Red Wixson OH, undated, Boulder City Public Library.

125  *at a moment's notice:* Allen, *Hoover Dam and Boulder City,* pp. 41–42.

126  *"the Bous family":* Ibid., p. 31.

126  *"You know what":* Saul "Red" Wixson OH, Boulder City Public Library.

126  *"At Jackson Lake":* Crowe to Mrs. Floyd Bous, Sept. 11, 1937, reprinted in Allen, *Hoover Dam and Boulder City,* p. 32.

126  *"Somebody [who] got caught sleeping":* Wixson OH.

127  *"He of course rode herd":* Elton Garrett OH, Nov. 10–11, 1986, Boulder City Public Library.

127  *"Safety Matter of Human Values":* LVRJ, Feb. 18, 1932.

128  *"I'm proud":* Tex Nunley OH. Nov. 10–11, 1986, Boulder City Public Library.

128  *When cut timber:* Paul, *Desperate Scenery,* p. 50.

129  *"I had spent":* "The Earth Movers—I," p. 103.

129  *Crowe's early years:* S. O. Harper, Walker R. Young, and W. V. Greeley, "Memoirs of Deceased Members: Francis Trenholm Crowe," *Transactions of the American Society of Civil Engineers,* Vol. 113, 1948, p. 1397; Rocca, *America's Master Dam Builder,* p. 4.

130  *"If I show up":* Harper, Young, and Greeley, "Memoirs of Deceased Members," p. 1398.

130  *bison skull and lariat:* Ibid.

130  *"I do not know":* Weymouth to F. H. Newell, Dec. 5, 1911, F. T. Crowe Official Personnel File, U.S. Office of Personnel Management (OPM).

130  *Arriving by train:* Rocca, *America's Master Dam Builder,* p. 14.

131  *"designed principally":* Paul, *A Ghost Town on the Yellowstone,* p. 137.

132  *Then James Munn:* Weymouth to H. N. Savage, October [?] 1906, F. T. Crowe file, OPM.

133  *Having been tipped to the trail:* Paul, *Desperate Scenery,* p. 61.

133  *Along for the ride:* Ibid., pp. 70–72.

134  *one murder:* Ibid., p. 218.

134  *a forest fire:* Ibid., p. 200.

135  *painful and afflicted pregnancy:* Rocca, *America's Master Dam Builder,* p. 35.

135    *six days' leave:* See Crowe, "Application for leave of absence," Oct. 17, 1911, and Weymouth to Newell, Nov. 24, 1911, F. T. Crowe file, OPM.

135    *Crowe had brought it in:* The $465,000 estimate is Weymouth's (Weymouth to Newell, Dec. 5, 1911); Crowe placed the figure at exactly $463,000 (Crowe to *Reclamation Record,* Oct. 2, 1914). Both documents are in the F. T. Crowe file, OPM.

135    *Arrowrock diversion tunnel:* Rocca, *America's Master Dam Builder,* p. 40.

136    *The Arrowrock system:* Ibid., p. 41.

136    *In this case Munn:* See ibid., pp. 45–46. Rocca writes that Crowe and Munn "agreed" to halt the concreting, but as weather conditions in Boise were no worse than they had been at Jackson Lake, it seems likely that Munn's authority was the deciding factor.

136    *Crowe stepped up the pace:* Ibid., p. 46.

137    *"distasteful":* Weymouth to A. P. Davis, Aug. 26, 1914, F. T. Crowe file, OPM.

137    *bureaucratic minutiae:* Rocca, *America's Master Dam Builder,* pp. 59–62.

137    *"I am simply":* Crowe to Weymouth, Oct. 4, 1919, F. T. Crowe file, OPM.

138    *death of John Crowe:* Rocca, *America's Master Dam Builder,* p. 106.

138    *Crowes in Denver:* Ibid., p. 124.

138    *"He makes no secret":* *Yakima Daily Republic,* May 10, 1924.

138    *"never-my-belly":* J. Muersinge, "Memories: Boulder City, Nevada, and the Workers Who Built the Hoover Dam," p. 13. The memoir is in the collection of the Boulder City Museum and Historical Association (BCMHA).

139    *"About a dozen":* Crowe, "James Munn: Builder of Men and a Foster Parent of M-K," *The Em-Kayan* (house organ of Morrison-Knudsen Co., Inc.), May 1943, p. 6.

140    *"Shooting of Dan McGrew":* Herbert Solow, "The Big Builder from Boise," *Fortune,* Dec. 1956.

140    *"a long, slim kid":* Frank Crowe, "James Munn," *The Em-Kayan,* May 1943, p. 6.

140    *"What have you got?":* Solow, "Big Builder," *Fortune,* Dec. 1956.

140    *The partners pared expenses:* Wolf, *Big Dams and Other Dreams,* p. 30.

140    Wattis offer: "The Earth Movers—I," p. 102.

141    *"Dam Hetch Hetchy!":* Muir, *The Wilderness World of John Muir,* p. 320. Muir's lines originally appeared in his book *The Yosemite,* published in 1912.

141 *San Francisco's credit:* Righter, *The Battle over Hetch Hetchy,* p. 144.

142 *remoteness of Deadwood:* Wm. Joe Simonds, "The Boise Project," U.S. Bureau of Reclamation, at www.usbr.gov/dataweb/projects/idaho/boise/history.html [accessed Sept. 23, 2008].

142 *"raised in a large tin tub":* Rocca, *America's Master Dam Builder,* p. 169.

142 *Conditions were already so bad:* Crowe to Catherine [sister], Dec. 26, 1929. The author thanks John Hollstein for providing a copy of this letter.

142 *Crowe returned the following March:* Rocca, *America's Master Dam Builder,* pp. 171–72.

142 *His first work crews arrived: Engineering News-Record,* July 23, 1931.

142 *The road remained unserviceable:* Ibid.; Rocca, *America's Master Dam Builder,* p. 172.

**CHAPTER 8: The Silver Spike**

144 *he had steamed in by private railcar:* John Cahlan OH, 1970, University of Nevada, Reno.

145 *Special trains carried: LAT,* Sept. 16, 1930.

146 *"Dusty trip":* This and all further diary entries are from the diary of John Chatfield Page, archived at the Boulder City Museum and Historical Association and in facsimile at www.library.unlv.edu/diaries_hooverdam [accessed July 3, 2009]. This first entry was made Sept. 14, 1930. Diary entries will henceforth be identified as JCP.

146 *Wilbur made his way to the center:* Elton Garrett OH, Nov. 10–11, 1986, Boulder City Public Library.

146 *Newsreel cameras:* JCP, Sept. 17, 1930.

147 *Bent double: LAT,* Sept. 18, 1930.

147 *"While I had never been":* Wilbur, *Memoirs,* p. 453.

147 *"Of course":* Winthrop A. Davis, in "Hoover Dam," transcript at http://www.pbs.org/wgbh/amex/hoover/filmmore/transcript/transcript1.html#wdavis [accessed July 3, 2009].

147 *federal public works budget:* Stein, *The Fiscal Revolution in America,* p. 20.

147 *"I am convinced":* Hoover, *Memoirs,* Vol. 3, p. 58.

148 *"Mr. Mellon had":* Ibid., pp. 30–31. The authenticity of the quotation attributed to Mellon, which appears nowhere save in Hoover's memoir, has been

challenged by some historians, although the sentiment attributed to Mellon appears accurate.

148 *"we should use"*: Ibid., p. 31.

148 *"From an economic viewpoint"*: Ibid., p. 43.

148 *Limited largely to the keeping*: Kennedy, *Freedom from Fear*, pp. 30, 55.

149 *"He has in respect"*: Lippmann, *Interpretations, 1931–1932*, pp. 67–68.

149 *"organized reassurance"*: Galbraith, *The Great Crash 1929*, pp. 137–38.

150 *"held up fairly well"*: Hoover, *Memoirs*, Vol. 3, p. 45.

150 *U.S. Steel became the first*: Kennedy, *Freedom from Fear*, p. 87.

150 *"to continue and even expand"*: Hoover, *Memoirs*, Vol. 3, p. 42.

150 *Peacetime construction spending*: Kennedy, *Freedom from Fear*, p. 57.

150 *Public, private construction spending*: Stein, *The Fiscal Revolution in America*, p. 22.

151 *"instituted systematic:* Herbert Hoover, State of the Union address, Dec. 3, 1929, at http://www.presidency.ucsb.edu/ws/index.php?pid=22021 [accessed July 3, 2009].

151 *Proposals for even larger programs*: Stein, *The Fiscal Revolution in America*, p. 23.

152 *Savage had compiled*: John L. Savage, "Present Status of Boulder Canyon Designs," Feb. 5, 1930, U.S. Bureau of Reclamation.

152 *Applications had arrived*: Wilbur and Ely, *The Hoover Dam Power and Water Contracts and Related Data*, p. 18.

153 *"an invitation"*: Northcutt Ely, "Dr. Ray Lyman Wilbur, Third President of Stanford University and Secretary of the Interior," address to the Fortnightly Club of Redlands, California, Meeting No. 1530, Dec. 16, 1994.

153 *"Start miserable little squabbling"*: Wilbur, *Memoirs*, p. 445.

153 *"from a stock company"*: Ibid., p. 446.

153 *explicit language of the statute*: The public power preference is embodied in the Boulder Canyon Project Act, H.R. 5773, at Sec. 5(c), incorporating Sec. 7(a) of the Federal Water Power Act, 49 Stat. 863.

154 *"champion and propagandist"*: Amos Pinchot, "Hoover and Power," *The Nation*, Aug. 5, 1931, p. 126.

154 *He dumped the matter*: Wilbur, *Memoirs*, p. 447.

154 *On their first pass:* See Wilbur and Ely, *The Hoover Dam Project and Water Contracts and Related Data,* pp. 18–20.

155 *"By coincidence":* LAT, Oct. 20, 1929.

155 *"We simply can't keep":* Ibid.

155 *It was another five months:* Wilbur and Ely, *The Hoover Dam Project and Water Contracts and Related Data,* pp. 22–25.

155 *Signed contracts and start of work:* Ibid., pp. 27–28; Wilbur, *Memoirs,* p. 449.

156 *"we have the Roosevelt Dam":* The speech text is at Wilbur, *Memoirs,* pp. 453–54.

156 *"the great crowd":* Ibid., p. 454.

156 *John Page recorded the event:* JCP, Sept. 17, 1930.

157 *Johnson felt the affront keenly:* The witness was Leland W. Cutler, who would himself play an important role in the creation of the dam. See Cutler, *America Is Good to a Country Boy,* p. 148.

157 *"Everybody would have accepted it":* Carr, "Memoirs," p. 152, Special Collections, UCLA.

157 *"the chairmanship":* Hoover, *Memoirs,* Vol. 3, p. 456.

158 *"Hoogivza":* LVRJ, May 10, 1947.

## CHAPTER 9: The Big Six

159 *Crowe worked late into the night:* Rocca, *America's Master Dam Builder,* pp. 184–85; Wolf, *Big Dams and Other Dreams,* pp. 6–7.

160 *More than one hundred:* See *The Taming of Black Canyon* [video], Bechtel Corp., 1981.

160 *The number of envelopes:* Cutler, *America Is Good to a Country Boy,* p. 150.

160 *"I consider it":* Ibid., p. 150.

161 *The government specifications:* Department of the Interior, Specifications No. 519, "Hoover Dam, Power Plant and Appurtenant Works," Dec. 17, 1930.

161 *"Who could tell":* Cutler, *America Is Good to a Country Boy,* p. 150.

162 *662 miles of piping:* C. J. Neilsen, "Boulder Dam," *Dams and Control Works,* U.S. Department of the Interior, Feb. 1938, p. 10.

162    *"so far as practicable"*: Specifications No. 519, "Hoover Dam, Power Plant and Appurtenant Works." The veterans preference is at p. 19, item 23; the Mongolian exclusion is at p. 13, item 2; the liability waiver cited by Cutler is at p. 14, item 12.

163    *"Frank and Hank"*: "The Earth Movers—I," *Fortune*, Aug. 1943.

163    *"we can raise"*: Ibid., p. 103.

163    *The ranch produced little*: Sessions and Sessions, *Utah International*, pp. 53–54.

163    *"Is he our kind?"*: "The Earth Movers—I," *Fortune*, Aug. 1943, p. 104.

163    *"If we can't"*: "The Earth Movers—I," pp. 103–4.

164    *leading tithe payer*: Hyman, *Marriner S. Eccles*, p. 24.

164    *division of Eccles estate*: Ibid., pp. 47–48; Sessions and Sessions, *Utah International*, p. 31.

164    *After witnessing Wattis in action*: Hyman, *Marriner S. Eccles*, p. 56.

165    *"I want you girls"*: Ibid., p. 76.

165    *Coffey and Humber*: *Time*, May 25, 1931.

165    *Eccles reached Wattis*: Hyman, *Marriner S. Eccles*, p. 75.

166    *first seven board meetings*: Six Companies Corporate Records, Bancroft Library, UC Berkeley.

166    *characteristics of Cuba job*: Foster, *Henry J. Kaiser*, pp. 39–40.

166    *"I lay awake"*: Leonard Lyons, "Unforgettable Henry J. Kaiser," *Reader's Digest*, April 1968, p. 213.

166    *traveling salesman of photography supplies*: Foster, *Henry J. Kaiser*, p. 17.

166    *"There's only one time"*: Lyons, "Unforgettable Henry J. Kaiser," p. 210.

167    *His first attempt at independence*: McCartney, *Friends in High Places*, p. 19.

167    *"I landed in Reno"*: Ingram, *A Builder and His Family*, p. 3.

168    *Dad painted the legend*: Ibid., p. 7.

168    *"I was standing alone"*: Henry J. Kaiser, address to Associated General Contractors of Northern California, 1928, cited in Heiner, *Henry J. Kaiser, Western Colossus*, p. 32.

168    *Bowman Dam: Building a Century*: Bechtel, *1898–1998*, pp. 23–24.

169    *"Henry, it sounds"*: McCartney, *Friends in High Places*, p. 30.

170    *Shea family inheritance*: Robert L. Bridges OH, 1997, Bancroft Library, UC Berkeley, p. 71.

170     *Shea and San Francisco arrangement:* Wolf, *Big Dams and Other Dreams,* p. 293, n14.

170     *"we never had a written contract":* "The Earth Movers—I," p. 104.

170     *"not only had an enviable reputation":* Cutler, *America Is Good to a Country Boy,* p. 152.

170     *Kahn family background:* "Industry's Architect," *Time,* June 29, 1942.

171     *"That made me one":* "The Earth Movers—I," p. 105.

171     *"It takes a great many halves":* Cutler, *America Is Good to a Country Boy,* p. 151.

171     *Cuban bonds:* Heiner, *Henry J. Kaiser, Western Colossus,* p. 48.

171     *She was repaid:* Herbert Solow, "The Big Builder from Boise," *Fortune,* Dec. 1956, pp. 202–3.

172     *"It hit us all the same":* LAT, March 5, 1931.

172     *The dam design:* John L. Savage, "Present status of Boulder Canyon designs" (report to chief engineer R. F. Walter), U.S. Bureau of Reclamation (USBR), Feb. 5, 1930, USBR archives, Boulder City, Nevada.

173     *"a structure of this unprecedented magnitude":* "Report of the Colorado River Board on the Boulder Canyon Project," Nov. 24, 1928, p. 5.

173     *the difference between the high and low figures:* "The Earth Movers—I," p. 106.

173     *Eccles was left behind:* Ibid., pp. 106–7; see also "The Constant Companions," speech by Edgar F. Kaiser, Pepperdine University, 1953 [?], Kaiser Papers, Bancroft Library, UC Berkeley.

174     *"The name just came to me":* "The Earth Movers—I," p. 107. *Fortune* identified the Chinese Six Companies as a tribunal that oversaw the tongs, a misconception that has been perpetuated by books and articles relying on the magazine as a source on the founding of Six Companies. (See, for example, Wolf, *Big Dams and Other Dreams,* p. 4.) Histories of the Chinese community in San Francisco, however, state that Six Companies and the tongs were distinct and, more often than not, mutually adversarial organizations. See Min, ed., *Asian Americans,* p. 131.

174     *Six Companies letterhead:* See Crowe to Emma Crowe [mother], Aug. 22, 1931. The author thanks John Hollstein for the use of this letter.

175     *The Six Companies partners met once more:* "The Earth Movers—I," p. 107.

175 *"considerable humor"*: LAT, March 5, 1931.

176 *It bears noting*: The three certified bids are in USBR, "Abstract of Bids: Construction of Hoover Dam, Power Plant and Appurtenant Works," USBR archives, Boulder City, Nevada. See Wolf, *Big Dams and Other Dreams*, p. 47, for a useful analysis of the unbalanced bids.

176 *"WE ARE THE SUCCESSFUL BIDDERS"*: Crowe wire to Melvin Holbrook (his brother-in-law), March 4, 1931. The author thanks John Hollstein for providing a copy of this wire.

176 *"We do not consider"*: LAT, March 5, 1931.

177 *"small, spry, white-haired"*: "Damn Big Dam," *Time*, March 23, 1931.

177 *"mild form of cancer"*: LAT, March 13, 1931.

177 *"I don't know when"*: "Damn Big Dam," *Time*, March 23, 1931.

177 *"OK FOR A JOB"*: Allen, *Hoover Dam and Boulder City*, p. 41.

177 *The next day*: Rocca, *America's Master Dam Builder*, p. 186.

177 *Six Companies payroll*: Six Companies Corporate Records, April 13, 1931, board meeting, Bancroft Library, UC Berkeley.

178 *"we must have a place"*: LAT, March 13, 1931.

## CHAPTER 10: Ragtown

179 *four million persons had become unemployed*: Kennedy, *Freedom from Fear*, p. 163.

179 *"You are making"*: Chernow, *The House of Morgan*, p. 326.

180 *"serious shock"*: Friedman and Schwartz, *A Monetary History of the United States*, p. 357.

180 *evicting bootleggers*: McBride, *In the Beginning*, pp. 10–11.

180 *"he was a rather cocky"*: Walker Young OH, June 23, 1975, Boulder City Public Library.

180 *Young had been fighting*: Young to Raymond F. Walter, Feb. 27, 1931, USBR archives, Box 26, Folder 4.7.3, National Archives and Records Administration (NARA), Laguna Niguel, California.

181 *"they all seem to be"*: Ibid.

181 *Within a few weeks*: McBride, *In the Beginning*, p. 9.

181 *"empire of squatters"*: Elton Garrett OH, Nov. 10–11, 1986, BCMHA.

181 *"Williamsville Town Topics"*: McBride, *In the Beginning*, p. 11.

# NOTES

182 *"That's what it looked like"*: Erma Godbey OH, BCMHA.

182 *"HELL HOLE"*: Victor Castle, "Well, I Quit My Job at the Dam," *The Nation*, Aug. 26, 1931, p. 207.

183 *"Well, I'll never"*: Godbey OH.

183 *"Packing boxes were mesmerized"*: Pettitt, *So Boulder Dam Was Built*, p. 28.

183 *"This man was so anxious"*: Godbey OH; Godbey, 31ers Discussion, Sept. 1973, Boulder City, Nevada; transcript courtesy of BCMHA.

184 *Butter could not be kept firm*: Helen H. Holmes OH, Boulder City Public Library.

184 *"They'd come with their kids"*: Murl Emery OH, UNLV.

185 *"Is there going to be a parade"*: T. C. Wilson OH, 1982, UNR.

186 *"stacked up like cordwood"*: John Cahlan OH.

186 *"A PITIFUL AND PATHETIC SIGHT"*: LVA, Feb. 10, 1931.

187 *"Everybody was starving"*: Wilson OH.

187 *"They'd line up"*: Ibid.

187 *"panic-stricken"*: Pettitt, *So Boulder Dam was Built*, p. 29.

187 *$50,000 to start construction*: Six Companies Corporate Records, Vol. 1, p. 102 (March 5, 1931), Bancroft Library, UC Berkeley.

188 *"ordinary American boys"*: Cutler, *America Is Good to a Country Boy*, p. 154.

188 *"Kaiser and Morrison"*: "The Earth Movers—I," *Fortune*, Aug. 1943, p. 212.

188 *"Isn't it wonderful"*: Ibid.

188 *shooting craps*: Ibid.

188 *"Drive over!"*: Ibid.

189 *MacDonald & Kahn had come under investigation*: LAT, Feb. 7, 1933, April 6, 1933, Feb. 22, 1938.

189 *"first hot argument"*: "The Earth Movers—I," p. 210.

190 *"Have your directors' meetings"*: Cutler, *America Is Good to a Country Boy*, p. 157.

190 *Through this arrangement*: Wolf, *Big Dams and Other Dreams*, pp. 38–39.

190 *armies of "peddlers"*: Ingram, *A Builder and His Family*, p. 35.

190 *On March 16*: McBride, *In the Beginning*, p. 6.

191 *"Here there is fertile soil"*: Elwood W. Mead, address at Massachusetts Institute of Technology, Jan. 9, 1931, reprinted in *NRE*, Feb. 1931, p. 22.

191    *The dam specifications:* See Specifications No. 519, "Hoover Dam, Power Plant and Appurtenant Works." The Boulder City provision is at pp. 23–24, item 34: "Boulder City will be under the exclusive administration and control of the Government."

191    *J. R. Smeal:* McBride, *In the Beginning,* p. 12.

192    *"My God, woman":* Godbey OH.

192    *Four women died:* Ibid., Nov. 7–8, 1986. In a separate oral history interview conducted in 1967, Godbey states that three women perished on that July day; this is her more detailed recollection, however.

193    *"The pit grew deeper":* Eccles, *Beckoning Frontiers,* pp. 54–55.

194    *"We can't break this run today":* Ibid., p. 59.

194    *"the failure of financial":* Marriner Eccles, address to Utah State Bankers Convention, June 1932, cited in Hyman, *Marriner S. Eccles,* p. 99.

195    *"I would if I could":* Hyman, *Marriner S. Eccles,* p. 88.

195    *"a welcome relief":* Eccles, *Beckoning Frontiers,* p. 63.

## CHAPTER 11: Rush Job

196    *Taking stock one day:* Carmody, "What the Reclamation Women Do in Las Vegas," *NRE,* Sept. 1931, p. 202. Carmody wrote five informative and atmospheric articles, primly bylined "Mrs. D. L. Carmody," for the Reclamation Bureau house organ before her untimely death from stroke in 1933 (*LVRJ,* July 20, 1933). The author is indebted to genealogist Diane E. Greene of the Boulder City/Hoover Dam Museum Archives for background information about Mrs. Carmody.

197    *Walker Young personally requested:* JCP, Sept. 24, 1930.

197    *"the calls from ladies":* Carmody, "What the Reclamation Women Do in Las Vegas," *NRE,* Sept. 31, p. 202.

197    *"sunk in a sea":* Ibid.

197    *"like a big yellow mushroom":* Carmody, "Impressions of an Engineer's Wife on Her First Trip to the Site of Hoover Dam," *NRE,* June 1931, p 136.

198    *"those strange mountains":* Ibid., p. 137.

198    *"Large, powerful cars":* Carmody, "A Visit to the Hoover Dam Site," *NRE,* Aug. 1931, p. 172.

200    *Five tunnels had to be bored:* "Difficult Railroad Construction, Boulder Canyon Project," *NRE*, Dec. 1931, p. 272.

201    *"God does not do business":* LeTourneau, *Mover of Men and Mountains*, p. 173. The author thanks J. David Rogers for bringing this memoir to his attention.

201    *"Even with power drills":* Ibid., p. 176.

201    *"Came the zero hour":* Ibid., p. 177.

202    *"too horrible":* Ibid., p. 178.

202    *Crowe's blasting scheme:* Norman Gallison, "Construction of the Hoover Dam: Details of the Driving of the Four Huge Tunnels," in *The Story of the Hoover Dam*, p. 49.

202    *Their only suitable landfall:* Ibid.

203    *Kaufmann was already abandoning:* See Richard Guy Wilson, "Machine-Age Iconography in the American West: The Design of Hoover Dam," *Pacific Historical Review*, Nov. 1985.

204    *"a complementary treatment":* Gordon B. Kaufmann, "The Architecture of Boulder Dam," *Architectural Concrete*, Vol. 2, No. 3 (1936), p. 3.

205    *"more . . . an artist":* Young to Mead, Nov. 23, 1931, NARA, Washington, D.C., Record Group 115, cited in Vilander, *Hoover Dam*, p. 10.

205    *"consume the entire time":* Ibid.

205    *whom he would personally escort:* Inscription, Bourke-White to Glaha, March 21, 1935. The author is indebted to Barbara Vilander for sharing this and other correspondence related to Glaha's work.

205    *"scarcely able to work":* JCP, July 7, 1931. Page's notations indicate that Glaha left for the mountains on July 9 and did not return until August 11.

205    *"coddled artist-photographer":* Willard Van Dyke, "The Work of Ben Glaha," *Camera Craft*, April 1935, p. 166.

206    *he shot pictures:* Ibid.

206    *innovative smokeless flash powder:* Norman Gallison to Mead, July 27, 1932, NARA, Denver.

206    *His workhorse still cameras:* Vilander, *Hoover Dam*, p. 14; Van Dyke, "The Work of Ben Glaha," p. 166.

206    *"any enlarging you wish can":* Mead to Young, Dec. 12, 1931, NARA, Washington, D.C.

206 *"This I feel sure"*: Ibid.

207 *"This work is highly spectacular"*: Young to Mead, Jan. 7, 1932, NARA, Washington, D.C., Record Group 115, cited in Vilander, *Hoover Dam*, p. 14.

207 *"Compositionally perfect"*: Van Dyke, "The Work of Ben Glaha," p. 171.

208 *the enlarged base would span*: Benjamin D. Rhodes, "From Cooksville to Chungking: The Dam-Designing Career of John L. Savage," *Wisconsin Magazine of History*, Summer 1989, p. 260.

208 *Savage dodged the issue*: Mead to Wilbur, "Memorandum re the Meeting of the Consulting Engineers to Approve Detail Plans of Boulder Dam," Dec. 28, 1929, NARA, Denver, Record Group 115; Boulder Canyon Project Final Reports, Part IV—Design and Construction, USBR 1941, p. 25, both cited in Donald C. Jackson, "Boulder Dam, Origins of Siting and Design," 2002, History Symposium, U.S. Bureau of Reclamation.

209 *"have not heretofore been satisfactorily solved"*: Mead, "Research Work of the Bureau of Reclamation," *RE*, May 1933, p. 54.

209 *This work was farmed out*: Ibid. The results of one compression test at the bureau's lab in Montrose, Colorado, can be seen in the photograph accompanying the article, ibid., on p. 57.

209 *Fred Noetzli had expressed contempt*: David P. Billington et al., "From Pathfinder to Glen Canyon: The Structural Analysis of Arched, Gravity Dams," from USBR, *Symposium on the History of the Bureau of Reclamation*, June 18–19, 2002, pp. 15–19.

210 *As an alternative*: Ibid., p. 19.

210 *The sixty-foot dam*: Kollgaard and Chadwick, eds., *Development of Dam Engineering in the United States*, pp. 257–61.

211 *Hoover Dam could be built*: Billington et al., "From Pathfinder to Glen Canyon," p. 25.

212 *"a thing of the past"*: Ibid., p. 29.

212 *"celebration of mass"*: The expression is Donald C. Jackson's; see his *Building the Ultimate Dam*, p. 246.

213 *Walker Young himself felt*: Young to Virginia (Teddy) Fenton, May 19, 1972, p. 4, BCMHA. Mrs. Fenton was a longtime resident and devoted amateur historian of Boulder City.

213 *"intimately acquainted"*: Annual Project History, Vol. 1 (1931), p. 151.

213   *Crain and Creel had expected:* See JCP, Jan. 27, 1931, to Feb. 3, 1931.

214   *as much as fourfold:* Petition for higher condemnation prices, H. B. Brown, attorney, Jan. 1932, USBR archives, NARA, Laguna Niguel, California, Group 115, Box 21.

214   *"ornamental and fruit trees":* Ibid.

214   *Even Young was tempted to concede:* See Young to Fenton, May 19, 1972, BCMHA, p. 4.

214   *But Mead, whose ambitious dam construction program:* Annual Project History, vol. 1 (1931), pp. 41–44; Imre Sutton, "Geographical Aspects of Construction Planning: Hoover Dam Revisited," *Journal of the West,* July 1968, p. 329.

214   *The three members issued:* Annual Project History, vol. 1, pp. 151–53.

215   *Mark Harrington had excavated:* Mark Harrington, "The 'Lost City' of Nevada—A Few Facts," *RE,* May 1935, p. 90.

215   *"an almost unbroken line":* Mark Harrington, "Archeological Explorations in Southern Nevada," *Southwest Museum Papers,* No. 4 (1930), p. 6.

215   *"long straggling":* Mark Harrington, "Ancient Tribes of the Boulder Dam Country," *Southwest Museum Leaflets,* No. 9 (1937), p. 12.

215   *"lapping at their feet":* K. J. Evans, "Mark Harrington," in Hopkins and Evans, eds., *The First 100.*

215   *The concept of salvage archaeology:* Sutton, "Geographical Aspects," p. 331.

216   *Six Companies had laid out $79,285:* Six Companies Corporate Minutes, vol. 1, April 9, 1931.

## CHAPTER 12: The Wobblies' Last Stand

217   *That baleful distinction:* J. G. Tierney's death is recorded at USBR, *Annual Project History,* Hoover Dam, Vol. 1, p. 342. The USBR official history acknowledges the earlier death of Harold Connelly, a USBR employee who died in a barge mishap on May 15, 1921. Connelly died in Boulder Canyon, however, not Black Canyon.

217   *His body was never recovered:* Walker Young to Virginia (Teddy) Fenton, May 19, 1972, BCMHA.

217   *Thirteen years later:* Patrick Tierney's death is recorded at USBR, *Annual Project History,* Hoover Dam, Vol. 5, p. 323.

217   *But Large and Lane: LAT,* May 18, 1931.

218   *The most grievously injured man: LAT,* May 9, 1931.

218   *"His ear was almost severed": LVA,* May 9, 1931.

218   *"no warning":* JCP, May 8, 1931.

219   *The visiting Nevada official:* JCP, May 9, 1931.

219   *"Gave them no information":* JCP, May 12, 1931.

219   *the company would pay off Lezie:* Six Companies Corporate Minutes, Vol. 2, p. 322, Nov. 16, 1931.

219   *Average temperatures:* Shea to Six Companies board, Six Companies Corporate Minutes, Vol. 1, p. 291, July 31, 1931.

220   *"It's getting hot here":* The Beals letters are in BCMHA.

220   *"The summer wind":* Elwood Mead, address at Massachusetts Institute of Technology, Jan. 9, 1931, reprinted in *NRE,* Feb. 1931, p. 22.

221   Mead life: See Paul Conkin, "The Vision of Elwood Mead," *Agricultural History,* No. 34 (1960), pp. 88–97.

221   *bivouac it dubbed River Camp:* Wilson, *The American Earthquake,* p. 368; Imre Sutton, "Geographical Aspects of Construction Planning: Hoover Dam Revisited," *Journal of the West,* July 1968, p. 322.

221   *On occasion boulders:* See Richard L. "Curley" Francis OH, Boulder City Public Library.

222   *"I tried to sleep":* Victor Castle, "Well, I Quit My Job at the Dam," *The Nation,* Aug. 26, 1931, p. 207.

222   *"an opaque yellow":* Wilson, *The American Earthquake,* p. 370.

222   *"consommé":* Pettitt, *So Boulder Dam Was Built,* p. 53.

222   *one batch of sandwiches: LVA,* July 12, 1931.

222   *The ferocious heat:* John H. Talbott and Jost Michelsen, "Heat Cramps: A Clinical and Chemical Study," *Journal of Clinical Investigation,* May 1933.

222   *"It was quite a sight":* Castle, "Well, I Quit My Job at the Dam."

222   *"We had what we called":* Robert Parker OH, BCMHA.

223   *"What we demonstrated":* Dr. David Bruce Dill OH, BCMHA.

223   *Sixteen deaths from heatstroke: Annual Project History,* vol. 1, 1931, p. 342.

223   *John Page morbidly noted:* JCP, July 20, 1931.

224   *"very trying conditions":* Shea to board, Six Companies Corporate Minutes, July 17, 1931, vol. 1, p. 261.

224    *"were unused to living"*: Annual Project History, vol. 1, 1931, p. 175.

224    *The Las Vegas coroner's jury*: LVA, June 29, 1931.

224    *"There is no question"*: The New Republic, Aug. 26, 1931, p. 48.

226    *preamble to the IWW constitution*: See Thompson, *The I.W.W.*, p. 4.

226    *IWW membership*: Renshaw, *The Wobblies*, p. 2.

226    *"miners, engineers, clerks"*: Quoted in Guy Louis Rocha, "Radical Labor Struggles in the Tonopah-Goldfield Mining District, 1901–1922," *Nevada Historical Society Quarterly*, Spring 1977, p. 7.

227    *"a bunch of bums"*: Thompson, *The I.W.W.*, p. 80.

227    *After weeks of testimony*: Renshaw, *The Wobblies*, p. 186.

227    *By 1931 its membership*: Ibid., p. 214; Thompson, *The I.W.W.*, p. 157.

227    *"The U.C. Co. and its two pimps"*: Industrial Worker, March 14, 1931.

228    *struck Utah Construction's Hetch Hetchy*: Thompson, *The I.W.W.*, pp. 145–46.

228    *"SIX COMPANIES THREATEN"*: Industrial Solidarity, May 19, 1931.

228    *"LIFE HELD CHEAP"*: Industrial Worker, May 30, 1931.

228    *Their leader was*: LVA, July 11, 1931.

228    *"a short strong-knit man"*: Wilson, *The American Earthquake*, p. 374.

228    *Anderson had hired on*: LVA, July 11, 1931; LVRJ, July 11, 1931. Anderson has frequently been described as a "truck tender," but this is certainly an error. No such job existed in Black Canyon. "Chuck tender," however, was a common job classification in mining and tunneling. The mistake may have originated with newspaper reporters who misheard Anderson's actual job title and substituted a term that sounded reasonable to their unschooled ears. It has been perpetuated by historians who relied on the newspapers as sources. Complete lists of all job classifications at the dam, and their wages, can be found in *LVRJ*, Aug. 14, 1931; Six Companies Corporate Minutes, vol. 1, April 13, 1931, p. 160; and www.usbr.gov/lc/hooverdam/History/essays/wages.html [accessed July 6, 2009].

229    *"Wobbly jauntiness"*: Wilson, *The American Earthquake*, p. 374.

229    *more than ten thousand unemployed men*: Blood statement, 1936 [?], p. 3, in Leonard T. Blood Papers, Special Collections, UNLV.

229    *running the sprinklers*: Castle, "Well, I Quit," *The Nation*, Aug. 26, 1931.

229    *Davis-Bacon exemption*: LVA, Aug. 28, 1932. The contract was signed March 25, 1931, by W. H. Wattis for Six Companies; on April 11 by USBR

chief engineer Raymond Walter; on April 13 by USBR commissioner Mead; and on April 20 by Interior Secretary Wilbur. See *NRE*, May 1931, p. 107.

229   *Big Six's wage scale:* Six Companies Corporate Minutes, vol. 1, April 13, 1931.

229   *"exactly the contrary":* Mead, letter to the editor, *The New Republic*, Aug. 26, 1931, p. 48.

229   *Central Labor Council:* LVA, Aug. 28, 1932.

230   *Crowe, reminded of this provision:* Blood statement, p. 5.

230   *"foremen were sending":* Ibid., p. 6.

230   *AF of L–Six Companies exchange:* Six Companies Corporate Minutes, vol. 1, May 12, 1931, p. 191.

230   *"nothing to discuss":* Industrial Worker, June 6, 1931; Judson King, "Open Shop at Boulder Dam," *The New Republic*, June 24, 1931.

230   *"systematic skimping":* Wilson, *The American Earthquake*, p. 370.

231   *meal costs:* Castle, "Well, I Quit"; Altus E. (Tex) Nunley and Dorothy Nunley OH, BCMHA; Six Companies Corporate Minutes, vol. 1, April 27, 1931, p. 180.

231   *Its practice of paying:* Industrial Worker, June 27, 1931.

231   *"exceptionally good business":* Six Companies Corporate Minutes, vol. 1, July 17, 1931, p. 259.

231   *Only after vehement protests:* LAT, May 11, 1933.

231   *"THREE MORE MEN":* Industrial Worker, July 4, 1931.

231   *cauliflower-eared:* Industrial Worker, July 25, 1931.

231   *"I.W.W. GROUP AT DAM":* LVA, July 11, 1931.

232   *Gracey and Setzer arrests:* LVRJ, July 11, 1931; *Industrial Solidarity*, July 28, 1931.

232   *The Wobblies' chattiness:* LVA, July 12, 1931.

232   *"free speech" campaigns:* Renshaw, *The Wobblies*, pp. 86–88; Thompson, *The I.W.W.*, pp. 48–49.

232   *At mealtime:* LVRJ, July 16, 1931; *Industrial Solidarity*, July 28, 1931.

233   *Assistant U.S. Attorney George Montrose:* LVRJ, July 11, 1931.

233   *"The whole thing":* LVRJ, July 13, 1931.

233   *T. Alonzo Wells:* John Cahlan, "Reminiscences," UNR, 1987.

233 *$28 a week: LVA,* July 16, 1931.

233 *This was rather better pay:* Castle, "Well, I Quit My Job," *The Nation,* Aug. 26, 1931.

233 *he ordered Anderson released: LVRJ,* July 16, 1931; *Industrial Worker,* July 25, 1931; *Industrial Solidarity,* July 28, 1931.

233 *The elated Wobbly press: Industrial Worker,* July 25, 1931.

234 *They shipped in clean drinking water:* Wilson, *The American Earthquake,* p. 372.

234 *greeted by a notice: Industrial Worker,* Aug. 15, 1931; memo, J. C. Page to Raymond Walter, "Six Companies' Strike—Boulder Canyon Project," Aug. 10, 1931, NARA, Denver. The author thanks Barbara Vilander for providing a copy of this document.

234 *Goaded by two Wobbly speakers: Industrial Worker,* Aug. 15, 1931; *Industrial Solidarity,* Aug. 18, 1931.

235 *"We're not wobblies": LVRJ,* Aug. 8, 1931.

235 *seven demands: LVRJ,* Aug. 8, 1931; *Industrial Worker,* Aug. 15, 1931; Page–Walter memo, "Six Companies' Strike," p. 2.

236 *At his office the next morning: LVRJ,* Aug. 8, 1931.

236 *Returned to camp:* Ibid.

236 *Although Crowe had given himself:* Ibid.

237 *"Pretty thin, Crowe": Industrial Solidarity,* Aug. 18, 1931.

238 *"a month or longer": NYT,* August 10, 1931.

238 *"We are several months": LAT,* Aug. 9, 1931.

238 *"then the men": Industrial Worker,* Aug. 15, 1931.

238 *The tunnels were not ahead:* For the pace and schedule of work, see Norman Gallison, "Construction of the Hoover Dam: Details of the Driving of the Four Huge Tunnels," in *The Story of the Hoover Dam,* p. 49.

239 *Charlie Shea would reveal:* See JCP, Oct. 14, 1931.

239 *"They will have to work": LVA,* Aug. 9, 1931.

239 *the wage provision: Engineering News-Record,* Dec. 15, 1932, p. 7.

239 *not until he arrived:* Page–Walter memo, "Six Companies' Strike," p. 3.

239 *Young spent the day:* JCP, Oct. 14, 1931.

239 *The only immediate result: LAT,* Aug. 9, 1931.

240 *At 3 A.M.:* Page–Walter memo, "Six Companies' Strike," p. 3.

240     *a check for 70 cents:* The check and a descriptive note from Norton are in BCMHA.

240     *Police Chief Clay Williams: LVA,* Aug. 11, 1931.

240     *At least one gambling hall:* Parker OH. Parker identified the casino as the Pioneer Club.

241     *The sale of guns:* Page–Walter memo, "Six Companies' Strike," p. 5.

241     *Rumors of Wobbly sabotage: LVRJ,* Aug. 11, 1931.

241     *Taking a reasonable precaution: LVA,* Aug. 11, 1931.

241     *"no disturbances":* JCP, Aug. 8–11, 1931.

241     *Doak phoned: LVRJ,* Aug. 10, 1931.

241     *two hundred strikers hunkered down: LVRJ,* Aug. 11, 1931; *LVA,* Aug. 11, 1931.

241     *Their only basis for hope: Industrial Solidarity,* Aug. 18, 1931; Wilson, *The American Earthquake,* p. 373.

242     *Montrose had earlier informed Shea:* Page–Walter memo, "Six Companies' Strike," p. 4.

242     *"silent as the Egyptian": LVRJ,* Aug. 11, 1931.

242     *"the present wage rate": LVRJ,* Aug. 9, 1931.

242     *"what [the strikers] really wanted": NYT,* Aug. 23, 1931. The author was Chapin Hall, who had earlier been one of Harry Chandler's favorite reporters at the *Los Angeles Times.*

243     *"You know where": LAT,* Aug. 9, 1931.

243     *"All these poor men":* Erma Godbey OH, UNR.

244     *"We know that the conditions": LVRJ,* Aug. 12, 1931; *LVA,* Aug. 12, 1931.

244     *"I hope": LVA,* Aug. 12, 1931.

244     *The Wobblies held:* Dabney, *Edmund Wilson,* p. 173.

244     *"Some people wouldn't believe":* Wilson, *The American Earthquake,* p. 374.

245     *Young stepped out of the car:* This account is drawn from ibid., pp. 376–78.

246     *"all past employees": LVRJ,* Aug. 12, 1931.

246     *"They did give it":* Emery OH.

246     *A hand-painted sign:* McBride, *In the Beginning,* p. 19.

247     *"rather sparingly": LVRJ,* Aug. 13, 1931.

247     *"rigidly adhered to":* Ibid.

247     *"no new men":* Ibid.

247    *"The Six Companies had"*: Industrial Solidarity, Aug. 25, 1931.

247    *"So you saw"*: Crowe to Emma Crowe, Aug. 22, 1931. The author thanks John Hollstein for providing a copy of this letter.

248    *Not until 1932:* Blood statement.

248    *Despite Crowe's stringent vetting:* LVRJ, Aug. 14, 1931.

248    *Once inside:* The wage schedule was published in LVRJ, Aug. 14, 1931.

248    *Las Vegas Airdome:* Guy Louis Rocha, "The I.W.W. and the Boulder Canyon Project: The Final Death Throes of American Syndicalism," *Nevada Historical Society Quarterly,* Spring 1978, p. 17.

249    *"Boulder Dam strike still on"*: LVRJ, Aug. 15, 1931.

249    *"State of Nevada"*: Rocha, "The I.W.W. and the Boulder Canyon Project," p. 18.

249    *"transfer the strike"*: Ibid., p. 19.

## CHAPTER 13: Ely's Kingdom

251    *Sims Ely reported for duty:* JCP, Oct. 3, 1931.

251    *A few months shy:* Ely was born Jan. 7, 1862. See affidavit of Calvin Ely [brother], in Northcutt Ely Papers, Stanford University.

251    *power of eviction:* Ray Lyman Wilbur, Jr., "Boulder City: A Survey of Its Legal Background, Its City Plan, and Its Administration" (master's thesis, Syracuse University, 1935), p. 251.

252    *"This was typical"*: Northcutt Ely, "My Father and His Search for the Lost Dutchman Mine," speech to the Fortnightly Club of Redlands, California, March 3, 1988, at http://www.redlandsfortnightly.org/papers/dutchmine. htm [accessed July 23, 2009].

252    *Ely background:* Ibid.; "Ely, Sims," *Who Was Who in America, 1951–1960;* Dennis McBride, "The Boulder City Dictator," in Hopkins and Evans, eds., *The First 100.*

252    *"would have full control"*: Wilbur, *Memoirs,* p. 458.

252    *"We threw him in there"*: Northcutt Ely related this anecdote during a speech at the Los Angeles Department of Water and Power in the early 1980s, while he was engaged in renegotiating the original Hoover Dam power contracts. It was repeated to the author by a member of the audience, Feb. 13, 2007.

# NOTES

253     *"coercion, blackmail"*: *The Nevadan Today (LVRJ)*, April 17, 1988.

253     *"It is quite true"*: *The Nevadan Today (LVRJ)*, May 15, 1988.

253     *"You know, you were the first Hitler"*: Page to Ely, Nov. 4, 1947, Northcutt Ely Papers, Stanford University.

253     *"an oasis in the desert"*: "Government Plans Model Town at Boulder City, Nevada," *NRE*, Feb. 1931, p. 28.

253     *He divided the city*: This description and the quotations are from S. R. De-Boer, "The City Plan of Boulder City," *National Municipal Review*, May 1931, pp. 253–55.

254     *Therefore Elwood Mead*: Stevens (*Hoover Dam*, p. 124) writes that Boulder City was redesigned by Young and Crowe in a single afternoon in the spring of 1931. The main source for this unlikely, even unimaginable, story may have been John Cahlan's "Reminiscences," an oral history prepared forty years after the fact. Authoritative sources make clear that the design of Boulder City remained from beginning to end exclusively in the hands of the Reclamation Bureau. John Page, an unimpeachable source writing contemporaneously, recorded that Mead approved the final design in December 1930, nearly three months before Six Companies won the construction bid—indeed, weeks before the bid documents were even issued (JCP, Dec. 19, 1930). Crowe would not have played any role, therefore, as Six Companies was not yet involved with the project. Indeed, Crowe regularly complained about Boulder City's layout to Young and Page, who consistently dismissed his objections (see JCP, April 4, 1931).

254     *DeBoer found these changes*: Imre Sutton, "Geographical Aspects of Construction Planning: Hoover Dam Revisited," *Journal of the West*, July 1968, p. 325.

255     *personally vetted by Gordon Kaufmann*: JCP, May 6, 1931.

255     *"all of them different"*: Mrs. D. L. (Stella) Carmody, "Under the Eagle's Wing," *NRE*, July 1932, p. 130.

255     *They were equipped*: "Notes for Contractors," *RE*, Jan. 1932, p. 10.

255     *"substantial villa"*: Dennis McBride, "Among the Lotus Eaters," *The Nevadan Today (LVRJ)*, Feb. 12, 1989, p. 12CC.

255     *the workers waited*: Alice Hamilton OH, at http://banyan.library.unlv.edu:8080/ramgen/audio/aliceaudio.rm [accessed July 8, 2009]. Hamilton

was Bud Bodell's girl Friday while he served as the Six Companies security chief.

255 *Six Companies threw up:* McBride, *In the Beginning,* pp. 31–32; Jean Page OH, BCMHA.

255 *For landscaping:* Carmody, "Under the Eagle's Wing," p. 129.

256 *"I have rented":* John H. Muersinge, "My Golden Wedding Speech," Feb. 17, 1973, BCMHA.

256 *unmarried male office workers:* E. H. Heinemann, "The Building of Boulder City," *NRE,* May 1936, p. 110.

256 *Six Companies records indicate:* Six Companies Corporate Minutes, Feb. 15, 1932, vol. 2, p. 345.

256 *It told the Reclamation Bureau:* Heinemann, "The Building of Boulder City." Page's estimate is in "Memorandum to Construction Engineer [Young]," Dec. 9, 1931, p. 14, RG 115, NARA, Denver. Young forwarded the memo to Mead on Jan. 8, 1932, with a cover letter erroneously dated Jan. 8, 1931.

256 *The discrepancy cannot:* For appliance costs, see "Notes for Contractors," *RE,* Jan. 1932, p. 10. The company's $5,000 monthly rent is set forth in the dam specifications, Department of the Interior, Specifications No. 519, pp. 23–24 (para. 34). The amortization schedule is from Heinemann, "The Building of Boulder City." Stevens also questions Six Companies' accounting, *Hoover Dam,* p. 285 n23.

257 *"principal complaint":* Page, "Memorandum to Construction Engineer," pp. 14–15.

257 *John Page's elder daughter:* Jean Page OH.

257 *"it was the weirdest place":* Dorothy Nunley OH, BCMHA.

258 *"[We] had three beds":* Ann Stebens-Vivian Russell OH, BCMHA.

258 *"almost unendurable":* W. R. Nelson, "Landscaping of Boulder City," *RE,* April 1932, p. 70.

258 *Weed background: Register-Guard* (Eugene, Oregon), Sept. 3, 1976.

258 *"cooperating with nature":* W. W. Weed, "Plant Behavior in Drought," *RE,* Nov. 1937, p. 260.

258 *"we have enough desert":* Ibid.

259 *orders for 9,150 trees:* Nelson, "Landscaping of Boulder City," p. 70.

259 *"took the shortest":* Weed, "Plant Behavior in Drought," p. 262.

259     *"planting a concrete lawn"*: Ibid., p. 263.

259     *dust storms*: Madeleine Knighten OH, cited in Allen, *Hoover Dam and Boulder City*, p. 124.

259     *the residents celebrated*: McBride, *In the Beginning*, p. 22.

259     *"Every time there was"*: Jean Page to Barbara Vilander, May 28, 1992. The author is grateful to Barbara Vilander for sharing this letter.

259     *delegation of fourteen Las Vegas pastors*: JCP, March 3, 1931.

260     *"the probable population"*: USBR, "Information Regarding Permits and Leases in Boulder City," May 18, 1931, reprinted in *NRE*, June 1931, pp. 118–20.

260     *"largely by guesswork"*: Ely, "Permits and Leases at Boulder City," *RE*, Aug. 1932, p. 137.

260     *"character, personality, age"*: USBR, "Information Regarding Permits and Leases in Boulder City."

261     *"respectable girls"*: Ray Lyman Wilbur, Jr., "Boulder City," p. 133.

261     *"undesirable literature"*: Ibid., p. 147.

261     *taxicab service*: See Young to U.S. Attorney General, Oct. 23, 1934, NARA Laguna Niguel; McBride; "The Boulder City Dictator."

261     *"Of course, [they] are not"*: Ely, "Permits and Leases at Boulder City," p. 139.

261     *"I had to take a day"*: Carl Merrill OH, Boulder City Public Library.

261     *"Because the rule"*: Sims Ely, "Causes for Expulsion," Dec. 28, 1932, in *Annual Project History*, vol. 3, 1933, p. 281.

262     *"I always think"*: Sims Ely to Northcutt Ely, Nov. 2, 1937, Northcutt Ely Papers, Stanford University.

263     *Some residents learned to use*: Dorothy Nunley OH.

263     *"He loved to see"*: Erma Godbey OH, UNR.

263     *"in trouble"*: Leroy and Lucille Burt OH, BCMHA.

263     *Residents assumed*: Godbey OH.

263     *"Mussolini" Bodell*: *Industrial Worker*, Dec. 8, 1931.

264     *He would later acknowledge*: Bodell OH, Special Collections, UNLV.

264     *Bodell's squad*: For Bodell and bootlegging, see his quotes in undated newspaper article, Bodell file, BCMHA.

264     *"rules the morals"*: Arthur Moore, "Boulder Dam Boom Fades into Distress," *Cleveland Press*, Jan. 15, 1932. This article was widely distributed by

the Scripps-Howard service; an identical version cited in Stevens, *Hoover Dam*, p. 154ff, is attributed to the *San Diego Union*, Jan. 17, 1932.

265  *"If they had bridge parties"*: McBride, "Among the Lotus Eaters."

265  *For this flagrant offense:* Walker Young OH, Boulder City Public Library.

265  *"Ely would have said"*: Elton Garrett OH, Boulder City Public Library.

266  *The city's birth rate:* The quotes are from Sims Ely, "Educational Facilities in Boulder City," *RE*, Nov. 1932, p. 188.

266  *a municipal census:* Ibid.

266  *$182,500:* Ray Lyman Wilbur, Jr., "Boulder City," p. 41.

266  *"This matter of high class schools"*: Ely to Mead, Feb. 13, 1932, NARA Laguna Niguel, RG 115.

267  *"This dam is to be built"*: Stiess to Hoover, Sept. 7, 1931, NARA Laguna Niguel, RG 115.

267  *Young eventually shamed:* See Young to A. E. Cahlan, secretary, Las Vegas Board of Education, Sept. 16, 1931, NARA Laguna Niguel, RG 115.

268  *"college graduates"*: Ely to Mead, Feb. 13, 1932.

268  *At first the board refused:* Six Companies Corporate Minutes, Jan. 30, 1932, vol. 2, p. 337.

268  *Ely's initial reaction:* Ely to Mead, Feb. 13, 1932.

268  *"fine public spirit"*: Ely, "Educational Facilities in Boulder City."

268  *"board felt poor"*: JCP, Aug. 10, 1932.

268  *cash dividend:* Six Companies Corporate Minutes, July 25, 1932.

268  *Norcross rejected:* See *Six Cos., Inc. v. De Vinney,* 2 F. Supp. 693, 699, Feb. 15, 1933.

268  *"one mile in length"*: Ibid., p. 697.

268  *Clark County immediately presented:* LVRJ, Feb. 15, 1932.

268  *The Big Six dodged:* Six Companies Corporate Minutes, Feb. 13, 1933.

269  *tax settlement:* Annual Project History, vol. 3, 1933, p. 113.

269  *The burgeoning population:* Ely, "Educational Facilities in Boulder City"; McBride, *In the Beginning,* p. 53.

269  *"On Thanksgiving Eve"*: RE, Jan. 1932, p. 12.

270  *"Did they eat"*: Ibid.

270  *"You couldn't have a flat tire"*: Vivian Russell OH, BCMHA.

## CHAPTER 14: The Jumbos

274 *"It was a job"*: Pettitt, *So Boulder Dam Was Built*, p. 75.

274 *"ex-sailors"*: Ibid.

274 *"A lot of these guys"*: Joe Kine OH, Boulder City Public Library.

274 *"brains and blood"*: *Industrial Worker*, Oct. 3, 1931, cited in Stevens, *Hoover Dam*, p. 164.

275 *Initially Williams toyed*: Allen S. Park, "Mammoth Drill Carriages Speed Hoover Dam Tunnel Work," in *The Story of the Hoover Dam*, pp. 45–46.

275 *The steel jumbo was studded*: Ibid.

276 *the sole days of rest*: Bud Keating OH, BCMHA.

276 *"What are you waiting for?"*: John Crowe, quoted in Rocca, *America's Master Dam Builder*, p. 203. John Crowe, Frank Crowe's nephew, was employed for several seasons on Hoover Dam.

276 *The first operational jumbo*: Park, "Mammoth Drill Carriages Speed Hoover Dam Tunnel Work," p. 45; N. S. Gallison, "Construction of the Hoover Dam: Details of the Driving of the Four Huge Tunnels," in *The Story of the Hoover Dam*, p. 52.

277 *Only three or four more blasts*: Gallison, "Construction of the Hoover Dam."

278 *copious bill of fare*: See Heinemann, "The Building of Boulder City," *RE*, May 1936, p. 111.

278 *"It was nothing"*: W. A. Whynn reminiscences, BCMHA.

278 *An order promptly came down*: For the Six Companies board's preoccupation with mess hall costs, see Six Companies Corporate Minutes, April 27, 1931, vol. 1, p. 180; Oct. 19, 1931, vol. 2, p. 318; Nov. 16, 1931, vol. 2, p. 322; Sept. 19, 1932, vol. 2, p. 374; April 16, 1934, vol. 2, unpag.

278 *"Big Berthas"*: These vehicles were the subject of many fond memories. Among others, see Marion Allen OH; Alfred Frank Baker OH; "Thirty-oners" (Joe Kine, Leroy Burt, Tommy Nelson) OH, Boulder City Public Library.

279 *"a good safe place"*: Allen OH.

279 *"so tough"*: Allen, *Hoover Dam and Boulder City*, pp. 49–51.

280 *"The main thing"*: Allen OH.

281 *Sidmore and Manning*: LVRJ, Dec. 15–16, 1931.

281   *That fate befell: LVRJ,* Jan. 10, 1933, at www.usbr.gov/lc/hooverdam/History/essays/fatbio.html [accessed July 11, 2009].

281   *The roof fell in:* Allen, *Hoover Dam and Boulder City,* pp. 53–57.

282   *"a fractured skull": LVRJ,* March 11, 1932.

283   *Kaiser-Mead marriage: NYT,* Aug. 25, 1932.

283   *It proved so popular:* Six Companies Corporate Minutes, vol. 2. Board meeting, April 16, 1934.

283   *"the facts are truthfully presented":* Kaiser in *Western Construction News,* Dec. 10, 1931, cited in Adams, *Mr. Kaiser Goes to Washington.*

283   *"the public will not know":* Young to Mead, Nov. 24, 1931, NARA Denver, RG 115.

283   *"the disgraceful conditions":* Mead to Young, Dec. 10, 1931, NARA Denver, RG 115.

284   *quarter-mile underground:* For progress on the main tunnels by footage, see Gallison, "Construction of the Hoover Dam," p. 52.

284   *"we would know the gas":* Richard "Curley" Francis OH, March 4, 1975.

284   *"I was called out":* Emery OH.

285   *"If they ever got you":* Tex Nunley OH, June 9, 1986, BCMHA.

285   *deaths from pneumonia:* Fatalities are recorded in the *Annual Project Histories* for 1931–1935.

286   *"If you said they died":* Mary Eaton OH, Nov. 15, 1986, BCMHA.

286   *"natural air currents":* Gallison, "Construction of the Hoover Dam," p. 53.

286   *Experienced mining hands believed:* See affidavit, J. P. Caulfield, Jr., Jan. 25, 1932, in *E. F. Kraus v. Six Companies, et. al.* (Eighth Judicial District Court, Clark Co., Nevada).

286   *"The food is excellent": Desert Sun* (Palm Springs, California), Dec. 4, 1931.

287   *"Physicians say that": Annual Project History,* vol. 3, 1933, p. 281.

287   *Gunnison Tunnel:* See David Clark, "Uncompahgre Project," Bureau of Reclamation History Project, 1994.

287   *It later calculated:* See *Six Companies, Inc. v. Stinson,* 58 F.2d 649, 652 (April 28, 1932).

287   *company lawyers swarmed:* Ibid., at 650.

288   *at several sampling points:* Caulfield affidavit, p. 10.

288   *"are laboring under"*: Affidavit, Fred L. Lowell, Jan. 28, 1932, NARA Laguna Niguel, RG 115, Box 6.

288   *"cool, clean, and pleasant"*: Affidavit [undated], Philip Samuel Williams, NARA Laguna Niguel, RG 115, Box 6.

288   *"various workmen"*: Affidavit, L. H. Duschek, Jan. 6, 1932, NARA Laguna Niguel, RG 115, Box 6.

289   *"tunnels not in mines"*: Six Cos., Inc. v. Stinson, 2 F. Supp. 689, 692, Feb. 15, 1933.

## CHAPTER 15: Turning Points

290   *They had driven through three miles:* See Mead, testimony before House Committee on Appropriations, May 31, 1932, p. 202.

291   *There were indications that familiarity:* Marion Allen's brush with disaster is drawn from his account in *Hoover Dam and Boulder City,* pp. 59–61.

291   *The one-day record:* The crews' progress is drawn from N. S. Gallison, "Construction of the Hoover Dam: Details of the Driving of the Four Huge Tunnels," in *The Story of the Hoover Dam,* p. 51.

291   *two of the shafts had been holed:* Ibid., p. 52.

292   *"Rainy & river rising"*: JCP, Feb. 9, 1932.

292   *"It was a nineteen to one bet"*: Hearings, House Committee on Appropriations, May 31, 1932, p. 225.

292   *"a wall of yellow mud"*: "The Earth Movers—I," *Fortune,* Aug. 1943, p. 210.

292   *Electrician George Carr:* LAT, Feb. 11, 1932.

293   *"Typical Colorado water"*: Allen, *Hoover Dam and Boulder City,* p. 59.

293   *The viscous slop:* Neil Holmes OH, Boulder City Public Library.

293   *A gallery of giant forms:* The description of the concrete jumbos is drawn from "Design of Lining Forms," *Engineering News-Record,* Dec. 15, 1932, pp. 15–20.

294   *To produce the 400,000 cubic yards:* C. H. Vivian, "Construction of the Hoover Dam" in *The Story of the Hoover Dam,* pp. 72–73.

294   *The initial results:* Allen, *Hoover Dam and Boulder City,* p. 71.

294   *Some first learned this fundamental principle:* Ibid, p. 73.

295   *Once the invert was poured:* The curing process is described in "Tunnel Concreting Procedure," *Engineering News-Record,* Dec. 15, 1932, p. 20.

295 *Two workers carrying:* Allen, *Hoover Dam and Boulder City,* p. 75. Allen's description corresponds to the death of Hiram A. Willis, who is listed in Reclamation records as having died of electrocution on May 30, 1932.

296 *"cruel, foolish":* Wilbur, *Memoirs,* p. 558.

297 *Mead seemed unable to explain:* See Hearings, House Committee on Appropriations, May 31, 1932, pp. 195–210.

297 *Shoreham Hotel:* See "Mr. Kaiser Goes to Washington," *Time,* Aug. 10, 1942.

297 *"patience, tolerance, and kindness":* Hearings, House Committee on Appropriations, May 31, 1932, p. 213.

298 *"You will force":* Ibid., pp. 227, 233.

298 *"The men that we employ":* Ibid., p. 234.

299 *"Who started that propaganda?":* Ibid.

299 *Never again:* See Kleinsorge, *The Boulder Canyon Project,* p. 212.

299 *Walter W. Waters:* Dickson and Allen, *The Bonus Army,* p. 5.

300 *"wasteful expenditure":* Ibid., p. 37.

300 *"mob rule":* Ibid., p. 187.

300 *"Well, Felix":* Smith, *An Uncommon Man,* p. 140.

301 *Hoover estimated his odds:* Ibid.

301 *"overcentralization":* Wilbur, *Memoirs,* p. 554.

301 *"I have no wish":* Wilbur, *Memoirs,* p. 560. The *Memoirs* were published by Stanford University in 1960, eleven years after Wilbur's death.

301 *In early fall:* Smith, *An Uncommon Man,* pp. 143–44.

302 *the GOP establishment:* Ibid., p. 146.

302 *"destroy the foundations":* Schlesinger, *The Crisis of the Old Order,* p. 434.

302 *the atmosphere on his westbound train:* Smith, *An Uncommon Man,* p. 148.

302 *"best night's sleep":* LAT, Nov. 10, 1932.

303 *pro-Hoover bunting:* Muersinge, "Memories," p. 9.

303 *"un-American":* The dispute over the polling places was covered in *LVRJ,* April 27 and 28, 1932.

303 *1932 Boulder City election results:* See LVA, Nov. 9, 1932.

303 *Young, Page, and Crowe:* JCP, Nov. 12, 1932.

303 *"They wouldn't stand up":* William D. McCullough, in Dunar and McBride, *Building Hoover Dam,* p. 107.

303    *He spent most:* Hoover, *Memoirs,* Vol. 2, p. 229; *LVRJ,* Nov. 11, 1932.

304    *"I never in my life":* Boyer, in Dunar and McBride, *Building Hoover Dam,* p. 107.

304    *The presidential train:* JCP, Nov. 12, 1932.

304    *nine thousand linear feet:* See "Tunnel Concreting Procedure," *Engineering News-Record,* Dec. 15, 1932, p. 18.

304    *Starting from the Nevada bank:* Wesley R. Nelson, "Account of the Building of the Cofferdams," in *The Story of the Hoover Dam,* p. 88; "Huge Blast Turns River into Diversion Tunnels," *Engineering News-Record,* Dec. 15, 1932, p. 9.

305    *"like a horse":* Pettitt, *So Boulder Dam Was Built,* p. 77.

305    *There was a grinding of gears:* Ibid.

306    *"an amazing celebration":* LVRJ, Nov. 14, 1932; JCP, Nov. 13, 1932.

306    *"She's taking it":* Pettitt, *So Boulder Dam Was Built.*

## CHAPTER 16: The Rising

307    *What had been a half-mile:* LVRJ, Nov. 21, 1932.

307    *Crews recovered:* LVRJ, Nov. 23, 1932.

308    *Pfc. Theodore Wells:* JCP, Nov. 16, 1932. In his journal Page incorrectly identified Wells's home station as San Diego; the 63rd Coast Artillery was stationed at Fort MacArthur from 1930. Wells's death was also reported in *LVRJ,* Nov. 18, 1932.

308    *"tim[ed] himself":* LVRJ, Nov. 22, 1932.

308    *"There wasn't much to it":* LAT, Nov. 27, 1932; the Carnegie Hero Fund records are at www.carnegiehero.org.

309    *"human pendulum":* LVA, Jan. 25, 1932, reprinted in *RE,* March 1933, p. 37.

309    *Scrugham visit:* JCP, Nov. 11, 1932.

310    *"bravely but utterly":* Time, Sept. 15, 1941.

310    *"dump Hoover":* Smith, *An Uncommon Man,* p. 140.

310    *naming him to the cabinet:* Kennedy, *Freedom from Fear,* p. 127.

311    *"In times such as these":* NYT, June 4, 1933.

311    *"Boulder Dam":* Memorandum, Secretary Ickes to Commissioner Mead, May 8, 1933, collection of BCMHA. See also Ickes, *The Secret Diary of Harold L. Ickes,* vol. 1, p. 38.

# NOTES

311   *"a number of insulting letters"*: Ickes, *The Secret Diary of Harold L. Ickes*, vol. 1, p. 37 [May 17, 1933].

311   *"sound public policy"*: See Ickes to Robert F. Crane, May 20, 1933, in Swing Papers, Special Collections, UCLA.

311   *Finally, he held that Wilbur*: Ickes, *The Secret Diary of Harold L. Ickes*, vol. 1, p. 38 [May 17, 1933].

311   *Hoover detected the hand*: Hoover, *Memoirs*, Vol. 2, p. 229, n1.

312   *"pettiness"*: Wilbur, *Memoirs*, p. 462.

312   *"a tall smiling gentleman"*: Jean Page OH, Boulder City Public Library.

312   *The cement cartel*: Adams, *Mr. Kaiser Goes to Washington*, p. 48.

312   *compromising on a discount*: See *The New Republic*, July 12, 1933, p. 220.

312   *The new bidder*: Adams, *Mr. Kaiser Goes to Washington*, p. 49.

313   *To protect themselves*: LVRJ, Aug. 29, 1932.

313   *Prostitutes in Las Vegas's*: Tex Nunley OH, BCMHA.

313   *"Everyone was supposed"*: Grant S. Allen OH, BCMHA.

313   *$45,000 a month*: LVRJ, Sept. 8, 1932.

313   *"Do you Dare"*: LVRJ, Aug. 29, 1932.

313   *"standard business practice"*: LVRJ, Sept. 8, 1932.

313   *two dividends*: See Six Companies Corporate Minutes, July 25, 1932, vol. 2, p. 365, and Aug. 15, 1932, vol. 2, p. 370.

314   *"Hearing Rushed"*: LVRJ, Aug. 29, 1932.

314   *"I believe that a man"*: LVRJ, May 8, 1933.

314   *the board immediately capitulated*: Six Companies Corporate Minutes, May 15, 1933, vol. 2, p. 416.

314   *the black population*: Figures from Roosevelt Fitzgerald, "Blacks and the Boulder Dam Project," *Nevada Historical Society Quarterly*, Fall 1981, p. 256.

315   *Colored Citizens Labor and Protective Association*: Ibid.

315   *"all assistance possible"*: LVRJ, May 27, 1932.

315   *"when and if"*: LVA, June 18, 1932.

315   *"I had never done"*: Joe Kine, quoted in Fitzgerald, "Blacks and the Boulder Dam Project," p. 257.

315   *the roster of black dam workers*: Roy Wilkins (assistant secretary, NAACP) to Ickes, May 12, 1933, NARA Denver, RG 115.

315   *"this question of Negro labor"*: LVA, July 8, 1932.

315    *Within a year:* Dennis McBride, "Among the Lotus Eaters," *The Nevadan Today (LVRJ)*, Feb. 12, 1989, p. 12CC.

315    *lowest pay grades:* Wolters, *Negroes and the Great Depression*, p. 200.

315    *The indignities:* Wilkins to Oscar Chapman, May 21, 1934, NAACP files, cited in ibid., p. 199.

316    *"Get rid of that colored cook":* Robert Parker OH, BCMHA. The Ely-Newland encounter is referenced in numerous other oral histories provided by contemporary Boulder City residents, attesting to its wide currency.

316    *"negroes would probably":* Page to Mead, July 27, 1931, NARA Denver, RG 115.

316    *Upon taking office, Ickes:* For the appointment of Foreman and Weaver, see Wolters, *Negroes and the Great Depression*, p. 142. Weaver became the first black cabinet member in U.S. history when Lyndon Johnson appointed him Secretary of Housing and Urban Development in 1966.

316    *He assured Ickes:* Mead, "Memorandum to the Secretary [Ickes]," May 16, 1933, NARA Denver, RG 115. The author is indebted to Barbara Vilander for bringing this document to his attention.

317    *"colored job seekers":* LVRJ, May 27, 1932.

317    *"I know of no way":* Ibid.

317    *As long as Negro workers:* Wolters, *Negroes and the Great Depression*, p. xiii.

317    *"color or religious affiliation":* McBride, "Among the Lotus Eaters."

318    *"The answers were":* LVA, Jan. 7, 1932, cited in Fitzgerald, "Blacks and the Boulder Dam Project," p. 257.

318    *In the first two weeks:* Fitzgerald, "Blacks and the Boulder Dam Project," p. 259.

318    *"telling description":* Ibid., p. 258.

319    *"having cast iron":* USBR, "Hoover Dam Power Plant and Appurtenant Works," Specifications No. 519, para. 81.

319    *"the maximum dimensions":* Ibid., para. 79.

319    *The greatest flood:* See ibid., drawing No. 3, "Hydrograph of the Colorado River/Lees Ferry." The graph shows that the 180,000 cubic feet per second flood was recorded in the third week of June 1921.

319    *Young turned him down:* JCP, Nov. 2, 1932.

320    *"at considerable length":* JCP, Nov. 23, 1932.

320   *The likely cause:* See USBR, Abstract of Bids, Specifications No. 519, March 4, 1931. The procedure for adjudicating the cost of change orders is specified by the construction contract between the U.S. Department of the Interior and Six Companies, Inc., April 11, 1931, articles 3 and 4.

320   *857,000 cubic yards:* See USBR, Abstract of Bids: Construction of Hoover Dam, Power Plant and Appurtenant Works, item 9 (March 4, 1931).

321   *Lookout Point blast: RE,* Oct. 1932, p. 168.

321   *The cable towers were themselves striking: The Story of the Hoover Dam,* pp. 92–95.

322   *six separate subcontracts:* The contracts are listed in *RE,* Oct. 1932, p. 174.

## CHAPTER 17: The Pour

323   *A Midwestern heat wave: LAT,* June 6, 1933.

323   *"the starting of the wheels":* "On the Purposes and Foundations of the Recovery Program," Fireside Chat, July 24, 1933.

323   *designated as Block J-3:* W. R. Nelson, "Progress of Construction at Boulder Dam," *NRE,* Jan. 1935, p. 11; see also Stevens, *Hoover Dam,* p. 190.

324   *C. W. "Wince" Bingham:* Richard E. Meyer, "A Lot of Water Has Gone over the Dam," *LAT,* June 7, 1983.

324   *eighteen months ahead of schedule:* The schedule written into the specifications called for the placing of mass concrete to begin in December 1934. See "Tentative Construction Program," Specifications No. 519.

324   *more than seventy trucks: Boulder Canyon Project Final Reports, Part IV—Design and Construction,* USBR, 1941, p. 87.

325   *Callville Wash:* J. David Rogers, "Hoover Dam: Impacts on the Engineering Profession, America, and the World," prepared for Association of Engineering Geologists, Sept. 21, 2005.

325   *a drill bit: LVRJ,* July 3, 1933.

325   *a primordial crevasse: Boulder Canyon Project Final Reports, Part IV—Design and Construction,* USBR, 1941, p. 91.

325   *"I'll let you know":* Allen, *Hoover Dam and Boulder City,* p. 163.

325   *the inner gorge:* Wm. Joe Simonds, "The Boulder Canyon Project," U.S. Bureau of Reclamation, at http://www.usbr.gov/history/hoover.html [accessed July 12, 2009].

326    *Owyhee Dam:* Gregg A. Scott et al., "Concrete Dam Evolution: The Bureau of Reclamation's Contributions," Reclamation Centennial History Symposium, 2002.

326    *230 separate columns: Annual Project History,* vol. 3, 1933, pp. 198–99.

326    *the scheme required 662 miles:* Nelson, "Boulder Dam Nears Completion," *NRE,* March 1935, p. 49.

327    *"We had 5,000 men":* "The Earth Movers—I," *Fortune,* Aug. 1943, p. 212.

327    *critical path management:* See J. David Rogers, "Hoover Dam: Impacts on the Engineering Profession, America, and the World," presentation delivered to the Association of Engineering Geologists, Sept. 21, 2005.

328    *"Oh, I'll tell you":* Richard "Curley" Francis OH, BCMHA.

329    *two patents:* U.S. Patent No. 2,202,284 (May 28, 1940) and No. 2,350,015 (May 30, 1944). Crowe also was awarded patent No. 1,560,895 in 1925 for an excavating bucket.

329    *They began the cycle:* The path of the bucket from concrete plant to pour is drawn from Lawrence P. Sowles, "Description of the Methods of Pouring the Concrete," *The Story of the Hoover Dam,* pp. 113–16.

330    *"Let it be said":* Ibid., p. 116.

330    *In the summer heat:* Steve Chubbs OH, Boulder City Public Library.

330    *keep the surface "live":* Sowles, "Description of the Methods of Pouring the Concrete," p. 117.

330    *Many lifts contained:* Ibid.

331    *Hoover Dam's grout curtain:* Wilbur and Mead, *The Construction of Hoover Dam,* p. 39. See also Specifications No. 519, paras. 85–89, pp. 47–49.

332    *"unusually good foundation":* A. W. Simonds and O. E. Boggess, Technical Memorandum 639, "Additional Grouting at Hoover Dam, 1938–1947," USBR. See also J. David Rogers, "Hoover Dam: Grout Curtain Failure and Lessons Learned in Site Characterization," presentation delivered to Association of Engineering Geologists, Sept. 23, 2005. The author is indebted to Dr. Rogers for his assistance with the technical details of the grout curtain.

333    *vast foundry: RE,* Jan. 1933, p. 12.

333    *eight hundred laborers: NRE,* July 1935, p. 139.

333    *Bechtel visit to Soviet Union:* McCartney, *Friends in High Places,* p. 45.

334    *"largest diameter plate rolls": RE,* Jan. 1935, p. 11.

334   *Then they were welded together:* Copeland Lake, "Huge Trailer Hauls Penstock Pipe at Boulder Dam," in *The Story of the Hoover Dam,* p. 130.

335   *Pitts and Johnson accident:* Pettitt, *So Boulder Dam Was Built,* pp. 96–98. Pettitt erroneously gives Jan. 3, 1934, as the date of the accident; see *LAT,* Jan. 5, 1935.

335   *Jackman death:* LVRJ, Oct. 2, 1933.

335   *Jameson death:* LVRJ, Nov. 8 and 9, 1933.

336   *His neighbors raffled off:* Meyer, "A Lot of Water Has Gone over the Dam."

336   *The form soared into the gap:* LVRJ, Sept. 19, 1933; Pettitt, *So Boulder Dam Was Built,* pp. 102–3.

336   *Reaves accident:* JCP, Feb. 21 and March 12, 1935; LVRJ, Feb. 21 and 22, 1935; Pettitt, *So Boulder Dam Was Built,* pp. 103–4.

337   *"There we were":* Allen, *Hoover Dam and Boulder City,* p. 97.

337   *"Sorry I had":* Ibid.

338   *the Six Companies board considered:* See E. J. Brockman (Six Companies supervisor of insurance) to Crowe, May 25, 1934, in Six Companies Corporate Records, vol. 5 (unpag.). Brockman's view that self-insurance "looks like a good bet" was overruled.

338   *"so far as practical":* Six Companies Corporate Minutes, Aug. 13, 1932, vol. 2, p. 369.

338   *"an engineer gave me":* Tex Nunley OH, Boulder City Public Library.

339   *"The keynote":* LVRJ, Feb. 18, 1932.

339   *thirteen thousand safety helmets:* Pettitt, *So Boulder Dam Was Built,* p. 62.

339   *"Safety was something":* Marion Allen OH, *Boulder City Public Library.*

339   *"It saved walking":* Pettitt, p. 99.

339   *One such daredevil stunt:* Ibid., p. 98; LVRJ, Feb. 20, 1935.

340   *The cookie-cutter lawsuits:* See LVRJ, Jan. 6, April 13, June 7, July 2, July 6, Aug. 1, 1933.

340   *"either die or get well":* LVRJ, Oct. 25, Nov. 2, 1933.

341   *contradicted by more than a decade of research:* Pankow, "History of Carbon Monoxide Toxicology," in Penney, ed., *Carbon Monoxide Toxicity,* p. 6.

342   *he had staged a wild chase:* LVRJ, Nov. 26, 1932.

342   *The ultimate blow:* LVRJ, Sept. 20, 1933.

342   *"one of the most widespread":* Ibid.

343    *Harry Austin arranged to defer:* Stevens, *Hoover Dam,* p. 208.

343    *"Kraus Case Is Tiresome":* LVRJ, Oct. 17, 1933.

343    *Its lawyers presented:* LVRJ, Oct. 19, 1933.

343    *After nearly seven weeks:* LVRJ, Nov. 29, 1933. Thanksgiving was not then fixed on the federal calendar and was designated variously by state laws as the fourth Thursday of November or the last Thursday of the month (Nevada's rule). Because November had five Thursdays in 1933, Nevada celebrated the holiday on the fifth, November 30.

344    *"I've seen some dumb":* LVRJ, Dec. 7, 1933.

344    *D. B. Burdick:* JCP, April 20, 1934.

345    *producing several ghastly impalements:* John F. Cahlan OH, UNR.

345    *He fed his data:* Sidney J. Williams to Frances Perkins, "Safety at Boulder Dam," Jan. 29, 1935, NARA Laguna Niguel.

346    *When the millionth cubic yard:* The Story of the Hoover Dam, p. 123.

346    *The second millionth:* LAT, June 2, 1934; Allen, *Hoover Dam and Boulder City,* p. 174.

346    *the third millionth:* NRE, March 1935, p. 50.

346    *Just over three weeks after that:* Allen, *Hoover Dam and Boulder City,* pp. 184–85.

346    *a pour lasting thirty-two months:* See "Tentative Construction Schedule," Specifications No. 519.

## CHAPTER 18: Reckonings

347    *The lookout point:* McBride, "Elks Point," *Boulder City Magazine,* June 2007.

347    *"Here man builds":* LAT, Feb. 20, 1932.

347    *A willowy Loretta Young:* LVRJ, Feb. 24, 1932.

348    *Every year brought:* Annual Project History, vol. 4, 1934, p. 24; McBride, *In the Beginning,* p. 75.

348    *Frank Capra:* JCP, Dec. 30, 1932.

348    *They were customarily escorted:* For a description of the formalities, see JCP, March 26, 1932.

348    *Privileged visitors:* The visitor totals and identities of VIPs are recorded in the Annual Project History, such as 1934, vol. 4, p. 24 (Shriners); and 1935, vol. 5, p. 36 (Mormon Tabernacle Choir).

348     *"severely interfered"*: Annual Project History, vol. 3, 1933, p. 92.

348     *Brothers was authorized*: Ibid.

348     *At Crowe's insistence*: Six Companies Corporate Minutes, April 16, 1934, vol. 2, unpag.

349     *they included a delegation*: LVRJ, April 8, 1933.

349     *"small town called Las Vegas"*: White, "Building the Big Dam," *Harper's Monthly Magazine*, June 1935, p. 118.

349     *Some 92,000 visitors*: RE, April 1935, p. 77.

349     *"Don't miss seeing"*: Rogers, *Will Rogers' Daily Telegrams*, vol. 3, p. 187 [Sept. 6, 1932].

350     *"over splendidly paved roads"*: LAT, June 18, 1933.

350     *"He has the physique"*: Ibid.

350     *"He demands"*: LAT, Oct. 22, 1933.

350     *"in the hitherto worthless"*: NYT, June 30, 1935.

350     *heroic raid*: RE, January 1933, p. 12.

351     *"The New Boulder Inn"*: Boulder City Journal, June 27, 1934.

351     *"The bootleg liquors"*: Young to Mead [memorandum], cited in Interior to U.S. Attorney General, Oct. 23, 1934, NARA Laguna Niguel, RG 115.

351     *"more thorough investigation"*: McCarran to [Assistant Secretary of the Interior] Theodore A. Walters, Aug. 3, 1934, NARA Laguna Niguel, RG 115.

352     *"quiet, good people"*: Young to Mead, Aug. 22, 1934, NARA Laguna Niguel, RG 115.

352     *"get rid of the girls"*: Ibid.

352     *"Bullets flew"*: Boulder City Journal, April 9, 1935.

352     *Overall employment*: RE, July 1935, p. 139.

353     *"On pages 34 and 35"*: Young to Joseph J. Barry, Aug. 25, 1934, NARA Denver, RG 115.

353     *"practically every change"*: Wallis to Young, Sept. 28, 1934, NARA Denver, RG 115. The author is indebted to Barbara Vilander for bringing this exchange of letters to his attention.

353     *"an unusually enthusiastic"*: Young to Mead, July 10, 1935, NARA Denver, RG 115. The author is indebted to Barbara Vilander for bringing this note to his attention.

354     *"It's thumbs down"*: Mead to Young, July 16, 1935, NARA Denver, RG 115.

354     *The first front opened:* JCP, Feb. 26, 1935.

354     *The charge originated:* LVRJ, Feb. 26, 1935.

355     *"somewhat of a man-eater":* Ickes, *The Secret Diary of Harold L. Ickes, Vol. 1,* p. 270.

355     *"stay in his own back yard":* Smith, *Building New Deal Liberalism,* p. 82.

355     *The limitation of an eight-hour workday:* The relevant federal law was the Act of June 19, 1912 (37 Stat. 137), which was incorporated in the Six Companies contract as Article 11(a).

355     *"there is evidence":* Annual Project History, vol. 5, 1935, p. 282.

355     *That did nothing:* JCP, Feb. 28; March 1, 2, 3, 9, 10, and 12, 1935.

356     *The last open diversion:* LAT, Feb. 2, 1935.

356     *Crowe hectored Page:* JCP, Feb. 15 and March 6, 1935.

356     *they hauled Page:* JCP, March 13 and 14, 1935.

357     *"physical derelict":* LVRJ, Feb. 19, 1935.

357     *Austin felt so confident:* See LVRJ, May 22, 1935 (nine lawsuits seeking $900,000 filed in Reno), and Aug. 6, 1935 (forty-eight suits in Reno and Las Vegas, totaling $4.8 million in claims).

357     *"We're the ones":* Affidavit, Hildebrand, *Norman v. Six Companies,* March 26, 1935.

357     *"We have at least":* Affidavit, Austin, *Norman v. Six Companies,* March 26, 1935.

358     *9–3 verdict:* LVRJ, March 18, 1935.

358     *Their sources told them:* See affidavits of Clarence Stocker and John L. Russell, March 26, 1935; and Jerome B. White, April 1, 1935, *Norman v. Six Companies.*

358     *Austin presented a sheaf:* LVRJ, March 27, 1935.

358     *Six Companies quietly settled:* LVRJ, Jan. 16, 1935.

359     *"Mr. Kaiser's telegraphic":* Ickes to Pittman, March 15, 1935, cited in Foster, *Henry J. Kaiser,* pp. 59–60.

359     *"Your personal assistant":* Kaiser to Ickes, March 26, 1935, cited in Foster, *Henry J. Kaiser,* p. 60.

359     *"hundreds of men":* Pettitt, *So Boulder Dam Was Built,* pp. 27–28.

359     *"On the average":* Ibid., p. 64. Pettitt's estimate was low. His formula of an average twenty-six per year in 1931 through 1935 would number the

fatalities at about 130. Reclamation's official figures, which are themselves assumed to be conservative, give the toll as 140, not counting pneumonia cases; adding them, the number rises to at least 167.

359 *"that every hour"*: Ibid., p. ii.

360 *"propaganda"*: Young to Mead, Dec. 24, 1935, NARA Denver, RG 115. The author thanks Barbara Vilander for bringing this memo to his attention.

360 *Pettitt to spend his honeymoon*: "George Albert Pettitt," In Memoriam, May 1977, University of California Academic Senate.

360 *Henry Luce*: Adams, *Mr. Kaiser Goes to Washington*, p. 109.

360 *net profit of $75,000*: LVRJ, Feb. 17, 1936.

361 *IWW historians*: Thompson, *The I.W.W.*, p. 159.

361 *Ragnald Fyhen*: Fyhen, "Labor Notes," Oct. 1968, Fyhen Papers, Special Collections, UNLV.

362 *"The language used"*: Ibid.

362 *unveiling of a tablet*: NRE, July 1935, p. 143.

362 *The culprit was*: Allen, *Hoover Dam and Boulder City*, p. 177. Sheldon Modglin's title is at ibid., p. 160. For B. Frank Modglin's role at MacDonald & Kahn, see Robert L. Bridges OH, Regional Oral History Office, Bancroft Library, UC Berkeley, pp. 75 and 91; and Wolf, *Big Dams and Other Dreams*, p. 251.

362 *Modglin unilaterally rescinded*: LVRJ, July 12, 1935.

363 *"touching off the spark"*: LVRJ, July 13, 1935.

363 *A rumor spread*: LVRJ, July 15, 1935.

364 *"little or no work"*: LAT, July 15, 1935.

364 *"The prospects are good"*: Letter, Mead to Young, July 16, 1935, NARA Denver.

364 *its board flatly rejected*: LVRJ, July 23, 1935.

364 *This was cold comfort*: Ibid.

365 *The wage issue was to be dumped*: NYT, July 26, 1935.

365 *Whether Ickes took*: For the Virgin Islands affair, see Ickes, *The Secret Diary of Harold L. Ickes*, vol. 1, pp. 399–411 [July 16–Aug. 6, 1935].

## CHAPTER 19: The Crest

366 *seventy staff aides*: Black, *Franklin Delano Roosevelt*, p. 367.

366 *"five bedrooms"*: NYT, Sept. 29, 1935.

366  *"all non-political pretense"*: LAT, Sept. 30, 1935.

366  *"first forced march"*: NYT, Sept. 29, 1935.

367  *pledged his support*: Moley, *The First New Deal*, p. 326.

367  *"yardstick"*: *The Public Papers and Addresses of Franklin D. Roosevelt*, Vol. 1 (Portland, Ore., Sept. 21, 1932).

367  *A constant irritant*: Schlesinger, *The Politics of Upheaval*, p. 349.

368  *outskirts of Boulder City*: LAT, Oct. 1, 1935; NYT, Oct. 1, 1935.

369  *"We had only"*: Recollections of Rupert B. Spearman, BCMHA.

369  *"We don't care"*: Walker Young OH, Boulder City Public Library.

369  *"There was the governor"*: Young OH; LAT, Oct. 1, 1935.

369  *"I could at least"*: Young OH.

370  *"Niagara of verbiage"*: Kennedy, *Freedom from Fear*, p. 114.

370  *"could see more"*: Ibid.

370  *"a community stranded"*: Pettitt, *So Boulder Dam Was Built*, p. 40.

370  *"gaily bedecked"*: LAT, Oct. 1, 1935.

371  *"I'm speechless"*: Ibid.

371  *The experience of staring up*: Cook, *Eleanor Roosevelt*, Vol. 2: *The Defining Years, 1933–1938*, p. 297.

372  *"Just as nature"*: RE, Nov. 1935, p. 209; LVRJ, Oct. 1, 1935.

372  *"more intimately associated"*: The text of the Ickes address is in RE, Nov. 1935, p. 209ff.

372  *"to try to nail down"*: Ickes, *The Secret Diary of Harold L. Ickes*, vol. 1, Sept. 30, 1935, p. 445.

372  *"This morning I came"*: RE, Oct. 1935, p. 193; LVRJ, Oct. 1, 1935.

373  *"Oh, I wanted"*: Madeline Knighten OH, Boulder City Public Library.

373  *"It was Hoover"*: LAT, Sept. 30, 1935.

374  *"It Can't Be Done"*: LAT, May 18, 1933.

374  *"And Still It Can't Be Done"*: LAT, Oct. 1, 1935.

374  *His was an expansive view*: Chernow, *Alexander Hamilton*, p. 258.

375  *"Sizzling hot today"*: Morrison, *Those Were the Days*, pp. 235–36.

375  *Later that afternoon*: See LAT, Oct. 1, 1935; John Cahlan OH UNR; Hugh Shamberger OH, UNR.

376  *"Patrick J. Crowe"*: Walker Young to Virginia "Teddy" Fenton, March 1, 1973, BCMHA.

377    *"He'd climb ladders"*: Robert Parker OH.

377    *"I Love Candy"*: LAT, May 30, 1979.

377    *His tenure lasted*: Parker OH.

378    *"Rough, tough, rock-hard men"*: LAT, May 30, 1979.

378    *Clarence Kailin background*: Giffey, ed., *Long Shadows*, pp. 301–2. As of late 2008, Kailin was still actively speaking out on social issues at the age of ninety-four.

378    *"I told him"*: LAT, May 30, 1979.

379    *His silhouette*: NYT, May 26, 2002.

379    *"oppressive monotony"*: See Allen Tupper True, "Color and Decoration at the Boulder Power Plant," *RE*, Jan. 1936, p. 12.

380    *"the look of eagles"*: Hansen, *The Sculptures of Hoover Dam* (USBR, 1968). The booklet was a reissue of articles Hansen wrote for the Feb., March, and April 1942 issues of the bureau's *RE*.

381    *Senator Pat McCarran*: NYT, April 22, 1947.

381    *"I didn't know Hoover"*: LAT, May 1, 1947.

381    *"Mr. Hoover as the only living"*: Swing to Harry Slattery, Sept. 3, 1947, Swing Papers, UCLA.

381    *"Vindication!"*: LAT, May 1, 1947.

382    *"It's one thing"*: "The Earth Movers—I," *Fortune*, Aug. 1943, p. 214.

382    *final profit*: Ibid.

383    *Change orders issued*: Stevens, *Hoover Dam*, p. 252.

383    *Crowe contract*: See Six Companies Corporate Minutes, Nov. 16, 1931, vol. 2, p. 323. The board advanced portions of the bonus to Crowe on Nov. 20, 1933 ($100,000); Nov. 9, 1934 ($75,000); and Dec. 16, 1935 ($75,000).

383    *"Take it, Ralph"*: NYT, March 1, 1936.

384    *"The dim-lit city"*: LAT, Oct. 10, 1936.

384    *"many weary days"*: Ibid.

## CHAPTER 20: Legacies

385    *Lake Mead depth*: Lake Mead's surface elevation, charted back to Feb. 1935 and updated monthly, is reported at www.usbr.gov/lc/region/g4000/hourly/mead-elv.html [accessed July 21, 2009].

# NOTES

385   *a timber raft:* Leo Dunbar OH, May 28, 1985, Boulder City Public Library.

385   *The results told them:* LAT, June 11, 1936.

386   *"The water in a pitcher":* RE, Jan. 1937, p. 8.

386   *There was no doubt:* LAT, May 19, 1939. For a technical discussion of Lake Mead's effect on earthquakes, see Daniel R. H. O'Connell, "Seismicity Near Hoover Dam" [2002], USBR, at www.nbmg.unr.edu/nesc/Presentations/usbr.pdf [accessed July 21, 2009].

386   *the most intense earthquake activity:* See J. David Rogers, "Hoover Dam Impacts," presentation prepared for conference on "The Fate and Future of the Colorado River," Huntington–USC Institute on California and the West, Nov. 1, 2008.

387   *"guesswork":* See Weaver and Bruce, *Dam Foundation Grouting*, p. 10.

387   *"not altogether unexpected":* A. W. Simonds and O. E. Boggess, "Additional Grouting at Hoover Dam, 1938–1947," USBR Technical Memorandum No. 639, March 1950, p. 2.

389   *The deepest hole:* A. W. Simonds, "Final Foundation Treatment at Hoover Dam," *Transactions,* American Society of Civil Engineers, Paper No. 2537 (Dec. 1951), p. 92.

389   *a cramped space:* See Rogers, "Hoover Dam Impacts," p. 35.

389   *"as if they had been shot":* Ibid., p. 106 (discussion by O. E. Boggess).

390   *uplift fell below the level:* Simonds and Boggess, "Additional Grouting at Hoover Dam, 1938–1947," p. 75.

390   *The bureau extracted the maximum publicity:* LAT, Aug. 7, 1941.

391   *The worst damage:* See http://www.usbr.gov/lc/hooverdam/History/essays/spillways.html [accessed July 19, 2009].

391   *This time the cause:* See Rogers, "Hoover Dam: Impacts on the Engineering Profession, America, and the World," presentation to Association of Engineering Geologists, Sept. 21, 2005, pp. 75–76.

393   *"camping space":* LAT, Aug. 1, 1983.

394   *But Arizona was also booming:* Reisner, *Cadillac Desert*, pp. 259–60.

394   *five Indian reservations:* Ibid., p. 262.

395   *tree ring data:* The key work in this field is C. W. Stockton and Gordon C. Jacoby, "Long-Term Surface-Water and Streamflow Trends in the Upper Colorado River Basin," National Science Foundation, 1976.

395    *In the twenty years:* See "Colorado River Basin Water Management: Evaluating and Adjusting to Hydroclimatic Variability," National Research Council, 2007, p. 96. This report is a groundbreaking effort to assess the effect of climate change on the Colorado watershed.

395    *340 witnesses:* Norris Hundley, Jr., "Clio Nods: *Arizona v. California* and the Boulder Canyon Act—A Reassessment," *Western Historical Quarterly,* Jan. 1972, p. 17.

395    *They ruled that Congress: Arizona v. California,* 373 U.S. 546.

396    *"a power and command":* Ibid., 546, 628.

397    *the age of abundance:* See Lisa Force, *The Colorado: A River at Risk,* Grand Canyon Trust, 2005, p. 15.

397    *In the desert reservoirs:* Ibid., p. 36.

397    *People kept coming:* Current population figures are from the U.S. Census, at www.census.gov.

397    *"unlimited population growth":* "Colorado River Basin Water Management," National Research Council, 2007, p. 52.

397    *An average 9.0 million:* See Terry Fulp, "Response of the System to Various Hydrological and Operational Assumptions," presentation at "Hard Times on the Colorado River: Drought, Growth, and the Future of the Compact," Natural Resources Law Center, University of Colorado (June 2005), p. 8.

398    *"reductions in snowpack":* Ibid., p. 91.

399    *"With this agreement":* Hon. Gale Norton, "Remarks at formal signing ceremony: The California Colorado River Water Agreement," Oct. 16, 2003, at www.doi.gov/secretary/speeches/hoover.html [accessed Nov. 6, 2009].

399    *Attending an irrigation congress:* Worster, *Rivers of Empire,* p. 132.

399    *"I tell you, gentlemen":* Stegner, *Beyond the Hundredth Meridian,* p. 343.

400    *"physical, economic": Colorado River Basin Water Management: Evaluating and Adjusting to Hydroclimatic Variability,* National Academy of Sciences 2007, at http://www.nap.edu/catalog/11857.html [accessed July 20, 2009].

401    *Geologists have mapped twenty-six faults:* Rogers, "The Boulder Canyon Project and Hoover Dam," Nov. 1, 2008.

401    *"maximum credible earthquake":* See Larry K. Nuss, "Seismic Analysis of Hoover Dam," presented to the U.S.-Japan Panel on Wind and Seismic Effects, Nov. 1998.

402    *Shea's company:* Robert L. Bridges OH, Bancroft Library, UC Berkeley.

402    *At Utah Construction:* Utah's wartime activities are detailed in Sessions and Sessions, *Utah International,* pp. 71–81.

402    *Corey transformed Utah:* Ibid., pp. 284–88.

402    *a cover story in* Time: "The Earth Mover," *Time,* May 3, 1954.

403    *Dennis Washington: Wall Street Journal,* June 6, 1996.

403    *construction of the first Liberty Ship:* "The Earth Movers—II," *Fortune,* Sept. 1943, p. 224.

404    *"When you're in trouble":* Bridges OH.

404    *Big Dig: Boston Globe,* Jan. 24, 2008.

405    *At the annual encampment:* McCartney, *Friends in High Places,* pp. 14–15.

405    *billionaires:* The Bechtels ranked ninety-first on the 2007 Forbes 400 list of the richest Americans, with a combined net worth estimated at $3.5 billion. See *Forbes,* Sept. 20, 2007.

406    *"sensationalism":* Young to Virginia Fenton, March 1, 1973, BCMHA.

406    *He died on April 23, 1982: LAT,* May 3, 1982.

406    *"a fine job out there":* Northcutt Ely to Sims Ely, April 8, 1939, Northcutt Ely Papers Stanford University; for references to Theodore Roosevelt, see Sims Ely to Harold Ickes, April 6, 1940, and Ickes to Ely, April 15, 1940, both in Ely Papers.

406    *Some members of its business community:* McBride, *In the Beginning,* pp. 95–97.

407    *the first bottle:* Ibid., p. 25.

407    *"My goodness, man": LVRJ,* Feb. 28, 1946.

407    *With war's end:* Rocca, *America's Master Dam Builder,* p. 345.

408    *He was sixty-two:* Ibid., p. 347.

408    *"My cow business":* Crowe to Mrs. Melvin Holbrook, Dec. 25, 1945. The author is grateful to John Hollstein for a copy of this letter.

408    *"If you want to see":* "By a Damsite," *Time,* June 19, 1944.

408    *"I had an idea":* Robert Parker OH, Boulder City Public Library.

# BIBLIOGRAPHY

## BOOKS

Adams, Stephen B. *Mr. Kaiser Goes to Washington: The Rise of a Government Entrepreneur.* Chapel Hill: University of North Carolina Press, 1997.

Alexander, J. A. *The Life of George Chaffey.* Melbourne: Macmillan, 1928.

Allen, Marion V. *Hoover Dam and Boulder City.* Privately printed, 1983.

Audubon, John Woodhouse. *Audubon's Western Journal: 1849–1850.* Cleveland: Arthur H. Clark, 1906.

Bieber, Ralph P. (ed.). *Southern Trails to California in 1849.* Glendale: Arthur H. Clark, 1937.

Bird, Stewart, and Dan Georgakas and Deborah Shaffer. *Solidarity Forever: An Oral History of the IWW.* Chicago: Lake View, 1985.

Black, Conrad. *Franklin Delano Roosevelt: Champion of Freedom.* New York: PublicAffairs, 2003.

Blake, William P. "Geological Report," in *Explorations and Surveys for a Railroad Route from the Mississippi River to the Pacific Ocean,* Vol. 5 (U.S. Senate Exec. Doc. No. 78, 32nd Congress, 2nd Session). Washington, D.C.: United States Senate, 1857.

Bohn, Frank (ed.). *Boulder Dam: From the Origin of the Idea to the Swing-Johnson Bill.* New York: Joint Committee of National Utility Associations, 1927.

Boyer, Diane E., and Robert H. Webb. *Damming Grand Canyon: The 1923 USGS Colorado River Expedition.* Logan: Utah State University Press, 2007.

# BIBLIOGRAPHY

Brands, H. W. *The Age of Gold: The California Gold Rush and the New American Dream*. New York: Doubleday, 2000.

Browne, J. Ross. *Report of the Debates in the Convention of California, on the Formation of the State Constitution, in September and October, 1849*. Washington, D.C.: John T. Towers, 1850.

*Building a Century: Bechtel 1898–1998*. San Francisco: Andrews MacMeel, 1998.

Camillo, Charles A., and Matthew T. Pearcy. *Upon Their Shoulders: A History of the Mississippi River Commission*. Vicksburg: Mississippi River Commission, 2004.

Chan, Loren Briggs. *Sagebrush Statesman: Tasker L. Oddie of Nevada*. Reno: University of Nevada Press, 1973.

Chernow, Ron. *Alexander Hamilton*. New York: Penguin, 2004.

———. *The House of Morgan*. New York: Simon & Schuster, 1990.

Clarke, Jeanne Nienaber. *Roosevelt's Warrior: Harold L. Ickes and the New Deal*. Baltimore: Johns Hopkins University Press, 1996.

Cook, Blanche Wiesen. *Eleanor Roosevelt*, Vol. 2, *The Defining Years, 1933–1938*. New York: Penguin, 2000.

Cory, Harry Thomas. *The Imperial Valley and the Salton Sink*. San Francisco: John J. Newbegin, 1915.

Cutler, Leland W. *America Is Good to a Country Boy*. Stanford: Stanford University Press, 1954.

Dabney, Lewis M. *Edmund Wilson: A Life in Literature*. New York: Farrar, Straus & Giroux, 2005.

Davis, Arthur Powell. *Report on Problems of Imperial Valley and Vicinity*. Washington, D. C.: Government Printing Office, 1921.

Davis, William C. *Jefferson Davis: The Man and His Hour*. New York: HarperCollins, 1991.

deBuys, William, and Joan Myers. *Salt Dreams: Land and Water in Low-down California*. Albuquerque: University of New Mexico Press, 1999.

deStanley, Mildred. *The Salton Sea: Yesterday and Today*. Los Angeles: Triumph, 1966.

DeVoto, Bernard. *The Course of Empire*. Boston: Houghton Mifflin, 1952.

Dickson, Paul, and Thomas B. Allen. *The Bonus Army: An American Epic*. New York: Walker, 2004.

Dunar, Andrew J., and Dennis McBride. *Building Hoover Dam: An Oral History of the Great Depression.* Reno: University of Nevada Press, 1993.

Eccles, Marriner S. *Beckoning Frontiers: Public and Personal Recollections.* New York: Alfred A. Knopf, 1951.

Erie, Steven P. *Beyond Chinatown: The Metropolitan Water District, Growth, and the Environment in Southern California.* Stanford: Stanford University Press, 2006.

Flint, Richard, and Shirley Cushing Flint (eds.). *The Coronado Expedition from the Distance of 460 Years.* Albuquerque: University of New Mexico Press, 2003.

———. *The Coronado Expedition to Tierra Nueva.* Niwot: University Press of Colorado, 1997.

Foster, Mark S. *Henry J. Kaiser: Builder in the Modern American West.* Austin: University of Texas Press, 1989.

Fradkin, Philip L. *The Great Earthquake and Firestorms of 1906: How San Francisco Nearly Destroyed Itself.* Berkeley: University of California Press, 2005.

———. *A River No More: The Colorado River and the West.* New York: Alfred A. Knopf, 1981.

Friedman, Milton, and Anna Jacobson Schwartz. *A Monetary History of the United States, 1867–1960.* Princeton: Princeton University Press, 1963.

Galbraith, John Kenneth. *The Great Crash 1929.* Boston: Houghton Mifflin, 1979.

Giffey, David (ed.). *Long Shadows: Veterans' Paths to Peace.* Madison: Attwood, 2006.

Gottlieb, Robert, and Irene Wolt. *Thinking Big: The Story of the Los Angeles Times, Its Publishers, and Their Influence on Southern California.* New York: G. P. Putnam's Sons, 1977.

Haase, John. *Big Red.* New York: Pinnacle, 1980.

Heffernan, William T. *Personal Recollections.* Calexico: Calexico Chronicle, 1930.

Heiner, Albert P. *Henry J. Kaiser, Western Colossus: An Insider's View.* San Francisco: Halo, 1991.

Hoover, Herbert C. *The Memoirs of Herbert Hoover,* Vol. 2, *The Cabinet and the Presidency, 1920–1933.* New York: Macmillan, 1952.

———. *The Memoirs of Herbert Hoover,* Vol. 3, *The Great Depression, 1929–1941.* New York: Macmillan, 1952.

———. *The State Papers and Other Public Writings of Herbert Hoover,* Vol. 1 (William Starr Myers, ed.) Garden City: Doubleday, Doran, 1934.

Hopkins, A. D., and K. J. Evans (eds.). *The First 100: Portraits of the Men and Women Who Shaped Las Vegas.* Henderson, Nev.: Huntington, 1999.

Howe, Edgar F., and Wilbur Jay Hall. *The Story of the First Decade in Imperial Valley, California.* Imperial, Calif.: Edgar F. Howe & Sons, 1910.

Hubbard, Preston J. *Origins of the TVA: The Muscle Shoals Controversy, 1920–1932.* New York: W. W. Norton, 1961.

Hundley, Norris, Jr. *Dividing the Waters.* Berkeley: University of California Press, 1966.

———. *Water and the West.* Berkeley: University of California Press, 1975.

Hyman, Sidney. *Marriner S. Eccles: Private Entrepreneur and Public Servant.* Stanford: Graduate School of Business, Stanford University, 1976.

Ickes, Harold L. *The Secret Diary of Harold L. Ickes:* Vol. 1, *The First Thousand Days, 1933–1936.* New York: Simon & Schuster, 1953.

Ingram, Robert L. *A Builder and His Family, 1898–1948.* San Francisco: Privately printed, 1949.

Ives, Joseph Christmas. *Report upon the Colorado River of the West.* New York: Da Capo, 1969 (facsimile of 1861 edition).

Jackson, Donald C. *Building the Ultimate Dam: John S. Eastwood and the Control of Water in the West.* Lawrence: University Press of Kansas, 1995.

———. *Great American Bridges and Dams.* New York: John Wiley & Sons, 1988.

James, George Wharton. *The Wonders of the Colorado Desert.* Boston: Little, Brown, 1907.

Johnson, Hiram W. *The Diary Letters of Hiram W. Johnson, 1917–1945.* New York: Garland, 1983.

Kahn, Otto H. *Our Economic and Other Problems: A Financier's Point of View.* New York: George H. Doran, 1920.

Kahrl, William L. *Water and Power.* Berkeley: University of California Press, 1982.

Kennan, George. *The Salton Sea: An Account of Harriman's Fight with the Colorado River.* New York: Macmillan, 1917.

Kennedy, David M. *Freedom from Fear: The American People in Depression and War, 1929–1945.* New York: Oxford University Press, 2005.

Klein, Maury. *The Life and Legend of E. H. Harriman.* Chapel Hill: University of North Carolina Press, 2000.

# BIBLIOGRAPHY

Kleinsorge, Paul L. *The Boulder Canyon Project: Historical and Economic Aspects*. Stanford: Stanford University Press, 1941.

Kollgaard, Eric B., and Wallace L. Chadwick (eds.). *Development of Dam Engineering in the United States*. New York: Pergamon, 1988.

Lane, Franklin K. *The Letters of Franklin K. Lane, Personal and Political*. (Anne Wintermute Lane and Louise Herrick Wall, eds.) Boston: Houghton Mifflin, 1922.

LeTourneau, Robert G. *Mover of Men and Mountains*. New York: Prentice Hall, 1967.

Lippmann, Walter. *Interpretations, 1931–1932*. New York: Macmillan, 1932.

——. *Interpretations, 1933–1935*. New York: Macmillan, 1936.

Lower, Richard Coke. *A Bloc of One: The Political Career of Hiram W. Johnson*. Stanford: Stanford University Press, 1993.

McBride, Dennis. *In the Beginning: A History of Boulder City, Nevada*. Boulder City: Boulder City Museum, 1992.

McCartney, Laton. *Friends in High Places: The Bechtel Story: The Most Secret Corporation and How It Engineered the World*. New York: Simon & Schuster, 1988.

McElvaine, Robert S. *The Great Depression: America, 1929–1941*. New York: Three Rivers, 1993.

McPhee, John. *The Control of Nature*. New York: Farrar, Straus & Giroux, 1989.

Min, Pyong Gap (ed.). *Asian Americans: Contemporary Trends and Issues*. Thousand Oaks, Calif.: Pine Forge, 2006.

Moehring, Eugene P., and Michael S. Green. *Las Vegas: A Centennial History*. Reno: University of Nevada Press, 2005.

Moeller, Beverly Bowen. *Phil Swing and Boulder Dam*. Berkeley: University of California Press, 1971.

Moley, Raymond. *The First New Deal*. New York: Harcourt, Brace & World, 1966.

Morrison, Ann. *Those Were the Days: The Diary of Ann Morrison*. Boise: Em-Kayan Press, 1951.

Muir, John. *The Wilderness World of John Muir* (Edwin Way Teale, ed.). New York: Mariner, 2001.

Mulholland, Catherine. *William Mulholland and the Rise of Los Angeles*. Berkeley: University of California Press, 2000.

Myers, William A. *River of Controversy: A Review of the Involvement of the Southern California Edison Company and Its Predecessors in the Development of the Colorado River, 1902–1942.* Los Angeles: Southern California Edison Co., 1982.

Nadeau, Remi A. *The Water Seekers.* New York: Doubleday, 1950.

Nash, Lee (ed.). *Understanding Herbert Hoover: Ten Perspectives.* Stanford: Hoover Institution Press, 1987.

Nelson, Gordon E. *The Lobbyist: The Story of George H. Maxwell, Irrigation Crusader.* Bowie: Headgate Press, 2001.

Olson, Reuel Leslie. *The Colorado River Compact.* Los Angeles: Published by the author, 1926.

Outland, Charles F. *Man-Made Disaster: The Story of St. Francis Dam.* Spokane: Arthur H. Clark, 2002 (facsimile of 1977 edition).

Paul, Elliott. *Desperate Scenery.* New York: Random House, 1954.

———. *A Ghost Town on the Yellowstone.* New York: Random House, 1948.

Penney, David G. (ed.). *Carbon Monoxide Poisoning.* Boca Raton: CRC, 2008.

———. *Carbon Monoxide Toxicity.* Boca Raton: CRC, 2000.

Petroski, Henry. *Remaking the World: Adventures in Engineering.* New York: Vintage, 1998.

Pettitt, George. *So Boulder Dam Was Built.* Berkeley: Six Companies, Inc., 1935.

Philbrick, Nathaniel. *Mayflower: A Story of Courage, Community, and War.* New York: Viking, 2006.

Pisani, Donald J. *From the Family Farm to Agribusiness: The Irrigation Crusade in California and the West, 1850–1931.* Berkeley: University of California Press, 1984.

———. *Water and American Government: The Reclamation Bureau, National Water Policy, and the West, 1902–1935.* Berkeley: University of California Press, 2002.

Powell, John Wesley. *The Arid Lands.* [*Report on the Lands of the Arid Region of the United States (1878).*] Lincoln: University of Nebraska Press, 2004.

———. *The Exploration of the Colorado River and Its Canyons.* New York: Penguin, 1987.

Quint, Howard H., and Robert H. Ferrell (eds.). *The Talkative President: The Off-the-Record Press Conferences of Calvin Coolidge.* Amherst: University of Massachusetts Press, 1964.

Reisner, Marc. *Cadillac Desert.* New York: Viking, 1986.

Renshaw, Patrick. *The Wobblies: The Story of the IWW and Syndicalism in the United States.* Chicago: Ivan R. Dee, 1999.

Righter, Robert W. *The Battle over Hetch Hetchy: America's Most Controversial Dam and the Birth of Modern Environmentalism.* New York: Oxford University Press, 2005.

Ritchie, Donald A. *Electing FDR: The New Deal Campaign of 1932.* Lawrence: University Press of Kansas, 2007.

Robinson, Michael C. *Water for the West: The Bureau of Reclamation, 1902–1977.* Chicago: Public Works Historical Society, 1979.

Rocca, Al M. *America's Master Dam Builder: The Engineering Genius of Frank T. Crowe.* Lanham, Md.: University Press of America, 2001.

Rockwood, Charles R. *Born of the Desert.* Calexico: Calexico Chronicle, 1909.

Rogers, Will. *Will Rogers' Daily Telegrams,* Vol. 3, *The Hoover Years 1931–1933.* Stillwater: Oklahoma State University Press, 1979.

Roosevelt, Franklin Delano. *The Public Papers and Addresses of Franklin D. Roosevelt,* Vol. 1. New York: Harper & Bros., 1938.

Roosevelt, Theodore. *Presidential Addresses and State Papers,* vol. 5. New York: Review of Reviews, 1910.

Rosenblum, Walter, and Alan Trachtenberg. *America and Lewis Hine.* Millerton, N.Y.: Aperture, 1977.

Schlesinger, Arthur M., Jr. *The Crisis of the Old Order, 1919–1933.* New York: Houghton Mifflin, 1957, 2003.

———. *The Politics of Upheaval: 1935–1936.* New York: Houghton Mifflin, 1960.

Sessions, Gene A., and Sterling D. Sessions. *Utah International: A Biography of a Business.* Ogden: Weber State University and the Stewart Library, 2002.

Smith, Jason Scott. *Building New Deal Liberalism: The Political Economy of Public Works, 1933–1956.* Cambridge: Cambridge University Press, 2006.

Smith, Jean Edward. *FDR.* New York: Random House, 2007.

Smith, Richard Norton. *An Uncommon Man: The Triumph of Herbert Hoover.* New York: Simon & Schuster, 1984.

Smythe, William Ellsworth. *City Homes on Country Lanes.* New York: Macmillan, 1921.

# BIBLIOGRAPHY

——. *The Conquest of Arid America*. Seattle: University of Washington Press, 1905.

Stegner, Wallace. *Beyond the Hundredth Meridian: John Wesley Powell and the Second Opening of the West*. New York: Penguin, 1992.

Stein, Herbert. *The Fiscal Revolution in America*. Washington, D.C.: AEI, 1990.

Stevens, Joseph E. *Hoover Dam: An American Adventure*. Norman: University of Oklahoma Press, 1988.

Stratton, Royal B. *Captivity of the Oatman Girls: Being an Interesting Narrative of Life Among the Apache and Mohave Indians*. New York: Carlton & Porter, 1858.

Sykes, Godfrey. *The Colorado Delta*. Washington: Carnegie Institute of Washington and the American Geographical Society of New York, 1937.

Terkel, Studs. *Hard Times: An Oral History of the Great Depression*. New York: Pantheon, 1970.

Thompson, Carl D. *Confessions of the Power Trust*. New York: E. P. Dutton, 1932.

Thompson, Fred. *The I.W.W.: Its First Fifty Years*. Chicago: Industrial Workers of the World, 1955.

Tout, Otis B. *The First Thirty Years, Being an Account of the Principal Events in the History of Imperial Valley, Southern California, U.S.A.* San Diego: O. B. Tout, 1930.

Twain, Mark. *The Autobiography of Mark Twain*. New York: Harper Perennial, 2000.

Twain, Mark, and Charles Dudley Warner. *The Gilded Age*. New York: Penguin Classics, 2001.

"Twelve Southerners." *I'll Take My Stand*. New York: Harper & Bros., 1930.

Tyler, Daniel. *Silver Fox of the Rockies: Delphus E. Carpenter and Western Water Compacts*. Norman: University of Oklahoma Press, 2003.

Vilander, Barbara. *Hoover Dam: The Photographs of Ben Glaha*. Tucson: University of Arizona Press, 1999.

Vinten-Johansen, Peter, et al. *Cholera, Chloroform, and the Science of Medicine: A Life of John Snow*. New York: Oxford University Press, 2003.

Wagner, Rob Leicester. *Red Ink White Lies: The Rise and Fall of Los Angeles Newspapers, 1920–1962*. Upland, Calif.: Dragonflyer, 2000.

Ward, Diane Raines. *Water Wars: Drought, Flood, Folly, and the Politics of Thirst*. New York: Riverside, 2002.

Warne, William E. *The Bureau of Reclamation.* New York: Praeger, 1973.

Waters, Frank. *The Colorado.* New York: Rinehart, 1946.

Watkins, T. H. (ed.). *The Grand Colorado.* Palo Alto: American West Publishing Co., 1969.

———. *Righteous Pilgrim: The Life and Times of Harold L. Ickes, 1874–1952.* New York: Henry Holt, 1992.

Weaver, Kenneth D., and Donald A. Bruce. *Dam Foundation Grouting.* Reston, Va.: ASCE, 2007.

Wehr, Kevin. *America's Fight over Water: The Environmental and Political Effects of Large-Scale Water Systems.* New York: Routledge, 2004.

Wells, H. G. *The Shape of Things to Come.* London: Penguin, 2005.

Wilbur, Ray Lyman. *The Memoirs of Ray Lyman Wilbur.* Stanford: Stanford University Press, 1960.

Wilbur, Ray Lyman, and Northcutt Ely. *The Hoover Dam Power and Water Contracts and Related Data.* Washington, D.C.: U.S. Government Printing Office, 1933.

Wilbur, Ray Lyman, and Elwood Mead. *The Construction of Hoover Dam.* Washington, D.C.: U.S. Government Printing Office, 1933.

Wilson, Edmund. *The American Earthquake.* New York: Da Capo, 1996.

Wilson, Neill C., and Frank J. Taylor. *The Earth Changers.* Garden City: Doubleday, 1957.

Wolf, Donald E. *Big Dams and Other Dreams: The Six Companies Story.* Norman: University of Oklahoma Press, 1996.

Wolters, Raymond. *Negroes and the Great Depression: The Problem of Economic Recovery.* Westport, Conn.: Greenwood, 1970.

Woodbury, David O. *The Colorado Conquest.* New York: Dodd, Mead, 1941.

Worster, Donald. *Rivers of Empire: Water, Aridity, and the Growth of the American West.* New York: Oxford University Press, 1985.

Wright, Harold Bell. *The Winning of Barbara Worth.* [1911] Gretna, La.: Pelican, 1999.

# ACKNOWLEDGMENTS

The designers and builders of Hoover Dam were actors in a grand drama of human endeavor and pioneers in the truest sense of the word. The documentary material they left to posterity, ranging from youthful personal letters treasured as family heirlooms to oral histories recorded in their twilight years, stands in vibrant counterpoint to the sanitized official histories of this monumental project. They preserve the words of the men who excavated the canyon and poured concrete in conditions of extraordinary hardship, and of the wives and children who lived the experience with them.

Much of this material is held at the archive of the Boulder City Museum and Historical Association, the indispensable first stop for researchers into the history of Hoover Dam. Located as of this writing in the basement of Boulder City's Boulder Dam Hotel, the archive is very much a labor of love for Dennis McBride, a native of the region and a meticulous archivist. I am indebted to Mr. McBride and his associate Diane E. Greene for their help in identifying items of special interest in the collection and providing me with access to relevant materials.

Among the museum's most important holdings is the original journal of John Chatfield Page, the Reclamation Bureau's office engineer at Boulder City from 1931 to 1935. Page's journal provides an invaluable daily record of the official and social life revolving around the dam project. (Sadly, the volume for 1933 has been lost.) The library of the University of Nevada, Las

# ACKNOWLEDGMENTS

Vegas, deserves special recognition for its initiative in digitizing all extant volumes of the journal and making them available online in facsimile form.

Most of the oral histories I used to research this book were produced by a cooperative effort of the Boulder City Public Library and the Las Vegas branch of the American Association of University Women; transcripts are held at the Boulder City Public Library. The histories from this collection most important to my research are listed at the end of this note, along with oral histories from other collections pertinent to this project.

I also made extensive use of memoirs and diaries by direct and indirect participants in the raising of Hoover Dam. Herbert Hoover deals with his namesake project at length in the second and third volumes of his memoirs, published in 1952. These are, however, marred by his characteristic defensiveness, his tendency to exaggerate his part in the development of the Boulder Canyon Project, and his evident desire to settle personal scores many years after the fact. The reader of Hoover's memoirs is well advised to measure his recollections of important events against those of other, possibly more objective, sources. A similar tendency toward self-justification colors the memoirs of Hoover's Interior Secretary, Ray Lyman Wilbur, a lifelong apologist for his friend and mentor. Both men's recollections are nevertheless highly revealing, if sometimes inadvertently so.

Among other important memoirs, Congressman Philip D. Swing's self-effacing recollection of his long struggle for enactment of the Boulder Canyon Act resides among the Swing Papers at the University of California, Los Angeles. Hiram Johnson's nearly daily communications with his sons and closest friends, published in seven volumes in 1983 as *The Diary Letters of Hiram Johnson,* chronicle this pugnacious and uncompromising politician's battle for progressive causes during his nearly three decades of service in the U.S. Senate, with the Boulder Canyon Project Act standing among his major preoccupations and principal achievements in the 1922–1928 period.

The staff of the United States Reclamation Bureau, Lower Colorado Region, gave unstintingly of their time and knowledge during my research for this book. I owe special thanks to Brenda Wilson of the USBR office in Boulder City for her hospitality and guidance during my lengthy sojourn among the office files, and Emme Woodward of the bureau's office at Hoover Dam for her assistance with the bureau's extensive photographic archive and for allowing me to tour, under her informed guidance, parts of the dam and its appurtenant facilities not accessible to the general public.

Numerous research institutions in the West and across the country hold materials relevant to the history of Hoover Dam. These include the special collections department of Young Research Library at the University of California, Los Angeles; the Bancroft Library of the University of California, Berkeley; the special collections department at Leid Library, the University of Nevada, Las Vegas; and the library of the University of Nevada, Reno. Important contributions to my research were made by material housed in the Water Resources Center Archives of the University of California, Berkeley; Special Collections, Stanford University Libraries; and the Hoover Institution Archives at Stanford University. The staff of the Sherman Library, Corona del Mar, California, under the direction of Dr. William O. Hendricks, provided me with access to rare documents relating to the Mexican ventures of Harrison Gray Otis and Harry Chandler. The arts library of the University of Southern California unearthed a hard-to-find copy of a vintage photography magazine with an important article related to the career of Ben Glaha. Considerable material relating to the history of the Bureau of Reclamation is stored at the National Archives and Records Administration, particularly at its repositories in Laguna Niguel, California, and Denver. My thanks go out to all these institutions.

Three individuals made especially noteworthy contributions to my research. J. David Rogers, Karl F. Hasselmann chair in geological engineering at Missouri University of Science and Technology, gave generously of his expertise in dam engineering in general and the designs of Hoover Dam and St. Francis Dam in particular. Dr. Rogers also shared with me a great quantity of primary and secondary source material dealing with the work of John Savage, the chief designer of Hoover Dam. John Hollstein kindly provided me with copies of personal letters written to family members by his distinguished granduncle, Frank Crowe. Barbara Vilander's graciousness in sharing material she compiled in preparing her book on Ben Glaha, lightened my research efforts considerably. Her peerless monograph *Hoover Dam: The Photographs of Ben Glaha* has done much to grant that unappreciated master his rightful place in the pantheon of photographic art. The interpretations in this book of material provided by these individuals are my own; it is my sincere hope that they find that the result justifies their time and assistance.

This project could not have been born, much less reached completion, without the support and counsel of many people. Sandra Dijkstra, my agent, perceived the richness of this story with her customary acuteness and helped drive it forward with her customary passion. Bruce Nichols contributed vital guidance during its early stages at Free Press. My editor at Free Press, Hilary Redmon, shaped the manuscript with her superb feel for pacing and eye for the telling detail.

My wife, Deborah, was my indispensable partner in research as she is in life. She reined in my stylistic excesses and saw me through the periods of uncertainty and self-doubt inevitable in a project of this scale. She and my sons, Andrew and David, were my inspiration, as always.

### ORAL HISTORIES

**Boulder City Public Library/American Assn. of University Women**
Grant Allen, Marion Allen, Alfred Frank Baker, Leroy and Lucille Burt, Steve Chubbs, David Dill, Leo Dunbar, Edna Jackson Ferguson, Richard L. "Curley" Francis, Elton Garrett, Erma Godbey, Alice Hamilton, Helen Holmes, Neil Holmes, Bud Keating, Joe Kine, Madeleine Knighten, Carl Merrill, Tommy Nelson, Altus E. "Tex" Nunley, Dorothy Nunley, Jean Page, Bob Parker, Dean Pulsipher, Vivian Clark Russell, Ann Stebens, the "Thirty-Oners" (Joe Kine, Elton Garrett, Bob Parker, Erma Godbey), Saul "Red" Wixson, Walker R. Young.

**Bancroft Library, University of California**
Robert L. Bridges

**Young Research Library, University of California, Los Angeles**
William Carr

# ACKNOWLEDGMENTS

**University of Nevada, Las Vegas**
Glenn (Bud) Bodell, Murl Emery.

**University of Nevada (Reno) Oral History Program**
Hoover Dam/Boulder City Pioneers (Marion Allen, Leo Dunbar, Erma Godbey, Carl Merrill, Mary Ann Vaughan Merrill); John Cahlan (interviewer: Mary Ellen Glass, 1970); John Cahlan (interviewer: Jamie Caughtry, 1987); Erma O. Godbey (interviewer: Mary Ellen Glass, 1967); Mary Ann Merrill (interviewer: R.T. King, 1987); Leon Rockwell (interviewer: Mary Ellen Glass, 1969); Hugh Shamberger (interviewer: Mary Ellen Glass, 1967); Thomas Cave Wilson (interviewer: Mary Ellen Glass, 1982).

# Index

# INDEX

# INDEX

# ABOUT THE AUTHOR

Michael Hiltzik is a Pulitzer Prize–winning journalist and author who has covered business, technology, and public policy for the *Los Angeles Times* for three decades. Currently the *Times*'s business columnist, he has also served as a financial and political writer, an investigative reporter, and a foreign correspondent in Africa and Russia. His previous books are *The Plot Against Social Security* (2005), *Dealers of Lightning: Xerox PARC and the Dawn of the Computer Age* (1999), and *A Death in Kenya: The Murder of Julie Ward* (1991). He received the 1999 Pulitzer Prize for articles exposing corruption in the entertainment industry. His other awards for excellence in reporting include the 2004 Gerald Loeb Award for outstanding business commentary and the Silver Gavel from the American Bar Association for outstanding legal reporting. A graduate of Colgate University and Columbia University, he lives in Southern California with his wife and two sons.